CITY BY THE BAY

A History of Modern San Francisco

1945 – Present

By Charles A. Fracchia

Library of Congress Catalog Number: 97-077579

ISBN: 1-886483-21-3

Published by Heritage Media Corporation.

Regional Offices

Los Angeles, CA, Denver, CO, and New York, NY.

Produced in Cooperation With

San Francisco Historical Society.

Publisher
Charles E. Parks

Author
Charles A. Fracchia

Photo Editor
Charles A. Fracchia

Managing Editor
Lori M. Parks

Art Director
Ann Hoff Scott,
Visual Antics

Production Manager
Deborah Sherwood

Assistant Production Manager
Christa DeMartini

Production Staff
Janet Craven
Sean Gates
Darlene Kocher
Simone Llerandi

National Sales Manager
Ray Spagnuolo

Partners in San Francisco Sales Coordinators
Kathee Finn
Tony Lucero
Roxanne Suntken

Partners in San Francisco Editorial Coordinators
Betsy Lelja
Susan Ikeda

Partners in San Francisco Contributing Writers
Wendy Belden
Nancy Bronstein
Eddie Foronda
Allen Gardiner
Lorilee Howard
Howell Hurst
Anne Marie Jordan
Rebecca Kuzins
Ellen Macauley
Daphne O'Neal
Debra Rahal
Chloe Rounsley
Caroline Scarborough
Melissa Schwarz
Julia Shure
Salinda Tyson

Administration
Michael Bayon
Regina Read
Caroline Whittaker

(Opposite Page)
Photo by David Wakely.

Acknowledgments

This book has been the result of the help of many people, some of whom I may have inadvertently forgotten to mention. To those, I can only say: "Thank you."

First, let me express my gratitude and appreciation to Deanna L. Kastler, my colleague on the board of directors of the San Francisco Historical Society, whose invaluable assistance in selecting the photos for this book and the accomplishment of so many tasks too innumerable to list makes her a virtual co-author.

Second, let me thank Sharon A. Moore for her careful reading of the manuscript and for her invaluable suggestions and corrections.

Third, let me thank Linda Toschi-Chambers, who put my manuscript into computer under very difficult time constraints and whose loving patience and good-humor I will always cherish.

Fourth, to family and friends, whose discussions about San Francisco and whose explorations of the city with me over the years have created in me an overwhelming love for the City by the Bay: my parents, Charles and Josephine Fracchia; my children, Laura and Michael Riviello, Carla and Michael Stening, Francesca and Grant Leschin, and Charles A. Fracchia, Jr.; my dear friends Greg and Kathy Calegari, George Bianchi, Everett and Louise Snowden, Jack and Peggy O'Brien, Bob and Gerayne Bianco, Peter Finnegan, Robert and Carol Sweyd, Stan and Irene Andersen, Kevin and Sheila Starr, Fred and Jena Ruhland, George and Edith Piness.

Fifth, to all those who spent time and energy in interviews, answering questions, tracking down photographs, and so many other tasks, let me say thank you: Ellen Carlin, Archana Chakrabarti, Eric Eiven, Joe Garity, Mary Sue Grant, Ivan Hudson, Hille Novak, Vicki Rosen, Janet Underwood, and Kathleen Woo of the Gleeson Library of the University of San Francisco, a library I have loved and used for over forty years; Fawn McInnis, Susan Goldstein, Pat Akre, Selby Collins, Khanh Nguyen and Robert Landazari of the History Center of the San Francisco Public Library; Phil Elwood; Richard Geiger and Gary Fong of the San Francisco *Chronicle*; Margaret Norton and Lee Cox of the San Francisco Performing Arts Library and Museum; Peter Dailey of the Port of San Francisco; Helen Sause, Marie Browning and Shirley Wysinger of the San Francisco Redevelopment Agency; Lynn Bonfield and Susan Parker Sherwood of the Labor Archives and Research Center, SFSU, The Names Project Foundation; Don Asher.

I dedicate this book to my greatest friend, my beloved wife, and dearest companion, Elizabeth Feaster Fracchia, whose love, support, and integrity have been the mainstay of my life.

Introduction

To research and write the first general and comprehensive history of modern San Francisco is indeed an awesome task. The more than five decades that have elapsed since World War II ended and San Franciscans rejoiced at the end of a decade and a half of tribulations — first depression, then war — have seen vast changes in both U.S. society and in that part of the country known as San Francisco.

These changes, to one such as I, who have lived through them, seem part of the scenario of one's life. One forgets many of the issues that were so important at the time they loomed over this urban landscape. Memory does not retain the physical changes within the city that seemed so momentous at the time: the restaurant that one so loved, and which had been around for generations, that closed its doors; the retail establishment, founded during the Gold Rush, that brought back such memories of shopping with one's mother, that announced it would cease business; the great landmark from the nineteenth century that seemed indestructible, that was pounded into rubble by the wrecking ball; the banal skyscraper that has taken the place of numerous small buildings that housed such old-fashioned businesses as a ship chandlery, a customs broker, or a family investment company.

Change. How subtle. How little noticed as one lives through it. Whatever happened to all those Irish families out in the Mission District? What ever became of those Russians on Potrero Hill? Those Italians in North Beach?

Slowly, inexorably, glacially, it seems, one's neighbors die or move away; new people — people with different physiognomies, different languages, different customs — move into the neighborhood; new

alliances are built up in the city; a new power structure emerges.

Household names — of those in business, of the socially prominent, of politicians, of eccentrics, of community activists — disappear, remembered only by the "old-timers"; new names take their place, new individuals are noted in the newspapers, talked about in "inner" circles.

Time seems to strain both the physical fabric and the personal reputations of any era. The 1920s eliminated most of the great Victorian mansions in Pacific Heights. The 1960s, 1970s, and 1980s transformed San Francisco's financial district from a small enclave to a far-flung district with soaring skyscrapers. No longer can one watch sacks of coffee being unloaded at the piers of San Francisco's bustling waterfront, smell the coffee beans being roasted at the nearby plants — Folgers, Hills Brothers, M.J.B. or drink a strong cup of coffee before dawn at the city's produce district (where the Golden Gateway now stands).

Compile a list of the one hundred most prominent San Franciscans between 1945 and 1960 and very few of today's residents of the city will have heard of them, much less know much about them.

Courtesy
Robert A. Eplett/OES.

Photo by
Deanna L. Kastler.

Columbarium.
Photo by
Deanna L. Kastler.

Never far from my mind as I researched and wrote this history of modern San Francisco were my own memories of growing up in the city: shopping with my mother at the Emporium, the City of Paris, the White House, O'Connor & Moffat, having a hot dog and root beer with her at the counter at Woolworth's, swimming with my father at Fleishhacker Pool and at the Sutro Baths, being taken by my grandfather to the old produce market, stupefied with sleepiness and cold in the pre-dawn fog, being seated in the cavernous, rococo-decorated Fox Theater on Market Street by a uniformed young usher, excited in the anticipation of seeing some long-expected movie, eating with a group of college friends at Johnny Kan's — my first experience of a Chinese restaurant.

Every one of the above-mentioned institutions is now gone.

And if we turn to the prominent personalities who peopled my youth — the likes of such politicians as Jack Shelley and Judge Ertola, business magnates Ben Swig, Charles Black, J.D. Zellerbach, Charles Blyth, Cyril Magnin, socialites Phyllis Fraser, Tommy Mein, Robert Watt Miller, Kenneth Monteagle, eccentrics Lloyd Downton, Jose Cebrian, Robert Downing-Olson it is not just death that has removed them: it is the fact that once formidable reputations have disappeared from view and from memory.

And the basis of history is memory; and its writing is to select from the infinite mass of detail of a peri-

od of time — in the present case, of somewhat more than half a century — and present in some coherent manner a narrative that will present a portrait of that age. What to select and how to present what has been selected has always been a great puzzle to any historian. I have not been exempt from this problem.

People, places, events: how many have existed, how many have taken place in San Francisco during this past half century. How very little of it all has been recorded. What an infinitesimal portion of it will find itself in this account.

I already anticipate how many times I shall be asked "Why didn't you mention this?" or "Why didn't you talk about that?" or "Why did you forget to bring out that…?"

Each of us has our own memories, our individual sense of what was important in any particular era, our own prisms of judgment as to what is significant.

And so, as I complete this book, I am cognizant that, despite all my efforts, despite countless hours of planning and subjecting my judgment to pitiless scrutiny, it cannot be a complete account of San Francisco's modern city. What I am hopeful it is, however, is a kaleidoscope, a mosaic, of this city's past half century, an account of the changes it has undergone from the end of World War II to the end of the twentieth century. The reader, hopefully, will learn the highlights of this past half century of the city's history, get some sense of the changing composition of the city during this period of time, and form a holistic impression of its essence as we get ready to enter the twenty-first century.

From this pioneering, general history of San Francisco's modern age, I hope there will be inspiration for others to refine this attempt, to bring out specialized studies, to provide in-depth analyses of specific aspects of this city's economic, sociological, demographic, religious, and political life.

The urban experience — whether in Rome, London, Paris, Buenos Aires, Rio de Janeiro, New York, Los Angeles, Tokyo, or Calcutta — is one of constant change, of teeming vitality, of experimentation, of triumph and tragedy. In obscure alleys and on broad boulevards, in tenements and in mansions, in churches, synagogues, mosques, and temples, and in office buildings and factories, in shops, restaurants, and places of entertainment, millions of peoples lead their lives, sometimes in the public eye, more often not. Some live in cities for a short time; others spend all their lives there. Foolish mistakes are made, both in individuals' lives and also in the corporate, civic life of the city; and sometimes there are judicious decisions made that benefit both the individual and the city.

Cities are people: people who happen to live and work within their confines, who go to sports events, musical performances, street fairs, and movies, who volunteer their services for worthy causes, who play on the streets, who attend their schools, who sit at desks in office buildings or who stand at lathes in factories, who dream up ideas or new products in technology, consumer services, or communications.

San Francisco partakes in every aspect of this urban experience. Whether it is one of these exquisite days, usually in Spring or Fall, when sunny, clear-blue skies bring out the delicate beauty of that intersection between water, hills, and the sky or whether it is a fog-shrouded late-afternoon, when a stiff, cold west wind pierces one, the life of this city is ever-changing, almost oblivious to the daily events of birth and death, only occasionally noting a place that is no more or one just constructed, usually too busy to notice what will later be described by historians as "trends," only occasionally bearing witness to how a particular neighborhood has changed in the past decade.

Retired longshoremen know little about the new technological business sprouting up in the old brick buildings in the South of Market area. Irish-American grandmothers in the Sunset District look out of their windows to see Chinese-American youngsters playing on the sidewalks. Two old Italian-American denizens of North Beach, sitting in Washington Square, watch as two young men walk by, holding hands and kissing each other as they stop at the corner.

"I remember when the 'Monkey Block' was here," remarks one old-timer to another, as they look up at the Transamerica Pyramid. "And there," pointing across the street to a tall modern building, containing condominiums, restaurants, and shops, "I used to eat at the Iron Pot."

People die. Buildings are destroyed. Events keep changing. And yet San Francisco continues to endure, to provide a place to live, to work, and to retire, a place to play, a place to learn.

It is this vital, changing, and enduring city, during the last half century, that I have attempted to portray in this book.

Charles A. Fracchia
Feast of the Assumption,
August 15, 1997
San Francisco

Courtesy
San Francisco Chronicle.
Photo by Gene Anthony.

Contents

(Left) *Courtesy Robert A. Eplett/OES.*

Pages 14-15, 92-93, 144-145, 164-165 courtesy David Wakely.

Pages 50-51 courtesy Tom Vano, Vano Photography.

Endsheet Painting by LeRoy Neiman, courtesy of Bowles/Sorokko Galleries

Partners' section openers by LeRoy Neiman, courtesy of Bowles/Sorokko Galleries

Chapter 1

1945–1960

Peace Comes to the City by the Bay

1 9 4 5 - 1 9 6 0

SAN FRANCISCO, MID-1945. A CITY THAT HAD SUFFERED THE CORROSIVE PANGS OF THE GREAT Depression for more than a decade, enduring during that period a bitter maritime strike and a general strike, as well as the hopelessness of massive unemployment, and then for three and a half years had undergone the losses, fears, and deprivations of a world war. A city that now looked confidently ahead to the end of the war, to the spending of the dollars that had accumulated during a period of total employment and high wages, to a normal life that meant more or less assured employment; back to the venerable stores that had purveyed goods to the city's residents and visitors since the nineteenth century; back to San Francisco women's beloved nylons and men's desire for new tires for their automobiles; to the welcoming home of sons, brothers, husbands, sweethearts and fathers who had been fighting in the military services of the United States around the world; back to the family Sunday drive to visit friends in San Mateo, Marin, or Alameda counties, no longer with gasoline under strict rationing; and back to real butter on one's bread, roasts for Sunday dinner, and sugar for one's coffee, without the restrictions and limitations of ration stamps.

San Franciscans were curious about the future. Would there be a depression, as there often was after a war? Or would the prosperity triggered by World War II become a continuing reality? How long before the military apparatus that ringed San Francisco Bay would be dismantled? When would rent control and rationing end? And what would happen to the behemoth of war industries — shipyards, steel factories, and armament depots that had transformed the quiet bucolic areas surrounding San Francisco and the hamlets that punctuated this countryside into the huge 24-hour-operating cavernous industrial sheds and the seemingly endless tracts of slap-dash, "temporary" housing to accommodate the thousands upon thousands of workers from the South and Midwest? And would the seemingly endless parade of men — and some women — in military uniforms truly cease?

How would the physical appearance of the city change after the peace had been won, San Franciscans pondered? Already, the Fillmore Street corridor had been transformed from a Japanese enclave and a Jewish section into a largely African-American neighborhood, reflecting the internment of Japanese-Americans in early 1942 and their replacement by Black workers from the South, who had migrated to the city to take advantage of the high wages in the war industries in the Bay Area. Would the city continue to grow? It already seemed to be bursting at the seams as a result of the massive migrations brought about by the war. Mansions in Pacific Heights, once housing one family, had been turned into boarding houses. Large, stately Victorians in the Mission District had been transformed into apartments. Ample flats had been subdivided into tiny apartments. There had been little or no new housing built in San Francisco — if one excepts the rapidly thrown up "temporary" housing overlooking the shipyards at the foot of Potrero Hill — since 1930; and much of the city had a dilapidated and blighted look, the result of the economic constraints of a decade and a half of depression and war.

But, after all, there were pockets in the physically-limited city for construction after the war. The "march to the ocean" — the development of the Sunset and Richmond districts — had not been completed by 1945. There were still dairy ranches on Twin Peaks — certainly archaic in the postwar city. And 162 acres of cemeteries had only recently been removed from the vicinity of the Catholic all-girls (as the expression then was) school of Lone Mountain College, an area now beginning to be called Laurel Heights. And, of course, why not tear down all those tumbling-down Victorians in the Western Addition and replace them with modern, convenient housing? Further, one could remove oneself from the perennially overcast

San Francisco weather and its congestion to the idyllic, bucolic surroundings of San Mateo and Santa Clara counties to the south, Alameda and Contra Costa counties to the east, and Marin County to the north. The Southern Pacific Railroad ran a commuter train from San Jose to San Francisco. From the East Bay one had a choice of the Key System over the San Francisco-Oakland Bay Bridge, completed less than a decade before, or, one could drive one's automobile over the bridge, or one could put oneself *and* one's automobile on a ferry. And from Marin County one could drive over that glorious "symphony in steel," the lightly-traveled Golden Gate Bridge.

How would the city be different after the war, San Francisco wondered? In truth, its demographic composition had been basically set during the Gold Rush and the subsequent Silver Age: a majority of Anglo-Saxon stock, very large components of German and Irish immigrants, smaller, but still significant, communities of Italians, French, Chinese, and Hispanics. For a large U.S. city, San Francisco had a relatively small African-American community and very, very few Eastern Europeans.

Also unusual for a large U.S. city, San Francisco had a very mild cleavage between socio-economic and ethnic groups: no large groupings of poor working class huddling in decaying tenements, no major tensions and hostilities between various ethnic groups. The Chinese, it is true, kept to themselves in their homes and businesses in Chinatown, where in 1945 all San Francisco Chinese lived, as they had for almost a century. The African-American community was also isolated: too new an immigrant group and too outside the established sections of San Francisco's demographic composition, most having been agricultural workers in the South.

Social mobility in San Francisco, perhaps reflecting its urban roots in the Gold Rush, was extensive; and opportunities for professional, social, and economic advancement for virtually every ethnic and every socio-economic group were seen as quite possible.

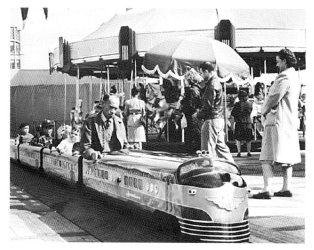

family values were very much in evidence in the immediate post-World War II period. This photo from 1947 shows parents and children in the Emporium's roof-top rides at Christmastime.
Courtesy
San Francisco
Public Library.

Neighborhoods were as well-defined in San Francisco in 1945 as they were in every large U.S. city. A sense of comfort, stability, mutual benefit, and community was generated by the practical desire of immigrants and the children of immigrants to dwell among "their own," The Irish lived in the Mission District; the Germans and Scandinavians lived in the Inner Mission; Italians in North Beach, Telegraph Hill, the Excelsior, and the Bayview-Hunter's Point area; Greeks in an enclave South of Market; Chinese and African Americans, as has been stated above, in Chinatown and along the Fillmore Street corridor, respectively.

Within 20 years after the end of World War II almost all of San Francisco's neighborhoods had drastically changed: not only in their composition, but in what they meant to those who lived there. Today there are some vestiges of such neighborhood communities — North Beach, for example (where, however, the great majority of children who attend the parochial school of the Italian national Roman Catholic church, Sts. Peter and Paul, are Chinese) — but the world of these "communities within a community" has evaporated during the past half century, with only a number of archaeological remains — and the memories of those who lived in them — as testimony.

This stable world of San Francisco in the immediate aftermath of World War II was politically, socially,

One of the periodic sales at the White House, another of San Francisco's prominent retail stores, in 1956.
Courtesy San Francisco Public Library.

and economically dominated and led by an urban coalition that included the leaders of labor unions, ethnic groups, and religious groups, most particularly of the latter, the Roman Catholic archbishop of San Francisco ("Check with Franklin Street," was frequently heard in City Hall — "Franklin Street" being the site of the rectory for St. Mary's Cathedral, then located on Van Ness Avenue), an oligarchy of German-Jewish and Anglo-Saxon business leaders, and certain representatives, mostly attorneys or judges, of an upper middle-class ascendancy among the Irish and Italian communities.

The decision-making process for the city was largely dictated by the hammered-out compromises of this disparate group, frequently acting through such organizations as the San Francisco Chamber of Commerce and the San Francisco Labor Council. Needless to say, this was not always a smooth process; and electoral and journalistic campaigns would frequently become rancorous.

Four daily newspapers served San Francisco and its surrounding communities: the *Chronicle*, the

Examiner, the *News*, and the *Call-Bulletin*. Each had a definite constituency; and each had a distinctive style. The impact of newspapers in the lives of everyone from youngsters to the elderly in those days before television can today be reconstructed only with difficulty. Newspapers would be read from cover to cover: international, national, and local news, syndicated columnists, the comics, sports news, vital statistics, social doings, business. The continuing adventures of "Joe Palooka," "Gasoline Alley," "The Phantom," "Prince Valiant," "Maggie and Jiggs," and other comic strip characters supplied the titillation and humor that television situation comedies and soap operas today provide.

On any Sunday morning, families throughout San Francisco could be found gathered together in living rooms, reading and then exchanging sections of the newspaper of choice — a process which could take some hours.

The post-war San Franciscan, now confident in the continuing health of the economy, job secure, and with the restrictions imposed by the war lifted, stepped out to shop with exuberance. Small neighborhood stores were still the major purveyors of groceries, of appliances, and of pharmaceuticals. For broader choices or for specialties, the San Franciscan (and those from throughout the Bay Area) headed downtown. "Downtown" for San Franciscans meant either the financial district — then situated principally along Montgomery Street from Sacramento Street to Market Street and extending two blocks east to Battery Street — or the retail district — situated then around Union Square and some adjacent streets and on Market Street from Fourth Street to about the Civic Center.

The kaleidoscope of venerable stores presented an array of options to San Franciscans. The Emporium, a huge store with an imposing facade on Market Street; the City of Paris, owned by the urbane, cosmopolitan Verdier family whose Normandy Lane gourmet foods and wine section, with its delectable cafe, was presided over by an elegant, mustachioed

The Emporium, in the late-1950s, was one of the principal retail stores in San Francisco. Its presence on Market Street was a landmark from the late-1890s until it closed in 1996. *Courtesy San Francisco Public Library.*

Roos Bros., a favorite men's store, in 1956. It is one of the many traditional San Francisco retail stores that closed in the period from the 1960s on. *Courtesy San Francisco Public Library.*

Poon de Rageen; the White House, and O'Connor & Moffat (purchased by Macy's in 1945) were general merchandise stores. Men would shop for clothes at such specialty stores as Roos Brothers, Bullock & Jones, Brooks Brothers, and Robert Kirk, Ltd. Women had a broader choice. I. Magnin & Co., its Pflueger-designed exterior dominating Union Square, presided over by the tasteful Grover Magnin and after 1950 the legendary Hector Escobosa, was the women's store of choice for the area's elite. A uniformed doorman would open the doors of chauffeured cars that would deposit well-coifed women from Pacific Heights, Nob Hill, Piedmont, and Hillsborough. Ransohoff's (the interior of which is seen so splendidly in Alfred Hitchcock's classic *Vertigo*) was yet another "high-end" women's store. Liebes and Joseph Magnin's catered to the pocketbooks of the middle class. Numerous boutiques — a feature of San Francisco's specialty store ethos — provided even greater choices.

Nathan Dohrmann & Company sold household wares; Gumps sold gifts and offered wedding registry to the city's elite; Shreve & Company sold jewelry.

For some years after the end of World War II there was no comparable shopping on the West Coast. Even the considerably larger city of Los Angeles did not compete with the elegant bazaars of cosmopolitan San Francisco. And, in the Bay Area, suburban shoppers would often make a weekly trek to San Francisco's stores or for appointments with doctors.

borhood had a modest shopping area, which usually included grocery stores, gift shops, clothing stores, a theatre, a five-and-dime store, pharmacies, and hardware stores. The area of Market Street and Union Square represented the most extensive and elegant of the city's shopping areas. But one of the most unique shopping areas of San Francisco was the Mission Miracle Mile — a stretch along Mission Street from Sixteenth Street to 24th Street. Known primarily for its enormous furniture stores — Redlich's, Sterling, and Lachman Brothers, among them — it also boasted Granat Brothers, a very large jewelry store and numerous large markets that prefigured the supermarkets that would soon be making their initial appearances throughout the country. Several movie theatres (as well as a strip-tease theatre) dotted the Miracle Mile: the El Capitan, now a gutted-hulk turned into a parking garage, seated 3,500 people.

Up until the 1960s virtually everyone wore a hat to work or play. Courtesy San Francisco Public Library.

On any given day, fedora-hatted men and, more predominately, hatted and white-gloved women could be seen glancing at goods on the counters and shelves of Union Square's and Market Street's stores (until well into the 1960s, no woman, no matter what her socio-economic status, would dream of going shopping downtown without wearing a hat and white gloves).

But it wasn't just the downtown area that drew San Franciscans. As mentioned above, each neigh-

founded during the Gold Rush by French immigrants, the City of Paris typified San Francisco's elegant retail trade — a cynosure for the shoppers from around the West. *Courtesy San Francisco Public Library.*

Since as early as 1911 car buyers would go to San Francisco's auto row, along Van Ness Avenue. Here, more than 20 dealers were housed in massive buildings with ornate showrooms. Willis Polk and Bernard Maybeck were among the architects who designed these auto "temples." Surrounding the elegant showrooms were scores of repair shops and body shops.

The importance of the Auto Row blocks along Van Ness Avenue was recognized as early as 1915, when the California State Automobile Association established its headquarters on Van Ness Avenue.

In the mad-cap advertising that marked the years after World War II, Auto Row achieved national notoriety when a dealer who called himself Horsetrader Ed sought and obtained a record for flagpole sitting when in 1948 he hired Milton Van Nolan to sit atop a flagpole at his dealership at 790 Van Ness Avenue. He would repeat the advertising stunt two years later, when a blonde Erma Leach repeated the feat.

Spurred on by Horsetrader Ed's raucous advertising and media coverage, thousands of Bay Area residents would stand around the dealership and gawk at the record-breaking pole sitters.

Entertainment has always been one of the most notable features of the life of major cities; and San Francisco had been known as one of the most important entertainment centers in the United States since the time of the Gold Rush.

San Franciscans had, despite depression and war, a wide array of entertainment options in 1945 and subsequent years — an array that would change considerably over the next half century.

The weekend drive — an automobile drive to adjacent counties to visit friends or just to "see the country" — was a standard feature of the post-war San Franciscan's Sunday entertainment fare. During the summer, such a drive would often culminate in such places as Alum Rock Park or Marin Town and Country Club, where family members and friends, or perhaps members of a fraternal lodge would congregate for a picnic, swimming, and games.

Mission Super was one of the immense stores on Mission Street's "Miracle Mile." *Courtesy San Francisco Public Library.*

Milton Van Nolan, who sat atop a flagpole for 70 days, 23 hours, and 33 minutes, to publicize Horsetrader Ed's used car business on Van Ness Avenue, gets a haircut before his descent. *Courtesy San Francisco Public Library.*

Church groups, fraternal organizations, and garden/art clubs represented a major factor in the social/entertainment life of the San Franciscan in the mid 1940s. Many of the activities of such groups also involved volunteer work for the poor, for those with health problems, and for schools.

The day-to-day entertainment centered around listening to the radio and the movies. Radio soap operas — morning, noon and night — and radio commentators had fans who would not think of missing an episode of "Stella Dallas," "One Man's Family," "Just Plain Bill," "The Cisco Kid," or, among commentators, Gabriel Heater or Walter Winchell.

The years immediately after World War II saw the peak years of movie attendance. Every neighborhood in San Francisco had one or two movie theatres, which would be thronged with children during Saturday and Sunday afternoon matinees, watching a double-feature film presentation, animated features, a serial, and a newsreel, and by adults in the evening.

But it was the huge, ornate movie palaces on Market Street that dazzled the imaginations of film-going San Franciscans: the Orpheum, the Warfield, the Golden Gate, the Paramount, and, most spectacularly, the Fox. Here, uniformed ushers would show you to your seats for long-awaited "first-run" showings of much ballyhooed movies. Rousing organ music would fill the cavernous buildings, each seating thousands. Going to the movies in such places was an event that bedazzled San Franciscans.

The Paramount Theater was one of the movie palaces that made Market Street the entertainment center of San Francisco. *Courtesy San Francisco Public Library.*

By the mid-1960s the movie industry was in a state of collapse. Movie studios were desperate to achieve any kind of technological development to entice people to return. *Courtesy San Francisco Public Library.*

The Golden Gate Theater was another of the movie palaces along Market Street. *Courtesy San Francisco Public Library.*

Loew's Warfield Theater (in 1922) was one of San Francisco's movie palaces, built in the aftermath of World War I. They would last into the 1950s and 1960s — after which movie attendance began to decline and the spectacular theatrical display of movie houses disappeared. *Courtesy San Francisco Public Library.*

The author's parents (the two on the right), Charles B. and Josephine Fracchia, celebrate with four friends at the Club Lido in San Francisco. Within a few years of this picture, the once popular supper clubs would be closed. *Courtesy Charles A. Fracchia.*

Sports events — the Seals, the '49ers (who began shortly after the end of World War II), the Shamrocks (ice hockey), boxing matches, and the extensive fare of local collegiate and high school athletics — provided yet another source of entertainment delight to San Francisco Bay Area fans.

An extensive and often exotic nightlife permeated the San Francisco of 1945 — a nightlife that had been going on since the years after World War I and which was sampled by socialite and working class alike. The hotels led the way: the Mural Room at the St. Francis Hotel, the Top of the Mark at the Mark Hopkins Hotel, the Persian Room at the Sir Francis Drake Hotel, and the Tonga Room at the Fairmont Hotel.

Supper clubs abounded: the Bal Tabarin, the Club Lido, the Club Moderne, the Forbidden City, the Sinaloa, Bimbo's 365 Club (with its notorious "Girl in the Fishbowl"), the Troc, the Chinese Skyroom, the Mocombo. Within a few years after V-J Day, most of these supper clubs would have closed.

The use of Golden Gate Park, swimming at Fleishhacker Pool, and an excursion to Playland-at-the-Beach were also among the ways in which San Franciscans would spend their leisure time in the aftermath of World War II.

Club life was a vital part of the upper-class San Franciscan's world. Until its demise in recent years, club life was at the very center of the city's social and business life. Reporters for the city's four dailies, public relations operatives, and advertising executives frolicked at the Press Club. Across the street, the Catholic Irish and Italian ascendancy dominated the Olympic Club. The business and professional oligarchy met at the Pacific Union Club in its quarters on top of Nob Hill, at the Bohemian Club (and in the summer at the Bohemian Grove on the Russian River), the Family, the Concordia-Argonaut, the Merchants' Exchange, the University Club, the Commercial Club, and the Engineers Club. These were all men's clubs at that time.

A singer at the Trocadero entertains San Franciscans in the late-1940s. *Courtesy San Francisco Public Library.*

The largest outdoor swimming pool in the world — Fleishaker Pool — was so large that lifeguards patrolled it by rowboat. *Courtesy San Francisco Public Library.*

Mom and dad and two kids in the bumper cars at Playland-at-the-Beach. Playland, a popular boardwalk at the Pacific Ocean's beach, was torn down in the 1960s. *Courtesy San Francisco Public Library.*

A plaque depicting a famous member from its inception in the 1870s, depicts Bret Harte on the Bohemian Club's city club facade. *Courtesy San Francisco Public Library.*

Women would gather at the Francisca Club, Town & Country, and the Metropolitan Club. (On Mondays, the city's female social elite would lunch at the St. Francis Hotel's Mural Room.)

Co-ed dining among the city's social elite would frequently bring them to the Burlingame Country Club or to the newly-founded Villa Taverna.

The Cotillion in December and part of August spent on estates at Lake Tahoe were part of the social rituals that dotted the lives of San Francisco's "upper crust,"

But 1945 and the end of the war represented the culmination of a lifestyle that had been formed around the time of World War I. The massive social and technological changes that followed World War II would transform San Francisco. The landscape would change — both in San Francisco and in the counties surrounding it.

How people spent their time would change. Customs, mores, outlooks would change. The demographic composition of the city would change.

In 1946 the famed cabaret and supper club, the Bal Tabarin, closed. In 1949 the Chinese Telephone Exchange, where Chinese women in traditional, ceremonial Chinese attire, and who had memorized the telephone numbers of all the Chinese in San Francisco who had telephones, closed — the victim of direct dialing. And in 1958 the last ferryboat plied the bay.

One by one the city's venerable retail establishments closed their doors. Hats and white gloves disappeared from Union Square by the late 1960s.

The city's population reached a peak of about 850,000 in 1948, before the trek to the suburbs reduced it by about 200,000. (By the end of the century it has stabilized at about 750,000.) Fewer and fewer children were to be seen playing in its streets. Old neighborhoods were slashed by freeways, deserted by their traditional residents, changed and often decayed.

Nostalgia for the "good old days" remains rampant; but no one can make a judgment on the quality of difference between the San Francisco of 1945 and of today. All cities, all societies, undergo constant organic change. The following is a chronicle of that change.

An operator at the Chinese Telephone Exchange on Washington Street. Each operator had memorized the names and telephone numbers of all subscribers in Chinatown.
Courtesy San Francisco Public Library.

The United Nations Is Born

Senator Tom Connelley signs the U.N. Charter, while President Harry Truman (left) and Secretary of State Edward Stettinius (second from left) look on. Courtesy San Francisco Public Library.

Spectators and delegates crowd the sidewalk in front of the War Memorial Opera House on April 25, 1945, for the opening of the conference which founded the United Nations. Courtesy San Francisco Public Library.

Fairly early during World War II the allies had discussed the creation of an international peace-keeping organization to take the place of the ineffective and now defunct League of Nations, which had been set up at the end of World War I. Proposals for the shape of such an organization were discussed in 1944 at the Dumbarton Oaks Conference and were further hammered out at the Yalta Conference, just before the death of President Roosevelt.

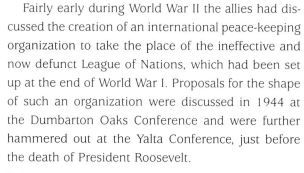

The site decided on for the organizational meeting of what came soon to be called the United Nations was San Francisco. On April 25, 1945, before either Germany or Japan had surrendered, the new U.S. president, Harry Truman, welcomed the delegates assembled in the Opera House. (The Opera House and the adjacent Veterans Building would be the nexus for the organizing conference.)

The news that a conference of such magnitude would be held in San Francisco threw the city into a tizzy. How to accommodate hundreds of delegates and their staffs in a city that was already bursting at the seams was a major problem. How to set up the logistical support for such a conference on such short notice was another.

It was fortunate that San Francisco's mayor in 1945 (elected in 1943) was white-thatched Roger

Lapham, a wealthy Easterner who had come to San Francisco in the 1920s as president of the American-Hawaiian Steamship Company. This competent executive was able to rapidly put together the logistical apparatus necessary for a successful conference.

The city was exhilarated by the promise of the aims of the conference and dazzled by the numbers of famous individuals who had come to San Francisco to draft the charter for this new organization. The city's society members were mobilized for receptions, dinner parties, luncheons, and tours for the delegates and their families — an exhausting and bewildering array of such events that strained even the capacities of San Francisco's social elite for parties.

Many of the delegates had been household names in the news even before the war; others had achieved prominence during the war. V.M. Molotov, the Soviet Union's foreign minister, and Andrei Gromyko represented Germany's successful opponent on its eastern front. Foreign minister Anthony Eden and deputy prime minister Clement Attlee represented brave Britain. T.V. Soong, acting premier and foreign minister of China, represented the country that had been longest at war with an Axis power. Georges Bidault, who would have a long and illustrious political career, represented France.

Prince Faisal, who would one day succeed his father, Ibn Saud, as king, represented Saudi Arabia. Paul-Henri Spaak, who would be elected the first president of the U.N. General Assembly, represented Belgium; and Trygve Lie, who would be elected the U.N.'s first secretary-general, represented Norway.

The Czech delegate, foreign minister, Jan Masaryk, scion of a family distinguished in that country's search for freedom, would, within a few years, be a casualty of the Soviet Union's determination to place his country within its bloc of satellite nations.

The U.S. delegation was headed by the country's secretary of state, Edward Stettinius, who also served as president of the conference. The tall, courtly, white-haired Stettinius was in the thick of the imbroglios

that developed between the U.S. and nations that favored its policies and the increasing intransigence being shown by the Soviet Union.

Within the nine weeks in which the conference met, despite quarrels between the Soviet Union and the United States and other Western nations and conflicts between the big-power countries and the smaller nations, a charter for the United Nations was drafted, voted upon, and, on Monday, June 25, 1945, signed by the delegates of the fifty founding nations.

Order of precedence for signing was by length of endurance in the strife against the Axis powers. Thus, T.V. Soong, using a brush pen, signed first: for China had been in conflict against Japan since the early 1930s.

On the next day, two months after he had welcomed them, U.S. President Harry Truman congratulated the delegates on the work they had done and spoke of the hopes and dreams that all humanity had for the emergent United Nations.

V-J Day Riot

At 4 p.m. on Tuesday, August 14, 1945, the official news that Japan had unconditionally surrendered flashed through San Francisco. Instantaneously, the city erupted in joyous delirium. Air-raid sirens, factory whistles, church bells, automobile horns joined to create a cacophonous bedlam. Vehicular traffic — both automobiles and municipal railway trolleys and buses — came to a halt, as tens of thousands of workers poured out of buildings to rejoice in the streets. Suddenly, strangers greeted each other; laughter and every kind of noisy demonstration of joy became a swelling rumble; hugging, kissing, and the attempt of military personnel to steal the ubiquitous hats of male civilians added to the manic festivities.

As it had been for many years at times of civic joy and gatherings — such as annual New Year's Eve celebrations — Market Street became the hub of San Franciscans' outpouring of relief and delight that the

war was finally over. From the office buildings and stores that lined Market Street and from those along Montgomery Street and the financial district came a cascade of shredded paper.

The celebration lasted until about 5 a.m. on Wednesday morning and then erupted again on that afternoon. This time, fueled by excessive drinking of

An overturned truck illustrates the out-of-control celebrations in honor of V-J Day in San Francisco on August 14, 1945. *Courtesy San Francisco Public Library.*

General Wainwright, a prisoner of the Japanese since the fall of Corregidor in the Philippines, receives a hero's welcome in San Francisco on September 9, 1945. *Courtesy San Francisco Public Library.*

The Hyde Street Cable Car heads toward the Hyde Street Pier where ferryboats are ready to take passengers to Sausalito. Alcatraz Island with its prison fortress dominates the bay. Courtesy San Francisco Public Utilities Commission, Charles A. Fracchia collection.

The Washington-Jackson cable car line ran along the ridge of Pacific Heights until the late-1950s. The westbound cable car shown here is at the corner of Jackson and Laguna streets. Courtesy San Francisco Public Library.

alcoholic beverages and by the unsupervised presence of thousands of sailors and soldiers, the celebration became an ugly riot. Drunken military men and civilian hoodlums smashed windows and street signs, stole and destroyed automobiles, overturned mailboxes, and looted businesses. It has been estimated that eleven individuals were killed and one thousand injured. Numerous women were raped.

Finally, civic and military authorities imposed order. Two thousand police under Chief Edward Dullea patrolled the city. The military police corralled all of the servicemen and returned them to their barracks or ships.

Almost instantaneously the constrictions of wartime began to disappear. Gasoline rationing, food rationing, and the other deprivations and inconveniences established during World War II came to a sudden end. San Francisco was very ready to enjoy the peace and to erase from its memory the corrosive years of the Great Depression and the fears and losses of World War II.

Riding a cable car excites natives and visitors alike. Andrew Hallidie's invention of the cable car in the 1870s allowed for expansion of the city to Pacific Heights. Courtesy San Francisco Public Transportation Commission, Charles A. Fracchia collection.

The Fight to Save the Cable Cars

The aftermath of World War II brought about a flurry of activity to bring back the economy to a peace-time footing and to rejuvenate the dilapidated infrastructure of the city, which had suffered from the deferred maintenance of a decade and a half of depression and war.

Factories were returning to the production of capital and consumer goods to accommodate the long-deferred needs and desires of a rapidly growing population. New housing was burgeoning in both San Francisco and its suburbs. Millions of young men who had been in the armed services were returning to college and to work. Most of the women who had gone to work during World War II had returned to household occupations and the raising of children.

The economy was exceptionally prosperous, as the industrial capacity of the United States strove to fill the pent-up needs of both its own citizenry and

those of the nations around the world, whose industries had been destroyed during the war. As a result, confidence was high. The desire to do away with the archaic, to rebuild, to build anew was the rage.

One of the objects of this desire to modernize was the city's transportation system, which had become lumbering, dilapidated, and not effective for the changes that were developing in San Francisco.

In 1944, even before the war's end, the city had finally been able to purchase the Market Street Railway — a privately-owned company that owned the bulk of San Francisco's non-municipal street transportation systems, including competing streetcar lines on Market Street and two cable car lines.

The cable cars, a distinctive San Francisco form of transportation that dated back to August 1873, and which dominated the city's street transportation system during the last quarter of the nineteenth century, had increasingly been seen to be obsolete from the early years of the twentieth century; and, given the initial impetus of the 1906 earthquake and fire, one by one the cable car lines were being replaced by, first, electric trolleys and then by buses. In the aftermath of World War II, in its attempt to revitalize and make modern and efficient San Francisco's transportation system, the Public Utilities Commission deemed that the remaining cable car lines were archaic and would have to go.

This position was announced by Mayor Lapham on January 27, 1947. But, immediately there was a public outcry against eliminating the cable cars. Most thought the outcry would die out, and that "the powers that be" would get their way. (Even *Chronicle* columnist Herb Caen, although lamenting their departure, was resigned to the fact that the cable cars would go.) However, on March 4, 1947, a joint meeting of the San Francisco Federation of

In 1964 San Francisco's cable cars were declared a National Historic Landmark, the only moving landmark in the country. *Courtesy San Francisco Public Utilities Commission, Charles A. Fracchia collection.*

In September 1982, Mayor Dianne Feinstein and singer Tony Bennett, close the cable car system for a major overhaul. Courtesy San Francisco Public Library.

The cable car turn-around at the corner of Powell and Market streets in the 1950s. Courtesy San Francisco Public Utilities Commission, Charles A. Fracchia collection.

the Arts and the California Spring Blossom and Wild Flowers Association announced the formation of the Citizens Committee to Save the Cable Cars. Spearheading the effort was a short, feisty woman by the name of Friedel Klussman.

Klussman mobilized squadrons of San Francisco matrons, and, since city officials showed no concern about saving the cable cars, garnered signatures from thousands of San Franciscans to place a measure to save the cable cars on the ballot.

Mrs. Klussman's efforts had galvanized San Francisco's desire to keep its beloved cable cars running. Despite such powerful opponents as the Real Estate Board, the League of Women Voters, and the mayor, seventy-seven percent of those voting on November 4, 1947, supported keeping the city's cable car lines running. (This was to be the first of seven ballots during the next several years.)

Five years later — in 1952 — the city took over the last private component of street transportation — the bankrupt California Street Cable Car Company, founded by railroad mogul Leland Stanford in the late 1870s. This new addition to the city's municipal transit system operated three cable car lines.

In 1954 new forces gathered to try to eliminate the cable car lines. Macy's, which had purchased O'Connor & Moffat, wished to make O'Farrell Street a one-way street and to have the city build a large parking garage at Ellis and O'Farrell Streets, the better to serve its increasingly auto-bound customers. City bureaucrats and politicians, despite the 1947 vote, continued to campaign for abandoning the cable car lines.

Thus, on May 16, 1954, the city shut down, despite extensive public protest, the O'Farrell, Jones and Hyde line, which went all the way to Presidio Avenue.

Then, the anti-cable car coalition had Proposition E put on the ballot in June 1954. Deviously crafted as a measure to save the cable car, Proposition E's public relations was handled by David Jones, a master of obfuscative advertising, who assembled a Save the Cable Cars Committee, backed by the Downtown Association, the San Francisco Chamber of Commerce, and other groups interested in eliminating the cable cars. Proposition E passed by fewer than 12,000 votes; and, as a result, a truncated California Street cable car line and a line made up of parts of the Washington-Jackson and the O'Farrell, Jones and Hyde lines were reconstructed. (Only the Powell-Mason line remained on its full original route.)

A counterattack by Mrs. Klussman's forces at the ballot failed in November of 1954. And on September 1, 1956, the remaining Washington-Jackson line, with its spectacular views of the bay from its Pacific Heights run, was shut down.

The remaining cable car lines were designated a National Historic Landmark on January 29, 1964.

The badly deteriorated system was shut down on September 21, 1982, for a total rehabilitation. Almost

$70 million was spent on the rebuilding of the cable cars themselves, the car barn at Washington and Mason Streets, and the street system. ($10 million of this was raised in private funds.) The full cable car system became operative again in June 1984.

Today no one thinks of eliminating the cable cars: for they have become an enduring icon of San Francisco and one of its major tourist attractions. San Franciscans, who may rarely or ever ride them, continue to glory in knowing that they remain part of the lore and physical fabric of the city.

International Thrusts in the Early 1950s

Just five years after the end of World War II the United States found itself again at war. Not called a war, but a "police action," the conflict in Korea, while on no level calling upon the resources of men and

material that World War II had, nevertheless made San Francisco once again a portal for the transmission of military personnel and war goods to the Far East. Once more, Fort Mason hummed with the activities of war and shipment of men to the barren land of Korea.

In the following year a living casualty of the Korean War briefly visited San Francisco, causing a spontaneous and tumultuous welcome that surprised the nation by its intensity. Dismissed as commander of the United Nations forces in Korea by President Truman, General Douglas MacArthur trekked back to the United States, where he had not been for well over a decade, and to retirement.

San Francisco Mayor Elmer Robinson, who had replaced Roger Lapham in the election of 1948, had invited MacArthur to visit San Francisco en route to Washington, D.C., where he had been invited to address the U.S. Congress.

General Douglas MacArthur, after his firing as commander of the U.S. forces in the Far East, received a tumultuous greeting in San Francisco on his return from Japan. He is shown here with San Francisco Mayor Elmer Robinson and California Governor Earl Warren. *Courtesy San Francisco Public Library.*

He arrived on April 16, and was met by dignitaries and a substantial crowd at the San Francisco International Airport. The next day, Wednesday, April 17, a welcoming parade in San Francisco, in which the general sat in an open car with Mayor Robinson and California governor Earl Warren, became a triumphal progress, as tens of thousands cheered the returning hero.

MacArthur addressed the crowds from the steps of City Hall. The streets surrounding San Francisco's municipal center, as well as the Civic Center Plaza, were packed with thousands who had come to watch the solemn general, still in his legendary trench coat and military hat that had become so familiar, deliver his well-crafted speech in stentorian tones.

Then he was off to Washington, D.C., where he delivered a speech — "Old soldiers never die" — that rivaled the speeches of Demosthenes and Cicero. Then retirement ... and obscurity.

The thrust of events in the Far East intruded upon San Francisco in the same year as MacArthur's visit. San Francisco had been chosen as the site for an international conference to conclude a treaty of peace with Japan. Fifty-two nations were represented.

By this time, the Cold War was already quite established and the conflict in Korea was a result of this hostility. The Russian delegation, which six years before had been troublesome at the conference to establish the United Nations, now bristled with hostility. Ensconced in a mansion in nearby Hillsborough, their dour faces marked the deterioration in relations between the Soviet Union and the United States since the end of World War II.

The Japanese delegation, headed by prime minister Shigeru Yoshida, arrived in San Francisco on Monday, September 4, 1951; and the next day the conference began. Both President Truman and his secretary of State, Dean Acheson, were present to write *finis* to the fierce hostilities between the two countries for almost four years and to the U.S. occupation of Japan.

Sessions of the conference took place at the Opera House over a three-day period; and on Saturday, September 8, forty-eight nations there signed the pact that admitted Japan once more to the concert of nations. At the same time the former enemies — Japan and the United States — signed a security pact: yet another move in the pitting against each other of the Communist bloc and the nations of "the free world."

Beatniks and the Beat Revolution

San Francisco, since the Gold Rush, had had an active literary environment. Newspapers, magazines, and books published the prose and poetry of San Francisco writers; and twice, once in the mid-1860s to the early 1870s, and again in the last years of the nineteenth century and the early years of the twentieth century, the city had achieved a national reputation for its writers: Bret Harte, Mark Twain, and Ina Coolbrith among those in the former age; Jack London, Frank Norris, and George Sterling in the latter.

Once again, in the early- and mid-1950s, San Francisco became the venue for a literary renaissance. This time, however, the experience was not limited to a literary movement, but also incorporated a lifestyle which was intended to be a scathing indictment of the postwar ethos and culture.

As was the case with the previous two literary "renaissances" in San Francisco, that of the mid-1950s was composed of virtually no native San Franciscans. Some of the writers associated with what has come to be called "the beat movement" had lived in San Francisco for many years; and continued to make their home in the city or its environs; and some only spent a short time there during the peak of the beat movement.

First, it would be profitable to examine the words "beat" and "beatnik." Steven Watson, in his *The Birth of the Beat Generation: Visionaries, Rebels, and*

Hipsters, 1944-1960's, states: "The word 'beat' originally derived from circus and carnival argot, reflecting the straitened circumstances of nomadic carnies. In the drug world, 'beat' meant 'robbed' or 'cheated'... Herbert Huncke picked up the word from his show business friends... and in the fall of 1945 he introduced the word to William Burroughs, Allen Ginsberg, and Jack Kerouac. He never intended it to be elevating, but the opposite: 'I meant beaten. The world against me.'

"The word acquired historical resonance when Jack Kerouac, in a November 1948 conversation with fellow writer John Clellan Holmes, remarked, 'So I guess you might say we're a *beat* generation.'"

Holmes was to write an article for the *New Yorker Magazine*, which appeared in November 1952, and which was titled "This Is The Beat Generation." "It involves a sort of nakedness of mind, and, ultimately, of soul," he wrote, "a feeling of being reduced to the bedrock of consciousness." Thus, the term was introduced to the mainstream public.

The word, by strictest definition, should be applied to William Burroughs, Allen Ginsberg, Jack Kerouac, Neal Cassidy, and Herbert Huncke, with the slightly later addition of Gregory Corso and Peter Orlovsky. However, says Watson, "By the most sweeping usage, the term includes most of the innovative poets associated with San Francisco, Black Mountain College, and New York's Downtown scene."

Although the above is technically true, the term "beat" is today most closely associated with those few years in San Francisco in the mid-1950s when a group of writers, mostly poets, both visitors to and longer-term residents of San Francisco, turned the North Beach section of San Francisco into a bohemian and literary cynosure.

The term "beatnik" was first publicly used by columnist Herb Caen in the April 2, 1958, issue of the *San Francisco Chronicle*. It was a made-up word to associate the launch during the previous October by the Russians of the first space vehicle, "Sputnik," and

the new bohemian type so prevalent in San Francisco, both being "equally far out."

If there is one event that provides the nexus for the experience of the "beat revolution" in San Francisco, it is the founding in June, 1953, of City Lights Bookshop by Peter D. Martin and Lawrence Ferlinghetti. The poet Ferlinghetti had come to San Francisco from New York in the early 1950's, and his imagination and energy were greatly instrumental in coalescing the young, avant garde writers who lived in or who floated in and out of San Francisco into some sort of dynamic community.

City Lights, named for the film starring Charlie Chaplin, in which the theme is man against machinery (or technology), was the first all-paperback store in the country. Located on the edge of San Francisco's North Beach, City Lights was also a publishing company, putting out many of the poems being written by the beat poets and a newsletter, which carried reviews that almost no other publication printed. (City Lights' newsletter was also one of the first publications to seriously review cinema as an art form, utilizing a young Berkeley woman by the name of Pauline Kael as its reviewer.)

City Lights Bookstore, founded in 1953 by Lawrence Ferlinghetti, who stands in front, and a partner, was the nexus of the beat experience in San Francisco during the 1950s.
Courtesy San Francisco Public Library.
Photo by John O'Hara.

One of the gurus of the North Beach bohemian scene was Henri Lenoir. He's shown here in front of a spoof on becoming a beatnik. *Courtesy San Francisco Public Library.*

San Francisco State Poetry Center, started by Ruth Witt-Diamont and inaugurated with a reading by W.H. Auden.

Around City Lights — in the North Beach area — would grow a bohemian complex that became the venue for the brief literary explosion that marked San Francisco in the mid-1950s. For many years North Beach had been part of the Italian ghetto of San Francisco. In the aftermath of World War II, in parallel with many of the city's neighborhoods, its denizens began to move to newer sections of San Francisco or to the suburbs. Attracted by the cheap rents for both residential and commercial space and by the Mediterranean quality of the low-rise, dilapidated buildings (built in the aftermath of the earthquake and fire of 1906) and the Italian presence of delicatessens, bakeries, and coffee houses, the beats gravitated to the area. Soon they had put their own, distinctive imprint on what had been a sober, but colorful, immigrant enclave.

Among the peculiar characteristics of the beat writers was their desire for the unconventional, to "epater les bourgeois," Not satisfied to break new ground in their writing, the beats led lives that horrified and provoked the ultra-conservative society of the late 1940s and the 1950s. In part, the lives of the beats — and their writings — were a protest

The relaxed atmosphere of City Lights made it a community center for the gathering bohemian tribe in North Beach. Browsers would sit for hours reading books plucked off the shelves. Chess players and kibitzers would linger on for the entire time the shop was open. Notices — seeking rentals, offering goods or services for sale, telling a friend of vacation plans, alerting someone as to where he or she should meet — littered the community bulletin board. Serious conversations about books, ideas, or happenings about the city were held in hushed tones. City Lights was the heartbeat of the Beat movement in San Francisco. It was in the bookstore tradition of Sylvia Beach's Shakespeare & Company in Paris and Frances Steloff's Gotham Book Mart in New York City.

In the year following Ferlinghetti's and Martin's opening of City Lights, another institution was founded which would augment what had come to be called the San Francisco Poetry Renaissance: the

The Cafe Trieste was one of the best-known coffee houses in North Beach. *Courtesy San Francisco Public Library.*

against the society in which they lived: against war, against materialism, against plundering the planet's resources, against what they saw as the constriction and hypocrisy of conventional relationships.

Yet another part of their lives can only be explained by certain pathologies of marginal individuals: mental illness, criminality, anarchistic attitudes. Sexual mores, certainly by the standards of the time, flouted every convention of the day. Behavior bordering on derangement, petty criminal and con-man sorties, the heavy use of drugs, living in squalor, and, rarely, if ever, seeking conventional employment, the beat convened his life on the order of the French tradition of the bohemian writers: Villon and Genet (and that quintessential U.S. writer who spent many years in Paris, Henry Miller).

In an age of conformity and uniformity, the beats and their camp followers personified, even in their attire, a desire to be "different," A black beret, goatee, and black jeans (or black tights, if female) were the costume of choice. A distinctive argot, developed from many sources, was soon being imitated by those who enjoyed the exotic.

Coffee shops, long a fixture in North Beach, now proliferated for the beats and the poets *manque*. Their tables were filled with young men and women, writing prose and poetry while sipping a cappuccino, discussing existential philosophy or the meaning of life, debating the relative merits of various avant garde writers. The abstract expressionist art of the day hung on the brick walls of these coffee houses; and in the evenings many turned into a venue for poetry readings.

The *viva voce* reading of poetry was a hallmark of the San Francisco Poetry Renaissance, much of it to the accompaniment of jazz (usually a sole saxophone, improvising to the rhythm of the poetry; in the case of Kenneth Rexroth's public, formal readings, a full jazz orchestra which had been rehearsed), which at this time was flourishing in major cities throughout the United States.

Translator, essayist, critic, and poet, Kenneth Rexroth disclaimed being a beat, but was a major bohemian presence in San Francisco for a few decades. *Courtesy San Francisco Public Library. Photo by Arthur Knight.*

The Cellar (576 Green Street), the Co-Existence Bagel Shop (1398 Grant Avenue), the Coffee Gallery (1353 Grant Avenue), the Caffe Trieste (606 Vallejo Street), the Iron Pot (639 Montgomery Street), Vesuvio's (255 Columbus Avenue, across the alley from City Lights), the Place (1546 Grant Avenue), known for its open social forum, called Blabbermouth Night, and that site of countless Italian-American wedding receptions, Fugazi Hall, were among the best known of San Francisco's beat coffee houses.

But it was not in a North Beach coffee house, but in a former auto garage in the very conventional Marina District that had been converted into an art gallery and venue for poetry reading, that the defining moment — and, according to some literary historians, the beginning of — the San Francisco Poetry Renaissance took place on October 13, 1955.

The former garage had been named the Six Gallery; and a painter associated with it had invited poet and essayist Kenneth Rexroth to organize a poetry reading. Rexroth enlisted the help of poet Michael McClure, who, in turn, sought the help of Allen Ginsberg.

About 100 mimeographed cards were sent out as invitations and numerous announcements were posted in the bars and coffee houses of North Beach.

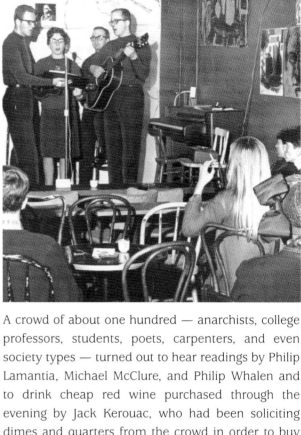

A crowd of about one hundred — anarchists, college professors, students, poets, carpenters, and even society types — turned out to hear readings by Philip Lamantia, Michael McClure, and Philip Whalen and to drink cheap red wine purchased through the evening by Jack Kerouac, who had been soliciting dimes and quarters from the crowd in order to buy the beverage.

Rexroth was the evening's master of ceremonies; and, at 10:30 p.m., after about two-and-a-half hours of readings, called for a break. Around 11:00 p.m., Ginsberg stood up and for the first time read from his recently completed poem "Howl," which he had begun the previous August in his apartment at 1010 Montgomery Street.

Steven Watson gives the following description: "Starting off in a calm and earnest voice that grew in intensity as he fed off the audience's enthusiasm, Ginsberg began to sway rhythmically, waving his arms, taking deep breaths to sustain him through each of the long verse lines. He sounded like a cantor, like a troubadour, and the audience had never heard such rawly extravagant language in public."

In 12 minutes of reading Ginsberg had sent an

electric shock through the poetic imagination of the United States: the orgiastic experience of this less than quarter hour exploded into a roaring ovation.

Much of the crowd went on to Sam Wo's for Chinese food and then on to The Place to drink. That night, Lawrence Ferlinghetti, echoing Emerson's message to Walt Whitman upon receiving *Leaves of Grass*, sent Ginsberg a telegram: "I greet you at the beginning of a great career. When do I get the manuscript?" In the following year — 1956 — City Lights published "Howl."

Ginsberg's searing indictment of society echoed the outrage of the classic Hebrew prophets, calling Israel to fidelity to its covenant with Yahweh. Some of this parallel is seen in his inspired, repetitive use of "Moloch" in the poem. It begins solemnly:

> I saw the best minds of my generation destroyed by
> madness, starving, hysterical, naked
> dragging themselves through the Negro streets
> at dawn
> looking for an angry fix, angelheaded hipsters
> burning for the ancient heavenly
> connection to the starry dynamo in the machinery
> of night, who poverty and tatters and hollow-eyed
> and high sat
> up smoking in the supernatural darkness of cold-
> water flats floating across the tops of cities
> contemplating jazz,
> who bared their brains to heaven under the El and saw
> Mohammedon angels staggering on tenement roofs
> illuminated, who cowered in unshaven rooms in
> underwear burning their
> money in wastebaskets amid the rubbish of mem-
> orable Berkeley manifestoes listening to the
> terror through the wall, who got busted in their
> pubic beards returning
> through Laredo with a belt of marijuana for New York,
> who passed through universities with radiant cool
> eyes hallucinating Arkansas and Blake-light
> tragedy among the scholars of war.

The second part of the poem begins:

> What sphinx of cement and aluminum bashed open
> their skulls and ate up their brains and imagination?
> Moloch! Solitude! Filth! Ugliness! Ashcans and unob-
> tainable dollars! Garbage heap of eyebrows
> and brains! Children screaming under the stairways!
> Old men weeping in the parks!
> Moloch! Moloch! Nightmare of Moloch! Moloch
> the loveless! Mental Moloch! Moloch the heavy
> judger of men!
> Moloch the incomprehensible prison! Moloch the
> crossbone
> soulless jailhouse
> and Congress of sorrows! Moloch whose buildings
> are judgment! Moloch
> the vast stone of war! Moloch the stunned
> governments! Moloch whose eyes are a thousand
> blind windows! Moloch
> whose skyscrapers stand in the long streets like
> endless Jehovahs! Moloch whose factories dream
> and croak in the fog! Moloch whose smokestacks
> and antennae crown the cities!

But, parts of "Howl" would include such raw language that was seen by his fellow poets as a radical departure from what had been acceptable to public writing and which would lead to the arrest and trial of Ferlinghetti and his then partner in City Lights for obscenity (a charge of which they would be acquitted).

The San Francisco Renaissance, which literary historians claim to have ended in 1960s with the publication of the last issue of *Beatitude* magazine, should not be seen as a "school" or a hard-and-fast movement. Some of the poets most closely associated with the renaissance — Rexroth and Ferlinghetti, for example — always insisted that they were not beat poets. Often obscured, also, are the antecedents of the San Francisco Renaissance in the amalgam of radical politics, poetry, and bohemian living in the 1920s, 1930s and 1940s. It should also be noticed that the avant garde poetry of those who participated in the San Francisco Renaissance relied on numerous different traditions. Literary historian Steven Watson writes:

"The San Francisco poets pursued the experiments of the earlier American generation in what was called open form poetry. They aspired in troubadour fashion to revive the spoken voice. This affected not only poetry's preferred form of presentation — public readings, often accompanied by jazz or simple percussion, rather than printed words — but also its sound.

"Several of the San Francisco poets shared the Beats' interest in confessional poetry, in consciousness-expanding drugs, and in sexual liberation. They also shared the bond of commitment to pacifism and to libertarian anarchism. Interest in Eastern religion, notably Buddhism and Taoism, tied many of the poets together. The natural environment figured prominently in their poems, depicted as endangered by mid-twentieth century civilization and as a beneficent environment for mankind. Poetry as an expression of the magical can be seen in the shared interest in the occult, Tarot readings, alchemy, automatic writing.

"Aside from shared aesthetic concerns and common themes, the Renaissance can be best described as overlapping constellations of poets who chose San Francisco for their home; their tightly knit relationships mattered as much as their writing."

These "overlapping constellations" can be seen in the individual lives of some of those who constituted the San Francisco Renaissance.

The first generation would include Kenneth Rexroth, William Everson (also known as Brother Antoninus), and Robert Duncan, who lived in Berkeley.

Rexroth came to San Francisco from Chicago, where he was born in 1905, in the late 1920s. The polymath Rexroth — essayist, poet, radical, book reviewer, and translator — was the elder statesman and "pontiff" of the group which assembled in San Francisco during the 1950s. Author of one of the best anti-war poems ever written, "Thou shalt not kill,"

Rexroth, who could be quite a prickly individual and could be quite dismissive and derisory of the younger poets. He came to loathe Gregory Corso and Jack Kerouac for their bad manners (and Kerouac for what he considered a pandering role in poet Creeley's affair with his — Rexroth's — wife). A classic dismissive statement of Rexroth's was: "They came to us late, from the slums of Greenwich Village, and they departed only for the salons of millionairesses."

The passion of Rexroth's *persona* is quite evident in his poetry. "Thou shalt not kill," for example, begins:

They are murdering all the young men.
For half a century now, every day,
They have hunted them down and killed them,
They are killing the young men,
They know ten thousand ways to kill them,
Every year they invent new ones.
In the jungle of Africa,
In the marshes of Asia,
In the deserts of Asia,
In the slaves pens of Siberia,
In the slums of Europe,
In the nightclubs of America,
The murderers are at work.

It ends:

And all the birds of the deep sea rise up
Over the luxury liners and scream,
"You killed him! You killed him,
In your God damned Brooks Brothers suit,
You son of a bitch"

William Everson (known also as Brother Antoninus, the name he took for the decade and a half he spent as a Dominican friar) is yet another poet who refused to identify himself as a Beat, rather pointing to Robinson Jeffers as having produced his intellectual awakening. "Jeffers showed me God," he said. "In Jeffers I found my voice."

A conscientious objector who spent World War II in a work camp in Waldport, Oregon, Everson became a fine printer (printing as an art has had a long tradition in San Francisco) and frequently printed his own poetry.

The younger generation would include Lawrence Ferlinghetti, Gary Snyder, Peter Orlovsky, Michael McClure, Bob Kaufman, Lew Welch, David Meltzer, Jack Micheline, John Wieners, Jack Spicer, and Kenneth Patchen.

Allen Ginsberg, Jack Kerouac, Gregory Corso, and Robert Creeley, despite their importance to the San Francisco Renaissance, can only be considered visitors to San Francisco. Ginsberg and Kerouac both arrived in San Francisco in 1954 to visit Neal and Carolyn Cassidy and left the city by late 1956.

Kerouac, whose masterpiece *On the Road* was published in 1957, wrote his first sequence of poems, "San Francisco Blues" in 1954 in the Cameo Hotel, in the midst of San Francisco's then "skid row," He would use the Iron Pot, a restaurant-bar hangout for artists and bohemians on Montgomery Street, near North Beach, as the setting for his novel *The Subterraneans* (the Iron Pot is a substitute for a bar in New York called the San Remo).

With the departure of Ginsberg and Kerouac in 1956 for Tangiers, where they helped William Burroughs in producing *Naked Lunch* and with that of Gary Snyder for one of his stints studying Buddhism in the Far East, the spiritual leadership of the San Francisco Renaissance was assumed by Bob Kaufman — a revered poet, particularly in Europe — who was the son of a German Orthodox Jew and an African-American Catholic from Martinique.

Kaufman was a merchant seaman from the age of thirteen until 1954, when he arrived in San Francisco. Steven Watson describes him:

"He played the shaman-like role often found in avant garde groups — the figure who is most purely disposed, most unimpeachably alienated.

"His commitment to anarchism and freedom of expression was total and he repeatedly clashed with the police."

By the late 1950s the Beats had become a celebrity group. The conventional media — *Time* and *Mademoiselle* among them — wrote articles about them. *Mad* magazine lampooned them. Hollywood made films about beatniks. Several beat exploitation novels appeared (including *Bang a Beatnik*, *Jesus Was a Beatnik*, and *Lust Pad*). The television situation comedy "The Many Loves of Dobie Gillis" had as a principal character Maynard G. Krebs, an aspiring beatnik.

Tour buses with gawking tourists threaded through North Beach. An ersatz beat culture developed in North Beach, with poets *manque* and "angry young men" displaying themselves in the cafes and coffee houses. Then came the end even of this ersatz culture. The North Beach haunts were being transformed into record stores and sandal and jewelry shops. The unauthentic moved away to Venice, (California), Bolinas (on the Northern California ocean shore), and to New York City. The media lost interest.

San Francisco, celebrated as the most visible venue for this literary spasm of the mid 1950s, returned to a quiet that would once more be disrupted by yet another revolution of the young in the following decade.

The Kingston Trio sings at Enrico Banducci's hungry i in the 1950s. *Courtesy San Francisco Public Library.*

*C*al Tjader at the
Blackhawk.
Courtesy San Francisco
Public Library.

*T*he Purple Onion was
one of San Francisco's
most popular venues
for fresh, young talent
in the 1950s.
Courtesy San Francisco
Public Library.

Parallel to the beat experience in North Beach was a new entertainment foray in the same area. In the early 1950s two nightclubs opened which became San Francisco legends and nationally acclaimed for their presenting new and fresh and unknown comic and musical talent that would in succeeding decades become great stars.

As the traditional San Francisco supper clubs closed their doors, the hungry i and the Purple Onion became crowded with natives and visitors alike.

The more famous of the two was Enrico Banducci's hungry i, located first in the cellar of the Columbus Tower and then at 599 Jackson Street. Banducci, a voluble bohemian bear of a man, always wearing a trademark beret, had an exquisite eye for young talent. Taking advantage of the young people's increasing taste for the informal, Banducci arranged the hungry i in the guise of one of North Beach's coffee houses. One went down a long flight of steps to enter an L-shaped bar and lounge, on the walls of which hung caricatures of patrons and of the comics and musicians who had appeared there.

Adjacent to the bar and lounge was a theatre that seated about three hundred individuals. A bare brick wall stood behind the stage.

And next to it was The Other Room, which had all the appearance of a traditional supper club (dinner was served there), where the likes of Bobby Short, Mabel Mercer, and Sylvia Sims would perform.

The ensemble that performed at the hungry i, frequently in their first public appearance, would encompass many who would become stars during the second half of the twentieth century. Among the comics were: Bill Cosby, Mort Sahl, Lenny Bruce, Elaine May and Mike Nichols, Shelly Berman, Bob Newhart, Jonathan Winters, Phyllis Diller, "Professor" Irwin Corey, Richard Pryor, Dick Gregory, Tom Lehrer, and Woody Allen.

And, among the musicians were: The Limelighters, the Kingston Trio, Barbra Streisand, and Peter, Paul and Mary.

The 1950s and early 1960s — which were the glory years for the hungry i — were a time of general contentment and the era, known as "the Eisenhower Years," was known for its conformity and its respect for authority. The beats certainly challenged this conformity; and, usually in a more low-key and satirical way, so did the comics who performed at the hungry i. Although today political satire has come to be ubiquitous, in the 1950s Mort Sahl's mordant political satire was considered to be quite daring.

Beyond the pale of any kind of gentility was the dramatic comedian Lenny Bruce. Bruce's corrosive humor, complete with an almost violent language and the use of words then deemed to be criminal if uttered in public, pushed back the frontiers of what was considered admissible public discourse. Silence on sexual matters, political conservatism, bigotry — all were considered anathema to Bruce, who skewered them in his skits.

In these tepid critiques and satire of the 1950s we see the beginnings of what would be the relentless criticism of government and society that would make the 1960s.

For such entertainment Banducci charged a cover charge of 25 cents on weekdays and 50 cents on weekends.

The hungry i's success brought little or no financial success to Enrico Banducci. As the talent he had showcased became famous, he could no longer afford to pay their escalated prices. The public taste was changing. Those who delighted in the combination of genial comedy and folk singing groups had gotten older, were raising families, had moved to the suburbs. The young, as the 1960s progressed, sought out the mega-concerts of rock music.

Yet another phenomenon of the post-World War II period was the renaissance in jazz which occurred in San Francisco. During the 1940s and 1950s San Francisco momentarily challenged New York's pre-eminence in jazz music.

This renaissance centered around two totally different movements. The earliest of these began in the early 1940s and was largely the work of trumpeter Lu Waters, who founded the Yerba Buena Jazz Band, which played at the Dawn Club at 20 Annie Street, next to the Palace Hotel.

Waters' band played a revival of what is called traditional jazz, or New Orleans jazz. It represented a turning away from the swing and bebop which had dominated earlier years. Nevertheless, this anachronistic revival, which indicated "West Coast jazz" in the east, was seen as retrogressive there.

When the Yerba Buena Jazz Band broke up around 1950s, Waters' mantle as the leader of the traditional jazz revival fell to trombonist Turk Murphy. Murphy would be a San Francisco fixture for many years, and his band playing at Earthquake McGoon's became a popular occupation for jazz fans in the 1960s and 1970s.

The second locus of jazz creativity centered around the unusual personality and music of Dave Brubeck. Brubeck, who grew up on ranches in Contra Costa and Amador counties, studied music at the University of the Pacific in Stockton and then, after a stint in the military during World War II, at Mills College in Oakland under Darius Milhaud.

Brubeck began to develop a controversial style of music which was founded on his studies of classical music, and which, despite the frequent carping of critics, has remained popular in both recordings and performances to the present.

While Lu Waters and Turk Murphy represented San Francisco's quixotic revival of traditional jazz, Brubeck was the leader of San Francisco's development of modern jazz; and from his various groups — the octet, the trio, the quartet — would come a number of musicians and composers who would give luster to the jazz music: Cal Tjader, a Swedish-American from the Midwest, became the father of Latin jazz on the West Coast, pianist Vince Guaraldi, and the now-largely forgotten Brew Moore.

Numerous jazz clubs provided venues for San Francisco's jazz musicians: the Jazz Cellar on Green

Dave Brubeck, one of the San Francico Bay Area's major jazz talents, performs in San Francisco in 1965. *Courtesy San Francisco Public Library.*

Street, the Jazz Workshop on Broadway, Jimbo's Bop City on Fillmore Street, The Tin Angel (where Kit Orey, Earl "Fatha" Hines, and Muggsy Spanier would play), the Hangover Club, the El Matador.

But, the most celebrated of these clubs was the Blackhawk on Turk Street (at Hyde). The club would see the likes of John Coltrane, Charlie Mingus, and the Modern Jazz Quartet play there; and it presented the rising Dave Brubeck and other local notables.(The Blackhawk is also known for fostering the beginning performances of a young San Francisco singer by the name of Johnny Mathis.)

The vibrant and vital jazz scene in San Francisco during the late 1940s, the 1950s and the early 1960s was to wither away as the decade of the 1960s progressed. Turk Murphy drew a dwindling audience of nostalgic jazz buffs at Earthquake McGoon's. Brubeck, Tjader, and Guaraldi continued to do well in their traveling concerts and recordings; but the San Francisco jazz renaissance had disappeared.

Many have attributed this demise to the rise of rock 'n' roll, but legendary jazz critic Phil Elwood disputes this, speculating that the jazz musicians

Turk Murphy's most famous venue was Earthquake McGoon's, where he performed for decades. *Courtesy San Francisco Public Library.*

themselves were at fault by electing to appeal to small, fringe audiences and seeing themselves almost as gnostic musicians, developing exotic music for the initiated few. When rock music began its ascent, it captured a young audience that was unaware of jazz.

At any rate, for two decades very little jazz could be heard in San Francisco. A revival in the 1980s, which continues to the present day, marks somewhat of a return to the passionate interest in jazz that characterized the decade and a half after World War II.

The late-1950s saw the end of the ferry boats plying San Francisco Bay. Here, the Alameda *docks in San Francisco after its journey from Oakland.*
Courtesy San Francisco Public Library.

Public Improvements

The post-World War II period was a time of vast public works throughout the United States. The economic constraints of the Depression and the focus on winning the war during the first half of the 1940s put aside public improvements. With the end of this decade and a half of financial inhibition and the accompanying economic exuberance following World War II, urban areas throughout the country borrowed great sums to augment their infrastructures.

The automobile would be the transportation phenomenon of the post-World War II period. A vast national program of highways was inaugurated; and the role of San Francisco as the hub of an expanding urban area made automotive access to the city a major priority.

Parkmerced, a planned community in San Francisco's southwestern section, filled in the city's barren wastes and agricultural area in the post-World War II era.
Courtesy San Francisco Public Library.

Union Square in 1953. A garage underneath the historic park accommodates shoppers to the center of the city's retail district. *Courtesy San Francisco Public Library.*

Union Square, with the St. Francis Hotel in the background, gets transformed with an underground garage. *Courtesy San Francisco Public Library.*

For a decade after World War II San Francisco was not only the site of major employment, but also the principal source for entertainment, shopping, and professional services. It was imperative that the outlying counties, increasingly dense suburbs, have easy automotive access to the city. This process had begun in the 1930s, with the construction of two bridges, and, in the aftermath of the war, wide highways would be built to link those bridges more effectively with San Francisco, as well as providing the increasing numbers of residents of San Mateo and Santa Clara counties with rapid and efficient automotive access to San Francisco. Multi-lane freeways began to be constructed that slashed through neighborhoods and dumped tens of thousands of automobiles into the city. (This subject will be discussed more extensively in the next chapter.)

Under the constant demand from San Francisco's merchants and employers for places to park these cars, the city embarked on a vast garage construction

The sparse two buildings of the airport. These two buildings would represent the airport until its expansion after World War II. *Courtesy San Francisco Public Library.*

program. City-built and operated parking garages began to dot the downtown area. Several-story garages were placed at strategic places near the retail areas and the business district. Parking garages were also built under city parks, such as Union Square and Portsmouth Plaza.

Yet another form of transportation that began to receive public attention after World War II was aviation. The San Francisco Bay Area had been a pioneer in the development of lighter-than-air flight since the 1860s. After the Wright Brothers' flight in 1906, the airplane became an increasing presence in Western Europe and the United States. Avid aviators in the Bay Area used golf courses, sand dunes, and other flat areas for taking off and landing their primitive aircraft. Two barnstorming pilots (one of whom died when his airplane plunged into the bay just off the Marina Green) were the sensation of the Panama Pacific International Exposition in 1915. Military use, utilizing airplanes to drop bombs, was first demon-

strated in 1911 in the Bay Area. An airport in the Marina District was contemplated, and military authorities did establish Crissy Field in the adjacent Presidio; but various geographical features rendered both of these sites as impractical. Aerial mail service was established in 1918.

It soon became apparent that aviation was not just a toy, but would be an important and integral part of modern transportation, having civilian commercial use as well as military use.

The first building of San Francisco's airport, built in 1927.
Courtesy San Francisco Public Library.

This recognition led to a charter amendment vote in 1926 in which San Franciscans overwhelmingly approved a plan by which the city would purchase land outside of its confines to develop an airport.

In 1927 Michael O'Shaughnessy, City Engineer, recommended the lease of one hundred fifty acres of land from the Mills Estate, an area fourteen miles south of San Francisco, in the town of Millbrae. The land had the advantage of being adjacent to a thousand acres of submerged wetlands which could be used for expansion.

The airport was named Mills Field and San Francisco Municipal Airport.

However, for the next decade and a half, San Francisco's airport staggered in its operations. San Francisco's voters turned down several bond issues to improve

Stonestown Shopping Center in the mid-1960s. Courtesy San Francisco Public Library.

San Francisco Fills In

The largest part of San Francisco had been developed by the beginning of World War II. During the 1920s, the 1930s and the 1940s, the western portion of San Francisco witnessed its sand dunes covered with block after block of individual houses, duplexes, and some apartment houses, the names of Doelger, Galli, and Gellert being among the principal builders of homes, as the city marched relentlessly toward the ocean.

In the early 1950s two major landmarks arose in the westernmost part of San Francisco: the Stonestown Shopping Center and Parkmerced Towers.

The Stonestown Shopping Center was the creation of two San Francisco builder-brothers, Ellis and Henry Stoneson; it began in 1948 and was completed in 1952. At the time, it was the fourth largest project of its type in the United States. It was the first shopping center — and remains the only one in San Francisco.

In the late 1980s the Stonestown Shopping Center underwent a massive renovation and transformation. A $55 million face-lift was designed by San Francisco architect John Field. A retail gallery, modeled after Milan's famous Galleria Victor Emmanuel, was part of the venerable shopping center's transformation.

At about the time that the Stoneson brothers finished the Stonestown Shopping Center, nearby, the Metropolitan Life Insurance Company was completing the final phase of its "city-within-a-city" — Parkmerced. Begun during World War II, Parkmerced was intended as a planned community within the urban confines of San Francisco. Two hundred acres of sand dunes were transformed into 1700 apartments and townhouses and eleven 13-story apartment buildings. Services for the community were (and are) taken care of by the housing corporation; and numerous entertainment additions to the complex implemented the plans for a self-sufficient urban housing center.

and expand the facility. Its operations lost money. Some airlines switched to Oakland. The depression of the 1930s made such public expenditures appear unnecessary and wasteful. It was contemplated that a new airport be constructed on the man-made island called Treasure Island, which after its use for the Golden Gate International Exposition in 1939-1940, would become San Francisco's airport.

World War II preempted these calculations. The military preempted Treasure Island. The federal government poured millions of dollars into improving and enlarging Mills Field. The war itself had shown the importance of the airplane.

The confidence and prosperity following World War II changed the voters' sentiments. They approved overwhelmingly a $20 million bond issue in November, 1945. Another bond issue — for $10 million — passed in 1949.

The lone terminal, with cows grazing in pastures adjoining the runways, was soon transformed into a huge complex. Many acres of bay wetlands were filled for the airport's expansion. The use of aviation for pleasure, business, and commercial cargo uses soared during the postwar years; and the San Francisco International Airport became one of the nation's busiest transportation nexuses.

Police drag water-soaked protesters down the Grand Staircase in City Hall. The riots occurred during the House Subcommittee on Un-American Activities meetings. *Courtesy San Francisco Chronicle.*

Riots in City Hall

The year 1960 was a presidential election year. After eight years in office, President Eisenhower would surrender his office to a successor. The national conformity that marked his administration had given his name — the Eisenhower Years — to the decade and a half after World War II. The youth of this era were known as "the silent generation."

But, in 1960, change was in the air. A youthful, vigorous, and imaginative senator from Massachusetts would be elected president in November of that year. The U.S. Supreme Court had already been handing down decisions of a liberal and progressive nature in the area of antitrust, civil rights, and personal liberties. College students at the beginning of the 1960s were beginning to become more vocal about what they considered to be inequities in society.

On Friday, May 13, 1960, a sign of these changing times took place in San Francisco's majestic city hall. The House Subcommittee on Un-American Activities decided it would hold hearings in San Francisco, and commandeered the board of supervisors' chambers in City Hall. Still influenced by the publicity-seeking and inflammatory methods of the now-censured Senator Joseph McCarthy, the subcommittee had become the principal target for those who objected to its Red-baiting, bullying tactics.

Students (and others) from around the Bay Area gathered in City Hall to protest the hearings. They were kept out of the supervisors' chambers by the subcommittee's careful control of who had access to the hearings; and, on the second day, Friday, May 13, tempers flared and the students became more unruly, singing, chanting, clapping, and stomping.

At about 1:15 p.m., the fifty-five policemen, who had leniently patrolled City Hall, suddenly became determined to end the demonstration. A fire hose was aimed at the students, and water flooded the marble floor and grand staircase of City Hall. The policemen's clubs subdued any resisting students, who were washed down or dragged down the staircase.

The mayor of San Francisco, the big, imposing George Christopher, spoke to the retreating students outside City Hall, saying that he had just come back from a trip to the Soviet Union and knew first-hand of the need for preserving order and obeying the law; but the shocked students booed him.

A municipal judge dismissed the charges against all but one of the sixty-four persons arrested, but chided the demonstrators for their unruly behavior and for creating a disturbance.

A controversy flared out after the riots, fueled by charges from members of the subcommittee that the riots had been caused by Communist agitators. Even Christopher, a conservative and certainly unfavorable to the demonstrators, was criticized by members of the subcommittee.

The subcommittee had subpoenaed television footage from the cameramen who had covered the riots and had a private firm produce a film called "Operation Abolition," (The name related to the film's theme that anyone advocating the abolition of the House Subcommittee on Un-American Affairs was either a Communist or a Communist dupe.) The obvious bias of the film sparked liberals and civil rights activists to attack its manipulation of the facts and its bigoted premise.

The controversy died down; but the demonstrations and riot of Friday, May 13, 1960, in San Francisco's City Hall were to be an omen of a decade and a half of tumultuous disaffection in San Francisco.

Chapter 2

1960—1978

Tumult and Disaffection

1 9 6 0 - 1 9 7 8

THE HOUSE UN-AMERICAN ACTIVITIES COMMITTEE RIOT IN CITY HALL IN MAY, 1960, USHERED IN a period of violence and volcanic upheaval in San Francisco. This violence and upheaval mirrored that of the nation and the world.

The election of John F. Kennedy as President of the United States inaugurated a time of optimism and a sense of national renewal. His death in November, 1963, shattered that optimism and confidence; and the subsequent assassinations of Martin Luther King and Robert Kennedy, the prolonged conflict in Vietnam, the highlighting of social and economic inequities in the United States through the War on Poverty, the incessant demonstrations on college and university campuses, and the riots in many cities created an atmosphere of lawlessness and disorder.

San Francisco was spared none of the divisiveness that distracted the nation. Its politics became driven by faction and incivility. A bitter strike by municipal employees indicated the end of the harmony that had marked the decade and a half after the end of World War II. The dramatic and drastic social changes — particularly among the young — that characterized the 1960s and 1970s astonished the community.

Physical and demographic changes created a new San Francisco. Familiar landmarks disappeared; and the modest skyline was transformed by what critics called "the Manhattanization of San Francisco". Traditional ethnic neighborhoods disappeared; and entire sections of the city became redeveloped into entirely transformed parts of San Francisco. The city's minority structure changed: an influx of Asians made that group one of the largest minorities in San Francisco; Hispanics, largely from Central America, dominated the Mission District, once largely Irish; homosexuals began to form a

community, residing mostly in the Inner Mission — the Castro area; and the power of the city's establishment — Anglo-Saxon corporate leaders, old German Jewish families, the Italian — and Irish — Catholic power brokers — began to dissipate. New groups and new alliances began to take their place.

Most of the city's small manufacturing businesses either closed their doors or left San Francisco. The venue for such businesses — South of Market — was re-created into an area of a convention center, tall skyscrapers, and a broad spectrum of housing.

A certain cosmopolitan elegance that had long characterized San Francisco also ended. The snap brim fedora that most men had worn for many years disappeared. And no longer did women — whether socialites or from the working classes — wear hats and white gloves every time they went shopping in San Francisco's retail district.

The cultural staples of several decades began to disappear. The ballads crooned by generations of singers, the songs that were sung on the Lucky Strike Hit Parade — "How Much Is That Doggie in the Window?", "I'd Love To Get You On a Slow Boat to China", and so many others — gave way to the harsh sounds of Janis Joplin and the amplified music of numerous rock 'n' roll bands.

Thousands flocked to the Fillmore Auditorium, where light shows, rock music, and the pervasive use of drugs had created an entirely new cultural landscape that would be replicated throughout the country.

Meanwhile, in San Francisco, in Berkeley, on countless college and university campuses, and in virtually every city in the United States, strident demonstrations and protests — against the war in Vietnam, against racial injustice, against capitalism, against virtually every value which had been held by the country's middle class and working class for generations — were in full swing. Never before in the history of the United States — with the exception of the Civil War — had such pervasive divisiveness so torn apart the nation.

As the 1970s progressed, however, the protests and demonstrations diminished. Students began to return to their studies. Interrupted careers were resumed. Young radicals turned to more mundane pursuits. Some drifted off to live in communes or to exotic foreign areas.

The stridency of the 1960s and early 1970s in San Francisco was replaced by a new phenomenon: the New Age. San Francisco became the City of Oz for a myriad of organizations that promised personal happiness and fulfillment and groups that organized the Sexual Revolution into a mandate for all who wished to be dominated by the pleasure principle. Whether down the Big Sur coast at Esalen or in San Francisco's Civic Auditorium, where the charismatic Werner Erhard proclaimed the e s t-ian revolution, the promise of heaven on earth became a major industry in San Francisco.

But, as what has been called "the Me Decade" dominated the sociological landscape of San Francisco, shifts of great complexity were beginning to transform the city's political world. The last few years of the era under examination in this chapter saw the beginning of the overthrow of the establishment coalition that had governed San Francisco for many years: an amalgam of conservative labor unions, "old" families, owners and managers of long-established, locally-based corporations, the conservative Irish-Italian-Jewish complex of voters, and conservative white-collar workers.

Slowly, but steadily, a change in demographics, the organization of young activists, the increasing popularity of an anti-growth, anti-business political agenda, and the gradual disappearance of the components of the previous ruling oligarchy changed San Francisco's political ruling structure into a progressive, even radical, coalition that has resulted in San Francisco's being dubbed "The Left Coast City".

Almost two decades after the HUAC riots at City Hall, the collective tumult and divisiveness erupted into twin tragedies that would result in further polarization, and would plunge San Francisco into the nadir of its municipal life and its national and international image. One was the murder of the city's mayor and one of its supervisors, a gay man, by a disgruntled former supervisor; the second was the mass suicide in the jungle of Guyana of a cult which had migrated there from San Francisco.

A sense of desperation, of hopelessness, of wonder at what many considered the anarchism and nihilism that had captured San Francisco, of stupefaction at the chaos that pervaded its municipal life took hold in San Francisco. Would the city self-destruct? Would the realities and values that had so long ruled in the city ever return? The disappearance of so much of the elegant, cosmopolitan, well-ordered San Francisco — including the traditional composition of its economy — surely meant that a type of Dark Ages was descending on the city.

And so, by the end of the 1970s, the sense of well-being that had so permeated San Francisco during the decade and a half after the end of World War II had gone; and in its place had come pessimism, gloom, and a sense of apocalypse.

Hippies in the Haight-Ashbury

The 1960s, aside from the HUAC riot, opened relatively quietly. After all, the clean-cut, clean-shaven, short-haired students in khakis and ties that got drenched in water and washed down the grand staircase in City Hall were hardly revolutionists. They were the sons and daughters of an affluent Bay Area middle class, protesting what they considered to be an infringement of civil liberties, protesting along the lines of the comics and folk singers who had come to be so popular among the collegians at that time.

Yes, the assassination of President John F. Kennedy had caused great anxiety in San Francisco, as well as the rest of the nation, but there were few if any signs of massive shifts in the social tectonic plates beneath the serene, affluent world of the early 1960s.

Then, in a working class district which had had a large number of Irish lower middle-class residents who lived near a neighborhood shopping street known as Haight Street, there began to emerge small signs of unconventional young men and women dressing and acting in a bizarre fashion.

The Haight-Ashbury, as the area was known, had been undergoing a post-World War II transformation. Long-time residents were either dying or moving out. The rather banal, ramshackle collection of wooden Victorian homes and those built in the first two or

Added to the local student population were a growing number of out-of-towners, many who were college drop-outs, many from poor or marginalized families in Southern California or the Southwest, many who were captivated by the British rock and roll sound now becoming popular among the young.

The usual rebellious nature of a generation against the generation before began to be seen in attire and appearance: Victorian and Edwardian clothing, as well as a shabby look of jeans and T-shirts, long dresses, often without underclothing, for women, long hair for both.

The invention of the contraceptive pill began to make sexual freedom more common among young singles; and the use of such drugs as marijuana and LSD, once taboo except among a few musicians and those totally alienated from society, became increasingly popular.

By 1964, such societal changes had become more visible in San Francisco. Organizers and icons had begun to appear. Among the first was Ken Kesey, a successful author noted for *One Flew Over the Cuckoo's Nest*, who in 1964 purchased a 1939 International Harvester bus, painted it in splotches of a dozen different colors, and gathered an entourage which he

The touring bus of Ken Kesey and his Merry Pranksters. *Courtesy San Francisco Chronicle. Photo by Gene Anthony.*

Multi-colored buses served as both homes and transportation for the peripatetic hippies. *Photo by Max Kirkeberg.*

three decades of the twentieth century had begun to acquire an air of urban blight. Rents were cheap; and San Francisco's growing college population had begun to discover the area as an inexpensive and charming place to live with an excellent location in the city's transportation system.

called the Merry Pranksters. This group proceeded to drive around the country, gathering media attention to their often drug-induced antics.

The attention of the San Francisco Bay Area began to focus on these changes, which, at first, had been dismissed as the bizarre behavior of a few young lunatics.

Helping the middle-class, older adults to see the pervasiveness of cultural change among the young were the potent demonstrations at the University of California at Berkeley in the mid-1960s. Student complaints about the university's banishment of left-wing recruiters from the campus, about issues of free speech, about the university's use of a certain parcel of its land seemed to galvanize the majority of students into protesters to such an extent that the mighty university was forced to temporarily close down.

Yet another component that was to emerge in the mid-1960s was the assemblage of rock and roll groups, many of whom would achieve international prominence and which were components of what would be called the San Francisco Sound. Concomitant with the rise of these musical groups was the

beginnings of mass audiences which would gather in parks and auditoriums, bespattered with the light shows that synchronized with the music, dancing with wild abandon to the amplified music, and often under the influence of drugs.

In 1964 a group, put together in a willy-nilly fashion by a promoter by the name of Marty Balin, played for the first time at a nightclub called the Matrix. They began to use the band's name in an advertising slogan: "The Jefferson Airplane Loves You". Receiving a favorable and perceptive review by San Francisco Chronicle jazz critic Ralph J. Gleason, the Jefferson Airplane began a march toward legendary stardom.

Yet another San Francisco group which began at this time (but made their musical debut in Virginia City, Nevada, at the renovated Red Dog Saloon) was the Charlatans, which cultivated an archaic Victorian/Edwardian look under the imaginative leadership of its founder, George Hunter.

Then, a group who had been at the Red Dog Saloon when the Charlatans had played there decided to put on some dances. The group, known as the Family Dog, rented the meeting hall of the International Longshoremen's and Warehousemen's Union near Fisherman's Wharf. A few mentions on the radio and a few silk-screened posters mailed out were the only advertisements for the event.

Someone was found to engineer the sound (no small feat in the large, octagonal hall); and it was decided that a new-fangled device known as a light show should be part of the program.

On October 17, 1964, a large crowd turned up at the Longshoremen's Hall for the event, most attired in outlandish clothing — from Mod clothes to Victorian suits, from granny gowns to pirate costumes — and, at the end of the evening, cleaned up after itself, picked up the litter, and deposited it in trash cans.

The Family Dog repeated the dance the following weekend, once again featuring the Charlatans, to which even more people came. The grapevine, coupled with

Long an iconoclastic institution in San Francisco, the San Francisco Mime Troupe had Bill Graham as its manager in the 1960s. Graham sponsored a rock and roll benefit for the troupe, which was the springboard for his success as a rock music entrepreneur. *Courtesy San Francisco Public Library.*

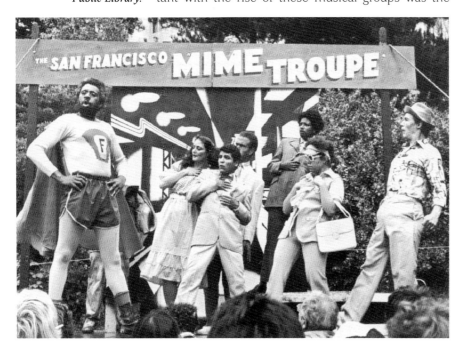

a glowing account of the previous dance in Ralph Gleason's column, ensured a sell-out crowd.

The format would be used again on November 6 in a loft on Howard Street, when a benefit (called the Appeal) was staged for the San Francisco Mime Troupe, whose manager was an actor *manqúe* by the name of Bill Graham.

The loft's limit of 500 persons was greatly exceeded, and Graham was forced to fast-talk the police into not clearing out the space because of the gathering's violation of fire code regulations.

On the same evening, the Family Dog had put on its third dance at the Longshoremen's Hall, and it too had been a great success. However, the group's business inexperience greatly hampered its ability to make any profit whatsoever.

This was not the case with the man who had staged the Appeal and who had instantaneously recognized the potential of rock dances as a money-making vehicle. Bill Graham rented an old auditorium in the Fillmore District for a December 10 benefit for the Mime Troupe. It would feature the Jefferson Airplane, Great Society (with its lead singer, Grace Slick), Mystery Trend, the John Handy Quintet, and the Gentlemen's Band.

A poster — the forerunner of the "psychedelic" posters that would in time become collector's items — advertised the event; and Graham also appropriated the Family Dog's use of a light show.

On the evening of the "dance-concert", as Graham billed it, there was a double line outside the auditorium's entrance at 9:30 p.m. There was still one at 1:00 a.m.

New music groups continued to form. A marijuana legalization activist by the name of Chet Helms, who would later take over the management of the Family Dog operation, put together a group at 1090 Page Street called Big Brother and the Holding Company. A group of kids from Palo Alto, who, like an increasing number of rock musicians in the Bay Area, were partisans of Ken Kesey and his Merry Pranksters and

Bill Graham on the telephone working deals with rock groups. *Courtesy San Francisco Chronicle.*

participants in their drug parties, formed a band known successively as Mother McCree's Uptown Jug Stompers, the Energy Crew, and the Warlocks. Led by a former bluegrass banjoist by the name of Jerome Garcia, they would undergo yet another name change to become known as the Grateful Dead. Yet another group of musical enthusiasts in San Francisco became known as the Quicksilver Messenger Service.

The Pranksters were responsible for yet another of the early innovative musical events in San Francisco, when, on January 8, 1965, they sponsored a musical dance event at the Fillmore Auditorium, to which 2,400 people came, jamming the huge dance floor and swigging from a baby bathtub filled with LSD-spiked punch.

The Family Dog dances were no longer the undisputed sole attraction. Ken Kesey, Stewart Brand, and Bill Graham had all gotten into the act. The various experimentation with various types of entertainment ended; the events coalesced into various bands playing loudly amplified music while thousands of teenagers and young men and women, arrayed in increasingly improbable clothing, danced wildly to the accompaniment of strobe lights and light shows.

The Grateful Dead (Jerry Garcia at the right) performed long after most of San Francisco's rock bands had dissolved. The group is shown here in 1977. *Courtesy San Francisco Public Library. Photo by Greg Gaar.*

As folk music had crowded out jazz as a popular musical medium in the late 1950s, so now rock and roll music destroyed the remainder of folk music in the mid-1960s. And, whereas both jazz and folk music were performed in relatively small nightclubs, rock and roll's amplification could be heard in the largest auditoriums, even in enormous outdoor spaces.

The beginning of the making of a San Francisco music icon took place on June 10, 1966, when Big Brother and the Holding Company performed at the Avalon with a singer whom Helms had imported from his native Texas. With bad skin, dull, stringy hair, and coarse features, Janis Joplin was no beauty. But her electrifyingly overwrought voice brought her and the band instantaneous fame.

The loud music, the flashing lights and images, the kinetic body motion, and, more often than not, the effect of drugs created a bacchanalian scene that frequently formed its own entertainment, as when men and women would step out of their clothes and dance only in their body paints.

Bill Graham's involvement in a weekend event known as the Trips Festival at the Longshoremen's Hall, where more than 6,000 were present, convinced him that he was confronted with a major entrepreneurial opportunity — one in which he was not slow to involve himself. Soon he would come to dominate San Francisco's rock and roll scene, with only feeble competition from Chet Helms and his Family Dog operation. It was Graham who was able to get a long-term lease on what was seen as the best venue for the suddenly so popular rock and roll dance-concerts — the Fillmore Auditorium; and within a short time, the "Fillmore" would become one of the most famous names in the United States. Helms would retreat to another ballroom in San Francisco — the Avalon Ballroom.

But, while regular rock and roll concerts were now a staple at the Fillmore Auditorium and the Avalon Ballroom, soon to be supplemented by huge outdoor concerts in Golden Gate Park and in the adjacent Panhandle, a conscious movement of youthful exclusivity was forming in the Haight-Ashbury. The new music — rock and roll — the use of drugs, a massive eruption of idealism, utopianism, and romanticism, and an augmented generational rebelliousness combined to suborn the two decades of post-war passivity, conformity, and uniformity. The canon of careers, marriage and children, hard study, discipline, traditional values became more than just old-fashioned; it became to the young who gathered in the Haight-Ashbury almost satanic in its evil.

Business thrived along the old shopping street. Psychedelic shops, crafts stores, exotic food shops, vintage clothing shops, and record stores catered to the increasing throngs of young people living in the Haight and relishing a communal life on its principal street. Dealing marijuana had become the economic base of the Haight, as the drug culture slowly began to seep into the adjoining middle class venues of San Francisco.

An old neighborhood movie theatre, the Haight Theater, built in the 1920s, had become as dilapidated as the neighborhood. Having failed as a neighborhood cinema, as a homosexual movie house, and as an Assembly of God church, the old Haight Theater now became the Straight Theater. Investors dreamed of yet another hippie palace: a dance floor, movie theater, and repertory theater.

As the Haight-Ashbury — and the hippie movement — continued to flourish, the Straight Theater became one of the focal points of community activity in the area. To the mainstream media and to the conventional middle-class of the Bay Area, the happenings at the Straight Theater, widely reported in the press, bizarre, revolutionary, and ununderstandable, represented the debauchery and chaos among the young, the breaking-down of society.

The Haight's community consciousness expanded as 1966 neared its end. The hundreds upon hundreds of young men and women (the latter often with flowers in their hair) who stood on the street handing out flowers to those who came to gawk at the phenomenon and saying to them "Love" or "Peace" steadily and increasingly fascinated the older residents of San Francisco and its suburbs.

On October 6, 1966, the denizens of the Haight held a "Love-Pageant-Rally" in the Panhandle, in order to lessen the misunderstanding between them and the "straight" world. Music, pageantry, and what many considered the amusing antics of the hippies created a successful event (albeit, probably without achieving its objective of harmony).

Into this equation came another component: the Diggers. Named after a seventeenth-century English millenarian, socialist, religious group, the Diggers arose out of one of the factions of the San Francisco Mime Troupe. It would introduce a political/social dimension to the individualistic "drop-out" scope of the hippie movement; and it did so by lambasting the capitalist system and profit motive and by distributing free food (gathered by the Diggers from numerous San Francisco shops and cooked by young women, mostly from Antioch College West) in the Panhandle, free clothing, and also free furniture and utensils.

Their Halloween event, a Full Moon Public Celebration, featuring nonsensical walking patterns at Haight and Masonic streets, caused a traffic disruption to which the police soon responded, resulting in a theatre of the absurd: the police arresting the eight-foot Mime Troupe puppets and those four Diggers who were operating them.

Such action was typical of the Diggers. On December 16 they mounted a Death of Money and Rebirth of the Haight Parade. When two Hell's Angels participants were arrested, the parade went to the South of Market jail to demonstrate for their liberation.

Events proliferated in the Haight-Ashbury and in the adjacent Panhandle and Golden Gate Park and in the musical venues in San Francisco. Thousands of young men and women, and many of those not "flower children" or hippies, attended one after another of such "happenings".

On January 14, 1967, leaders of the San Francisco hippie community and of the Berkeley politically radical community sponsored such a "happening" to unify both groups into a common effort to bring into effect a new age: "A Gathering of the Tribes" and "A Human Be-In" were the names given to it.

Jerry Rubin, one of the organizers, told a press conference a couple of days before that the common aim of the hippies and the radicals was to drop out of

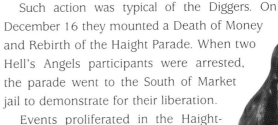

A principal impressario of the rock music revolution in San Francisco, Chet Helms sponsored many legendary rock singers and bands. *Courtesy San Francisco Public Library.*

"games and institutions that oppress and dehumanize" and to create communities where "new values and new human relations can grow".

Allen Cohen, editor of the *Oracle*, the principal publication of San Francisco's hippie community, wrote out a statement of purpose:

"A union of love and activism previously separated by categorical dogma and label mongering will finally occur ecstatically when Berkeley political activists and hip community and San Francisco's spiritual generation and contingents from the emerging revolutionary generation all over California meet for a Gathering of the Tribes for a Human Be-In.... Now in the evolving generation of America's young the humanization of the American man and woman can begin in joy and embrace without fear, dogma, suspicion, or dialectical righteousness. A new concert of human relations being developed within the youthful underground must emerge, become conscious, and be shared so that a revolution of form can be filled with a Renaissance of compassion, awareness and love in the Revelation of the unity of all mankind."

To such grandiloquent language the *Berkeley Barb* added: "The spiritual revolution will be manifest and proven. In unity we shall shower the country with waves of ecstasy and purification. Fear will be washed away; ignorance will be exposed to sunlight; profits and empire will lie drying on deserted beaches; violence will be submerged and transmuted in rhythm and dancing."

The Human Be-In took place at the Polo Field in Golden Gate Park. Thousands listened to Allen Ginsberg and Gary Snyder, connections to the 1950s beatnik scene in San Francisco, chant Buddhist and Hindu mantras; to Timothy Leary recite his "Turn on, tune in, drop out" formula; to Lenore Kandel read from *The Love Book*; and to the Quicksilver Messenger Service, Big Brother and the Holding Company, the Grateful Dead, the Jefferson Airplane, and several other bands play their music.

Hippie Hill in Golden Gate Park. A favorite rendezvous for hippies from the Haight-Ashbury, Hippie Hill featured non-stop music...and non-stop drug-taking. Courtesy San Francisco Public Library. (Right and Opposite Page)

As the sun set in the late afternoon, the crowd began to drift away — many to the beach, where they built fires and chanted. Others joined Allen Ginsberg in a massive clean-up of the park.

From such prognostications of love as the supreme component of the new age, a tough, Irish-born cop who had become San Francisco's chief of police, during a meeting between leaders of the Haight's hippie community and himself and members of the police hierarchy, Thomas Cahill asked the hippies, "You're sort of the Love Generation, aren't you?"

Whereas Gertrude Stein named the Lost Generation and Jack Kerouac the Beat Generation, it was a supreme irony that a conservative chief of police with a thick Irish brogue named it the Love Generation.

On April 5, 1967, the inevitable happened: the Gray Line Bus Company began a "San Francisco Haight-Ashbury District 'Hippie Hop' Tour", which it advertised as "the only foreign tour within the continental limits of the United States". The tour even offered a pamphlet which contained "A Glossary of Hippie Terms."

The increasing national media attention was both an attraction to unhappy teen-teenagers throughout the nation who thought that slipping away to the Haight-Ashbury would solve all their problems and also to matrons from Nebraska and conventioneers from Florida, who chuckled in amazed disbelief as the Gray Line bus plowed through the thick throngs of young men and women in the Haight.

Joel Selvin, in his history of the rock and roll development of San Francisco, *Summer of Love*, writes:

"The Haight had changed greatly. ... No longer a sunny, quiet confluence of long-haired acidheads from S.F. State living in the neighborhood's old Victorians, it was now a knotted mass of dreamers and schemers, artists and con artists, the devout and the jive, and growing daily. A carnival seemed to be taking place on every block. Clowns wearing costumes were everywhere. An explosion of color and character had taken place. Teenage runaways mingled with dealers. Hell's Angels were a ubiquitous part of the streetscapes, esteemed colleagues of many of the musicians. The salty Mediterranean air that hung over the district hummed with electricity. As many as 100,000 people were expected to descend on the little mecca the coming summer [of 1967]."

This was to be the Summer of Love. Some 100,000 newcomers were expected to flood San Francisco's Haight-Ashbury. The great majority would be bereft of any economic resources. How would they be fed? Housed? Kept from the clutches of those who would exploit them? Kept free of disease?

The Haight's more responsible denizens rallied by forming groups to handle the influx; but the rampant factions that marked the hippies and radicals alike criticized their motives.

Some of these questions were being partially resolved by committed individuals, dedicated to helping out the young men and women of the Haight. A Haight-Ashbury switchboard got hundreds of calls a day. And Dr. David Smith's founding of the Haight-Ashbury Free Medical Clinic provided much needed medical help to the throngs of hippies.

The Summer of Love began with the Monterey Pop Festival, which featured a kaleidoscope of virtually all the U.S. and British rock bands, blues and folk groups, and such entertainers as Ravi Shankar. It was estimated that 100,000 had crowded into the Monterey Fairgrounds, where the event was held; and, like Woodstock, it became one of the defining moments in contemporary music.

The massive crowds that had been expected to inundate the Haight failed to show up, or, more accurately, failed to stay. Many came, and then departed: back to their homes, to communes in rural areas of Northern California, trekking to "spiritual" areas such as India and Nepal. Nevertheless, it became almost impossible to drive or walk the streets of the Haight-Ashbury. Tourists thronged to the Haight, as did the locals. The shifting crowd of hippies filled the sidewalks. The original Edwardian and Wild West attire had been joined by tie-dye vestments, denim, sheets, Indian garb, and second-hand shabby attire.

They smoked marijuana and ingested drugs in the Panhandle, on Hippie Hill (in the eastern portion of Golden Gate Park), on the street, and in their "pads".

Panhandlers became a common scene in the Haight. The more responsible sold

There was a big sale of furnishings in the Fox Theater shown here just before its demolition. Thousands of San Franciscans mourned the loss of this elegant movie palace. *Courtesy San Francisco Public Library.*

copies of the *Berkeley Barb* or the *Oracle*… or dealt drugs. Runaways, disheveled, malnourished, often hooked on drugs, looking pathetic and lost, clutching puppies and kittens, were very much in evidence.

Amphetamine and heroine use was on the rise. Strong-arm crime was increasing. Wars between drug dealers were now a staple of the Haight. Rape became common. The promised peace and love seemed illusory.

It was estimated that 75,000 teenagers and young men and women came to the Haight during the Summer of Love. (The duration of stay and how many denizens of the Haight simultaneously left, of course, is not known.) By early September many of the newcomers were leaving San Francisco.

The end of the Summer of Love had left the Haight a different place. Crime, factionalism, disease, and disillusionment had left a bitter taste; almost like coming off a "high". Various individuals and organizations decided to commemorate this transformation by holding a Death of Hippie ceremony on October 6. The press release read:

"The media casts nets, create bags for the identity-hungry to climb in. Your face on TV, your style immor-talized without soul in the captions of the *Chronicle*. NBC says you exist, ergo I am… and the reflections run in perpetual and circuits and the FREE MAN vomits his images and laughs in the clouds because he, the great evader, the animal who haunts the jungles of images and sees no shadow, only the hunter's gun, and knows sahib is too slow and he flexes his strong loins of FREE and is gone again from the nets. They fall on empty air and waft helplessly on the grass."

Charles Perry, in *The Haight-Ashbury: A History*, describes the actual ceremony:

"… the funeral procession began atop Buena Vista Hill at sunrise on Friday. 'Taps' was played, candles were held aloft. Hippie and media emblems were consigned to a fire: copies of daily newspapers and the *Barb*, beads, reputed marijuana. Some eighty people took part in a procession down Haight Street, which was adorned for the day with a banner that read, 'Death of Hippie Freebie, i.e., Birth of the Free Man'. They bore a cardboard coffin with a representative hippie inside. After a 'kneel-in' at the corner of Haight and Ashbury, the procession moved on to its destination, the Psychedelic Shop, where a record player was turned up loud to drown out the unscheduled screams of a girl bumming out on acid. The Psych Shop window was filled with signs: 'Be Free', 'Don't Mourn for Me, Organize', 'Nebraska Needs You More.'"

By 1968 the Haight-Ashbury was in a state of disintegration. The Flower Children were no longer in evidence; the Love Generation had destroyed itself.

The escalation of the war in Vietnam, beginning in 1965, had begun to bitterly divide the country; the young were turning from love and peace to violence to protest the conflict in Southeast Asia.

The Haight's hippies were leaving: some to jobs,

excessive drug use. The once-colorful Haight, by 1969, was reduced to a dilapidated slum: stores stood empty, steel gates cushioned others from constant burglary, trash littered the streets, derelicts slept in the doorways of buildings, drug addicts careened listlessly along Haight Street.

The Straight Theater closed and was demolished in 1981. One by one the dance/concert halls closed: the old Fillmore, the Avalon, Winterland, Fillmore West. Most of San Francisco's bands were no longer; and, although rock and roll became increasingly a big business, the zestful integration between the bands and their listeners was no longer.

Riots became the order of the day. Inner cities burned. Napalm rained down on the jungles of Vietnam. Terrorist bombings and terrorist organizations became commonplace. Demonstrating students were shot, wounded, and killed on college campuses.

The sunny optimism that had marked the early days in San Francisco's Haight-Ashbury hippie experience had evaporated.

The Physical Transformation of San Francisco

Every city is always in the process of organic change. Buildings are torn down; new ones are built. Streets are widened; new streets are constructed, sometimes many feet off the ground (and are called freeways). Institutions that have served generations — such as stores, theatres, and restaurants — suddenly exist no more.

Often cities try to arrest this process, opting to keep as much of their historical fabric as they can, determining to keep a certain "look" or a certain texture.

Thus, San Francisco, albeit caught up in the post-World War II frenzy of urban growth and change, early on began to pass legislation which would miti-

gate this growth and change. After losing numerous Victorian houses in the aftermath of World War II to the construction of banal, stucco apartment houses and several buildings of great historical and architectural significance, the city passed an historical preservation ordinance that has nearly ended the erosion of its historical fabric.

After massive redevelopment projects — notably, in the Western Addition and South of Market — caused criticism and divisiveness in San Francisco, the mood of the city and its leaders swung away from such huge, planned clearing away of entire neighborhoods and their reconstruction in totally different ways.

And, after the financial district of San Francisco expanded by many blocks and huge skyscrapers thrust upwards that had transformed the once-low skyline of the city, community activists, after several failures, were able to enact what has been considered the most stringent slow-growth legislation of any city in the United States.

All that remained of San Francisco's greatest movie palace, the Fox Theater on Market Street, was the facade, soon also to be destroyed. A banal complex of offices and apartments took its place. Courtesy San Francisco Public Library.

The baroque style of the Fox Theater made it one of San Francisco's premier movie houses. Courtesy San Francisco Public Library.

Playland-at-the-Beach being demolished in 1972. *Courtesy San Francisco Public Library.*

Laughing Sal laughs maniacally no more. Sal delighted and scared several generations of children and adults who visited Playland-at-the-Beach. *Courtesy San Francisco Public Library.*

San Francisco's population in 1998 is probably less than it was in 1948. At this point, it shows no desire to increase its residential density by tearing down single-family homes and erecting high-rise residential construction.

It continues to be the consensus in San Francisco that its citizens prefer to live on a small physical urban scale, on a human scale, with fewer congested streets, less residential density, not so many high-rises. The last quarter century has seen San Franciscans more and more prone to vote for regulating legislation that would insure such a lifestyle.

There was little consciousness of historical preservation in San Francisco for two decades after the end of World War II. One of the oldest houses in San Francisco, a landmark on Russian Hill, the Humphreys house was torn down in 1948. Its site became an ugly apartment house. Playland-at-the-Beach, a boardwalk entertainment center facing the Pacific Ocean, so much enjoyed by generations of San Franciscans, was torn down in 1972: its acres covered by condominium buildings. Fleishhaker Pool, the world's largest outdoor swimming pool, was filled in and covered over for a parking lot in 1980. The 1853 Montgomery Block, probably the second most historically and architecturally significant building in San Francisco, was torn down in 1959 for a parking lot. The Transamerica Pyramid now stands on the site. In the 1960s and early 1970s, the San Francisco Redevelopment Agency's attempts to remake the Western Addition resulted in block after block of Victorian row-houses, dilapidated but capable of restoration, being obliterated.

A rising realization of the importance of the city's historical physical fabric, fueled by the publication in 1968 of *Here Today*, a pioneering study of San Francisco's remaining historical buildings, produced by the Junior League of San Francisco, prompted an ordinance that was passed by the Board of Supervisors in 1967, creating legislation for the preservation of San Francisco's historical buildings and setting up a San Francisco Landmarks Preservation Advisory Board (advisory to the Planning Commission) to designate historical and architectural landmarks.

Yet another feature of historical preservation in 1960s and in subsequent years was the process by which those enamored of Victorian homes would buy these shabby, often mistreated, structures, and painstakingly rehabilitate and restore them. Most of these Victorians were in marginal urban areas: the Western Addition, the Mission, the Haight-Ashbury, the fringes of Pacific Heights; and those who bravely moved into these restored houses often had to suffer the inconveniences of living in a "rough-and-tough" area.

By the late 1990s, however, this process of "gentrification" of formerly dilapidated Victorian buildings had sparked a renaissance in many of San Francisco's neighborhoods.

The aftermath of World War II was an era of confidence and of affluence. The federal, state, and local governments all operated under the premise that the resources of the United States could be galvanized to end poverty, hunger, and all other ills. (Two decades

later Lyndon Johnson and his administration would pursue the same chimera.) One of the legislative results of this optimism was that of redevelopment: in which process federal funds would be made available to major cities for them to implement the objective of purchasing large tracts of urban land (under eminent domain) and, in partnership with private enterprise, level the buildings that were there and replace them with modern housing, shops, etc. Poor people would then have the amenities of life, went the reasoning, that would "jump-start" them into the productive middle-class.

In some cases, San Francisco's redevelopment projects were common-sense utilizations of resources to improve an area. In other cases, the end result was to create a banal ghetto, a neighborhood of crime, drugs, and continuing poverty, with prison-like buildings constituting the housing stock. In all cases, the projects were controversial.

The first of the projects was the redevelopment of Diamond Heights. In the middle of the City and County of San Francisco, on the slope of Twin Peaks, almost all of Diamond Heights lay undeveloped and uninhabited at the middle of this century. The project began in the mid 1950s and was completed in 1978. The result was a residential neighborhood with supporting schools, parks and playgrounds, shopping facilities, and churches.

Courtesy San Francisco Public Library. (Following page)

One of the popular attractions at Playland-at-the-Beach — the Diving Bell. *Courtesy San Francisco Public Library.*

The next project began the pattern of controversy. It was called the Western Addition Area A-1. This project began with the widening of Geary Street into a boulevard in the mid-1950s. It was decided that the blighted blocks adjoining the thoroughfare, which now appeared to be a chasm definitively separating one side of it from another, should be torn down and new construction put up.

The project went from Franklin Street on the east to a bit beyond Broderick Street on the west and from Post to Eddy Streets. Block after block of superb Victorian houses were leveled, and 2009 new housing units — one third for subsidized housing, the remainder for market-rate housing were put up.

In addition to residential construction, the A-1 fostered medical construction (by doctors affiliated with Mount Zion Hospital), playgrounds, public and private schools, St. Mary's Cathedral (the previous cathedral, on Van Ness Avenue, had burned down in 1962), commercial and retail facilities, and the Japanese Cultural and Trade Center (situated in the midst of what had been, until 1942, the Japanese enclave in San Francisco).

Many considered the destruction of hundreds of irreplaceable Victorian homes and commercial buildings, the construction of banal residential units and disparate other buildings, and creating the ugly barrier of Geary Boulevard not to be an enhancing aspect of San Francisco's growth.

The Sutro Baths, a popular entertainment spot in the 19th century, lost favor with the public in the early 20th century. Even when ice skating was offered, there was little interest. Slated to be torn down, Sutro Baths burned to the ground in 1966. *Courtesy San Francisco Public Library.*

The Sutro Baths—for almost three quarters of a century one of San Francisco's most notable landmarks—burned down in 1966. The ruins still remain adjacent to the Cliff House. *Courtesy San Francisco Historical Society. Photo by Rudolph E. and Betty Peterson.*

The Montgomery Block was the largest office building in the
West when it was built in 1853. It survived the earthquake
and fire of 1906, but was demolished in 1959.
Courtesy San Francisco Public Library.

The next project was the Chinese Cultural Center, which entailed tearing down the old Hall of Justice (the icon for the "Ironsides" television series) and constructing a 27-story Holiday Inn, into which was incorporated a 20,000 square foot space occupied for a nominal rent by the Chinese Cultural Foundation of San Francisco. One of the more flamboyant aspects of this development was the construction of a 28-foot wide pedestrian bridge over Kearny Street into Portsmouth Plaza.

One of the most visible of San Francisco's redevelopment projects is that known as the Golden Gateway. Its location is northeast of the city's traditional financial district (of which it is now a part) and on the former location of the old, congested marketplace for wholesale produce. (Most of the produce firms were re-established in the modern produce terminal built for them near Islais Creek, in the southeastern part of the city.)

The project began in 1962 and was completed in late 1986. Its physical scope was from California Street to Broadway and from Battery Street to the Embarcadero. Some 1400 new housing units, five high-rise office buildings (which also contained shops and restaurants, a hotel, and public plazas) were constructed as part of this redevelopment project. Today, the Golden Gateway apartments and townhouses are eagerly sought-after residences; and the Alcoa Building and the four Embarcadero Center buildings are part of San Francisco's business/financial center.

One of the most ambitious of the redevelopment projects — and one of the most controversial — was the Western Addition A-2 project. Approved in 1964, but, because of legal difficulties, not begun until 1966, the A-2 went from Grove/Ivy Streets to Bush Street and from Van Ness Avenue to St. Joseph/Broderick Streets. Once more, as in the A-1, block after block of Victorian buildings were torn down. It included the development of 5670 new housing units, the retention and rehabilitation of 3965 units, the construction of 2727 units of market-rate housing, the revitalization of the Nihonmachi (Japan Town) and Fillmore business districts, construction of new commercial buildings, churches, and community recreational and cultural facilities.

But, the most controversial, the most litigation-beset, and the most divisive of San Francisco's

Transamerica Pyramid, built on the site of the Montgomery Block, was once disliked for replacing a historic landmark. It is now a San Francisco favorite.
Courtesy
San Francisco
Convention and
Visitors Bureau.
Photo by
Bruce Kliewe.

The demolition of the Western Addition by the Redevelopment Agency laid waste to block after block of Victorian homes. *Courtesy San Francisco Public Library.*

The stained glass rotunda of the elegant City of Paris—a retail establishment started by a French family in 1850. A victim of the suburbanization of the Bay Area, it closed in the 1960s. *Courtesy San Francisco Public Library.*

redevelopment projects was the Yerba Buena Center. The eighty-seven acres that were redeveloped by the San Francisco Redevelopment Agency in the South of Market area — now known as the Yerba Buena Center — was essentially a blighted area of dilapidated residence hotels, commercial and industrial buildings, increasingly obsolete for business purposes, and open parking lots.

The original concept for a rehabilitation of this area came in 1954 from Ben Swig, real estate mag-

Victorian homes were torn down in the 1960s and 1970s. In the background can be seen St. Paulus Church, which burned down in the mid-1990s, and the Opera House. *Courtesy San Francisco Public Library.*

nate, philanthropist, and community leader. These plans called for a convention center, sports stadium, high-rise office building, and large parking garage.

Nothing came of Swig's plan; but, in the mid 1960s, Justin Herman, the aggressive and hyper-kinetic executive director of the San Francisco Redevelopment Agency, had eight-seven acres designated a redevelopment area. The area went from Market Street to Perry Street (a small street one block south of Harrison Street) and from Second Street to Fifth Street. Almost immediately, a coalition of labor unions, some businesses in the area, and South of Market residents organized to oppose the project; and, what in earlier days would have been a "done deal", became enmeshed in almost a decade and a half of litigation, aided by a squadron of public advocacy attorneys, representing the groups opposed to the project.

As the Yerba Buena Center nears completion (in 1997), the passions that flared during the 1960s and 1970s over this project seem to have abated; and, while some lament the failure to implement the original Kenyo Tange design, most now seem pleased with the result of the compromises reached in the late-1970s.

Union opposition, which was stilled by Mayor Joseph Alioto in the late 1960s, had begun because it was felt that the demolitions would drive more small businesses out of the city with the resulting loss of blue-collar jobs. In reality, taxes, bureaucratic regulations, and economic inefficiencies were already driving the last vestiges of such traditional businesses as printing, commodity companies (such as coffee roasting), and those related to the maritime trade out of San Francisco.

The matter of the displacement of residents was a more complex one. The pro-growth advocates of the project attempted to convey the idea that the area was only a Skid Row: the reality was that only a small portion was such. There were a large number of residents who were quite poor and living in cheap rooms in residence hotels.

Although one can debate, according to one's ideological lights, whether it is appropriate to demolish such moldering buildings for such a purpose as a convention center and other uses, thus also demolishing the communities that exist in these buildings and neighborhoods, what was not subject to debate was the federal law that mandated replacement housing for those displaced by a redevelopment project; and it was the failure of Justin Herman and others involved in this project to understand how seriously this mandate would be taken by the

tenants and their lawyers, as well as the courts; and the Redevelopment Agency's high-handed tactics in evicting tenants that would lead to the years of delay, vast changes to the project's design, and an incalculable increase in costs.

Even though the unions had ceased to oppose the Yerba Buena project, the tenants continued to resist. They coalesced with the local merchants to

A Victorian hoisted on a hugh flatbed truck is driven down the street to a new location in the middle of the night. *Courtesy San Francisco Redevelopment Agency.*

This Victorian is being prepared for removal to a new home. *Courtesy San Francisco Redevelopment Agency.*

San Francisco's Produce District—where the Golden Gateway now stands—was a crowded and busy place. The city finally succeeded in locating it elsewhere and redeveloping the site. *Courtesy San Francisco Public Library.* (Opposite Page)

form the Tenants and Owners in Opposition to Redevelopment (TOOR) and fought the project in the courts.

Herman and the Redevelopment Agency thwarted Mayor Alioto's efforts to negotiate an out-of-court settlement; but, after Herman died in 1971, Alioto negotiated a settlement in 1973 that called for two thousand units of replacement housing.

However, this endless journey was not yet finished. Richard Edward De Leon's *Left Coast City* gives an excellent summary of the complexities of completing this project:

"Five years [since TOOR's lawsuit, which was filed in 1968] of complicated legal battles, protests, and bureaucratic in-fighting then gave way to another five years of the same, this time around issues involving project design, financing schemes, and

environmental impacts. In 1978, after scaling down the project, securing voter approval, and settling remaining lawsuits, the city received a green light to begin construction."

Almost two decades after this "green light," the project is virtually completed.

Other redevelopment projects took place in San Francisco during the past three decades: Hunter's Point, in the southeastern portion of San Francisco, the India Basin Industrial Park, the Rincon Point — South Beach area. Other redevelopment areas are proposed. Although the era of the Redevelopment Agency's massive projects has probably come to an end, it will continue to redevelop smaller pockets of San Francisco, continuing to be part of that ongoing organic change that continuously transforms cities.

The hours before dawn were the busiest for San Francisco's produce market (now the site of the Golden Gateway), when hundreds of trucks would line up to buy fruits and vegetables for stores and restaurants throughout the Bay Area. *Courtesy San Francisco Public Library.*

Diamond Heights before development begins. The cross on Mt. Davidson, city-owned land, became the focus of controversy in the mid 1990s because of the question of separation of church and state. In 1997 voters approved a ballot measure to sell the cross and a small plot of land on which it sits to an Armenian group.
Courtesy San Francisco Redevelopment Agency.

The streets of the Diamond Heights development follow the contours of the land in contrast with the grid pattern of most of San Francisco's streets.
Courtesy San Francisco Redevelopment Agency.
(Opposite Page)

Ben Swig with his conception for redevelopment.
Courtesy San Francisco Public Library.

Moscone Convention Center takes shape near the Yerba Buena Center. The two buildings of the convention center draw thousands of visitors to San Francisco each year, making tourism the largest product the city has to offer.
Courtesy San Francisco Redevelopment Agency.

Freeways, Freeway Revolts, and Bart

The end of World War II, with its rising affluence, its increasing expansion of suburbs, and its expanding automobile culture, saw a nationwide determination to use the nation's resources to aid auto transportation. Thus began an explosion of building of highways throughout the country: no place more persistently than in California.

Los Angeles became the U.S. model for the "new city" — one binding itself with the most highway (or, "freeway" as highways are called in California) mileage of any city in the country.

During the early-1950s San Francisco was as eager as the next city to link its downtown area to the growing suburbs to the north, east, and south. In 1953, the Bayshore Freeway opened from Army to Bryant/7th streets, nearing a direct link with the San Francisco-Oakland Bay Bridge (a linkage which would be completed somewhat later).

The Central Freeway was completed in 1959; and by 1958 the Embarcadero Freeway was about to begin construction.

The state highway builders decided to build an elevated freeway which slashed across the northern waterfront — much to the disgust of most San Francisans.
Courtesy San Francisco Public Library.

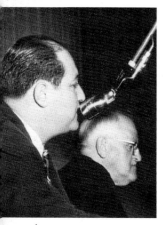

Supervisors William Blake and James Leo Halley hear protests against the Western Freeway in May, 1956.
Courtesy San Francisco Public Library.

The Central Freeway that slashed through San Francisco, closed after the Loma Prieta Earthquake in 1989. Its future, as of 1997, is uncertain.
Courtesy San Francisco Public Library.

But, by the mid-1950s, San Franciscans, despite the usual pro-growth forces (which included many politicians, the downtown interests, and, usually, the labor unions) urging on the state's highway construction program, began to doubt the wisdom of criss-crossing the city with huge concrete freeways, displacing homes and businesses, cutting across parks, and creating gigantic barriers between one section of the city and another.

Various neighborhood groups began to protest against the continuation of the freeway program; and these groups found their spokesperson in the person of William Blake, a cranky businessman who had been appointed to the board of supervisors by Mayor Elmer Robinson.

In 1959, the Board of Supervisors voted to cancel seven of ten planned freeway routes through the city, much to the shock of the state Department of Highways and state government.

But the state highway builders were not defeated: over the next several years they would continue to resurrect new routes and to vigorously campaign for

Market Street under construction for the BART tunnel.
Courtesy San Francisco Public Library.

BART at the Orinda Station.
Courtesy Bay Area
Rapid Transit District.

freeways in San Francisco, against which plans and propagandizing San Franciscans would continue to protest and attempt to block.

The city's own planners produced in 1960 a comprehensive plan for freeways, cited as a model of reasonableness. Once again, there was a public outcry; and, once again, Supervisor Blake was able to convince his colleagues to vote unanimously against one of the two proposed freeways — the Western Freeway.

With its San Francisco pro-growth allies, however, the state's highway bureaucracy counter-attacked, attempting to salvage a future freeway plan for the city.

In 1962 emerged yet another freeway proposal: the Panhandle Freeway. The situation was, however, more perilous at this time for the anti-freeway forces: for the board of supervisors had lost four anti-freeway members during the previous two elections.

For two-and-a-half years the Panhandle Freeway proposal roiled San Francisco's politics. The proposed freeway was to extend the Central Freeway up the Oak/ Fell corridor, slice sixty per cent of the Panhandle for the roadway, and tunnel under the north edge of Golden Gate Park before turning onto Park Presidio Boulevard towards the Golden Gate Bridge.

In May, 1964, thousands gathered in Golden Gate Park for a rally against the proposed freeway. Then, on October 13, in a dramatic six votes against the freeway to five votes for it, the

A Longshoreman unloads sacks of coffee on San Francisco's waterfront. The coffee roasting plants, such as Folger's, Hills Bros., and M.J.B., were just a couple blocks away. *Courtesy San Francisco Public Library.*

plans for a Panhandle Freeway were dashed. (Blake was joined in opposition by supervisors George Moscone, Roger Boas, Leo McCarthy, Clarissa McMahon, and Terry Francois. Jack Morrison, Joseph Casey, Jack Ertola, Joseph Tinney, and Peter Tamaras were in favor.)

This was the defining moment of the "freeway revolt."

Still, the advocates of additional freeways for San Francisco did not give up; and politics at the local, state, and federal levels combined to keep open the option that two freeways could still be built. A joint committee of city and state planners came forth with the recommendation that both freeways be built. The opponents of the freeways continued their all-out efforts to derail the recommendation; and, finally, on March 21, 1966, the San Francisco Board of Supervisors defeated the state's freeways for a sixth and last time.

A rising national tide against the proliferation of highways and the determined action of numerous San Franciscans and civic groups were able to defeat the state highway bureaucracy and their pro-highway allies in San Francisco.

The initial impetus for some sort of Bay Area rapid transit project came in 1947, when a joint Army-Navy commission recommended that the area build an underwater transit tube beneath San Francisco Bay.

Three years later the state's legislature created a special commission to study Bay Area transportation problems; and, in 1957, it created a five-county Bay Area Rapid Transit District.

The Embarcadero Freeway effectively isolated San Francisco's northern waterfront from the rest of the city. *Courtesy San Francisco Public Library.*

During the next five years the directors of the Bay Area Rapid Transit District (BART) moved steadily toward the implementation of an objective of building a rapid transit system that would link San Francisco, San Mateo, Alameda, and Contra Costa counties; but, in 1962, both San Mateo and Marin counties withdrew from BART. The three remaining counties carried on alone.

In that same year almost $800-million of general obligation bonds were approved by voters in the three counties, and in 1964 construction began on the project.

The financing for the project, in addition to the proceeds from the sale of the general obligation bonds, came from an addition to the existing sales tax in the three counties and large amounts of federal funds, expended in those days of U.S. Government largesse.

San Francisco's Market Street was excavated, beginning in July 1967, for the subway on that street, and, for the next few years, crossing from north to south of Market would present problems.

In August, 1969, the trans-bay tube structure was completed; and, on September 11, 1972, the first twenty-six mile part (out of the original seventy-five mile plan) of the BART track opened for service (between Fremont and Oakland). The BART system had begun to operate.

In the quarter century since the first section of BART began service, its importance to Bay Area transportation has become more evident. Extensions have been pushed into more eastern sections of Contra Costa and Alameda counties and into San Mateo County, which had originally opted out of the system.

BART has been a major component in transportation cooperation and interface in the Bay Area, working with San Francisco's municipal railway system and the East Bay's AC Transit to coordinate and make more efficient the region's mass transportation system.

Although the citizens of the three counties involved in the BART system voted additional taxes to pay for its construction and operation, and, although during the early years of BART's construction and operations problems were endemic (e.g. — huge rises in costs because of hyper-inflation, design problems due to the fact that BART was the first mass-transportation system in the U.S. designed and constructed for a half century), BART is today a principal component in the Bay Area's mass transportation and in lessening the gridlock and pollution brought about by the ever-increasing use of the automobile.

The Port Returns to San Francisco Ownership and Control

In 1863 the State of California acquired ownership and control of San Francisco's waterfront and port. This was the result of a group of San Francisco financiers and speculators' scheme of gaining control of the port by a private monopoly. The state aborted such a move at the behest of the opponents of the monopoly by itself taking over control and ownership of San Francisco's port.

A State Board of Harbor Commissioners, exempt from local control, guided the port from the early days of the Comstock bonanza until 1968, when the Burton Act transferred ownership and control to San Francisco. The legislation required that the city assume responsibility for $55 million in general obligation bonds and agree to invest $100 million (later reduced to $25 million) for harbor improvements.

However, what was once the third busiest port in the United States had become in 1994 the twenty-sixth in rank; and further decline was predicted.

What had happened that such a busy and prosperous port had so precipitously deteriorated? A number of factors had occurred to hasten this decline. Many of the port's piers were constructed between 1912 and 1930, when break-bulk shipping flourished and countless vessels were serviced at Port facilities. In the post-World War II period, however, the dominance of the waterfront by industry, maritime operations, and railroad terminals began to decline. The completion of the two bridges in the 1930s led to a dramatic reduction in the once thriving ferry boat industry. Technological innovations in the shipping industry, particularly the shift from break-bulk cargo to containerized cargo, further reduced demand for port facilities. The rise of foreign competition in shipbuilding and ship repair dealt another blow to maritime activity at the port; and, with the decline of these prime industries, maritime support activities also declined.

The State Board of Harbor Commissioners was slow to respond to the evolution from break-bulk to containerized cargo shipping; and, while San Francisco's port authorities dawdled, Oakland was strenuously building modern container terminals. In 1964 — four years before the local take-over — Oakland and San Francisco had the same tonnage receipts. Thirty years later Oakland was the fifth busiest port in the United States; San Francisco was the twenty-sixth.

In the late 1960s and early 1970s, immediately after San Francisco had taken control of the port, a "catch-up" in modernization was attempted: the first LASH (lighter aboard ship) terminal on the West Coast was built, improvements were made to the break-bulk piers, modern container terminals were built. But San Francisco could never regain its pre-eminence over Oakland; and the Port of San Francisco's facilities are utilized at only a fraction of their capacity. Most experts believe that, despite the surge in Pacific Rim trade and shipping, San Francisco will never again become a major port.

In the thirty years since the City and County of San Francisco has recovered the ownership and control of the port there has arisen an on-going public discussion of what the city's plans for the waterfront's development should be. Various proposed developments, such as the fifty-story U.S. Steel Office Building, the Ferry Port Plaza at Piers 1, 3, and 5, and a residential condominium project at Pier 45, were laid aside as a result of state decisions that they were incompatible with the public trust provision of the Burton Act or in violation of the tenets of the San Francisco Bay Conservation and Development Commission (BCDC).

And so, in the mid-and late-1990s the San Francisco Port Commission constructed a plan for the future development of the 7.5 mile waterfront and submitted it for public discussion. It became the plan's theme to reunite the city with the waterfront; and, to accomplish this, the plan called for the following objectives: continued cargo shipping and ship repair operations along the southern waterfront, modernized fishing operations in historic Fisherman's Wharf, expanded opportunities for recreational boating and water activities throughout the waterfront, expanded ferry boat and new water taxis operations at the Ferry Building, with satellite facilities to save other waterfront areas, excursion boat services from downtown, Fisherman's Wharf, and other key visitor locations, passenger cruise ship operations on the northern waterfront, historic ship berthing at Fisherman's Wharf and other highly visible locations, and ceremonial and temporary berthing throughout the waterfront.

Thus, San Francisco has turned its back on intensive commercial office building and residential development on its waterfront, recognized the reality of its future situation as a port, and has produced a plan which will revitalize the area and make it an attractive addition to the city for the benefit and utilization of residents and visitors alike.

Of Riots and Invasions

The late 1960s saw political and social upheaval throughout the Western world. The war in Vietnam and social, economic, and political disaffection, particularly among the young, saw cities convulsed in riots, which included large-scale looting and burning of the inner cities, university and college campuses paralyzed in endemic tumult, and almost constant protests everywhere. Not since the 1870s had disaffection been so publicly proclaimed.

Although San Francisco did not undergo as severe tribulations as did other cities — Detroit, Los Angeles, and Chicago (during the 1968 Democratic convention) among them — one of its principal institutions of higher learning was almost destroyed by riots which began in late-1968.

San Francisco State University had been a campus of liberal and progressive sentiment in the 1950s, with an excellent reputation for its courses in the theater arts, creative writing, and other liberal arts. The rising disaffection that became evident in the mid-1960s was magnified at the university. The campus was in turmoil, beginning in about 1966, but the diplomatic work of its president, Dr. John Summerskill, had been able to alleviate most problems.

But, the increasing conservatism of older residents of the state, the concerns of its governor and his appointees about the spreading chaos on campus, and the intransigence of radical student leaders on the campus made obsolete Summerskill's attempts at harmonious solutions. He was replaced by Dr. Robert Smith.

The first demands of the students were made in the early Fall of 1968: the abolition of the campus ROTC and the rejection of campus recruiting by Dow

Chemical. To these were added a litany of radical demands (including one that stated that any minority student who applied for admission should be admitted, regardless of his or her qualifications) by the Black Students Union and the Third World Liberation Front.

Some students had already shown the ferocity of their feelings when they entered the office of the school newspaper, the *Daily Gator*, and beat up its editor, Jim Vasgho, in November of the previous year. These students had objected to his not being sympathetic to the demands of the radical students.

The radical students called a strike to begin on November 6, 1968. During the first days of the strike, African-American students and faculty members invaded classrooms and took them over in attempts to "educate" still-teaching faculty and those students still attending classes.

A week after the strike had begun — the campus was relatively quiet; but onto it marched a large force of club-bearing, helmeted police — the San Francisco Police Tactical Squad. The reasons for their entrance onto the campus remain unclear, but the result was increased fury on the part of the students.

Smith ordered the campus closed and made futile attempts at arbitration and meeting the demands of the students. But he was caught in a cross-fire: the radical students asserted that their demands were non-negotiable and the state university system's trustees and chancellor ordered that the campus be re-opened and that no negotiations take place until order was restored. In late November, Robert Smith resigned as president of San Francisco State University.

The chancellor appointed as acting president the well-known semanticist S.I. Hayakawa, who was a professor at San Francisco State and who had had no previous administrative experience.

Hayakawa immediately plunged into the task of restoring order. He issued a set of emergency regulations. He closed the campus early for the Thanksgiving holiday and reopened it on December 2. On that day the campus erupted. Police were called in to stop the strikers' demonstrations. Hayakawa himself climbed atop a truck containing sound equipment to broadcast the strikers' chants and speeches, and, with his trademark tam-o'-shanter perched on his head, tore out the wires from the equipment. (This image of Hayakawa, spread on television and in newspapers, would result in his being elected a U.S. senator for California within a few years.)

But December 2 saw the campus in a full-scale riot, as six hundred policemen, including mounted police, with helicopters overhead, battled the demonstrating students in a bloody melee.

The battle continued the next day, which became known as "Bloody Tuesday."

On December 16, many faculty members went on strike, and the hope for any kind of settlement drifted away. Hayakawa decided to close the school a week early for the Christmas break.

When school reopened on January 6, 1969, the strike continued; and, on January 23, a Black Students Union rally resulted in four hundred fifty four students being arrested.

The strike became a magnet for outside concern and agitation. Inflammatory comments by African-American leaders, notably Assemblyman Willie Brown, the Rev. Cecil Williams, and publisher Carleton Goodlett, supported the cause of the radical students. Mayor Joseph Alioto left not a stone unturned in his efforts to effect a compromise settlement and an end to the rioting.

The intensity of the strike — its violence and vandalism — began to abate; and on March 21, 1969, a compromise settlement was hammered out.

But, a once thriving college was now riven with divisiveness and anger. For many years, faculty members who had been on different sides of the issues refused to speak to each other. A diminution of academic standards was another result of the days of strife. And the learning process would become a handmaiden to the ideology of various groups.

On November 20, 1969, some ninety Native Americans boarded a boat in Sausalito which took them to the historic island of Alcatraz, "the Rock," in San Francisco Bay. There, they brushed aside the lone caretaker and announced that they were claiming Alcatraz — a place, they claimed, their ancestors had occupied for thousands of years.

Alcatraz had been a possession of the U.S. Government since the 1850s. During the 1860s it had become a detention center for Confederate prisoners and had been fortified against possible incursions by Confederate raiders. After World War I it had become a federal penitentiary.

The famous prison was closed in 1963, after which numerous proposals were put forward for new uses for this surplus government property, notably one by Texas multi-millionaire Lamar Hunt, which proposed a casino and a vast entertainment center.

The invasion of Alcatraz was led by Richard Oakes, a twenty-seven year old Mohawk who was a Native American studies student at San Francisco State University; and its purpose was both to call attention to the wrongs done to Native Americans and to extract substantial funds for a Native American university.

The strategy worked well. Federal requests to leave the island were refused; and, although a Coast Guard blockage of the island was ordered — and an ineffective one — the U.S. Government took no further steps to eject the Native Americans. Media coverage was extensive; and numerous individuals and organizations donated food and money to the invaders.

But the Native American occupation of Alcatraz did not go well. The demands of the Native Americans were too diffuse and ill-focused; and, despite a great deal of compassion for Native Americans by the U.S. public, these demands became impossible to settle.

Two months after the occupation, Richard Oakes' twelve year old daughter fell from one of the Alcatraz buildings where she had been playing. A few days later she died from her injuries. Oakes left Alcatraz and the leadership of the occupying Native Americans.

Factions and disputes grew among them. A heavy use of alcohol and drugs, dreadful sanitation, and an ebbing of the initial publicity reduced the declining number of occupiers to pathetic impotence.

Vandalism of the buildings increased; and on June 1, 1971, fire destroyed the warden's house and several adjacent buildings.

On June 11 federal marshals landed on Alcatraz and peacefully removed the fifteen remaining Native Americans.

None of the elaborate proposals for Alcatraz was ever implemented; and today, as part of the Golden Gate National Recreation Area, it is one of the most popular tourist attractions in San Francisco. Numerous visitors each year take a ferry to the notorious former prison to view its massive cell-blocks and to hear about its lurid past.

DEATH IN THE JUNGLE

San Franciscans, during the 1970s, gradually became aware of a group called the People's Temple and its leader, the Reverend Jim Jones. What they knew was rather vague and ambiguous. The group didn't exactly fit in the usual religious categories: Protestant, Catholic, Jewish. But, then, since the 1960s, so many strange groups had surfaced in San Francisco that one more didn't seem to make much difference.

What they did know was that Jones, who had come down to San Francisco from Mendocino County, had gathered a sizable flock among the city's poor, many of them African-American. Headquartered in a former synagogue on Geary Street, the People's Temple formed a community — a portion of this community living communally — that was a powerful political force. Jones could turn out thousands of workers for the campaigns of liberal candidates whom he favored. George Moscone's close election as mayor, many asserted, was due to the People's Temple efforts; and many politicians, among

Indians on Alcatraz.
Courtesy San Francisco
Chronicle.

them flamboyant Assemblyman Willie Brown, incessantly praised the work of Jones and his adherents.

Occasionally, rumors and allegations would surface that there was more about the People's Temple than met the eye: that there were ritual humiliations and beatings of members, that Jones insisted that income and assets of members be turned over to the Temple, that its leader treated women members as his wives, and that it was some sort of cult.

Jim Jones had been rewarded with a position on the Housing Authority, of which he became president, by a grateful Mayor George Moscone. Aside from Brown, District Attorney Joseph Freitas and Supervisor Harvey Milk, praised his work. Stories in the local press were adulatory of Jones and his People's Temple.

Two investigative reporters, Phil Tracy and Marshall Kilduff, began to investigate the allegations and rumors that the People's Temple was a dangerous cult. *The Chronicle* killed their story. Liberal politicians turned a deaf ear to requests from the reporters for interviews. Finally, a San Francisco-based magazine, *New West*, agreed to run their story — a piece which incorporated the allegations from former members of the People's Temple that it was indeed a cult under the fanatical leadership of Jones.

When it became certain that the story would be published in *New West*, Jones, who had orchestrated a campaign to stop its publication, decided to move to the Latin American country of Guyana, where he had purchased a twenty-seven-thousand acre enclave. One thousand members of his flock followed him there.

But the People's Temple story was not finished. Members of the families of those who had followed Jones to Guyana peppered politicians and the media with stories that their relatives were being kept against their will in the People's Temple compound. A grandstanding congressman from San Mateo County, Leo Ryan, decided to investigate. Jones said he could visit and bring back any person who wished to leave. Ryan and his entourage flew to Guyana and left with

An unused synagogue on Geary Street was recycled into the People's Temple, where cultist Rev. Jim Jones presided over his flock.
Courtesy San Francisco Chronicle.

a handful of those who wished to defect from the compound. At the airstrip in Guyana, Ryan and four members of his group were killed as they prepared to leave by fanatical zealots of the Rev. Jim Jones.

As the story exploded in the media throughout the world, it was followed by news even more grotesque: on Sunday, November 19, 1978, fragmentary bulletins began to circulate that Jones and his followers had committed mass suicide by drinking cyanide-laced punch.

During the next several days the full horror of the event became evident; and by Thanksgiving Day the details of an increasing body count — almost one thousand members of the People's Temple had,

Supervisor Harvey Milk.
Courtesy San Francisco Chronicle.

Mayor George Moscone.
Courtesy San Francisco Chronicle.

Dianne Feinstein, president of the board of supervisors, leads a silent prayer on the day following the murders. *Courtesy San Francisco Chronicle. Photo by Jerry Telfer.*

on Sunday, November 19, 1978, fragmentary bulletins began to circulate that Jones and his followers had committed mass suicide by drinking cyanide-laced punch.

During the next several days the full horror of the event became evident; and by Thanksgiving Day the details of an increasing body count — almost one thousand members of the People's Temple had, under the order of their insane leader, committed suicide. Their bodies were stacked in the tropical heat of the Guyana jungle — men, women, and children — creating a hellish stench.

The man who had

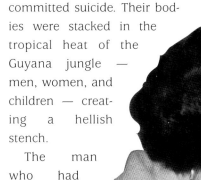

The caskets of Mayor George Moscone and Supervisor Harvey Milk lie in state in the rotunda of City Hall.
Courtesy Associated Press.

been extravagantly praised by San Francisco's liberal political establishment, by the city's press, from the *Chronicle* to the *Bay Guardian*, by such philanthropists as the man known as "Mr. San Francisco," Cyril Magnin, had led his followers into an apocalyptic death-trap, a *götterdämmerung* of death, lest he be humiliated or imprisoned for his deeds as an evil guru of those who trusted him to lead them to better lives.

The Guyana tragedy was to rivet the attention of the world on San Francisco, from whence the People's Temple had emanated. An event a week

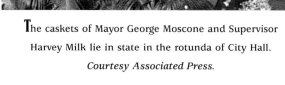

Dan White under arrest after he shot Moscone and Milk.
Courtesy San Francisco Chronicle.

(Next Page)

Two men of very different backgrounds were elected in the subsequent elections. From District 5, largely composed of sections of the Inner Mission, including the Castro area, came a New York Jew who had come to San Francisco as a securities analyst and who had become a hippie and an anti-war activist. He was brash and arrogant, had a dramatic flair, and had no qualms about using guerrilla tactics on his opponents. His name was Harvey Milk; and he was gay.

From District 8, largely composed of the south central portion of San Francisco, including Visitacion Valley, came a very young man who had been born and raised in an Irish-American working class family in that area. His father had been a fireman, and this family typified the Irish-American force in San Francisco's politics, its fire and police departments, and its social structure, that was in the 1970s withering away.

The newly elected supervisor, Dan White, was a repressed, tightly wound individual, who had not attended college, was a veteran of Vietnam, had been a policeman, and was, at the time of his election, a fireman (a job which, upon his election, he had to give up).

The two men had very different agendas. Harvey Milk, the first openly homosexual elected official in the United States, was deeply committed to enhancing the status of the large — and growing — number of homosexuals in San Francisco and to a liberal program beyond that.

Dan White ran for the office of supervisor because he lamented the changes that had been wrought in his native San Francisco during the past decade: the collapse in the power and numbers of the Irish and Italian Catholics, the rise of a gay culture, rampant crime, the increasing obscurity of the city's traditional working class.

Police car on fire in front of a besieged City Hall on the night of May 22, 1979, when gays rioted after hearing the verdict of the Dan White case.
Courtesy Associated Press

Despite the chasm between the two men's personalities and their political views, Dan White put aside his strong anti-gay views and attempted to befriend Milk. Milk did little to disguise his scorn for Dan White: his politics, his personality, his background. And, in a couple of instances, whether due to a genuine misunderstanding or due to White's political naiveté, White felt that Milk had betrayed him by reneging on promises to vote for positions about which he felt strongly.

This personal and political confrontation was exacerbated by Dan White's financial travail after he was elected supervisor. He was recently married; his wife was pregnant with their first child; he had a mortgage on a house; and his salary was only $9600 per year.

Some supporters arranged for the developer of Pier 39, Warren Simmons, to lease him a spot on this tourist magnet to begin a fast food outlet. And, because of White's conservative position and votes on the board of supervisors, a number of San Francisco political money sources — the Chamber of Commerce, the real estate interests, the Police Officers Association — paid off his election indebtedness and showed eagerness to otherwise financially aid him.

Such supporters triggered assertions — in the press and elsewhere — that Dan White had abandoned his working class constituency for San Francisco's moneyed interests.

These events were played out in the mayoral administration of George Moscone, a handsome, charming Italian-American native son, whose intensely liberal politics and whose alliance with the Burton brothers and Willie Brown made him anathema in the conservative ethos from which he had sprung.

On top of this, Moscone had a reputation among San Francisco's conservative elements as a moral leper: a constant philanderer who sought out black prostitutes and who used marijuana and cocaine.

Moscone, who had barely beaten conservative supervisor John Barbagelata for his position as San Francisco's mayor (in an election which featured a

Courtesy of San Francisco Chronicle.
Photo by John Storey.

good deal of fraud favoring Moscone), could not muster a liberal majority on the board of supervisors. He was constantly being beaten 6-5; and one of those six votes was that of Dan White.

The fevered, tempestuous politics of this era, the failure to understand politics as compromise, the pressures on his life, and his already tortured, complex personality combined to further depress Dan White. He sank into a deep lassitude, neglecting his constituents, becoming paranoid, lashing out at his critics.

Then, on November 10, 1978, Dan White resigned as a supervisor for the City and County of San Francisco, hand-delivering a letter of resignation to Mayor Moscone.

The diligent clerk of the board of supervisors filed the report for the following Monday's weekly meeting of the board for action, when it was accepted.

But there were those who were appalled by White's action. An ex-aide and a current assistant urged him to reconsider; his moneyed political supporters worried about a shift in the board's current conservative majority with a liberal appointment by Moscone now in the offing.

White was finally convinced to take back his resignation, and, after he approached Moscone, the mayor agreed to give him back his letter of resignation. However, the letter had already been acted upon by the board of supervisors, and a vacancy existed. White could only return if Moscone appointed him; and Moscone had agreed to do this if the city attorney decided that indeed a vacancy had been created.

However, a backlash by many disgruntled constituents in District 8 and heavy lobbying by Mayor Moscone's liberal followers, most notably Harvey Milk, and White's inability to vow future fealty to Moscone's political agenda combined to have the mayor abandon his promise to White. The mayor decided to appoint someone else. And, perhaps as humiliating to White, Moscone forgot to call to tell him so. White found out from a reporter.

Furious, humiliated, his repressed, fragile personality crumbling, White, on November 27, 1978, called one of his aides to pick him up at his home and to drive him to City Hall, where he wished, he said to her, to expostulate with Moscone and accuse Milk of his downfall.

When he arrived at City Hall, White had with him a loaded revolver and several additional bullets in his pocket. Not wishing to pass through the metal detector at the entrance, White ducked into a basement window and made his way to the mayor's office, where he requested a meeting from his secretary. The mayor agreed to see White, but when Moscone wished to defuse the obviously emotional White by offering him a drink and to defend his own actions by a barrage of charming palaver, White took out his revolver and shot him several times.

White reloaded and headed out the back entrance of the mayor's office to the offices of the supervisors. He saw that Harvey Milk was in his office, and asked him to join him in what had been his own office. Milk did so, and when White upbraided him for his role in his not being appointed to the seat he had vacated, Milk smirked. Once more, White fired his revolver; and Milk lay dead.

Startled supervisors and city employees saw an obviously agitated White leave his old office and exit City Hall. White retrieved his car and drove to the nearby Doggie Diner, a fast-food restaurant. There he called his wife, who was working at their place on Pier 39, and asked her to meet him at St. Mary's Cathedral. In that cavernous church, White told his long-suffering wife what he had done. Together they walked the short distance to the Northern Station, the regional police station where White had once been a policeman; and there he confessed to friends and former colleagues his crime.

Several months later Dan White's trial took place in a San Francisco courtroom. The lead prosecutor for the district attorney's office, Thomas Norman, was confident that he could prove first-degree murder;

but his confidence became arrogance, and his case was ineptly presented.

Meanwhile, White's defense attorney, a youthful Douglas Schmidt, brilliantly conceived and presented a strategy of diminished capacity, the so-called "Twinkie defense," that tried to convince jurors that, despite the appearance of rational intention to kill, White, because of depression, intensified by a diet of junk food, was not legally capable of committing first-degree murder.

The jury bought the assertion of diminished capacity, and on Monday, May 21, 1979, brought in the verdict of voluntary manslaughter for the two killings — a verdict that held a maximum sentence of a bit more than seven years.

The verdict was announced to a surprised San Francisco at about 5:30 p.m. An hour later a leader of the gay community in San Francisco, Cleve Jones, began to harangue a gathering crowd at Castro and Market streets, inflaming its disappointment at the verdict into a belligerence that grew as the crowd expanded and marched towards City Hall.

The mob that now stood before the beautiful, Beaux Arts City Hall confronted very few policemen (the majority of the police force, who worked during the day had already gone home). The gays began to blow the whistles they carried with them to alert passersby that they were being beaten by "gay-bashers" and began to throw rocks and bottles at the policemen and at the glass doors of City Hall. Some of the rioters began to tear off the grillwork from around the doors of the building.

The new mayor, Dianne Feinstein, who had been a twice unsuccessful candidate for mayor and had been the president of the board of supervisors at the time of the killings, was in her office, paralyzed with fear.

The police chief, Charles Gain, an aloof outsider who was despised by the police force and who had been appointed by George Moscone, ordered his men to do nothing, which infuriated the hapless police besieged in City Hall.

Fires began in the vicinity of City Hall. The numerous police cars parked around City Hall were set afire by the enraged homosexual crowd. A fire truck was stopped from entering the area. The entire Civic Center area began to be vandalized. Still, Chief Gain held his men back, despite pleading from the mayor.

Finally, two hours after the first rock had shattered a glass door at City Hall, Gain gave the order to the police, maddened with frustration and hurt and impotence, to disperse the crowd. They responded with pent-up fury, their clubs flailing. Just before midnight Civic Center was quiet — a surreal sight of burned-out police cars, fires, and an enormous blanket of broken glass.

Police cars were dispatched to the Castro area, where the enraged, frustrated police ran amok through the streets and even into the bars, leaving Castro Street littered with clubbed and kicked men and women.

At 2 a.m. Gain ordered his men out of the Castro, much to the disappointment of his rampaging policemen; by 3 a.m. San Francisco's streets were empty.

Dan White served less than 4 years at Soledad Prison in protective housing, impregnating his wife on one of her conjugal visits (the child was born with Down's Syndrome). In January, 1984 he was paroled to the Los Angeles area for one year. His return to San Francisco in 1985 was to a sterile life as a pariah. Several months after his return, he did what his religiously devout wife had feared he would do when she had accompanied him from St. Mary's Cathedral to the Northern Station: he committed suicide in the garage of his house by carbon monoxide asphyxiation.

No one could more dramatically have signaled the end of an era in San Francisco nor the shift in its power structure than Dan White.

Chapter 3

Ghirardelli

1978 — The Present

The Transformation

1 9 7 8 - T h e   P r e s e n t

SAN FRANCISCO IN THE LAST QUARTER OF THE TWENTIETH CENTURY IS A CITY TRANSFORMED from the city that witnessed the end of World War II.

Its demographics have changed drastically; its politics have radically altered; its ability to achieve consensus has turned into fractious interests struggling against each other; long familiar institutions have disappeared; social structures that long dominated the city are no more; the city's economic structure has substantially changed.

Much of this change is not peculiar to San Francisco, but is part of the change that has occurred in the United States and the developed world since 1945. However, San Francisco's susceptibility to new ideas and to change have made these changes more pronounced than in many other cities.

As the city lost whatever manufacturing base it had in the years after World War II — its food products companies, its printing and lithography companies, its shipping companies — its "blue-collar" working class evaporated. The rugged unions that contained this working class have shriveled; and their place as labor influences in San Francisco's power structure had been taken over by public employees' unions (reflecting San Francisco's swollen bureaucracy), service unions (reflecting the city's dependence on the tourism and convention trade), and teachers' unions.

And, although San Francisco has always been considered the financial capital of the West, the recomposition of the city's economy during the past century has made finance an even greater component in its business life. San Francisco has spawned during its postwar era several major investment banking/brokerage firms that have achieved national status (albeit that these firms during the late 1990s, in a time of consolidation of financial companies, seem to be being acquired by large banks). The West's two largest banks — Bank of America and Wells Fargo Bank — are headquartered in San Francisco. Numerous large and successful mutual fund companies and money management firms are also located in the city.

This massive financial complex has been a catalyst to the explosion of support businesses, most notably law firms. Established firms have increased many times over the number of attorneys in their employ; and many new firms have been started.

The huge growth in tourism and the convention business has created thousands of new hotel rooms and the rehabilitation of many dilapidated, small hotels to accommodate those who come to "everybody's favorite city." New restaurants have sprung up with startling rapidity — and old ones have closed — to serve both tourists and Bay Area residents who no longer cook at home and for whom food has become a mystical experience.

The city's retail stores — from the very elegant to the most "schlocky" — cater to the tourist and convention trade. Stores on Union Square will stay open after hours to serve those attending a convention, hoping that these free-spending conventioneers will boost their sales.

The social structure that dominated the immediate postwar period has almost totally evaporated. It is not uncommon for residents of a neighborhood not to know any of their neighbors. The institutions that were once at the heart of San Franciscans' social community — churches, fraternal organizations, school and civic groups — have either disappeared or have drastically diminished in importance. Gone are the Young Men's Institute, the Knights of Columbus, the Elks, the Parent Teachers Association, and various garden clubs. In their place have come the ubiquitous health club and, for the young and single, bars and coffee houses on Chestnut or Union streets in the Marina District and dance clubs south of Market.

In 1987 Pope John Paul II made the first-ever papal visit to San Francisco — a rather subdued event that

San Francisco from Twin Peaks in the mid-1950s offered a skyline of very few skyscrapers.
Photo by Max Kirkeberg.

A decade later shows the beginnings of a built-up downtown area.
Photo by Max Kirkeberg.

The International Hotel became a battleground during the 1970s between proponents of business growth and those who felt that the lodging rights of marginalized individuals in society were being threatened.
Photo by Max Kirkeberg.

By 1992 (the date of this photograph) the city's downtown financial area had both expanded across Market Street (the dark line in the right of the photograph) and had a large number of skyscrapers. Voters a few years before — in 1986 — had voted to severely limit such future growth.
Photo by Max Kirkeberg.

The New Main Library was built in the mid 1990s by renowned architect I.M. Pei. The state-of-the-art building combines open spaces with the latest computer technology. *Photos by Deanna L. Kastler.*

Cardinal Agostino Casaroli, Archbishop Quinn and Pope John Paul II, accompanied by Secret Service Agents, return from viewing the Golden Gate Bridge during the 1987 papal visit.
Courtesy San Francisco Catholic. Photo provided by Papal Consortium.

For the second time in its history, in 1987 the Golden Gate Bridge was officially closed to motor vehicles. To celebrate its fiftieth anniversary, thousands flocked from the north and south entrances to meet in the center of the bridge causing the span to flatten out, much to the consternation of bridge engineers. *Courtesy San Francisco Chronicle. Photo by John O'Hara.*

cost the Archdiocese of San Francisco millions of dollars. A few years later the archbishop of San Francisco announced the closing of several churches in the city — the victim, he claimed, of many fewer Catholics and of declining church attendance and involvement in the life of parishes.

As the city changed, its politics became more and more contentious. The strife that began in the 1960s — the protests that characterized that decade — became crystallized and institutionalized during the subsequent decades. A massive strike by city workers in 1974 — one in which unions representing municipal railway and BART refused to cross picket lines — shut down San Francisco. In the following year the city's police and fire forces went on strike.

San Franciscans were sufficiently outraged to pass a series of anti-labor ballot measures in 1976.

The progressive-liberal ascendancy in politics, most visibly seen in this bloc's attempt to achieve slow-growth legislation, was asserted in numerous ways; and, as the twentieth century comes to a close, its agenda has been largely victorious. Domestic partners legislation, "set-asides" in city contracts for minority and women-owned businesses, an entire spectrum of affirmative action measures, the renaming of Columbus

A "centipede" snakes up the Hayes Street Hill as part of the whimsical celebration of the Bay to Breakers race. *Courtesy San Francisco Chronicle. Photo by Brant Ward.*

A giant fish is part of the annual Bay to Breakers bash. *Courtesy San Francisco Chronicle. Photo by Lea Suzuki.*

Day to Indigenous Peoples Day, that old chestnut, district elections (passed again in 1997), and stringent rent control (except, thus far, on vacant units) have been but a few of the demands of the city's increasingly liberal voters that have been met and passed into law.

The ballot box has not been, however, the only place where liberal propagandists and ideologues for various causes have battled for their ideas. In the late 1970s, after legal action was exhausted to spare the International Hotel (a dilapidated residential hotel in an area between Chinatown, North Beach, and the financial district) from demolition, protesters battled San Francisco's sheriff and his deputies from serving eviction notices to the handful of mostly elderly Filipinos who inhabited the hotel, and then later to prevent demolition.

The riot by San Francisco's gays that followed the announcement of the Dan White verdict was followed by less violent protests that marked the announcement of the Rodney King verdict and the decision of the United States to push Iraq out of Yemen.

ACT UP is a group that attempts to disrupt the rhythms of urban life to publicize what it sees as the need for greater resources to stop AIDS. It has stopped traffic on the Golden Gate Bridge for hours and interrupted musical events at the Opera House. Critical Mass is a group that seeks more public action in encouraging the use of more mass transportation and greater access and safety standards for bicyclists. Once a month this group will select a place in San Francisco where hundreds of bicyclists will ride, clogging city streets and disrupting traffic.

Thus, not just peaceful assembly to urge some action or to protest some governmental action, but disruption of cultural events, stopping of traffic, and outright vandalism, have become tools of those advocating some change.

On the other hand, there are events which can paper over these fractious politics for a moment and give a semblance of festive unity. The celebration of the 50-year anniversary of the Golden Gate Bridge in

1987, when hundreds of thousands shoe-horned themselves onto the bridge cast an aura of love for San Francisco among the city's innumerable factions. Two years later, tragedy gave a unifying solidity in the face of the Loma Prieta Earthquake. The response to the Black and White Ball, a long-standing benefit for the San Francisco Symphony, and the annual ritual of the *Examiner*-sponsored Bay-to-Breakers run are among those events which showcase the exuberance of San Franciscans and their love of participation in such civic rites.

San Francisco probably suffered less than any other city in California during the economic stress of the recession of the early 1990s. While communities in Southern California saw prices of both commercial and residential real estate plummet, San Francisco experienced virtually no decline in the value of residential real estate; and its commercial real estate was somewhat insulated by the slow-growth provisions of Proposition M, passed in 1986.

As a result of this economic stability, and even, as the 1990s progressed, San Francisco, in the mid- and late-1990s underwent a municipal "renaissance" of sorts. Liberal bond issues to seismically retrofit and rehabilitate several public buildings, such as City Hall, the Opera House, and the Veterans' Building, to locate the Asian Art Museum in the old Main Library on Civic Center, and to build a new Main Library were enthusiastically passed by at least the two-thirds of the voters required.

The election of the former speaker of the California State Assembly, the dapper, elegant, ultimate power broker, Willie Brown, as mayor of San Francisco in 1995 added to the upbeat mood of San Francisco. Given to a love of festivities as part of municipal rituals, Brown presided over celebrations such as honoring Herb Caen — his eightieth birthday and his reception of a Pulitzer Prize — shortly before Caen's death, Brown spent large sums of money on his inaugural (privately raised) and on the city's hosting of the mayors' conference in 1997, and envisaged the rehabilitation of City Hall more for ceremonies, entertaining, and celebrations than for the housing of the municipal bureaucracy.

Brown's resounding victory in 1995 and his expert use of power (somewhat aided by a new charter, passed by the voters effective July 1, 1996, the first new charter since that of 1932, which gave the mayor some additional power) convinced many San Franciscans that an era of a more purposeful and efficient operation of the city was at hand.

Certainly, his ability to tamp down the political agenda of the more militantly liberal of San Francisco activists has done a great deal to lessen the divisiveness of San Francisco politics.

And so, as San Francisco prepares to enter the twenty-first century and to commemorate the sesquicentennial of the Gold Rush, which transformed a small, somnolent trading village into an instant metropolis, and of its incorporation as a city (1850-2000), it is a very different city than that of a half century ago. For those who remember the San Francisco of the 1940s and 1950s, that city is held dear in a romantic haze; for baby-boomers and newcomers to San Francisco, there is present life to be lived in the city.

Change is a constant in any living organism; and San Francisco will continue to change. There will be an on-going attempt by some to hasten that change; while others will exert their efforts to contain it. But, on those days when warm sunshine highlights blue skies, incandescent, sparkling air, and the interplay of hills and water, it seems that no changes will ever change the beauty and the spirit of the City by the Bay.

The Sexual Revolution and the New Age Take Place in the City by the Bay

The ferment that marked the 1960s carried on in various strands throughout the following decades of the twentieth century; and in no place in the United States did new ideas take root and sprout as they did in the San Francisco Bay Area.

What has been termed "the sexual revolution" was a phenomenon that came out of the 1960s' upheaval and the persistent overthrow on a mass scale of traditional authority and values. Soon, what had been done in the back seats of parked cars or in dingy motel rooms was done openly in college dormitories, on beaches, and in woods.

The advent of the Pill had coincided with the eagerness to experience sex that characterized the 1960s and the aftermath of that decade.

This new openness toward sexuality found its most hedonistic and even academic nexus in San Francisco, which became the "capital of the sexual revolution" in the United States.

One of the aspects of this outburst of sexuality was the salacious side: the work of imaginative businessmen. Striptease dates back to the nineteenth century; but even the most provocative striptease shows had the performers keep on pasties and "G-strings". It was in San Francisco that some aggressive businessman came up with the idea of topless women: and the idea caught on, as places proliferated featuring topless shows of various types.

This phenomenon began in the 1960s, and it began in what had been San Francisco's original "naughty" area: the Broadway portion of the Barbary Coast. Broadway, during the late nineteenth century, had swung from its unsavory mix of low saloons and brothels to an Italian entertainment enclave, serving the surrounding Italian-American ghetto of North Beach and Telegraph Hill with restaurants, nightclubs, and social halls. By the 1960s, as the Italian-American population of the area was diminishing, Broadway was ready for a transition.

The next logical step in this progression of entertainment was total nudity, and, once more, San Francisco was the pioneer.

The topless craze did not confine itself to a nightclub-type scene; but soon there were topless shoe shine stands and restaurants where topless waitresses served food and beverages. One nightclub at Broadway

A depiction of Carol Doda, San Francisco's famous silicone-enhanced nude dancer at the Condor, where she was a star attraction for many years. *Photo by Max Kirkeberg.*

Carol Doda gives a press conference. *Courtesy San Francisco Chronicle. Photo by Ken McLaughlin.*

and Columbus Avenue even advertised one of its performers as "a topless grandmother of eight."

Perhaps the most famous of the Broadway nightclubs was the Condor, which featured a nude dancer by the name of Carol Doda. Doda's fame came from her enormous silicone-enhanced breasts. For many years, the neon sign that glowed on the corner of

Broadway and Columbus Avenue was one of the icons of San Francisco.

Across town from North Beach, on the edge of the Tenderloin, two brothers who had been making pornographic films in a warehouse South of Market, now began a pornographic empire, centered on a theater called the O'Farrell. Jim and Artie Mitchell were graduates of San Francisco State University, and had decided that the expanding interest in sexuality during the 1960s would also expand the market for pornographic films.

At first, their products were little different from the stag films of previous years; but they soon discovered that pretty and wholesome-looking coeds were willing to perform in their films, the lure being the money or the unusual excitement, and they envisaged an even greater market as the result of being able to obtain "the girl next door" as an actress.

This perception was brilliantly realized when they produced *Behind the Green Door*, starring a blonde model by the name of Marilyn Chambers, who happened to be at that time on the box of Ivory Snow soap. The irony of this young woman being on millions of boxes of Ivory Snow — "99 44/100 % pure" — and also being the star of a pornographic film brought the Mitchell brothers much publicity and the film

record attendance. *Behind the Green Door* became an adult film classic.

However, the Mitchell's soon gave up film-making and devoted their energies to making the O'Farrell Theater into an adult entertainment complex. A theater continues to show films; but the most popular attractions there are the "live theaters."

These sexual transformations that began in the 1960s soon spawned a minor industry in San Francisco: nude massage parlors, shops selling adult videos and sex paraphernalia, and other such sex-oriented businesses.

It was in the late 1960s and early 1970s that human sexuality began to enter the psychoanalytical world and the fringes of medicine; and, once more, San Francisco was at the center of this movement. Several institutes, devoted to enhancing one's sexual pleasure, were begun — one even associated with the University of California at San Francisco, one of the

Jim Mitchell, who killed his brother, Art, several years ago, continues live entertainment at the Mitchell Brothers O'Farrell Theater. Brightly painted with a jungle scene, it still offers nude and X-rated shows. *Photo by Deanna L. Kastler.*

The cult-like figure of e s t founder Werner Erhard sits in his office at Franklin House. *Courtesy Associated Press.*

most formidable medical research centers in the United States.

As Pacific Heights couples had begun to attend pornographic films at the O'Farrell Theater during the 1970s, prompting the term "porno chic," so did thousands of middle-class San Francisco couples and singles flock to their various therapeutic organizations for guidance on better sex.

Part of the purpose of these institutions, usually staffed by health professionals, was to help the disadvantaged — usually impotent men or disabled men and women — achieve sexual release. For the men suffering from impotence, there was often the use of surrogate sex partners in attempts to eliminate the problem.

By far the largest number of participants in these sex institutes were young or middle-age couples or single individuals who were seeking ways of achieving the highest pleasure possible from the sex act itself or other forms of sexual activity.

The extension of this focus on sexuality from the legitimate institute described above was the proliferation of sex gurus in the San Francisco Bay Area during the 1970s and 1980s. In private homes or in rent-

ed halls, various men and women would proclaim themselves sexually enlightened and advertise seminars or tantric yoga classes that promised a spectacular increase in one's sexual enjoyment.

These innumerable groups lasted for several years, leading to recreational sex among large numbers of Bay Area citizens. To visitors to San Francisco who participated in such experiences it reinforced their impression of the city as the Oz of hedonism.

Emerging from the optimism and confidence of the 1960s in the perfectibility of the human being came a movement that sparked yet another revolution in the United States in the 1970s and 1980s: what was known as the New Age or as the human potential movement. San Francisco, once more, became the center of this movement.

There were a number of factors that had contributed to this phenomenon: the presence south of San Francisco, on the Big Sur coast, of the Esalen Institute, whose classes, seminars, massage workshops, and idyllic setting, where participants walked around the grounds without clothes and would gaze at the Pacific Ocean from the hot tubs at the edge of a cliff; the increasing popularity of the thoughts of such psychology gurus as Wilhelm Reich, Abraham Maslow, Carl Rogers, and Fritz Perls; the collapse of traditional religious groups in conveying a sense of salvation; the strains which had come from the tumult and change of the 1960s.

San Francisco, with its constant effervescence in dealing with new ideas, became, in a sense, the "corporate headquarters" for the movement. Thousands of couples and singles drove down the coast to Esalen to find the key to changing their lives in a positive way. When they returned, they remained hungry for the sense of community they found there, for additional insights from the humanistic psychology that had prevailed in the classes, seminars, and workshops in which they had participated, and for the life of extraordinary happiness which had been implied could be theirs.

Thus, there sprung up a myriad of seminars, classes, and workshops in San Francisco and in adjacent areas that promised happiness and fulfillment. The lure of this promise soon drifted to other urban areas in the country.

One aspect of this New Age-seeking was a revival of ancient superstitions — tarot card reading, the I Ching, astrology, psychic readings, the use of crystals. They became ubiquitous throughout the Bay Area.

But, while such practices were frequently done "tongue-in-cheek," many of the groups which organized under the impetus of the human potential movement garnered the status of religious groups or cults.

No group in the United States ever achieved the fame, wealth, and status of the San Francisco-based organization called *e s t* (officially, Erhard Seminars Training, Inc.).

Founded in the early 1970s by a Philadelphian with a fondness for aliases, Werner Erhard, whose real name was Jack Rosenberg, was a car salesman who had abandoned his wife and four children and had come to California to start life anew with a woman he had bigamously married. *e s t* captured the imagination not only of San Franciscans and Californians, but of "seekers" throughout the country and throughout the world.

Erhard's flight to California entailed a sharpening and refinement of the aggressive sales techniques he had acquired as a car salesman in Philadelphia. Work as an encyclopedia salesman and as a "trainer" for a group called Mind Dynamics began to polish the former car salesman. He was a sponge for the human potential ideas and concepts then becoming popular, and soon he started his own group: thus was *e s t* founded.

The *e s t* seminar took place during two consecutive weekends. Each weekend began on a Friday night and ended late on a Sunday night. No one could leave during the sessions, whether it was to respond to the call of nature, to smoke a cigarette, or to have a drink of water. The sessions were composed of slick, dramatic, and emotional harangues on Erhard's vision of life and how to live it, along with "sharing" and questions by the participants. On the final Sunday night there was a "graduation," and those who had completed the seminar were deluged with congratulations and good wishes from those who had previously completed the seminar.

Erhard's clever use of graduates of his seminars as unpaid workers and proselytizers for *e s t* was the mainstay of his success. Usually seeking community, or having a need to feel important or wanted, or caught up in a gnostic search for happiness and fulfillment, these acolytes would volunteer many hours each week. They would bring family members, friends, neighbors, and co-workers to an *e s t* introductory session, and would sign up for one of a myriad of "graduate" seminars that promised even greater insights into how to achieve any dream or fantasy one could conjure up.

Soon, thousands upon thousands were flocking to *e s t* seminars and "graduate" seminars. Erhard chose and trained additional "trainers" to leverage his growing empire.

San Francisco's Civic Auditorium would be filled with eager seminar participants; similar venues throughout the United States soon resounded with the unmistakable *e s t* jargon: "You just don't get it.", and "Handle it."

Werner Erhard not only became wealthy, his devoted followers provided him with a phalanx of unpaid workers prepared to follow his simplest request, from cooking and serving for his dinner parties to cleaning his houses and staffing the *e s t* offices. Meanwhile, the *e s t* propagandists continued to urge all they knew to take the *e s t* seminar and follow-up courses.

In the late 1980s and early 1990s, however, trouble began to appear for Werner Erhard and his kingdom. He had become a guru-figure in a cult, an incessant womanizer and more and more insistent on adulation from his followers. His second wife filed for divorce. Allegations of financial irregularities began to appear in the press; and, most damaging, allegations that he had sexually abused one or more of his daughters began to surface.

A name change of *e s t* to the Forum took place; but, if that was done to distance his money machine from the Erhard name, it did not succeed. Attendance began to plummet and Werner Erhard's empire began to unravel.

Amid continued charges of impropriety and of self-serving in his business dealings, Erhard attempted to sell the Forum. As the controversies swirled around him, Werner Erhard left the United States. Mention of him virtually disappeared from the media.

And while Werner Erhard's controversial life tended to dampen enthusiasm for similar human potential movement groups, the movement lingers on in the San Francisco Bay Area.

A Turn-of-the Century Kaleidoscope: San Francisco's Changing Ethnic and Nonconformist Neighborhoods

According to Brian J. Godfrey in his well-researched *Neighborhood in Transition*, "World War II marked a historic watershed for San Francisco: only the Gold Rush, and arguably the earthquake and fire, had greater impacts on the cultural landscape."

In the more-than-half-century since the end of World War II San Francisco has been transformed from the city that existed in 1945. Constant transformation is a fact of life for cities, as well as individuals; but such processes are sometimes so gradual and subtle that they make but a small mark on the historical radar screen.

Much of historical commentary on the heterogeneity of urban areas focus on ethnic diversity; increasingly, such commentary needs to incorporate nonconformist diversity as well, as can readily be seen in San Francisco.

So pervasive has been the demographic change — ethnic and nonconformist, alike — that one can say that the city of the very last years of the twentieth century is totally unlike that of 1945.

If one looks at the census information of the 1940s and 1950s and compares it with that of 1990 or presumed updates with the end of the century, one is stunned by the changes.

Where now is the sizable Greek community that existed South of Market around Third Street? Where now is the once vigorous Maltese community centered around its church, St. Paul of the Shipwreck, in the Bayview area? Where now are the "Mission Irish" or the Italians of North Beach? Whereas, in the nineteenth and first half of the twentieth century, the greatest bulk of foreign-born or foreign-parentage residents of San Francisco were European, at the end of the twentieth century the greatest bulk is Asian or Latin American.

Such changes have had great economic, cultural, social, and political results in San Francisco; and they will continue to influence the patterns and rhythms of this city's urban life.

If we begin in the northern part of San Francisco, we look at two well-known communities: Chinatown and North Beach. Chinatown was a ghetto almost in the medieval sense of the word, and was the exclusive place of residence for San Francisco's Chinese residents. Today, Chinatown is one of the most densely inhabited areas in the United States and is home mainly to poorer Chinese and to recent Chinese immigrants. The Chinese community, which, since the abrogation of the 1882 Chinese Exclusion Act in 1943 and the total change in immigration laws since the mid-1960s, has soared in numbers, perhaps today numbering about one quarter of the city's population. And, if one speaks of an Asian community, largely expanded by the influx of Southeast Asian refugees, that percentage would be larger.

The Chinese in San Francisco have expanded out of the confines of Chinatown and have established businesses in the traditional Italian enclave of North Beach, which, aside from some restaurants and

Clement Street in the Richmond District of San Francisco is an example of a district that has undergone many changes over the years. Shown here in the 1940s, a streetcar line ran down the center of the street past the Colosseum, a neighborhood theater, surrounded by a mix of shops and residential housing. Today's Clement Street shows the remnants of the Colosseum Theater, closed and boarded up since the Loma Prieta earthquake of 1989, along with a closed Woolworth's store. Many Chinese grocers and restaurants have opened to serve a growing Chinese population in the Richmond District. *Courtesy San Francisco Public Library.*

shops along Columbus Avenue and Stockton Street, has very little Italian presence. (There are probably fewer than 2000 Italians or those of Italian forbearers in North Beach today.) They have established a major presence on the slopes of Russian, Nob, and Telegraph hills; and huge sections of the Richmond and Sunset districts are now inhabited by Chinese. There are several blocks on Clement Street, in the Richmond District, in which all shop and restaurant signs are in Chinese, and where one rarely hears English spoken.

As one approaches the Western Addition, one is reminded of the tiny African American representation in San Francisco before World War II. African

Americans constituted less than one percent of San Francisco's population in 1940. Then, thousands upon thousands of African Americans left the South during World War II for the war industries jobs on the West Coast. Earlier African Americans lived primarily in the Western Addition, mainly along the Geary corridor between Japantown (denuded of Japanese during 1942, as a result of Executive Order 9066) and what were then the Laurel Hill cemetery lands. African Americans coming to find wartime employment began to fill in the abandoned Japantown and in the area of lower Fillmore Street, which had once been a primarily Jewish area. In addition, African Americans began to live in the vicinity of the Hunter's

Point shipyard, from whence they expanded into the adjacent area known as the Bayview District.

Eventually, an expanding African American middle class began to occupy homes in the Ingleside District.

Today, African Americans constitute about 10 percent of San Francisco's population. Although areas of African American population concentration at the end of the twentieth century continue to be almost the same as they were in the 1940s, the Western Addition, as a home for African Americans, has been greatly reduced due to redevelopment and other factors.

San Francisco's Hispanics have the longest history — except, of course, for Native Americans, very few of these earliest inhabitants of San Francisco who survive today — of any group in San Francisco. But, the relatively small group of Hispanics who resided in what is today San Francisco during the Spanish and Mexican periods were soon swamped after the takeover of California by the United States in 1846.

However, Hispanics began to migrate to San Francisco during the Gold Rush, where they resided in the area of Telegraph Hill and North Beach. After World War II the Hispanic population of San Francisco was relatively small, but during the subsequent decades it expanded greatly, as thousands of Mexicans and citizens of Central American countries began to pour into the city. Although the Hispanic population in San Francisco scattered throughout the city, it was mainly concentrated in the Inner Mission and in the eastern side of the Outer Mission. In these areas they displaced the Irish, Germans, and Scandinavians who had previously lived there.

It is difficult to ascertain the numbers of Hispanics in San Francisco, because as is common with the contemporary Hispanic experience in the United States, many are undocumented. However, San Francisco's Hispanic population is today sizable: probably in excess of 10 percent.

One of the fastest growing ethnic groups is that of San Francisco's Filipino community. The earliest migrations were in the 1920s and 1930s, mostly male, and living in the area of Kearny Street, just off the city's financial district.

The next wave of Filipinos arrived in the several years after the end of World War II and resided largely in the Inner and Outer Mission districts, as well as in the Richmond District. The third wave came, and continues to come, in the wake of immigration law changes in the mid-1960s. These newer residents live in the South of Market area and in the south-central part of San Francisco (with a large continuation into Daly City, to the southwest of San Francisco).

A small, but increasing, segment of San Francisco's population consists of a category called Pacific Islanders: Samoans, Guamanians, and others. Small, but important economically, are such groups as Koreans, East Indians, who own many of the residential hotels in the city, and Arabs (mostly Palestinians), who own and operate most of San Francisco's combination liquor-grocery stores.

One of the components of San Francisco's demographics is its young — single or married — professional caste. Most of these come from other parts of the country, coming to San Francisco to find jobs or having been transferred here by their companies. Some will continue to live in San Francisco, others will move to other parts of the Bay Area, and still others will move on to other cities as part of their corporate odyssey.

These young men and women have begun to fill the Marina District and the relatively new housing complexes in the South Beach portion of the South of Market area. Somewhat older, usually married, professionals can be found buying houses in what have been previously working class areas: Noe Valley, which, because its denizens tend to be politically liberal and socially conscious, has been called "the brown rice belt," the Excelsior District, and Bernal Heights.

There is not a neighborhood in San Francisco that has not been totally transformed or at least touched by the rapid changes of the post-World War II era. Pacific Heights, the premier residential district in San

Francisco, has a number of recent arrivals from other parts of the United States, some who have inherited fortunes, others who are making large sums of money as investment bankers, lawyers, or Silicon Valley entrepreneurs. A sprinkling of wealthy Chinese can now be seen living in houses built by the city's "movers and shakers" of the late nineteenth and early twentieth centuries.

San Francisco has always provided a tolerant home for nonconformists. In the 1860s and 1870s, and again in the last years of the nineteenth century and the early years of the twentieth, bohemians, writers and artists tended to congregate in what is now known as the Jackson Square area. Beatniks in the 1950s found home in North Beach; and the hippies of the 1960s in the Haight-Ashbury. There does not seem to be today a similar abode for such nonconformists in San Francisco.

However, what could be incorporated in the term "nonconformist" is San Francisco's gay community. This community had been growing in San Francisco since World War II. Since many of the beat poets were homosexuals, there was an overlap of the beat and gay communities in the 1950s in the North Beach area, where such legendary places as the Black Cat and Miss Smith's Tea Room, catered to a homosexual clientele.

From North Beach, homosexual gathering places gravitated to Polk Street and then to the South of Market and Castro areas. What is now simply known as "The Castro" has become not only a predominantly gay area, but nationally known as a dynamic gay enclave, with numerous businesses catering to a homosexual clientele. This formerly Irish Catholic neighborhood has been largely gay since the first migrations into it began in the late 1960s.

It would be a mistake, however, to place all — or even most — of San Francisco's homosexual population in "The Castro": for gays live throughout San Francisco. Estimated at between 15 and 25 percent of San Francisco's population, the city's gay population

tion has probably leveled off or even slightly declined. Part of this can be attributed to the AIDS epidemic which began in the early 1980s; another factor is the increasing acceptance of homosexuals throughout the United States, thus reducing the lure of the freedoms of San Francisco.

The demographic changes which have so transformed San Francisco's neighborhoods have also changed the physical fabric of these neighborhoods. A dreary neighborhood bar that once served an Irish Catholic clientele on Castro Street has now been redecorated, and serves an entirely gay clientele. Drab Victorian houses that reflected the blight of the Western Addition have been rehabilitated and now sparkle with fresh paint. The schoolyard of Sts. Peter and Paul Church, the Italian national church in North Beach, is now thronged with Chinese-American children. A store which sold shoes to generations of Irish and German residents in the Mission District now sells tacos to the Hispanics who live in the vicinity.

While earlier immigrants have assimilated and moved to new habitations throughout the Bay Area, new migrants bring new languages, new customs, and new values to San Franciscans, replacing their immigrant predecessors, but, in many ways, recreating their immigrant experiences.

The Rebuilding of San Francisco and the Transformation of Its Politics

There was little in 1945 — or, in 1960 — that indicated that in the 1990s San Francisco would be repeatedly referred to as "the People's Republic of San Francisco." The city, in 1943, had elected as mayor a wealthy, conservative Republican by the name of Roger Lapham. His two-term successor, Elmer Robinson, elected in 1947, was yet another conservative, as would be his successor, George Christopher, who would be mayor until early-1964 and who would be San Francisco's last Republican mayor. (Although the office of mayor of San Francisco is a non-partisan one, party affiliation has

Roger Lapham, a wealthy shipping magnate who came to San Francisco in the 1920s, was chosen to run for mayor in 1943 by the city's conservative interests. He served for one term, as the nation came out of World War II and began its peacetime transition. He is shown here driving a Municipal streetcar at a time when public transportation was going through critical times. Courtesy San Francisco Public Library.

IT IS DANGEROUS AND UNLAWFUL
TO RIDE ON FENDER

973

traditionally been stated to indicate whether a candidate was a liberal or a conservative.)

In the mid-1960s a Democratic labor leader and Congressman by the name of John Shelley was elected mayor. Shelley, whose old-fashioned liberal, trade-union politics seemed anachronistic in the turmoil of the mid- and late-1960s, served only one term. Anointed to succeed him was a state legislator by the name of Eugene McAteer, but, when McAteer dropped dead of a heart attack on an Olympic Club hand-ball court, the leaders of the conservative elements of the city's Democrats chose a successful trial attorney by the name of Joseph L. Alioto as their can-

didate — a candidacy which was successful and led to Alioto's being mayor for eight years.

Then, in 1975 came a political revolution with the election of state senator George Moscone as mayor. Moscone, a dedicated progressive, brought the upheaval of a new kind of political coalition in San Francisco to the city's politics. He largely swept away "the movers and shakers" who for decades had dominated the city's commissions and filled those commission seats with ethnic minorities, gays, and women.

However, George Moscone was never to fully implement his progressive agenda: for a majority of six on the board of supervisors was able to veto his legislation.

The murder of George Moscone in November, 1978, put an end to this progressive experiment; and it put into the office of mayor a woman who had unsuccessfully run for mayor three times before: Dianne Feinstein.

A wealthy, ambitious woman, Feinstein essentially reversed the policies and practices of George Moscone. The well-known "movers and shakers" came back, albeit with larger numbers of minorities, gays, and women than had been common before the administration of George Moscone.

Feinstein followed in the well-trod path of such conservative Democrat former mayors as Jack Shelley and Joe Alioto; and, like Alioto, she was pro-growth and pro-business.

The decade in which Feinstein was mayor saw many of the rifts, divisions, and controversies in the urban body politic papered over; and she was successful in helping to rescue San Francisco from its grief and depression following the Jonestown tragedy and the killings of Moscone and Milk. But, the mayoral election of 1987 saw the upset victory (over Supervisor John Molinari, who was very much in the Alioto/Feinstein mold) of a state legislator by the name of Art Agnos, who was

elected by a progressive coalition of neighborhood activists, environmentalists, ethnic minorities, and working class liberals. George Moscone's experiment now had a new proponent as mayor.

Agnos' divisive, troubled, and unsuccessful administration ended with his defeat by a rather improbable candidate — former police chief Frank Jordan.

George Christopher was mayor from 1956 to 1964, and was the last Republican mayor of San Francisco. He is shown here working a jackhammer for the building of the Fifth and Mission Garage. Christopher's eight years as mayor will be a time of critical transition for San Francisco. *Courtesy San Francisco Public Library.*

Rarely have dedicated followers of a successful candidate so turned against that candidate as did those who had elected Agnos in 1987 and then rejected him in 1991.

Jordan seemed to have trouble grasping the complexities of mayoral politics. No longer a candidate who was a lodestone for the disaffection against Art Agnos, his administration seemed a bumbling one from the beginning; and in 1995 he was defeated by the former speaker of the assembly, a powerful and wily politician by the name of Willie Brown, who would be San Francisco's first African-American mayor.

The "sturm und drang" of San Francisco's politics during the past half century — but, particularly, from the late-1960s to the present — usually has been centered on the physical make-up of the city; and, from this principal controversy, others arose: the relationship of big business to the city, accessibility to the political process of gays, ethnic minorities and women, an expansion of the rights and benefits of what had previously been marginalized groups.

For at least two decades after the end of World War II, there was little or no opposition to the big business-led oligarchy that ruled San Francisco and to the policies this oligarchy put forward. Even the populist revolt inspired by Friedel Klussmann to save San Francisco's cable cars was limited by the continuing — and often successful — attempts by downtown interests and their political allies to reverse her initial victory.

There was little or no opposition to the decision to build Candlestick Park in the late-1950s; there was none to the initial proposals for urban redevelopment; and nobody blinked when, in the late-1950s, there began the tearing down of existing buildings in the downtown area and their replacement with an ever-increasing number of skyscrapers, which, in the following quarter century, would transform San Francisco's downtown and its skyline.

The combination of shifting demographics in San Francisco during the past half century and the chal-

lenge to existing authority that exploded in the 1960s and their aftermath led to increasingly confrontational politics and to progressive demands that were far in advance of virtually any other part of the United States. As a result, the governing process of San Francisco became, in the words of Richard De Leon in his excellent analysis *Left Coast City: Progressive Politics in San Francisco, 1975-1991*, an "antiregime" — capable of vetoing many things, but not capable of taking part in a coherent process of governance.

The recognition that the largely business-dominated vision of San Francisco as a venue for continuous growth was filled with danger and problems emerged slowly in San Francisco. Its earliest manifestation was in Friedel Klussmann's cable car revolt. Then, it was seen in the freeway revolt. Later, it began to crystallize in a series of campaigns to limit high-rise construction in San Francisco.

What began late in the post-World War II cycle of downtown construction and relatively modestly in the tearing down of some dilapidated post-1906 earthquake and fire buildings along Montgomery Street and their replacement by banal post-modern high-rises sparked little or notice in the late-1950s or the early 1960s. In fact, until the mid-1970s, slow-growth opposition to the pro-growth regimes that ruled San Francisco was still embryonic. After all, "growth" and "progress" were seen as good for the community. The building of office skyscrapers meant jobs and increased tax revenues for the city. Very few stopped to think of the problems of transportation gridlock, the banal, dehumanizing sense of scale and aesthetics, the consumption of public economic resources, the threats to the urban quality of life.

Such a minority consideration was seen in the overwhelming rejection by voters in 1971 and 1972 of two successive ballot propositions sponsored by liberal businessman Alvin Duskin to stop the "Manhattanization" of San Francisco by allowing only low-rise construction in the future.

However, in 1971 opposition to the proposal by

U.S. Steel to build a twenty-five-story hotel and a forty-story office building on the waterfront was able to thwart this project (local opposition abetted by that of the Bay Conservation and Development Commission).

The election of George Moscone united liberals, activists, and environmentalists to forge a progressive, and, consequently, slow-growth administration. However, the board of supervisors was able to stop much of Moscone's agenda. Then, in November, 1976, voters finally passed a measure to bring into effect district elections, which was seen by progressives as the key to passing progressive legislation. (Shortly thereafter, voters reversed themselves and brought back elections at large. District elections were then brought back by the voters in 1997.)

Moscone's death in November, 1978, brought Dianne Feinstein to the mayor's office. A centrist Democrat who was definitely pro-growth, Feinstein set about dismantling the progressive changes that had been brought about by Moscone. (One of the most visible of her moves was to fire the unpopular police chief, Charles Gain, and repaint the police cars black-and-white from a powder blue.) She vetoed domestic partners legislation and advocated the home-porting in San Francisco of the *USS Missouri*. Her unambiguous support for downtown development programs resulted in the rapid sprouting of skyscraper office buildings. (It has been estimated that the number of such buildings erected between 1979 and 1985 was the equivalent of thirty-seven Transamerica Pyramids.)

It is ironic that it was during the administration of this fiercely pro-growth mayor that San Francisco's slow-growth forces were finally able to achieve a major electoral victory to attain their ends.

There were a number of reasons for this. First, the pro-growth regime was crumbling. The business leaders that had so dominated San Francisco's political agenda for four decades following the end of World War II had died or retired from business. Their embattled successors had less commitment to a pro-growth vision of San Francisco, and, consequently, were less prone to expend their resources and those of the corporations they headed to staying the slow-growth forces.

Second, it was becoming more evident by the mid-1980s that San Francisco had developed an excess of office space. Third, the more compliant residents and workers in San Francisco of the decades following the end of World War II were being replaced by a young, professional middle class and what De Leon describes as a "postindustrial petty bourgeoisie," whose sensibilities were affronted by the overbuilt and congested environment in which they worked and lived. "They formed the nucleus," De Leon writes, "of a slow-growth coalition that expanded to include neighborhood activists, tenant union leaders, small business owners, and disillusioned ethnic minorities."

In 1979, the first full year of Feinstein's near-decade as mayor, Proposition O was placed on the ballot. It called for a reduction of the height and bulk of new buildings, but set up a bonus system by which these limits could be exceeded by developers willing to contribute to public transit improvements, energy conservation designs, additional affordable housing, and other measures mitigating the impact of growth on the city's infrastructure and quality of life.

An aggressive campaign was mounted against Proposition O, regaling voters with fears that its passage would discourage business, eliminate jobs and tax revenues, and promote urban sprawl. Nevertheless, Proposition O garnered 46 percent of the vote.

However, in 1981, the mayor and the board of supervisors instituted a fee of $5 per square foot on new buildings in order to defray such costs as increased public transportation that would be incurred by these developments.

In 1983 slow-growth forces placed the San Francisco Plan Initiative — Proposition M (but not to be confused with the Proposition M of 1986) — on the ballot. Once more the pro-growth forces battled this proposition, and did so by releasing its vaunted Downtown Plan as a means of deflecting the proposition's harsher provisions. Still, Proposition M obtained a near victory — 49.4 percent of the vote.

Legal suits, notably by attorney Sue Hestor, became the venue by which slow-growth advocates attempted to lessen the building of skyscraper office buildings; and in 1984 voters overwhelmingly approved Proposition K, which mandated that new construction could not obstruct year-round, all-day sunlight in the approximately seventy parks and open spaces under the city's jurisdiction.

The slow-growth forces became divided in 1985 when neighborhood activist Joel Ventresca sponsored Proposition F — a draconian measure that demanded an immediate and total suspension of high-rise construction projects. Many slow-growth advocates distanced themselves from Proposition F, and it obtained only 41 percent of the vote.

By early 1986 the slow-growth forces had begun to achieve a broad coalition for their agenda. Two of the three components of the city's progressive front (what De Leon calls "the three Lefts") — the environmentalists and the neighborhood populists — had come together in a loose alliance for yet another attempt at a slow-growth initiative. The result was a Campaign for Accountable Planning and a ballot initiative,

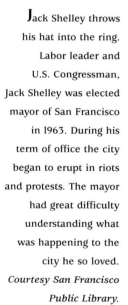

Jack Shelley throws his hat into the ring. Labor leader and U.S. Congressman, Jack Shelley was elected mayor of San Francisco in 1963. During his term of office the city began to erupt in riots and protests. The mayor had great difficulty understanding what was happening to the city he so loved. *Courtesy San Francisco Public Library.*

once again labeled Proposition M, which would go before the voters on November 4, 1986.

Proposition M imposed a permanent citywide limit on new construction of 950,000 square feet per year (on any building or conversion of 25,000 square feet or more) and contained provisions to limit construction to less than that amount until the pipeline was cleared of projects already approved. It assured that the loopholes in the Downtown Plan were plugged: for voters had to approve of any exception to the provisions of Proposition M.

In addition, Proposition M called for eight priority policies that were to guide the Planning Commission, which included the preservation of neighborhood character, the preservation of landmarks and historic buildings, and the preservation and enhancement of affordable housing.

Although union leaders continued to argue a pro-growth position, as a process by which jobs were maintained and increased, an increasing number of union members were being influenced by the arguments of the slow-growth advocates.

Feinstein led a spirited campaign to defeat Proposition M, despite a dispirited big business community. She tried a tactic which was intended to split the slow-growth coalition by recruiting the Reverend Cecil Williams, a prominent African-American leader. Williams responded by claiming that Proposition M would be detrimental to the poor population in San Francisco.

It was a brilliant tactic, which along with others of the "No on M" forces nearly cost the slow-growth coalition its eventual victory; but, on November 4, 1986, Proposition M passed — just barely — by 5,311 votes. San Francisco had enacted the most restrictive growth-control measure of any large U.S. city. It was a major turning point in the city's political history: one that opened new vistas for local popular control of land-use and development policy.

The progressive forces now sought to capture the city's political machinery as well; and, in 1987, they elected Art Agnos mayor — a progressive mayor who intended to follow in the footsteps of George Moscone. The centrist policies of Dianne Feinstein would now be repudiated.

Agnos won the election by a clever campaign that bundled the liberal/progressive agenda with an extraordinarily effective grass roots effort. It destroyed the

Mayor Joseph Alioto gives a press conference during the San Francisco police strike in 1975. Rose Marsha Pistol Drag Queen follows in the procession.
Courtesy San Francisco Chronicle.
Photo by Vince Maggiora.

inept campaign of Supervisor John Molinari, who had been favored to win, but, who, on December 8, 1987, was defeated in a landslide, 70 percent to 30 percent.

Issues were a major factor in the 1987 campaign, and Agnos' mobilization of a small army of precinct workers was based upon his adherence to the progressive agenda espoused by neighborhood activists, environmentalists, and others who saw his election as the way in which this agenda would be implemented. Vacancy control of rental units, growth limits (and the inviolate nature of Proposition M), and district elections were primary causes for the city's growing number of progressive voters. Here was an opportunity for the partnership between a progressive mayor and a progressive board of supervisors to make this agenda a reality.

Agnos entered office with very positive circum-

stances to effect the changes that he and his progressive constituency desired: a landslide vote, relative social tranquility, a liberal/progressive board of supervisors, a slow-growth mandate effected by the voters. But, there were some negative circumstances, as well: a large revenue shortfall of $180 million he had inherited from Feinstein's last budget, the diminution of state and federal aid, and the endemic government fragmentation and political disorder that continued to afflict San Francisco.

Nor was the mayor helped by his own personality: he appeared humorless and vindictive, he was given to backroom deals, a common occurrence for a legislator in Sacramento, but not acceptable in San Francisco's politics; and he became unable to maintain the level of communication with the constituency that had gotten him elected.

Art Agnos, in his finest moment as mayor of San Francisco, speaks to an owner of a collapsed building in the Marina District after the 1989 earthquake. *Courtesy San Francisco Chronicle. Photo by Darcy Padilla.*

Once again, it was San Francisco's land use and development policy that became the lightning rod for political disaffection and the tumult of Agnos' mayoral administration.

Art Agnos, upon becoming mayor, seemed to have turned his back upon the slow-growth philosophy that permeated his constituency and had begun to be the conventional wisdom in San Francisco.

It was probably the economic stringencies under which he had to operate which probably turned Agnos into a Feinstein clone on the issue of real estate development. His political situation was further aggravated by his frequent trips to Sacramento and Washington, D.C., to seek funds from the federal and state governments to aid his city: for he began to be accused of having been an outsider and of being frequently absent from San Francisco.

There were two, very visible controversies which separated Agnos from his constituency. The first of these had to do with the building of a new ballpark for the San Francisco Giants. Robert Lurie, scion of a wealthy San Francisco real estate owner, had pur-

chased the San Francisco Giants to prevent the team from moving to another city. In an attempt to staunch his losses from his ownership of the franchise, Lurie demanded a new stadium from the city. In November, 1987, Proposition W, intended as an expression of public support for a new stadium to be built at Seventh Street and Townsend Street, was defeated. Lurie then sought a stadium site in Santa Clara. Agnos, as with any mayor, did not want to be tarred as the mayor who lost a major sports franchise; and he swung into action in a last-ditch effort to save the Giants for San Francisco. It did not stand well with his followers that, when he was campaigning, Agnos expressed opposition to a stadium being built at Seventh and Townsend and was generally hostile to public funds being used to aid private enterprise.

Agnos and his advisors now convinced Lurie to choose San Francisco over Santa Clara by coming forward with a proposal to build a stadium in China Basin.

In 1989, San Francisco's offer was formulated in Proposition P (simultaneously, a proposition was put

Reverend Cecil Williams, pastor of Glide Memorial Church, and champion of the poor and homeless, leads a crusade to better the lives of his flock. *Courtesy San Francisco Public Library.*

Mayor Frank Jordan, standing on the Grand Staircase of City Hall's Rotunda, contemplates the awesome task of being chief executive officer of probably the most fractious city in the United States. *Courtesy San Francisco Chronicle. Photo by Scott Sommerdorf.*

to the voters — Proposition V — that would modernize Candlestick Park). Agnos became an aggressive and vehement champion of Proposition P, even releasing the team from its lease on Candlestick Park. Strong opposition to Proposition P developed — opposition which Agnos labeled anti-growth and anti-business. Concerns about traffic and parking problems he dismissed by declaring "If you want a bucolic existence, move to Bolinas."

Less than a month before the election, the Loma Prieta earthquake hit. The city was paralyzed, and, when it began to recover, much of its sentiment felt that its resources should not be expended on a new baseball stadium. Then, just a few days before the election, a new group called the "No on P/Yes on V" committee emerged, sending out a mailer to all households, playing up the destruction of the earthquake with the theme "Now is not the time." It turned out that the money behind the campaign came from a Sacramento developer, Greg Luckenbill, who had built a stadium there to which he was hoping to entice a baseball team.

(So furious was Agnos by this mailer that he had the district attorney attempt to press criminal charges against the five leaders of the mailer — the so-called "Ballpark Five." A judge subsequently dismissed all charges.)

In a surprisingly high turnout election, Proposition P was defeated 49.5 percent to 50.5 percent. The defeat also marked the beginning of significant alienation of Art Agnos from his progressive constituency.

The next step in this process of alienation was involved with the Mission Bay project. This project was essentially a huge real estate development to build what had been touted as "a city within a city" on 315 acres that belonged to the Southern Pacific Railroad (eventually spun off into a company called Catellus Development Corporation).

Originally, when the project was first set out in 1980, it called for the construction of three forty-story towers and several twenty-to-thirty-story build-ings, creating 11.7 million square feet of office space to hold more than forty-six thousand workers and housing for twelve thousand.

The process of approving the Mission Bay project dragged on, and, as it did so, the 1980 plan was radically altered. Finally, in 1986, Proposition M passed, after which, the Mission Bay project would need to apply piece by piece for the annual "beauty contest" for space approval or it would have to present the entire package to the voters for an exemption to Proposition M. The developers chose the latter alternative.

Thus, in 1990, Proposition I came onto the ballot; but the "No on I" forces — a combination of large-scale developers such as Walter Shorenstein, who did not want competition from Mission Bay for his properties, and slow-growth activists such as Calvin Welch — defeated it 51 percent to 49 percent.

The matter was back to the drawing boards. A Mission Bay plan has, as of this writing, yet to be implemented.

While Agnos' role in the Mission Bay plan was minimal (although he was accused of negotiating in private on this matter), his role in the development of the waterfront was much more aggressive.

San Francisco's waterfront, as indicated above, had ceased to be a port. (Even the port of Richmond, California, had bypassed it in terms of tonnage processed.) Since the Port was required to be self-supporting, and, most importantly, the Port's properties (i.e., the waterfront) were exempt from Proposition M, Agnos saw in the waterfront a pullet to be plucked for revenues.

In 1989 he appointed Michael P. Huerta as the new port director. Agnos felt Huerta would be his "point man" in the development of the port.

During Feinstein's last year in office, an outraged citizenry was able to stop the building of a hotel on Pier 45. The building of Underwater World at the entrance of Pier 39 was, however, approved in 1990.

Then, Piers 24-26 and 30-32 were put up for development; and disgruntled slow-growth advocates put forward Proposition H on the ballot. Labeled the Waterfront Land Use Plan Initiative, it called for a ban on hotels as an unacceptable nonmaritime use of waterfront property, required the city to prepare a waterfront land-use plan, and prohibited it from taking any action on development proposals until the plan was completed and made public. On November 6, 1990, San Francisco voters approved Proposition H by 51 percent to 49 percent.

Slow-growth advocates had been able to save the waterfront from the rampant development proposed by Art Agnos and had been able to deflect his aggressive efforts to defeat Proposition H; but these former followers of the mayor's were now seeing him as a problem, not as the solution to San Francisco's urban problems. So embittered did these individuals and groups become that many of them now sought any way of getting him out of the mayor's office. Their chance came in 1991.

Art Agnos faced two fellow liberal/progressives in the primary election: Angela Alioto and Richard Hongisto. To his right were two moderates, Supervisor Tom Hsieh and former chief of police Frank Jordan. His campaign never got off the ground. His erstwhile supporters attacked him mercilessly or voted for him without enthusiasm. Meanwhile, the campaign of Frank Jordan, a pro-business moderate who had little sympathy for growth controls, social reform or left-wing progressivism, caught fire. His campaign swings against San Francisco's dirty streets, aggressive panhandlers, and the so-called homeless who lived in parks and other public spaces captured the imaginations — and vented the antagonisms that many residents felt — of San Franciscans.

Hsieh and Alioto were eliminated; and in the final contest, with Jordan emulating Agnos' precinct drive four years before, Jordan defeated Agnos 51.7 percent to 48.3 percent. From winning by a land-slide in 1987, Agnos was narrowly defeated in 1991.

The four year mayoral administration of Frank Jordan was a sad one for the mayor. Faced with a hostile board of supervisors, not much of his agenda was passed into legislation. There were minimal development controversies, as the progressive agenda had been largely ensured by the passage of Proposition M and kindred ballot measures. But, it was Jordan's inability (and, probably, the inability of any mayor to do so) to make good on his campaign promises to end panhandling, to clean up the streets, and to do something about the "homeless" problem that caused a backlash against him. He began to look more and more like an ineffective mayor.

In addition to the appearance of ineffectiveness, Jordan also gave the appearance of being bumbling and inept. It was said that his new wife — an aggressive and successful businesswoman — interfered in his decision-making and in his relations with staff and political advisors. His lack of political experience and his temperamental indecisiveness caused him numerous problems and resulted in many cases of troubled relations (and even enmity) between him and political advisors.

By the end of his four-year term, Jordan's support had eroded. Former backers were now switching support to a contender for the office of mayor whom they saw as a "winner". Even an Hispanic lesbian whom he had appointed to a vacancy on the board of supervisors endorsed his principal rival in the re-election campaign of 1995.

This rival turned out to be one of the most powerful politicians in the United States — Willie Brown. Brown had been elected to the state assembly in the 1960s — during an era of a shift from conservative Democrats to a younger, more liberal set of politicians. He became the speaker of the assembly — one of the most powerful political positions in the country — but during the late-1990s, with term limits ending his tenure as an assemblyman and a Republican majority in that body ending his reign as speaker, Brown was casting about for other political challenges. He decided to run for mayor of San Francisco.

The always elegant Willie Brown, with an unidentified companion, attends a GQ fashion show given by his close friend, clothier Wilkes Bashford. *Courtesy San Francisco Chronicle. Photo by Brant Ward.*

A ubiquitous "Richmond special" looms like an ugly thorn amongst a group of roses. The charm of a row of Edwardian cottages is spoiled by a non-descript building in their midst in the Richmond District. *Photo by Deanna L. Kastler.*

The election once more eliminated all candidates except for Brown and the incumbent; and, in the run-off, in December, 1995, Brown won with a substantial majority.

Less than two years (at this time of writing) have elapsed since Brown, San Francisco's first African-American mayor, was elected; and, thus, an assessment of his administration is premature. However, already his willingness to use his power as mayor has become a principal feature of his mayoral style. Confident of a compliant board of supervisors, a reasonably sympathetic media, and a broad spectrum of support, Brown has fired or demanded the resignations of top city bureaucrats and brooks no opposition from city employees or politicians.

Yet another aspect of his style is a sense of panache. His personal style of elegance has been carried into his administrative style. He loves civic parties, he insisted on a stylish program for entertaining the nation's mayors, gathered in San Francisco in 1997, and he advocated the use of a refurbished City Hall for lavish entertainments.

And also emerging in 1997 is Willie Brown's pro-growth stance and sympathy for development projects. Whether this inclination will garner him the enmity of San Francisco's slow-growth, progressive forces, as it did Mayors Dianne Feinstein and Art Agnos, cannot yet be determined. As yet, Mayor Willie Brown enjoys halcyon days as San Francisco's chief executive.

It could be that San Francisco's ability to enact slow-growth legislation is "running out of steam." Since the late-1970s, when election after election brought forth an ultra-liberal board of supervisors, the land-use issue was at the heart of the progressives' political agenda. The San Francisco business community became more and more reconciled to the ballot victories of the slow-growth forces. The catalogue of the board's votes on such foreign policy matters as making San Francisco a nuclear-free city or a sanctuary for protesters against the Persian Gulf conflict or its concern with providing equal rights for transgenders seemed harmless enough; it might provoke jibes from "the religious right" or jokes from comedians, but it had virtually no practical impact.

The use of land, on the other hand, was central; it enjoined an old controversy as to the rights of private property owners relative to the community as a whole. Nor was this controversy confined to the downtown area. It was a burning issue in the city's western sections, as well. The so-called "Richmond special," where an older, single home would be torn down and replaced with two or more units, has been fought by neighborhood and preservationist groups who have protested the change of character in a neighborhood and the ungainly, ugly appearance of the replacement construction.

This controversy, in turn, has pitted preservationists and neighborhood activists against the city's Asian community, which has largely favored the replacement construction.

It is too early to tell if the changing kaleidoscope of San Francisco's slow-growth coalition will hold.

The Fourth Annual AIDS Candlelight March in 1987. The march began at Castro and Market streets and ended at the Civic Center. *Courtesy San Francisco Chronicle. Photo by Deanne Fitzmaurice.*

The lull in the pressures from pro-growth forces from the mid-1980s through most of the 1990s may be ending; and, if that is the case, the coalition assembled during the 1970s and early-1980s will once again have to redeploy their forces.

Gay by the Bay

One of the most astonishing of San Francisco's post-World War II transformations has been its emergence as the "Gay Capital of the World."

For two decades after the end of World War II, homosexual culture in San Francisco was virtually invisible. Under severe social and economic stigma, a smirking, derisory attitude on the part of non-homosexuals, as well as the fact that sexual acts between those of the same gender were felonies under both state and local criminal codes, very few homosexuals desired to declare themselves such.

It was rare for two homosexuals to live together and rare for one to state that his or her sexual preference was for one of the same sex. One could be socially ostracized. Jobs could be lost. One could be the subject of derision.

Mounted police patrols in the western portion of Golden Gate Park waited to swoop down on homosexuals engaged in sexual activities. Those bars known to be hang-outs for homosexuals, such as Montgomery Street's Black Cat Cafe (also a bohemian spot) were regularly raided. Watch-holes in restrooms and dressing rooms in retail stores were used to spy upon possible sexual criminality. Politicians would occasionally demand a "crack-down" on "perverts" and "deviates" in the city.

Dr. Karl M. Bowman (pictured) and Bernice Engle of the Langley Porter Clinic in San Francisco published *The Problem of Homosexuality* one of several reports published in the 1950s and 1960s which used wartime research to determine the cause and treatment of homosexuality. *Courtesy San Francisco Public Library.*

Participants in the Gay Freedom Day Parade march down Market Street. *Photo by Max Kirkeberg.*

San Francisco had had, at least since the Gold Rush, a small homosexual subculture. This subculture grew during the twentieth century, especially during and after World War II, always, of course, as a silent, fearful group of men and women.

The gay lifestyle in San Francisco received an impetus during the literary renaissance of the mid-1950s with the coming to the city of homosexual beatnik poets such as Allen Ginsberg.

Also, during the 1950s and early 1960s, San Francisco became the headquarters for several prominent homophilic organizations, seeking to end the criminalization of homosexual sexual activity and the bigotry against gays.

The Mattachine Society, founded in Los Angeles in 1950, relocated its national offices to San Francisco in 1957. In 1955, four San Francisco lesbian couples founded the Daughters of Bilitis.

Extravagant costumes
are a feature of the Gay
Freedom Day Parade.
Photo by Max Kirkeberg.

The rainbow has
become an iconic symbol
of the gay liberation
movement — seen here
in one of its multiple
representations at the
Gay Freedom Day Parade.
Photo by Max Kirkeberg.

But continued harassment of gay bars by the police — almost one hundred individuals were arrested in a raid at the Tay-Bush Inn in 1961 — and a scandal in which police and state Alcoholic Beverage Commission officers were caught taking bribes from gay bar owners for not raiding their establishments — led to the founding of the Tavern Guild in 1962. It was the first gay business association in the United States; and ventured to protect both bar owners and patrons from police harassment.

By the mid-1960s San Francisco's homosexual community had begun to take on a different look than it had in previous years. The anti-authoritarian stance of young men and women and the focus of a large segment of the population on individual liberties began to create an atmosphere of greater tolerance for homosexuals.

The Gay Freedom
Day Parade inspired
whimsical costumes.
*Courtesy
San Francisco Chronicle.
Photo by Mike Macon.*

A gay group — "The Sisters of Perpetual Indulgence" protest at the University of San Francisco in 1980. *Courtesy San Francisco Chronicle. Photo by Steve Ringman.*

faux nuns — "the Sisters of Perpetual Indulgence" — humorously dressed as nuns, ride on motorcycles in the Gay Freedom Day Parade. *Photo by Max Kirkeberg.*

This situation in society at large changed the world of homosexuality, and particularly changed it in San Francisco. More gays began to gravitate to San Francisco. And more men and women openly declared themselves to be homosexual. Instead of anonymous and furtive connections, gay men and women now had a broad network of social venues in which to meet and date. Many began to pair off into committed relationships and live together, as was becoming more and more common in the heterosexual community, beginning in the 1960s.

By the late-1960s organized protests against the criminalization of homosexual sexuality, the treatment of homosexuality as a medical disorder by the psychiatric community, and the hostility and bigotry against homosexuals began to become frequent in large urban areas. Gay liberation became a buzz-word.

The police raid in 1969 at the Stonewall Inn on New York City's Christopher Street, and the subse-quent organization of homosexuals in that city, is looked on as the beginning of the gay liberation movement; but gay ferment against institutionalized anti-homosexuality had been a factor in San Francisco for several years before that event across the continent.

In 1969, gays, under the leadership of an organization called the Committee for Homosexual Freedom, began to picket the States Steamship Lines, which had fired an employee for publicly declaring his homosexuality.

In 1970, after a number of years of quietly attempting to influence sympathetic members of the mental health profession to push for the depathologization of homosexuality, the more assertive, less apologetic style of the new gay liberation movement was demonstrated by its "gay invasion" of the American Psychiatric Association's annual meeting, held that year in San Francisco.

The AIDS quilt dramatically captures the extent of the plague which has taken so many lives. The complete AIDS quilt was on display in the Mall in Washington, D. C. in October 1996. *Courtesy NAMES Project Foundation. Photo by Paul Margolies.*

The AIDS quilt, which originated in San Francisco, shown here on display in the city's convention facility, Moscone Center. *Photo by Max Kirkeberg.*

Meanwhile, a more liberal judiciary and the impact of organized homosexual political action began to achieve positive results for homosexuals. The decriminalization of homosexual sexuality occurred in the early-1970s, a cause fought for and led by one of San Francisco's state legislators, Assemblyman Willie Brown.

The election of George Moscone as mayor in 1975 meant that a large number of homosexuals were appointed to city commissions and to politically appointed jobs in San Francisco.

Two years later the first openly gay individual was elected to public office (a "first" for the nation, as well as for San Francisco). Harvey Milk was able to take a seat on the board of supervisors after the passage of a charter amendment that mandated district elections.

Gay enclaves began to develop in San Francisco. During the early 1970s, these could be identified as Polk Street, the Haight-Ashbury, the Tenderloin, and South of Market. But, as the 1970s progressed, the largest and most visible gay enclave developed in what is known as the Castro area, actually a part of the Inner Mission district which had been an Irish working class area of the city.

It would be the Castro area that provided the most enduring of the iconographic visions of San Francisco's gay community: protests emanating from the area, bars filled with men, men walking down Castro Street, *holding hands and kissing*, in rather *outre* attire, and the famous Halloween celebrations.

The 1970s and onward represented steady strides in non-discrimination for San Francisco's gay community. Local legislation passed ordinance after ordinance ending discrimination against gays in housing, jobs, and any other area where such discrimination might exist.

Even marginalized groups within the gay community managed to elicit protective legislation: transgenders, for example.

Such legislation reached its apex in the late-1990s, when San Francisco passed legislation mandating equal coverage in health benefits for "domestic partners." In other words, city workers and employees of companies that wished to do business with the city were to provide their employees equal benefits for both heterosexual married couples, as well as for straight or gay couples who had filed an affidavit proclaiming themselves "domestic partners."

Then, in the 1990s the activism, political organization, and sheer numbers of gays in San Francisco (some estimates in 1997 claim somewhere between 150,000 and 250,000 gays in San Francisco — the latter figure would compute at about one-third of the city's population) brought about the near-dominance of gays in San Francisco's politics in the 1990s. Members of the board of supervisors, a member of the state assembly, and an increasing number of municipal and superior court judges have been among the gays elected in recent years.

Aside from the political arena, the city's gay community has been an increasingly powerful factor in its economic life and in its cultural life.

On June 27, 1970, twenty to thirty gays marched down Polk Street from Aquatic Park to City Hall to commemorate the previous year's Stonewall Uprising. The next day larger numbers attended a "Gay-In" at Golden Gate Park. No organized public commemoration of Stonewall took place in 1971; but gays from San Francisco took part in a rally in Sacramento to support Willie Brown's consenting-adults bill. In 1972, however, 50,000 people took part in a Stonewall commemoration called "Christopher Street West."

But, in 1973, two commemorative events took place: the "Gay Freedom Day Parade" and a rival "Festival of Gay Liberation." Their coalescence by the mid-1970s gave rise to a national phenomenon: the "Gay Freedom Parade," whose 1997 attendance was estimated at 700,000 and whose texture is one of humor, whimsy, and diversity. Beginning with the spectacular Dykes on Bikes, the "Gay Freedom Day Parade" has become one of the largest annual outdoor events in the United States.

But, it was not entirely a smooth path to end discrimination of gays; for homosexuals were outraged by the killing of Harvey Milk in November, 1978, and they erupted in violence and vandalism the following year, when Dan White, Moscone's and Milk's killer, received a verdict of voluntary manslaughter at the conclusion of his trial. Homophobia and violence against gays still continued, paradoxically, in this most liberal of cities.

What afflicted San Francisco's gays more than such incidents, however, was the plague that began in the early-1980s — the AIDS epidemic that has raged furiously in gay communities for the past two decades.

At first, the medical community was puzzled. Then it was labeled "gay cancer." (AIDS can be — and is — contracted by heterosexuals, largely those who are drug-users and share needles.) Soon, medical research began to bear down on this virulent

The Giants were one of the first sports organizations to help with the AIDS epidemic. Shown here is the franchise's "Until There's a Cure" kick-off. Courtesy San Francisco Giants. Photo by Andy Kuno.

disease and to analyze its dimensions. One San Francisco author was even able to trace its origins to Africa and to the ur transmitter — a promiscuous, gay airline steward.

The eruption of the disease, the long period of suffering, and the eventual deaths devastated San Francisco's gay community. The cumulative necrology was a stunning "gutting" of the city's creative enterprises.

San Francisco began to concentrate on ways to impede the plague: and one of its recommendations was to close the city's gay bathhouses, where anonymous and indiscriminate sex was seen as a fertile field for spreading AIDS. And, although the result of this recommendation was to divide the city's gay community in a rancorous way, the San Francisco Department of Public Health used its emergency powers to order the bathhouses closed on April 9, 1984.

The death-toll from the AIDS virus led to an even more aggressive stance on the part of gays, who felt that there were insufficient public funds being expended on medical research to find a cure for the disease and in the care of those stricken with the disease. Thus, ACT UP and the Queer Nation were to provide an "in-your-face" aggressive approach to demonstrating for their agenda, staging sit-ins on local bridges and paralyzing traffic, and other dramatic, disruptive moves to publicize this agenda.

As the twentieth century comes to an end, it has been only a third of a century since homosexuals have garnered their civil rights and have become a potent force in urban centers. In no U.S. city has the homosexual culture become as powerful and as ubiquitous as in San Francisco. And yet, as the battles for these civil rights and for acceptance have been largely won, the future remains vague. Will homosexuals as a whole continue to be part of the city's liberal, progressive establishment, or will a gay conservative constituency emerge? Will the gay community continue to support a distinctive homosexual system, or will a movement toward assimilation in a broader, heterosexual environment take place? Such questions cannot be answered presently; only the continuation of San Francisco's urban organic changes will reveal the answers.

The Earth Shook: Some of the City Burned

Those of reasonable age in 1963 will frequently be heard to declare, "I can still remember what I was doing when I heard that President Kennedy had been assassinated."

Those who were of reasonable age in 1989 who were living in or working in or visiting San Francisco will spend the rest of their lives declaring, "I can still remember where I was and what I was doing on the day of the earthquake."

As the earthquake and fire of 1906 has taken on mythic dimensions, so it is that the second worst earthquake to hit the San Francisco Bay Area — that at 5:04 p.m. on Tuesday, October 17, 1989 — has begun to become part of the cherished memories of those who experienced the convulsion of the earth on that sunny late-afternoon in the Fall of 1989, while the attention of the nation was riveted on the first-ever Bay Area

San Francisco's Ferry Building which had survived the 1906 earthquake, has a crooked flag and a stopped clock after the 1989 earthquake. *Courtesy San Francisco Chronicle. Photo by Fred Larson.*

At 5:04 p.m. on Tuesday, October 17, 1989, the second worst earthquake in San Francisco's history shook the Bay Area.

Courtesy Robert A. Eplett/OES.

A car dangles precariously between the fallen portions of the upper deck of the San Francisco-Oakland Bay Bridge after the Loma Prieta earthquake.
Courtesy
San Francisco Chronicle.
Photo by
Scott Sommerdorf.

World Series — the third game of the baseball pageant between the San Francisco Giants and the Oakland Athletics.

Earthquakes have been endemic in California throughout its history. In the very first year of European colonization — 1769 — one was recorded by the leader of the expedition, Don Gaspar de Portola. In 1812 one virtually destroyed Mission San Juan de Capistrano. Severe damage to San Francisco was done by one in 1868; and, the "Big One," in 1906, with its resultant three days of fire, destroyed the entire business district and rendered more than half of the city's residents homeless.

Numerous earthquakes have also devastated different parts of Southern California during the twentieth century.

Even with such a history of earthquakes, there is not a Californian who is not shocked and surprised when he or she experiences one.

And so it was, on October 17, 1989, when a 7.1 (on the Richter scale: each point on the scale represents a geometric increase, not an arithmetic increase) earthquake hit the San Francisco Bay Area (and south to the Santa Cruz Mountains, whose communities suffered considerable damage), San Franciscans, whether at Candlestick Park, driving on the streets and freeways, at home preparing dinner, in shops, walking, in skyscraper office buildings, or in elevators leaving work for the day, the impact of the earth's tremor was a stunning surprise.

Radios and televisions stopped working. Telephones did not work. Electric power in San Francisco did not operate. Refrigerators began to warm. Hospitals turned on their generators. Elevators stopped. Electrically-operated transportation ceased to run.

Radios and televisions which were battery-operated began to trumpet the news of the results of the tremor; but, because of disruption in communications and

The earthquake registered 7.1 on the Richter Scale, and some families registered devastating losses as their homes crumbled.
Courtesy
Robert A. Eplett/OES.

Days after the earthquake, San Franciscans resumed their daily activities amid reconstruction efforts. *Courtesy Robert A. Eplett/OES.*

the difficulty of garnering news of an event of such a magnitude, the "news" frequently turned out to be wrong (e.g., one broadcast asserted that the San Francisco-Oakland Bay Bridge had collapsed into the bay with hundreds dead).

San Franciscans gathered in knots around operating radios and televisions, shocked, confused, and desperately trying to comprehend the dimensions of the disaster.

Bridges and freeways had indeed been among the most devastated areas as a result of the earthquake. A weak link in the upper deck proved the undoing of the San Francisco-Oakland Bay Bridge. A fifty-foot section collapsed onto the lower deck, causing, surprisingly, only one fatality. Thus, the main artery between San Francisco and the East Bay was closed.

Not so fortunate were motorists on the section of I-880 in Oakland, known as the Cypress Freeway. A one-and-one-half mile stretch collapsed, the upper deck pancaking down onto the lower deck. For days afterwards, rescue workers burrowed through the tangled mass of steel and concrete rubble, searching for the dead, the injured, and the survivors.

Although some 42 people died in the collapse of the Cypress Freeway, it had been expected that the death toll there would have been much greater.

Throughout the Bay Area, freeways buckled and cracked, although not to the same extent as the Cypress Freeway; and one of the features of the post-earthquake era was that of closed, torn-down, and seismically retrofitted freeways. (The damage done to San Francisco's Embarcadero Freeway, which for more than three decades had provided an ugly gash across a stretch of the city's northern waterfront, allowed authorities to tear it down — a feat which has led to a beautification of the area where the freeway had stood. A ballot measure some years earlier to tear down the freeway had been defeated by San Francisco voters.)

Throughout San Francisco there was damage as a result of the earthquake. Cracks appeared on the

facades of houses and on terrazzo steps; glass windows shattered, and, along Union Square, glass from the windows of the upscale shops rained down on passersby; brick from the facades of houses or forming the exteriors of post-1906 commercial buildings crumbled.

As had happened in 1906, the most serious damage from the earthquake took place in areas where coves, lagoons, or marshland had been filled. In 1906, these areas were those of the old Yerba Buena Cove (then the area of the financial, wholesale, and produce districts) and the old Mission Bay (a chunk of the area South of Market).

In 1989 the old Yerba Buena Cove area had become fairly stable because of greater awareness of the need to render buildings built on filled land safer from earthquake damage. Thus, although a number of old brick buildings built after the 1906 earthquake and fire were severely damaged, the newer skyscrapers escaped with little or no damage. In the South of Market area, many of the post-1906 brick buildings were also severely damaged: the wall of one collapsed onto an adjacent parking lot, where five people were killed.

But it was the Marina District, which was built on land filled for the 1915 Panama-Pacific International Exposition, and, which was, in the 1980s, transitioning from an Italian-American enclave (many Italian-Americans moving there from North Beach after the Marina was developed during the 1920s) to a section of the city desirable to young professionals, that was the most devastated.

Virtually every building in the Marina was in some way damaged: chimneys collapsed, steps crumbled, windows shattered, furniture, artifacts, and bookcases tumbled about, cracks developed, cornices fell. But, a number of houses, flats, and apartment houses simply collapsed, tumbling, one story upon another, falling into the fronting streets, compacting automobiles. Other buildings tipped so precariously that they were ordered torn down immediately.

Work to restore the San Francisco-Oakland Bay Bridge began almost immediately. *Courtesy Robert A. Eplett/OES.*

Because of broken gas mains, fires began in the Marina district; and, as in 1906, because of broken water mains, water to fight the fires was scarce. Water began to be pumped in from the bay. Professional firemen, as well as residents, fought the blazes well into the evening. Water was still being poured on the smoldering ruins the next morning.

Rescuers, both professional and compassionate residents, sought to extricate the trapped, the injured, and the dead (fortunately, only five persons died in the Marina district) from the shattered buildings. Specially-trained dogs and various listening devices were employed for this massive and complex task.

The Marina Green and a local middle school became centers for the numerous victims of the earthquake to assemble for food and shelter. And, then, began the agonizing wait to determine whether one's home — whether individual house, flats, or apartment house — could be re-occupied or even visited to remove valuables.

The day of October 18 saw the Marina District a shattered neighborhood: some buildings burned out, some collapsed, others were teetering precariously, all damaged in some way, sidewalk and street pavements shattered. The eerie scene of destruction was heightened by the huge piles of personal belongings, rescued from homes, piled up on the sidewalks and in front of buildings. Many residents had slept out on the street the evening before in order to protect these belongings. Stunned, shocked, and disheveled, they looked like refugees in a city bombed-out during World War II.

Building inspectors visited buildings to determine which were safe for immediate reoccupancy, which could be entered briefly (fifteen minutes was the time allowed) to retrieve valuables, and which would be demolished immediately. For residents of the latter, their belongings would not be saved: they became part of the rubble of the demolished buildings.

The Marina was cordoned off from sightseers; only legitimate residents could enter the devastated area. Almost immediately, the clean-up began. Those whose homes were temporarily or permanently unavailable to them found new places to live, into which they moved whatever possessions they could salvage. Within days construction and demolition crews were working feverishly in the Marina. Salvageable buildings were being repaired; those that were not were being demolished and the rubble hauled away. Owners of buildings made repairs that would lessen the devastation to them in the event of a future earthquake. The Pacific Gas & Electric Company put forth heroic efforts to insure the resumption of gas and electric service in record time (which led to the never-before-seen proliferation of signs in the area that proclaimed, "Thank you, P.G. & E.").

The Monday following the earthquake downtown San Francisco was back to work. (The Pacific Coast Stock Exchange had opened the day after the earthquake, using candles in the early morning to process trades.) Commuters from the East Bay, 300,000 automobiles which had used the Bay Bridge not being able to utilize that form of transportation, used ferries or drove a long route across the Richmond-San Rafael Bridge to reach their jobs in the city.

Ten days after the earthquake the World Series resumed at Candlestick Park, a number of those singled out as having provided heroic services during the disaster throwing out the first balls.

San Francisco slowly returned to a normal life. The dead were mourned; those dispossessed of their homes and belongings struggled to put together their lives; homes and offices were repaired; businesses strove to contain the disruption to their operations; and those responsible for attracting conventions and visitors to the city put forth great efforts to convince the nation and the world that earthquakes were rare occurrences.

The cataclysm of October 17, 1989, brought forth the best in San Franciscans, whose compassion, help, and mighty efforts tended to alleviate the suffering of those who had been dispossessed from

Fire rages in San Francisco's Marina District after the October 17, 1989, earthquake. *Courtesy San Francisco Chronicle.* *Photo by Vince Maggiora* (Opposite page)

their homes, suffered the loss of their material goods, and had their livelihoods imperiled. Neighbors who had been strangers met and became friends. They laughed at the television network anchors who rushed by airplane and stretch limousines to San Francisco, wearing jungle fatigues, to report on the disaster, and then rushed away to the next world event. They braved the aftermath of the catastrophe with patience and good humor.

The warm, sunny day of October 17 was soon replaced by early rains. They could not dampen the spirits of the city's residents. Instead, they bought by the thousands T-shirts that proclaimed, "I Survived the Great Earthquake of 1989."

Politicians raced to fix blame and to mandate preparation for "the next one." Very few listened: San Franciscans slowly put their lives back together, resumed the customed rhythms of their lives, and told stories about their experiences during the "Great Earthquake of 1989."

Rescue workers used search dogs in attempts to locate those alive or dead in collapsed buildings.
Courtesy San Francisco Chronicle.
Photo by Fred Larson.

Chapter 4

Sports

Sports

S AN FRANCISCO HAS ALWAYS BEEN A SPORTS-ORIENTED CITY. FROM THE DAYS OF BULL-AND-BEAR fights at Mission Dolores, during the Mexican era in California, to the big business aspects of professional football, baseball, and basketball in today's urban San Francisco, sports has been a major concern of the city's residents.

Racetracks dotted San Francisco during the nineteenth and early twentieth centuries. Boxing was the darling of sports enthusiasts, even when it was illegal; many leading boxers came from the San Francisco Bay Area and many significant boxing matches were held locally until well into the 1950s. The interest in baseball as "America's pastime" was mirrored in the fascination with the sport that goes back to the nineteenth century. In 1946 a professional football franchise was founded in San Francisco.

Tennis, swimming, golf, and numerous other sports have champions that come from the Bay Area. As early as the 1860s, the Olympic Club, which still flourishes, was founded to encourage amateur athletics. Golden Gate Park plays host to scores of minor sports: lawn bowling, croquet, archery, model boat racing, among them.

The first half of the twentieth century saw the "Golden Age" of amateur teams in virtually all areas of sports — leagues were formed of teams from fraternal organizations, factories or other places of work, church groups. Organizations such as the South End Rowing Club, founded in the nineteenth century and still thriving at the end of the twentieth, represent very popular sports activities during the last century and the early part of this century.

High school and local college sports were avidly followed in San Francisco well into the second half of the twentieth century. Thousands would pour into Kezar Stadium to watch football games between

Prologue

rivals St. Ignatius High School and Sacred Heart High School or Lincoln and Washington. The Little Big Game was between college rivals St. Mary's College and the University of Santa Clara.

A great deal of press space would be given to such high school and college football and basketball teams (and, to a lesser extent, baseball).

Today's San Franciscan does not live in a world of local high school and college rivalries. Only parents of students participating and the most avid sport enthusiasts among the alumni of a school will go to its games today. Nor does a San Franciscan partici-pate on a scale common during the first half of the

Polo in Golden Gate Park was a popular sport in 1948 when the California All-Stars played against the Texas Rangers. *Courtesy San Francisco Public Library.*

Kezar Stadium was built in 1925 on the outskirts of Golden Gate Park for high school football games. For many years it was the "home" stadium for the San Francisco 49ers. It could seat up to 60,000 fans. *Courtesy San Francisco Public Library.*

Seals Stadium, at 16th
and Bryant streets in
San Francisco's Mission
District, was built in the
mid-1920s and demol-
ished in 1960. Many
San Franciscans felt that
Seals Stadium would
have been a better ball-
park for the Giants than
the cold and windy
Candlestick Park.
*Courtesy San Francisco
Public Library.*

twentieth century in amateur sports leagues: in baseball, basketball, bowling.

San Franciscans are today caught up in the tele-
vised presentations of big business professional
sports — primarily, football, baseball, and basketball —
and in more solitary, non-competitive athletic
endeavors: "working out," bicycling, hiking, running.

Boxing, once so popular, has disappeared as a
sport in the San Francisco Bay Area. After hosting
two successive local ice hockey teams, the only Bay
Area ice hockey team is located in San Jose. Swimming, once one of the most followed sports in San
Francisco, has today virtually no aficionados in the city.

Whether today's search for community will encourage more participation in amateur sports, seen
in leagues based on work or associations, is not yet
evident. But, even in today's complex competitive climate, where an individual has such a multiplicity of
demands on his or her time, sports continue to be

one of the most discussed
and most followed endeavors
in the city.

The San Francisco Seals

Organized, professional baseball in the West Coast has its origins in the nineteenth century, when
various inter-urban leagues were
founded. In 1903, a new league
was formed — a minor league of
West Coast cities that was called
the Pacific Coast League. Among
the teams in this league was the
San Francisco Seals.

Three years after the league was
founded, the earthquake and fire of
1906 forced the Seals to play in the

Joe DiMaggio's fabled
career with the New
York Yankees was pre-
ceded by his years with
the San Francisco Seals.
*Courtesy San Francisco
Public Library.*

Candlestick Park
(now 3Com Park) hosts
the San Francisco Giants.
Courtesy
San Francisco Giants.

The legendary
Willie Mayes at bat.
Courtesy
San Francisco Giants.

rival Oakland Oaks' home — Idora Park in Oakland. When they returned to the city in 1907, they would play at Recreation Park at 14th Street and Valencia. In 1931 they began to play at the newly-built Seals Stadium at Sixteenth and Bryant streets, which would be the Seals' home until the end of the team's existence.

The Seals were a powerful team in the 1930s. In 1933 the team would be joined by a lanky, eighteen-year old son of a local crab fisherman — Joe DiMaggio, who would become one of the icons of United States sports.

DiMaggio first played the shortstop position, but was shortly thereafter placed at right field. He quickly became a sensation. (Although DiMaggio's 1941 record fifty-six game hitting streak with the New York Yankees continues unbroken, he had a sixty-one consecutive game hitting streak with the Seals in 1933.)

One of the legendary figures of the Seals during the 1930s and 1940s was the team's manager (and occasional player) Frank "Lefty" O'Doul, a gregarious native San Franciscan from what used to be called "Butchertown." A brilliant manager, a man who has been called "The Father of Japanese Baseball", and a bon vivant who was frequently seen walking the streets of San Francisco or sitting in one of its restaurants, O'Doul was the principal source of the Seals' revival after he became the team's manager in 1934.

The end of World War II saw a resurgence of interest in baseball, and the sport flourished. In 1946, the Pacific Coast League applied to be recognized as a third major league, but the plan was rejected by owners of the National and American leagues. Despite the fact that attendance at PCL games was quite high, that it produced a large number of players for the major leagues (and managers, as well), and that the

Willie McCovey, one of the Giant's greatest players, gets a hit at Candlestick Park. *Courtesy San Francisco Giants*.

One of two Western cities to obtain a major league baseball franchise in the late-1950s the other was Los Angeles, San Francisco welcomed the former New York team in 1958. San Francisco Giants, penant contenders in 1959, paraded before 250,000 cheering fans along Market Street. *Courtesy San Francisco Public Library.*

WELCOME S.F. *Giants*

Barry Bonds, son of
Giants great Bobby Bonds,
came to the Giants as
the highest-paid baseball
player at that time.
Courtesy
San Francisco Giants.
Photo by
Martha Jane Stanton.

population of the West Coast was soaring after the war, recognition of the PCL as a major league was not forthcoming.

But, if the PCL could not become a major league, by the end of the 1950s the major leagues would be coming to the West Coast. The changes in business economics and in lifestyles that came in the post-World War II era saw the half century of major league stability end, as teams in weak markets or in cities with more than one team began to move to other cities.

After the 1957 seasons both the Brooklyn Dodgers and the New York Giants decided to move to the west coast — the Dodgers to Los Angeles, the Giants to San Francisco. The two teams would use the stadiums of their predecessors until new stadiums could be built.

The Seals franchise moved to Phoenix; the Dodgers bought out the Los Angeles Angels franchise. Other PCL teams moved away: the Oakland Oaks to Vancouver, the Hollywood Stars to Salt Lake City.

After the 1959 season the Giants were able to move into Candlestick Park. Within a few days after the end of the season, Seals Stadium, which, for almost thirty years, had seen baseball played in the sunny Mission District, was torn down.

The San Francisco Giants

By the late-1950s baseball attendance was falling victim to television. New York City, with three franchises, would be the starting point for a revolution in major league baseball: a reshuffling of the geographical venues for teams and an end to the decades of stability. Baseball teams would now fan out to homes throughout the United States (and two in Canadian cities).

The first team to leave New York was the Brooklyn Dodgers, who departed for Los Angeles. Almost immediately thereafter, Horace Stoneham, whose family owned the Giants for 57 years, announced that the New York Giants would relocate to San Francisco. They would play the 1958 season in Seals Stadium, which, for over a quarter century, had been the home of the San Francisco Seals.

Stoneham and San Francisco's Mayor George Christopher had reached an agreement by which the Giants would move to San Francisco and the city would build the team a new baseball park.

The selling of a new ballpark to San Francisco's voters was an easy affair in the late-1950s compared to what would happen in subsequent years. In those confident and ebullient years after World War II there was virtually no opposition to paying for a major league baseball team with a municipally-funded ballpark.

Despite a slight flurry of disgruntlement over the fact that one of the best politically-connected contractors in San Francisco — Charles Harney — sold the site for the ballpark to the city — land that he had purchased for a fraction of what he sold it to the city for — and then proceeded to obtain the contract to build the stadium — this conflict was soon papered over and the city proceeded to welcome the Giants.

For their first consecutive fourteen seasons in San Francisco, the Giants were an exciting team and a winning team. The 1958 team included baseball great Willie Mays, Orlando Cepeda, and Felipe Alou. The next year they would be joined by Willie McCovey.

The 1960 season was the first at Candlestick Park, where a new pitcher by the name of Juan Marichal began his brilliant career.

In 1962 the Giants overcame a four-game deficit with only seven games left in the season to tie the downstate (and traditional New York) rivals the Los Angeles Dodgers.

In the best-of-three playoffs the Giants came from a 4-2 deficit in the ninth inning to win the series by beating the Dodgers 6-4 in the third game. The Giants had won their first National League pennant since they had moved to San Francisco.

The 1962 World Series was against the formidable New York Yankees. Tied three games each, the two teams faced each other in the ninth inning at Candlestick Park with the Yankees leading 1-0. With two outs

and Matty Alou on third base, the batter was Willie McCovey. The slugger slammed a screeching liner that landed in the glove of Yankee second baseman Bobby Richardson. The Giants had fought valiantly.

The year 1971 saw the Giants win the National League Western Division Championship, but only to lose the pennant to the Pittsburgh Pirates.

In the following year the Giants had their first losing season in San Francisco (69-86) and the next few years were also dismal ones. Attendance was down, and Horace Stoneham decided to sell the team to Canada's Labatt's Breweries. The Giants seemed headed for Toronto.

Thanks to a restraining order obtained by Mayor George Moscone, enough time was obtained for the Labatt deal to fall through and the Giants to be purchased in the mid-1970s by San Francisco real estate mogul Bob Lurie and Arizona cattleman Bud Herseth.

The Giants were a mediocre team until the mid-1980s, when Lurie brought in Al Rosen as general manager and Roger Craig as manager. The improvements in the team ushered in by these two men brought about a 1987 National League Western Division flag and a 1989 National League Championship.

In what was dubbed the "Bay Bridge Series," San Francisco was matched against the American League champion, the Oakland A's.

Oakland swept the first two games, and, then, at 5:04 p.m. on October 17 — only minutes away from the start of Game 3 at Candlestick Park — a major earthquake jolted the Bay Area. A national television audience watched as power went out in the region and far-reaching damage was reported. Commissioner Fay Vincent announced that the World Series would be postponed until further notice.

After ten days the Series resumed, but the Giants' fortunes hadn't changed. The A's won the next two games to sweep the Giants.

Three years later Lurie's decision to sell the Giants duplicated the 1976 crisis, when it appeared that the Giants would move to Toronto. This time it was

The Loma Prieta
Earthquake on
October 17, 1989,
stops the third game
of the World Series
at Candlestick Park.
*Courtesy
San Francisco Giants.*

Florida. But, once again, there was a last-minute local purchase: a syndicate of wealthy San Francisco investors, led by Safeway CEO Peter A. Magowan, purchased the Giants.

While the Giants (through the 1996 season) remained a mediocre team, they won an off-field victory on March 16, 1996, when the San Francisco voters passed a measure that allowed the Giants to lease land in China Basin for a privately-financed 42,000 seat stadium, which should be complete by April 2000.

During the thirty years since the removal of the franchise to San Francisco, the Giants have been an inconsistent team; but, even in this inconsistency, the team has managed to employ an impressive array of players, who, even in a losing season, could give baseball fans a display of superb ball-playing.

The San Francisco 49ers

As a professional sport, football is a comparative "Johnny-come-lately." Why two San Francisco contractors, Tony Morabito and his brother decided to start a professional football team in the city in 1946 is a puzzle. Placed in the now-defunct All American Football Conference, the San Francisco 49ers, as they named the team, was a "poor cousin" to the collegiate rivalries that was football in the Bay Area in the post-World War II period: the Big Game was Cal Berkeley vs. Stanford; the Little Big Game, which was played in the 59,000 seat Kezar Stadium at the edge of Golden Gate Park, was St. Mary's and Santa Clara. (This latter game, played on a Sunday, took precedent over the professional football team, which had to play on a Saturday.) University of San Francisco completed the quintet of popular Bay Area college football teams.

So popular was college football that the Morabitos sought to hire football players who had been stars on their respective Bay Area college teams as a way of attracting fans to watch the 49ers play.

The 49ers' first coach (1946-1954) was an innovative offensive coach, Buck Shaw, far ahead of his time; and his imaginative offense, along with the playing of the "cream" of the players from the local colleges, made for exciting football.

Then there was the lessening of interest in local college football, as, one by one, the three, small Catholic colleges — St. Mary's, Santa Clara, and U.S.F. — dropped their football programs.

Shaw's coaching and the running of the T-formation by that ball-handling magician quarterback Frankie Albert created increased interest in 49ers by Bay Area football fans, and large numbers would listen to radio broadcasts of the games in those pre-television days or make the trek to the football stadium in cars, trucks, campers, or public transportation, parking and often picnicking in Golden Gate Park. Into Kezar Stadium would pour almost 60,000 people, taking with them coolers filled with beer and liquor, and, if unhappy, would throw bottles onto the field, or, if the 49ers lost, pour beer onto the players as they ran into a tunnel under the stands to get to the dressing room.

Long before the days of Montana, Rice, and Ronnie Lott, the 49ers had their stars: Frankie Albert, Y.A. Tittle, John Brodie, Bruno Banducci, Hugh McElhenny, Joe Perry, R.C. Owens, Jimmy Johnson, Abe Woodson.

While the 1940s and 1950s had talented and exciting players and excellent coaching, the title eluded them. The 1960s and 1970s saw a collapse in the San Francisco 49ers' ability to win games, although there would be the occasional resurgence.

Then, in 1979, the former coach of Stanford University, a soft-spoken man by the name of Bill Walsh, became the coach of the San Francisco 49ers. This followed by about two years the purchase of the franchise from the Morabito family by the DeBartolo family of Youngstown, Ohio, represented by Edward J. DeBartolo, Jr.

The intense desire of this wealthy Midwestern family (the late DeBartolo, Sr., had made a fortune in real estate development) to produce a championship team became a relentless bid to purchase the best talent possible.

Walsh's first two seasons were dreadful: 2-14 and 6-10. But, his concentration on building up the team's defensive capacities, on which the 49ers had never previously focused, began to produce results. At the same time, Walsh crafted an offensive strategy that was primarily implemented by the team's new starting quarterback, a former Notre Dame University player by the name of Joe Montana and a receiver by the name of Dwight Clark. Then in 1981, after his two losing seasons, Walsh had a team that was a major contender for the championship. In one of the most dramatic events in football history, a pass from Joe Montana to Dwight Clark, leaping high in the endzone, for a touchdown against Dallas, which won them the NFC title that year — an event that will always be known as "The Catch" — set them up to win the Super Bowl that year. San Francisco exploded in joyous triumph that evening with the first-ever championship win for the franchise.

The 49ers would win two more Super Bowls under Bill Walsh, who retired in 1988 (he would return to the 49ers in 1996 as administrative assistant to the coaching staff). His successor, George Seifert, developed the best winning percentage in NFL history; and would lead the 49ers to an additional two more Super Bowl championships — a total of five for the franchise.

Even though both Walsh and Seifert were principal contenders in each season during which they coached, the 49ers owner was not satisfied with five Super Bowl titles in the eighteen years of their collective coaching. Walsh was forced out in 1988; Seifert in 1997.

The year 1997 brought the 49ers a new coach — Steve Mariucci, who had been the head coach at the University of California at Berkeley — and a contro-

versial election which sought $100 million from the taxpayers of San Francisco as the city's contribution to the building of a new football stadium next to the present 3 Com Park (formerly known as Candlestick Park).

Unexpected opposition to the city's spending $100 million (plus interest for the bonds) for a private enterprise developed; and the issue became a hotly contested one. The 49ers and their allies spent unprecedented amounts of money campaigning for the stadium. The lascivious birthday party of Jack Davis, the political consultant running the campaign, became part of the controversy surrounding the campaign.

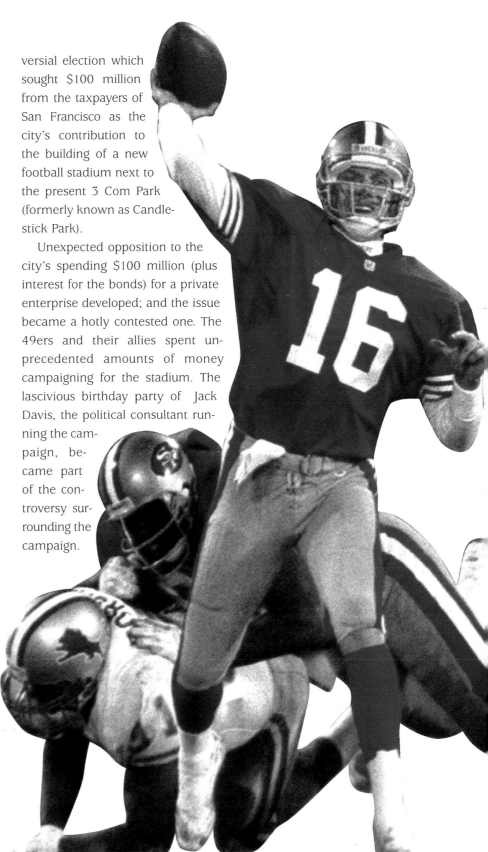

Joe Montana, wearing his number 16 jersey, tosses the ball for a touchdown. *Courtesy San Francisco Chronicle.*

Although for a while it appeared that the bond issue would lose, a vigorous 49er campaign for the stadium, the energetic and effective campaigning of Mayor Willie Brown, and the residual positive sentiment for the San Francisco 49ers combined to eke out a narrow victory for the new stadium.

San Francisco Warriors

As with all sports franchises in the late 1950s and during the 1960s mobility had become common. So it was that in 1962 Eddie Gottlieb, who had owned and nurtured the Philadelphia Warriors since the team's inception, sold the franchise to a partnership of Diner's Club and Franklin Mieuli. The team was moved to San Francisco.

A year later, when the Warriors appeared to be having financial problems, Diner's Club walked away from the investment, leaving Mieuli as the sole owner.

During their first season, the San Francisco Warriors played at several different sites, including the Cow Palace, Civic Auditorium, and the University of San Francisco's Memorial Gym, as well as playing "home" games in San Jose, Oakland, and Bakersfield. (In fact, so confusing did these changes become, that some players would sometime show up at the wrong place.)

This new team in San Francisco contained some prestigious names, among them Wilt Chamberlain and Tom Meschery (a local who had attended Lowell High School). In 1963 Nate Thurmond was acquired; and in 1965 Rick Barry, drafted out of the University of Miami, came to play.

It wasn't until the 1966-1967 season that the team began to obtain local recognition and garner local fans and attendance.

Despite some years of memorable playing and an excellent record, the Warriors never won an NBA championship; and then there were years of desolation, when they ranked at the bottom of their division. The team never reached the "dynasty" status of such teams as the Los Angeles Lakers, the Philadelphia 76ers, the New York Knicks, the Boston Celtics, or the Chicago Bulls.

In 1971 the San Francisco Warriors came to an end. Owner Franklin Mieuli moved the team across the bay to Oakland, where, playing in the stable venue of the Oakland Coliseum Arena, they became the Golden State Warriors. The Warriors thus became a regional team, with no name of a city attached to the franchise; and, although the team continued to have fans in San Francisco, it could no longer be considered a San Francisco basketball team.

Hockey

Hockey has not been able to thrive in San Francisco. The lack of snow and ice in the mild climate of San Francisco cannot be used as an excuse: for Los Angeles' ice hockey team does well.

The city had a minor league team — the San Francisco Shamrocks — during the late 1940s. Playing at Winterland, that team eventually disappeared.

Then, in the 1960s, the San Francisco Seals made their appearance. That franchise moved to Oakland and then to Salt Lake City.

Finally, in the 1990s, the Spiders, a minor league team, came to San Francisco.

But, when major league hockey finally came to the Bay Area, it was not to San Francisco, but to San Jose, where that community had given great support to the Sharks. This team also has disappeared from the area.

cultural Life

Cultural Life in San Francisco

B Y "CULTURAL LIFE," ONE'S CONSCIOUSNESS SETTLES ON SUCH FACETS OF URBAN LIFE AS OPERA, museums, ballet, and other such forms of "high culture." In reality, culture is truly anything which stimulates the intellectual and emotional responses of a community; and, although urban culture does incorporate such musical institutions as its opera company, symphony, and ballet, it also encompasses street fairs, ethnic festivals, and other aspects of entertainment.

San Francisco's multi-cultural diversity, its affluence, and its penchant for a broad array of entertainment activities have combined to invest this city with a broad kaleidoscope of cultural activities. Whether it is San Francisco's opera, symphony, ballet, or plethora of chamber music offerings, or, whether it is the Hispanic community's Cinco de Mayo annual parade or its Day of the Dead (November 2) commemoration, or whether it is the St. Patrick's Day Parade, the Columbus Day Parade, or the Gay Freedom Day Parade, or, whether it is the mania for physical activities or the flocking of young singles to the dance clubs in the South of Market area, the rich texture of San Francisco's culture has few rivals among cities in the United States.

The 1990s have provided a boon for many of the city's cultural institutions. Following a merger between the city's two fine arts museums — the M.H. de Young Memorial Museum and the California Palace of the Legion of Honor Museum — and the seismic retrofitting and rehabilitation of the latter, the reorganized Fine Arts Museums of San Francisco, under the directorship of Harry Parker, underwent a significant positive change in the development of its collections and in their presentation.

The need for a new building to replace the de Young's home in Golden Gate Park is now under consideration; and private individuals have come forth with offers of substantial financial support for the proposed building.

Prologue

The Dragon is one of the iconic features of the annual Chinese New Year's Day Parade. "Gung Hoy Fat Choy."
Courtesy San Francisco Public Library.

The Asian Art Museum was also the beneficiary of San Franciscans' largesse during the 1990s. One of the largest collections of Asian art in the world, voters gave the museum a new quarters: the former Main Library of the San Francisco Public Library at Civic Center. This structure is, as of this writing, beginning to be rehabilitated for its new purpose.

San Francisco's third major museum — The San Francisco Museum of Modern Art — was able to move out of its cramped quarters in the Veterans' Building in Civic Center and into an exquisitely designed new museum in the revitalized South of Market area. The museum was now able to display much more of its collection and to enjoy the amenities of a space designed to be a museum. And its location in what is rapidly becoming a major cultural center in San Francisco has sent its attendance soaring.

Another venerable San Francisco cultural institution — the San Francisco Public Library's Main Library — found a new home in the 1990s. Once again, San Francisco's voters were generous. First, they voted a ballot measure that assured the Library

Three colorful
dragons in the
Chinese New Year's
Day Parade.
Photo by Peter Ng.

a certain percentage of the city's revenues, effectively doubling its budget. Second, it voted $100 million in bonds to build a new library. A considerable amount of money was also raised privately to furnish the new Main Library.

But such benefactions did not result in harmony at the San Francisco Public Library. Activists began to criticize the head librarian for "looting" the branches for the Main Library, of throwing out books and advanc-

ing technological information retrieval at the expense of the printed word, and of fiscal irresponsibility.

The librarian resigned, and now efforts are being made to rectify many of the problems brought forward by the move of the Main Library to its new home.

But, it is not just museums and libraries, opera and symphony orchestras, that make up the fabric of San Francisco's cultural experiences. On many weekends one can attend a street fair, participate in an

A birthday cake sits on Civic Center Plaza in front of San Francisco's City Hall in 1950 to commemorate the centennial of California's admission to statehood.

Courtesy San Francisco Public Library.

In 1954 Douglass Cross and his lover George Cory wrote their famous song about San Francisco. In 1962 Tony Bennett's recording made the song famous.
Courtesy San Francisco Public Library.

ethnic festival, such as Japantown's Cherry Blossom Festival, go to that San Francisco phenomenon, "Beach Blanket Babylon" — a humorous musical revenue that has packed in audiences for more than twenty years.

A comprehensive study of San Francisco's culture since World War II could only be contained in a separate book: this chapter seeks a more modest goal, that of presenting a brief summary of a few of the more prominent cultural institutions.

Critical Mass is a gathering of thousands of bicyclists on the last Friday of the month to promote the need for more bike lanes and safer bicycle traffic.
Photo by Chris Carlsson.

Mural art, popular in San Francisco during the 1930s, has seen a revival during the past quarter century, especially in the Mission District. *Photo by Deanna L. Kastler.*

The annual Cinco de Mayo parade flashes with the bright colors of the costumes and exciting music of the Hispanic community. *Courtesy San Francisco Chronicle. Photo by Steve Ringman.*

Cinco de Mayo has become a major celebration for Hispanics in San Francisco. *Photos by Peter Ng.*

In the mid-1990s San Francisco's Museum of Modern Art, long inhabiting a crowded space in the Veterans Building, moved into a Mario Bota-designed structure in the South of Market area, sparking a huge increase in its attendance. *Photo by Deanna L. Kastler.*

$\int$an Francisco edifices are featured in the extravagant hat that marks the finale of "Beach Blanket Babylon" — the musical review that has been continuously entertaining San Franciscans and tourists alike for a quarter century.

Courtesy "Beach Blanket Babylon."

The annual Cherry Blossom Festival is one of the many ethnic celebrations in San Francisco.

Courtesy San Francisco Public Library.

Traditional Japanese drummers take part in the parade.

Photo by Arai Kazuyoshi.

The carnival celebration — preceding the time of Lent — has long been a major festival in such cities as Rio de Janiero in Brazil and New Orleans in the United States. It is becoming year-by-year an increasing extravaganza in San Francisco. *Photos by Eric Brooks.*

(Opposite page)
Photos by Paul Cartier

Lew Christensen and Jaqueline Martin in "Swan Lake".
Courtesy San Francisco Performing Arts Library and Museum.

ʃan Francisco Ballet in "Swan Lake".
Photo by Marty Sohl.
(Previous page)

The San Francisco Ballet

Although the ballet has a long tradition in Europe, it is a relative cultural newcomer in the United States. Founded in 1933, the San Francisco Opera Ballet (the name was changed to the present San Francisco Ballet in 1942) is the oldest professional ballet company in the United States.

The pioneer ballet company's early history is closely associated with three brothers — Willam, Harold and Lew Christensen, who from its earliest days provided directorial and artistic leadership.

In 1951 Lew Christensen became the Ballet Company's director. Five years later it made its East Coast debut, and the following year — 1957 — toured eleven Asian nations, marking the first performances by a U.S. ballet company in the Far East. In 1958 the company toured Latin America and in 1959 the Near East, the same year in which it toured California for the first time.

Thus, the national and international outreach that began in the 1950s reflected the innovations that had begun shortly after it was founded: the U.S.' first full-length production of "Coppelia" (1939), the country's first production of "Swan Lake" (1940), and the nation's first production of "Nutcracker" (1944).

In 1972, after performing in various theaters throughout San Francisco, the San Francisco Ballet settled in the War Memorial Opera House for its annual residency. (As opposed to its infrequent presentations in its early years, the San Francisco Ballet today offers in excess of one hundred performances annually.)

In 1973, Michael Smuin became the company's associate artistic director (he became co-artistic director with Lew Christensen in 1976); and the new partnership with Lew Christensen was commemorated with a full-length production of "Cinderella."

But problems loomed for the company. By 1974, the San Francisco Ballet faced bankruptcy. But the company and the community responded with an extraordinary grassroots effort called "S.O.B." (Save

(which attracts students from all over the world and trains approximately three hundred students annually) and houses the company's administration.

In 1985, Helgi Tomasson arrived as artistic director (Lew Christensen had died the year before), leading to an ever-expanding reputation for the company's excellence.

In 1995, the San Francisco Ballet Company hosted twelve ballet companies in a festival to commemorate the fiftieth anniversary of the signing of the United Nations Charter. The San Francisco Ballet Company's performance of the world premiere of Mark Morris' "Pacific" prompted critic Clive Barnes to write: "... San Francisco Ballet itself came out covered with roses. If Tomasson had planned his San Francisco adventure to demonstrate that his own company was now indeed a world-class troupe comfortably capable of holding its own amid any international hierarchy, he could hardly have planned it better."

Thus, six-and-a-half decades after its imaginative, but modest, beginning the San Francisco Ballet Company is now recognized as one of the three largest and most important ballet companies in the United States.

Linda Meyer and David Anderson in "Beauty and the Beast". Choreography by Lew Christensen. *Courtesy San Francisco Performing Arts Library and Museum.*

Sergei Prokofiev's "Romeo and Juliet," choreographed by Michael Smuin. *Courtesy San Francisco Performing Arts Library and Museum.*

Our Ballet), which focused national attention on the company, raised a great amount of funds for it, and successfully brought it back from the brink of bankruptcy and endowed with new vitality and resources.

Emmys were garnered on two occasions: for "Romeo and Juliet," the first full-length ballet ever to be shown on PBS' television series, Dance-In-America and for the "Tempest," when it was broadcast across the nation, Live from the Opera House.

The company was able to build a $13.8-million facility, the first ever in the U.S., created expressly to house a major dance institution, which offers rehearsal accommodations for the company and its school

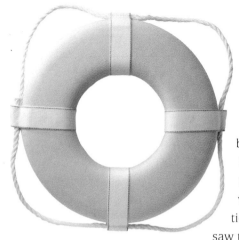

The Choral Tradition Thrives

One could probably trace the tradition of choral music in San Francisco back to the eighteenth century, when local native American converts sang at the liturgies at Mission Dolores. But, it was the Gold Rush, with its immigration from throughout the world, that saw the beginnings of formal choral music. This was largely the work of the large number of German immigrants in San Francisco, who started music societies in the bustling city, implementing their musical traditions in their new home.

In the late-twentieth century San Francisco remains a national center for the choral tradition in music and some of the locally-spawned and headquartered groups have achieved international reputations.

Founded in 1978 by tenor Louis Botto, who died in 1997, Chanticleer, the only full-time classical vocal ensemble in the United States, had its inaugural concert in 1978 at Old Mission Dolores — a candle-light concert to a packed crowd in the small, adobe church.

During the next twenty years, Chanticleer has become internationally recognized for its interpretation of vocal literature, from Renaissance to jazz, from gospel to venturesome new music; and the

Captain Corcoran and Dick Deadeye — characters in Gilbert and Sullivan's "H.M.S. Pinafore" — performed by the Lamplighters. *Courtesy San Francisco Performing Arts Library and Museum.*

company is in great demand throughout the country and throughout the world.

Chanticleer performs more than one hundred concerts each year and has maintained, since 1994, an increasingly active recording schedule.

In the very same year as the popular duo in London produced one of their all-time favorites, "H.M.S. Pinafore," a pirated production was performed at San Francisco's Bush Street Theatre. The year was 1878, and, while W.S. Gilbert and Arthur Sullivan may not have received any royalties from this — or subsequent — performances of their repertoire, it is almost certain that their shades are pleased by the continuing popularity of their witty and humorous musical plays.

In 1952, two San Franciscans who had been active in performing in the Gilbert and Sullivan repertoire, decided to form a company that would perform this repertoire more consistently than had been done in

the past. Orva Hoskinson and Ann Pool MacNab little realized the herculean efforts that awaited them.

Opening in a theater in San Carlos, the company, named The Lamplighters, began with that perennial favorite, "H.M.S. Pinafore," which was repeated shortly thereafter at the Crossroads Theatre at 1470 Washington Street. "Mikado" was to be the next offering.

Unlike the instant success that came to Chanticleer, however, the Lamplighters would spend almost two decades seeking stability and viability. For a number of years the company incessantly sought for a theater where they could consistently produce their offerings. Finances were uneven; and the company subsisted on loans from its members.

The homelessness of the Lamplighters and its chronic shortage of money, both factors which led to an irregular schedule of performances, led to the leasing of a boarded-up neighborhood theater on Divisadero Street near Hayes — the Harding Theater.

Part of the cast of the Lamplighter's production of "H.M.S. Pinafore." *Courtesy San Francisco Performing Arts Library and Museum.*

185

This would be the home of the Lamplighters for the next seven years.

At this time a volunteer by the name of Spencer Bemen would join the supporters of the company. One day he would be named executive director, would see the Lamplighters through dark days, and finally would oversee its ascent into financial viability, critical success, and venue stability.

In 1965 the Lamplighters merged with an organization named Opera West. It was a difficult transition for the purveyor of Gilbert and Sullivan, with its casual organizational culture, to adhere to new business and administration techniques and to broaden its repertoire. But, somehow, the transition worked, painfully, but well.

New problems began to surface. The area of the Western Addition where the Lamplighters performed at the Harding Theater was becoming increasingly blighted and dangerous. There was no parking available. Audiences stayed away in droves. Finances once again become precarious.

In 1968 the Lamplighters decided to lease a five hundred-seat theater at Presentation High School — a Catholic girls school on Turk Street, near Masonic.

The superb professionalism and expert staging of productions that had marked the Lamplighters from the company's beginnings in the early 1950s now could be utilized in a well-located, permanent home.

Soon, productions became sold out; and the Lamplighters became known as the premier interpreter of Gilbert and Sullivan repertoire in the United States. Patrons stepped forward to support the company; grants helped it to expand. Stability and viability came at last to the Lamplighters in the 1970s.

In the 1990s a venue change transpired. Presentation High School closed, and the University of San Francisco bought the property. Soon, U.S.F. had its

Davies Symphony Hall, framed by a modern sculpture.
Courtesy San Francisco Symphony.

own plans for the use of the theater. The theater at Riordan High School — a Catholic boys high school — was secured: the Lamplighters continue to delight its audiences with its superbly crafted productions at this new location.

One of the emerging choral group "stars" in San Francisco is the Instituto Pro Musica de California (Coro Hispano de San Francisco). Founded in 1975 by Juan Pedro Gaffney, the son of a long-time state legislator from San Francisco, the Instituto presents throughout the state programs of Hispanic music from Spain's empire in the Americas.

The San Francisco Opera

Opera, probably the most complex and difficult to perform of all the performing arts, was first presented in San Francisco in 1851, only three years after the discovery of gold. During subsequent years, irregular, but frequent, performances of operas provided part of the entertainment fabric in the city. (One of the enduring stories from San Francisco's past is the touring Metropolitan Opera's performance of Carmen, starring Enrico Caruso, on April 17, 1906, the eve of the earthquake and fire of that year).

It was not until 1923, however, that San Francisco had its own opera company, when, in that year, the San Francisco Opera was incorporated. The conductor and director — and presiding musical impresario — was Gaetano Merola.

Performing in the Civic Auditorium (and, occasionally, at Dreamland Auditorium), the San Francisco Opera began

James Morris as Wotan, holding the ring, from Wagner's epic cycle of operas. Courtesy San Francisco Performing Arts Library and Museum.

its innovative and distinguished institutional history with Merola's importation directly from Europe of leading singers.

Finally, a group of San Francisco's business and professional elite decided that the company needed its own opera house; and, in 1932, during the depths of the Depression, the opera season opened in the new Beaux Arts War Memorial Opera House, opposite City Hall, which had been designed by John Bakewell and Arthur Brown, Jr. Merola conducted "Tosca" starring Claudia Muzio on opening night.

As the depressed 1930s continued, to be followed by the war years of the first half of the 1940s, support for the San Francisco Opera continued, and the company was able to add new operas to its repertoire and to continue to import leading singers from Europe.

With Merola's death in 1953, Kurt Herbert Adler began a long and distinguished reign as the leader of the San Francisco Opera. (He would retire twenty-eight later, in 1981.) Adler became known for his fierce pursuit of perfection in the presentation of operas, for his openness to presenting more modern operas, and for his keen eye in obtaining young, emerging European and U.S. singers, many of whom would sing their signature roles for the first time during San Francisco Opera performances (e.g., Leontyne Price's first-ever "Aida" of her career in 1957).

In 1965, the season included a galaxy of the principal leading ladies of the day: Renata Tebaldi, Pilar Lorengar, Mary Costa, Marie Collier, Evelyn Lear, Leontyne Price, and Dorothy Kirsten.

The 1970s saw the debuts of "the three tenors" — Jose Carreras, Placido Domingo, and Luciano Pavarotti. New, exciting sopranos — among them, Renata Scotto, Katia Ricciarelli, and Montserrat Caballe — were paired off with these young tenors.

Following Adler's retirement in 1981, Terence McEwen became the company's general director in 1982. Ten years later he would be succeeded by Donald Runnicles.

In 1989, the season was interrupted by the Loma-Prieta earthquake. For the first time since 1932 the company was forced out of the Opera House, and it gave performances of "Aida" and "Idomeneo" at the Masonic Auditorium.

The damage caused by the earthquake and the "wear-and-tear" of more than a half century led to the municipal decision to seismically retrofit and to rehabilitate the War Memorial Opera House. The 1996-1997 season was spent in its old venue from the 1920s and early 1930s — the Civic Auditorium — with some performances at the Orpheum and Golden Gate theaters. In the Fall of 1997, the new season returned to the redecorated, retrofitted, and rehabilitated Opera House.

For three quarters of a century the San Francisco Opera has been the premier performing arts institution in the San Francisco Bay Area. Despite opera's reputation as an exotic art form, opera-lovers are a widely diverse group of individuals: rich and poor, straight and gay, old and young, and from every nationality and race. Poor but avid opera-lovers, unable to afford the high prices of tickets, will stand in line for hours to obtain standing room tickets.

Thus, the success of the San Francisco Opera mirrors the broad popularity of opera in Southern Europe.

And, yet, San Francisco's opera is frequently depicted as the hostage of the city's wealthy and its social elite. This, of course, is understandable: glittering socialites sitting in the boxes of the Opera House, the stunning array of business, professional, and social power on the opera's board of trustees and other opera association boards of directors, the splendid pageant of the season's opening night.

It has been this attraction of the city's opera for its social and business elite that, of course, has provided the substantial financial resources that has allowed the San Francisco Opera to continue to be one of the foremost companies in the country.

On opening night of the season, which is extensively reported in the local press, and on the subsequent evenings during the season attended by socialites, there are numerous attendees who do not know Puccini from pastrami. Some even make an aggressive display of their ignorance of and their dislike for this performing art. Nevertheless, year after year, they put on couture dresses and white tie and tails and go to the opera, have themselves photographed for the society pages, and attend gala suppers following the performance.

For such an affirmation of their social status, these men and women give substantial sums towards the support of the opera.

Nor has such a society/wealth connection been confined to "old" San Francisco families. New wealth in the city and the creators of fortunes in the Silicon Valley have joined the parade of opera supporters: a fact that has ensured the continuing excellence of the San Francisco Opera.

The San Francisco War Memorial Opera House was renovated and seismically upgraded in 1997. *Photo by Deanna L. Kastler.*

The San Francisco Symphony

Symphonic music in San Francisco dates back to the Gold Rush, when, in 1854, there was an orchestra organized for public concerts. The San Francisco Symphony Society was organized in 1897; and that group was reorganized in the aftermath of the 1906 earthquake and fire into the organization that now maintains and governs San Francisco's symphony orchestra, the San Francisco Symphony Association.

Under the conductorship of Alfred Hertz (1915-1930) the orchestra became a distinguished and stable institution in San Francisco's cultural firmament.

But the Great Depression brought financial problems; and in 1934 San Franciscans voted to spend a portion of the city's tax revenues to support the Symphony, thus ensuring its continuance.

Another distinguished conductor joined the Symphony in 1936, and would conduct the orchestra until his death in 1954. Pierre Monteux, who had been a notable conductor in France since the early part of the century, was to give the San Francisco Symphony a much-needed revitalization from the depths of the Depression, through the years of World War II, and for several years after the end of the war.

Monteux would be succeeded by Enrique Jorda (1954-1963), Josef Krips (1963-1970), Seiji Ozawa (1970-1977), Edo De Waart (1977-1985), Herbert Blomstedt (1985-1995), and then by Michael Tilson Thomas.

From 1932 to 1980 the San Francisco Symphony performed in the War Memorial Opera House. But, seeking to play an expanded schedule and to be in an environment that was more specifically suitable to a symphony orchestra, the San Francisco Symphony sought its own orchestra hall.

Seiji Ozawa, in his trademark white turtleneck and love beads, conducts the San Francisco Symphony Orchestra. *Courtesy San Francisco Performing Arts Library and Museum.*

Michael Tilson Thomas, the guest conductor of the
San Francisco Symphony in the 1970s. Years later he
will be named the orchestra's music director.
Courtesy San Francisco Performing Arts Library and Museum.

Seiji Ozawa conducts the San Francisco Symphony in the War Memorial
Opera House, the orchestra's home before it got its own building.
Courtesy San Francisco Performing Arts Library and Museum.

This campaign became focused in the 1970s, and, with the generous help of the widow of a successful businessman, construction began on a site in Civic Center. Louise M. Davies' contributions of about $.3 million were sufficient to name the new building after her — the Louise M. Davies Symphony Hall.

The Symphony played in its new home in the 1980-1981 season.

For many years of the post-World War II period, criticism of the San Francisco Symphony as a mediocre orchestra was quite vocal. As the years went by, concerted efforts to improve the quality of the orchestra began to obtain results; and, as the twentieth century comes to an end, the San Francisco Symphony is recognized as one of the most distinguished in the country.

San Francisco Newspapers and the Herb Caen Phenomenon

When World War II ended San Francisco had four daily newspapers and a plethora of neighborhood, weekly, and ethnic newspapers. The four dailies — the *Chronicle*, the *Examiner*, the *Call-Bulletin*, and the *News* — each had a distinctive personality, carrying both local and nationally syndicated columnists and all giving extensive coverage to local events.

In keeping with San Francisco's almost total dominance of the Bay Area at the war's end, there was little or no coverage of happenings in the suburbs. The news or events there would be covered by supplemental newspapers: the small suburban papers.

The principal rivalry was between the *Chronicle*, San Francisco's oldest daily, and its largest newspaper, the *Examiner*, which was the flagship of the Hearst empire. The somewhat staid *Chronicle* — in

the mid-1940s — had been overtaken in circulation by the more imaginative and innovative *Examiner* some years before.

But, as the expression goes, "turnabout is fair play." In the 1960s, under the editorship of the flamboyant Scott Newhall, the *Chronicle* began to change its staid format into that of a sensation-seeking tabloid. In 1965 Newhall conceived of an ersatz story which was featured day after day in the *Chronicle*.

The story was titled "The Last Man on Earth," and its presumption was that a nuclear holocaust had occurred and a family had been spared. This family — the Boyds — was, according to the *Chronicle*, to go into the Sierra Nevada wilderness with virtually no tools, equipment, and provisions and live "off the land." The Boyds' story, said the newspaper, would be told by them as they experienced this harrowing feat.

The *Chronicle*'s clever advertising fueled great interest in the story, and, while the story was still being run, the *Chronicle*'s circulation surpassed that of the *Examiner*.

The problem — at least in terms of quality journalism — was that the Boyds' encampments were provided with every sort of convenience. Boyd himself wrote and sent to the *Chronicle* most of his accounts from his home in Marin. In short, the series was a fraud.

The circulation wars between the *Chronicle* and the *Examiner* were costly; and the two newspapers began to discuss ways in which their competitiveness would not erode profits.

What was contrived in 1965 was the Joint Operating Agreement. The *Chronicle* would be the sole morning newspaper; the *Examiner* would fill the afternoon slot. The two newspapers would produce the expanded Sunday newspaper. All revenues and expenses would be shared, and net profits would be divided evenly between the two newspapers. In other words, a cartel was set up that would eliminate competition.

However, during the third of a century since the Joint Operating Agreement was signed, circumstances have changed for the two newspapers. The trend in circulation is downward. Suburban newspapers have gotten an increased readership in those fast-growing areas. Television and radio have become the preferred vehicles for news transmission for many.

In addition to this uncertainty which is affecting the newspaper business throughout the country, the holding company for the *Chronicle* and other media ventures itself faces an uncertain future. With the death several years ago of the last child of M.H. deYoung, the co-founder of the *Chronicle*, the trust that held the company's shares came to an end and the stock was distributed to the heirs. Shortly thereafter, the company's largest shareholder engineered a vote among the family shareholders that excludes all family members from managerial participation in the company and put into place a professional management. It remains to be seen what the impact of this decision, of inevitable estate taxes, and of an expanding family will have on the *Chronicle* media empire. Will the *Chronicle* and the other media properties be sold? Will the local ownership that has owned the newspaper for well over a century be no more?

For almost sixty years a native of Sacramento, California, by the name of Herbert Eugene Caen, wrote a column for the San Francisco *Chronicle* (and for several years of those nearly six decades for the San Francisco *Examiner*) that became an institution,

Herb Caen, San Francisco's legendary chronicler,
with his "Loyal Royal."
Courtesy San Francisco Public Library.
(Left Page)

as Herb Caen, who died in February, 1997, himself became a San Francisco legend.

Chosen in 1938 by the then editor of the *Chronicle* to write an entertainment column, Caen soon transformed the column into a San Francisco gossip column. His mentor and hero was Walter Winchell: his style, he proclaimed, was three-dot journalism. With the exception of his stint in the U.S. Army during World War II and his last days, as he slowly died of cancer, Caen cranked out a daily column on San Francisco.

Breezy, chatty, and witty, the column had certain constants. Foremost, there were the personalities: unknowns and major figures, politicians, socialites, the forgotten former stars, the shoe-shine man he may have taken a liking to, the restaurateur whose company he enjoyed. Thousands and thousands of these passed through his columns.

Second, there were the games. Cute firm names, only in Marin stories, odd nomenclature — those were but a few of the ever-fresh items that peppered Caen's columns.

Third, especially as he got older, there was the nostalgia for an earlier San Francisco. No one could catch in prose the flavor of the ever-changing city, from the time he first came to live and work in it during the late 1930s, the last days of the Great Depression, when he was still a teenager, to his death at 80 in 1997. His ability to create the mood of a vanished city — its departed citizens, its departed restaurants and businesses, the sense of fog and foghorns, sun, wind, hills, and cable cars — arose from his palpable love for San Francisco and its denizens.

As the years went on, Caen would receive each day a cascade of mail, telephone calls, *viva voce* tips, faxes, and e-mail. He responded to every letter; and he would frequently answer the telephone.

Caen's power as a columnist was awesome. A restaurant he praised would be filled for months. A movie or a play would witness the demand for seats increase if he essayed a positive opinion. A business could flourish on his recommendation.

The man himself fancied himself a *bon vivant*, especially in his earlier years. Fancy cars, showgirls on his arms, a heavy smoker and a heavy drinker, Caen's energy, both day and into the very late night, was prodigious. As an older man, he sought a more stable and even staid life.

He was a complex man, who would annually bore his readers with endless columns detailing his recent vacation. Redolent with accounts of his staying at the most expensive hotels and eating at the most expensive restaurants, the columns became a dreary litany of conspicuous consumption abroad or in large U.S. cities.

He could turn on an erstwhile friend, as in the case of where a successful real estate broker would annually book Maxim's in Paris for a New Year's Eve party for wealthy San Francisco socialites and would include Caen and his lady friend of the moment. When the broker fell out with the city's social set and was himself dying, Caen would print some cruel comments about him in his column.

His columns would deride Republicans and their policies and praise Democrats and their social agenda, declaim against a society that had homeless and poverty, while he himself preferred the company of rich socialites, eating in fancy restaurants, extravagant travel, and plush living quarters.

The popularity of his column was a factor in every socio-economic group, to newcomers and old-timers in the city, in Pacific Heights and in the Sunset, among

Cyril Magnin, known
as Mr. San Francisco,
performs for friends.
*Courtesy San Francisco
Public Library.*

the young and the old. Part of the reason for this was that it was amusing and a quick read. Neither radio nor television could duplicate these qualities, and thus it was able to overcome this competition. Whether one was a retail clerk or a secretary or an investment banker or a business magnate, San Franciscans loved to read Caen's quick takes on personalities, places, and events in the city. It reduced a large city to the dimensions of a small village. No matter who you were, you felt you knew Louis Lurie or Cyril Magnin or Melvin Belli. Even if you never went out to eat, you knew of lunching at El Prado or dining at Ernie's. And, as a recent resident or one who had lived all of his or her life in San Francisco, you relished the memory for the possibility of being tied into the earlier city: the San Francisco of the 1930s, 1940s, and 1950s. The consummate wordsmith, Herb Caen made you feel part of Bagdad by the Bay, the mythopoeic city of San Francisco.

J.J. Brookings Gallery Illustrates Bay Area Art Scene

SAN FRANCISCO HAS NEVER BEEN A MAJOR ART-BUYING METROPOLIS. UNLIKE NEW YORK OR LOS ANGELES, which seem to breed numerous art collectors, San Francisco has been much more conservative. Although there are several galleries in San Francisco that have international reputations and have done exceptionally well, most of their revenues come from out of this city.

"That's because San Francisco is a stage," says J.J. Brookings Gallery's art consultant Julian Wyler. "Its citizens prefer the performing arts — the opera and the symphony — as places to put their money."

Wyler goes on to say that art-collecting in the San Francisco Bay Area is dominated by corporations. "It's akin to the Medici in fifteenth century Florence," says Wyler, "where private interests bought or commissioned art for public viewing. Corporations now buy art not just to hang on their walls, but to present to the public."

The J.J. Brookings Gallery was founded in San Jose in 1970, and moved to San Francisco in the mid-1990s. Located in what is now a thriving museum area, in the South of Market near the Museum of Modern Art, the Brookings Gallery displays art in all media: photography, sculpture, oil painting, and works on paper. Its large premises enable the gallery to hang several shows at once.

Brookings Gallery owner Tim Duran has changed the traditional rhythms of art gallery presentations. "We've become much more involved," he says. "The Moscone Center is just a block away from us, and many companies use our gallery to introduce new products during conventions. And we bring our artists to where people are, not just keeping them contained in the gallery."

Both Duran and Wyler discern changing international perspectives in the art world: more foreign artists are displaying their work in U.S. galleries and more foreigners are buying in U.S. galleries. "The global nature of the art collecting world has become much more pronounced in recent years," states Wyler.

Both Duran and Wyler see the J.J. Brookings Gallery as a harbinger, as a catalyst in the merchandising of art. "We tend to be more visionary," says Duran, "more interested in trying new means of introducing art and artists to new buyers."

A photograph entitled "Dark Tower, Golden Gate" by Nicholas Pavloff is one of many beautiful pieces in J.J. Brookings Gallery. *Courtesy J.J. Brookings Gallery.*

PROFILES OF BUSINESSES

THAT HAVE CONTRIBUTED

TO THE BEAUTY,

STRUCTURE, ECONOMIC

BASE AND PLEASURE

FOR THE RESIDENTS

AND VISITORS OF THE

"CITY BY THE BAY"

In San Francisco

Partners

Contents

Partners

SAN FRANCISCO'S

REAL ESTATE AND

CONSTRUCTION

COMPANIES SHAPE

TOMORROW'S

SKYLINE, PROVIDING

WORKING AND

LIVING SPACE

FOR ITS PEOPLE.

Building a Greater

Commercial & Interior Construction, Inc.

Andrea G. Minutoli (right) standing next to his partner, Pietro Grassi. Surrounding them is the clay model used to form the decorative portico of the Market Street entry to San Francisco's famous Fox Theater, the largest and grandest of the west.

For the past century, the Minutoli family has influenced the shape and style of San Francisco.

Between the years of 1895 and 1907, the Minutoli family emigrated to America from Riposto, Sicily and Montecatini, Italy, and shared in the dream of building up their new land. In 1907, amidst San Francisco's post-fire construction boom, Giuseppe Minutoli, a graduate naval architect, joined a partnership to form the Cooperative Marble & Mosaic Company. In 1909, he and his brother-in-law Pietro Grassi left this firm to form a terrazzo company which, by 1914, had become the West's largest firm specializing in prefabricated terrazzo.

By 1916, Minutoli had developed a new product that he called Travertite Marble to compete with both natural stone and terra cotta. Natural stone was very expensive and difficult to work with, and terra cotta was a poor substitute that was not able to be made into large panels. Minutoli's new product, originally made from Italian Travertine marble aggregate and Portland or Lumnite cement, was San Francisco's first architectural precast concrete.

The Ferry Building, constructed in 1895, sustained significant damage during the Loma Prieta earthquake of October 1989. CICO is in the process of seismically retrofitting the building.

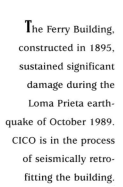

The Travertite Marble Works in San Francisco quickly grew to become the largest and most prestigious ornamental plaster and cast stone manufacturer in the West, employing over 300 men. Travertite stone looked like natural stone but was more durable, more adaptable, more easily polished or tooled, and less expensive. Minutoli gradually created a wide variety of synthetic stones to ornament San Francisco's buildings, and also became the region's leader in ornamental plaster, terrazzo, and mosaic.

San Francisco blossomed into a center of excellence for ornamental precast stone and the Minutoli family pioneered the industry. Their work has accented the most famous buildings in San Francisco's history, including Grace Cathedral, the Fox Theater, the Pacific National Bank Building, and the Financial Center Building. In 1930, they completed the largest terrazzo project ever undertaken, laying 37 miles of floor and base for the General Hospital of Los Angeles. Awarded the Gold Medal at the 1929 Bologna International Exposition on Treasure Island in 1939, their ornamental stone was recognized for its contribution to the arts.

Andrea Minutoli retired in 1950, and leadership passed to his son Joseph. As architectural Modernism spread, ornamental cast stone never returned to its pre-war greatness, though Joseph and his sons — Andrea, Steve, and Rebello — directed hundreds of projects over the ensuing years. In 1967, they completed San Francisco's largest ornamental cast

stone project of modern times — the renovation of the Palace of Fine Arts, which was originally constructed for the Panama Pacific International Exposition of 1914.

The Palace of Fine Arts renovation was the culmination of Joseph's work, and marked the rise of the third generation. During the project, his eldest son, Andrea ("Ray"), became the company's chief draftsman and estimator. Ray developed several new methods of fabricating and installing precast and pre-stressed concrete, and in 1968 was elected president of the Northern California Precast Concrete Association. That same year he assumed presidency of the Travertite Stone Products Company. By 1974, however, the demand for ornamental stonework had dwindled to obscurity. The Minutoli family closed their plant and turned their attention to new ventures.

Ray earned his general engineering and building contractor's licenses and, in 1975, opened his own firm specializing in construction management. His early projects included hi-tech light industrial and manufacturing facilities, historic renovations, and numerous collegiate recreation facilities. Ever interested in innovative construction techniques, Ray devised new ways of controlling the competitive tolerances for NCAA certified collegiate swimming pools.

In 1980, Ray established the Construction Division of Lucasfilm, Ltd. under his license and, as Director of Construction for Skywalker Development Company, managed the design and construction of all Lucasfilm projects from 1980 to 1983, including the renowned Skywalker Ranch and Industrial Light and Magic in San Rafael, California. He subsequently joined with a local developer and managed the construction of over 500,000 square feet of new office space in Marin, Sonoma and Alameda counties.

Ray founded Commerical & Interiors Construction, Inc. (CICO) in 1984. CICO has since done hundreds of projects around the Bay Area, ranging from small tenant improvement projects to multi-million dollar seismic, institutional, and commercial renovations. CICO, known for its lean and accessible staff, meticulous attention to detail, and on-time completion, uses the most modern and efficient information systems to control each project from beginning to end.

Recent seismic renovation projects have included the San Francisco International Airport, the California Academy of Sciences in Golden Gate Park, and the historic Chinatown Branch Library. Its current contracts include seismic renovation of the Ferry Building, a new library for the Piedmont High School, and the remodeling of the Claremont Country Club in Oakland. Also specializing in design build projects, CICO is currently constructing the Pier 35 cruise line passenger terminal. Its previous design/build projects include BART's Central Control Room at its systemwide headquarters at Lake Merritt Station, the BART Embarcadero Station Escalators in San Francisco.

Ray's children share in the family's historical values and traditions while playing important roles in the firm. Katsuko Minutoli is the company's bookkeeper, Marianne Minutoli Hill has served as both Chief Financial Officer and as President; Kristina Minutoli Thuma created the company's safety program and office management procedures; Alicia is Vice President and Corporate Secretary; and Joseph has been a field operations coordinator and has recently graduated from law school at the University of San Francisco.

The fourth generation is now carrying on the Minutoli legacy, guided by a timeless dedication to value and quality.

In 1967, from their workshop in the building that is now the Exploratorium, Joseph Minutoli supervised what was probably the most complex casting and molding operation in modern times— The Palace of Fine Arts. (Upper right corner)

The Cooperative Marbles & Mosaic Company, loading stone for the entry foyer to the bank of Italy in 1907.

Edward Scott Electric Co., Inc.

The history and growth of "Scott Electric" is paralleled by the growth and development of San Francisco and the Bay Area. Much has changed over the years, yet each can trace their roots back to very early times.

Edward J. Lynch was born in San Francisco in 1882, and by his early 20s was a recognizable man about town. At age 17, he began his electrical career as an apprentice for Slattery Electric, which became Lynch and Slattery Electric in 1912. Early newspaper accounts publicized many new developments in the fledgling electrical industry and Ed was always in the limelight. His most recognized work was the wiring of the Palace of Legion of Honor for the 1915 Pan Pacific Exposition. In 1921, Ed formed Lynch Electric located on Sutter Street. One of his first projects was the new US Post Office at Embarcadero and Sansome Streets. Newspaper accounts also reference several warships built on the waterfront "with the electrical portion under the guidance and direction of Master Electrician Edward J. Lynch." This launched a long relationship between the firm and the Department of Defense.

By night, though, Ed pursued his first love, the boxing game. He quickly became a promoter and held fights in large warehouses on the waterfront or in tents in Golden Gate Park. Admission was five cents and, always in need of a bouncer to watch the back door, Ed brought along his young brother-in-law, Edward Scott. For this, many a night both men went home with swollen knuckles, but always with money

in their pockets. By the late 20s, the boxing game was rapidly losing popularity due to the death of fighters in what was the end of the "bare knuckles era." Ed Lynch taught Ed Scott the electrical business and when Ed Lynch died in 1934, Ed Scott went on his own as Edward W. Scott Electric Company. Lynch Electric continued under the direction of Ed Lynch's wife, Violet, and their oldest son Edward. They also had help in afternoons and summers of Edward's two teenage brothers, Ray and Leonard.

With the coming of World War II, the two firms joined forces as Lynch and Scott Electric, and worked on the rapid development

Ray and Leonard Lynch on a "shakeout" cruise with the U.S. Navy in 1982 in recognition of their involvement in Department of Defense work.

Early stage of the Codernieu Winery in Napa Valley in 1992. Upon completion, the entire facility was covered over with dirt to blend in with the hilltop.

going on at several bulging military bases in the Bay Area. Following the conclusion of WWII, the firms split up and young Raymond Lynch, fresh out of the Army, joined his uncle Edward Scott and the young firm began to spread its wings. One of the first major clients was the California Packing Co., which later became Del Monte Foods. Numerous large fruit packing plants were built throughout the Sacramento and San Joaquin Valley. This involvement led to further work at facilities such as the Gladding Beam Plant in Ione, one of the first plants to manufacture large wood beams and trusses. As all of the work in the Central Valley was going on, the Department of Defense work still was the major backbone for the firm. With the eventual Korean War developing, the firm was hired to facilitate the immediate reopening of the huge Hunter Leggitt Army Base in Southern Monterey County.

The Army needed the decommissioned Base up and running for 50,000 new recruits in four months. The ability to complete the work led to numerous other military contracts throughout the Korean War and into the Cold War period.

Company archives reveal long forgotten missile silos installed all over the Bay Area, even by the Great Highway in San Francisco. In order to utilize the missiles, large tracking stations were built up and down the West Coast. One in particular was important in the firm's history, located at Point Arena on the Mendocino Coast. This remote facility, built on a mountaintop high above the fog line, could track the eminently arriving Russian Bombers as far away as Hawaii. The 40 electricians lived in old hunter's cabins for two years, coming home on the average of once a month.

This is an early flight simulator for TWA at its new facility at San Francisco International. Would this instill the utmost confidence in your flight?

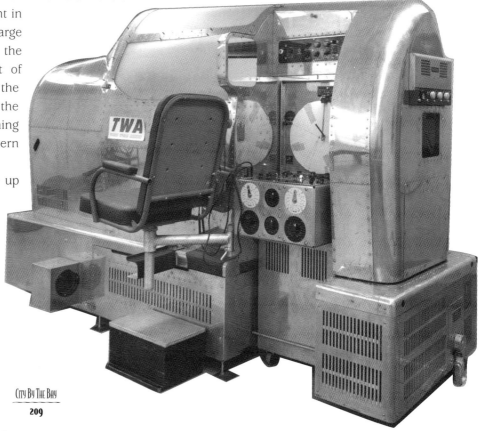

While all of this was going on outside the City, young Leonard Lynch, Ray's younger brother left Lynch Electric in 1959. Leonard's first big project was the dramatic expansion and buildout of what was a very small University of San Francisco. Coupled with new major clients such as Bank of America, Southern Pacific Railroads and Automatic Tube Company, the firm flourished. The Automatic Tube Company crews were sent to sites across the country such as Omaha, Kansas City, New Orleans and Wheeling, West Virginia, to install hospital control systems.

Closer to home, crews worked on the first Stanford Linear Accelerator, built to aid cancer research. This lead to work at many local hospitals such as Stanford Hospital and Marin General and Novato General. Meanwhile the Defense Department awarded large contracts for Long Beach Naval Supply and a large Fuel Storage Facility in Antiqua in the Caribbean.

In the 1970s, the third generation of the Lynch family began to join the business. This included Ray Jr., Eileen and Steve Lynch, children of Ray Lynch Sr. and their cousin Leonard Lynch Jr. In the 1980s Ray Jr., Steve and Eileen were joined by their brothers Greg, John and Brian and Leonard Jr. was joined by his brothers Jerry and Mike. In 1981, Ray Sr. retired and Leonard Sr. followed suit in 1982, now leaving the operation of the Company to the next generation.

In the 1980s the business opened a branch office in Santa Rosa and participated in the ongoing business expansion in the North Bay. The company began doing work for several of the wineries in Napa such as Chateau St. Jean,

The Nike Missile installation at the Great Highway. Native San Franciscans will recognize the San Francisco skyline.

Beaulieu Vineyards and the new Cordorniu Winery as well as several large shopping centers such as Santa Rosa Plaza, Larkspur Landing, the Village at Corte Madera and Vintage Oaks in Novato.

Scott Electric formed two subsidiaries in the late 1980s. Scott Controls Inc. focused on new developments in the teledata and telecommunications industry. E.W. Scott Electric capitalized on the deregulation of power companies by specializing in power distribution and underground facilities. Current clients include the San Francisco International Airport, the remaining military bases in Northern California and anyone who wishes to upgrade their high voltage network system.

A high profile project was the enclosure of Candlestick Park and movable bleachers in right field (the first time a movable section of a stadium had been created). Another noteworthy project was installing emergency back-up power for the Golden Gate Bridge in 1993. In the event of a power outage, the tollbooths, bridge and transmitter lights will continue to function and allow vehicle and vessel traffic to continue to operate.

Within the past two years, Scott Electric has completed a number of Seismic Retrofitting projects in historic San Francisco Buildings, including the US Customs House on Battery Street, the San Francisco Opera House, the War Memorial Building and the Bill Graham Civic Auditorium. Across the bay, the Company retrofitted the Oakland City Hall. These retrofitting jobs have been financed with special funds allocated in the wake of the 1989 Loma Prieta Earthquake. Generally this work involves lifting the building off its foundation and replacing it with an elastic foundation system, followed by installation of state-of-the-art phone, data and life safety electrical systems. Recent San Francisco projects include a $50 million project for the Mt. Zion Cancer Research Facility, and complete upgrade of

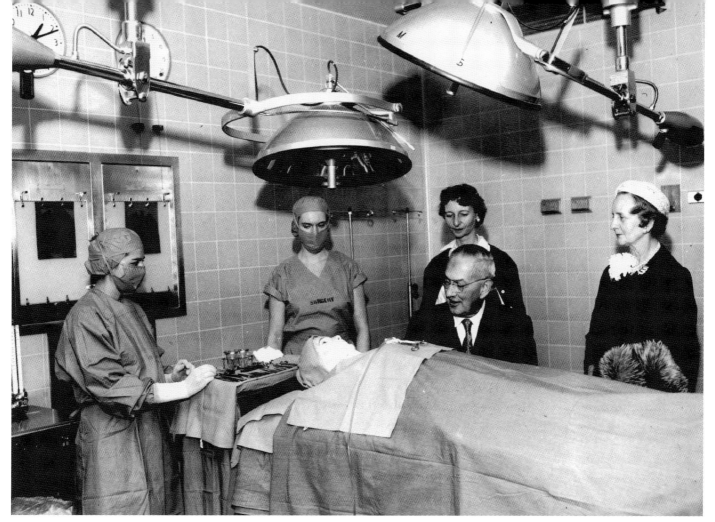

Classic operating room from St. Francis Hospital in San Francisco.

the U.C.S.F. Medical Center Campus to provide its power needs into the 21st century. Another major project underway is part of the $2.4 billion expansion of the San Francisco International Airport, as it completes plans to double its pedestrian capacity within the next five years. Scott Electric is completing work on the American Airlines private passenger terminal as well as substantial upgrades to the main terminal and back-up power.

The Company has been involved in the Bay Area Rapid Transit (BART) expansion in the East Bay, doing design/build parking structures and BART Stations in Walnut Creek and Concord. Scott Electric has also performed work for East Bay Municipal Water District (EBMUD), Marin Municipal Water District, Vallejo Sanitation and Solano Municipal Water District, to upgrade their operations to comply with a number of regulatory clean water acts. The company is now working for the Santa Cruz Waste Treatment Facility. The work allows for the transmitting of data on every working piece of equipment, pumps, grinders, conveyor belts, etc via satellite to a monitoring station in Corvallis, Oregon.

The Company is also doing a substantial amount of work continuing the upgrades for Bay Area Schools and Universities, including the San Francisco School District. The major focus is the bring all the schools to current or better levels of teledata and telecommunications capabilities, as well as to meet safety/security requirements.

Scott Electric has 175 employees, with its San Francisco office as Headquarters. Coinciding with the next major wave of expansion of high tech companies in Silicon Valley, the Company has opened an office in San Jose. The Company is now doing a substantial amount of work there, including an $8 million High Tech Museum of Innovation in San Jose.

The Company routinely maintains a sufficient back log of work, and it treats its employees well. Therefore a large number of the best electricians in the San Francisco Bay Area have continuously worked for Scott Electric. We have been able to sustain continued growth and continue to provide quality services to our clients.

George Goodwin Realty

George Goodwin Realty is a full service company specializing in residential properties throughout San Francisco. The firm sells single family homes, duplexes and apartment houses, as well as commercial buildings.

The company has built some houses and is currently building two condominiums, with spectacular views of the City, in the Noe Valley neighborhood. George Goodwin Realty also offers apartments and other rental properties throughout the City. It provides property management services to rent-controlled apartment houses, duplexes, single-family homes and other properties. The firm arranges loans for buyers, sellers, builders and investors.

A third generation San Franciscan, George Goodwin was born in the City's old Children's Hospital in 1922. He was raised in the Richmond District, attending Sutro and Alamo Grammar Schools, Presidio Junior High School and Washington High School.

He graduated from high school in 1940, then landed a job at Crocker Bank, working five-and-a-half days a week and earning $65 per month. "If your accounts didn't balance at the end of the day, you had to stay overtime, without pay, until you found the error," he recalls.

After the Japanese attack on Pearl Harbor, Goodwin enlisted in the United States Navy and trained to be an aviation machinist's mate. He was sent to Pearl Harbor in 1942, a year after the attack, and was first stationed at Ford Island Naval Air Station and later at Barber's Point Naval Air Station. During his enlistment, he qualified for officers school and was sent to the School of Mines in Butte, Montana. When World War II ended, he continued in the Naval Reserve, eventually attaining the rank of lieutenant.

After the war, Goodwin returned to San Francisco to begin civilian life again. The first thing he did was marry his high school sweetheart, Marjorie Krase; 52 years later, they are still happily married.

He finished his college education at the University of San Francisco, earning a Bachelor of Science degree.

While attending college, he worked for his uncle in the real estate business. He worked full-time in that business after he graduated and, to this day, is still working full-time in the real estate business. When he began fifty years ago, homes in The Sunset area of the City were selling for $9,000 to $12,000; the same houses are now selling for $250,000 to $300,000.

Throughout his fifty years in business, Goodwin has dealt with every kind of person there is. But his clients share one common trait: they are responsible people who have worked hard to save money and buy a home. George Goodwin Realty assists these people in achieving their dream of home ownership.

From its office in The Sunset, George Goodwin Realty provides a full gamut of real estate services.

Gordon Reid
L'habitat companie

From the winding streets of exclusive Telegraph Hill, to the elegant stone mansions of Pacific Heights, few housing markets in the world present as much allure and challenge as San Francisco's.

Adeptly poised to offer its wide-ranging expertise is a small upscale firm, Gordon Reid, L'habitat companie, with a fresh approach to real estate. A client-focused firm, this company prides itself on the human approach it takes to home sales and purchases while also emphasizing the use of technology to deliver the highest level of service.

As members of the San Francisco and Marin County Associations of Realtors, Gordon Reid is linked to the Multiple Listing Services (MLS) in both counties with current information on market trends and analyses. They do everything from assessing the nuances of a neighborhood to match a client's eclectic tastes, to evaluating local schools, to helping clients stage their homes to maximize value. Thus the tag line to their name, L'habitat companie — "home company" — loosely borrowed from the French, to clarify where their focus is trained. Gordon Reid is in the business of taking care of its client's home needs.

At the same time, these Realtors are committed to the housing needs of the larger community. To that end, Gordon Reid offers its clients an unusual opportunity once a transaction moves toward finalization. Clients are asked to choose a charity that assists the homeless or supports other home-related causes. A donation is then made (deducted from Gordon Reid's commission) in the client's name.

Gordon Reid is comprised of three well matched colleagues. Adrian Gordon is a lawyer and CPA with an extensive background in tax and real estate law. He has negotiated transactions as large as several hundred million dollars and has a broad understanding of what it takes to complete the complex real estate transaction of today.

Lynn Reid has a masters degree in social work. Formerly the director of a key department in a San Francisco hospital, Lynn is a skilled listener, negotiator and coordinator. Her manner is a comfort to clients as they undergo what is often one of life's more stressful moments. Beyond that, her knowledge of San Francisco's neighborhoods provides clients with the insightful information they need to choose the right home.

With offices in San Francisco and Marin Counties, realtors (from left) Ginger Foote, Adrian Gordon and Lynn Reid of Gordon Reid L'habitat companie serve clients on both sides of the Golden Gate Bridge. *Photo by Keith Silva*

Ginger Foote is based in Mill Valley. Her presence there expands Gordon Reid's reach over the Golden Gate Bridge into Marin County. With 20 years experience in large corporate brokerages, she brings her training in contract management, property valuation and market analysis to the firm. Among her numerous specialties, Ginger has developed an expertise working with seniors contemplating a change in home and lifestyle.

While many brokerages today are looking to grow rapidly, Gordon Reid prefers to remain small, accommodating and flexible. Their size allows them to customize the work they do for each client and offer top quality professional services in the process. Further, Gordon Reid maintains flexibility in the amount of commission charged for their work.

For Gordon Reid, residential real estate is a business of and about people as well as property. To achieve optimal results and remain responsive to each client's needs, Gordon Reid selects its clients carefully and limits the number of transactions engaged in at any one time. The payoff is in the integrity of their work and the lasting personal and business relationships they forge.

HCV Pacific Partners

The Resort at Squaw Creek, Olympic Valley, California, the first year-round destination resort and conference center developed in North America.

HCV and its investors own this Class A commercial building at 625 Market Street in the heart of San Francisco's financial district. (Far right)

and service — to its investors, tenants, residential purchasers and hotel guests.

The activities of the company are directed by Geoffrey Yeh, Chairman of Hsin Chong, a diversified construction and real estate development company based in HongKong, and Randall J. Verrue, President and Chief Executive Officer of HCV PacificPartners. With over 20 years of experience in the California real estate market, HCV's management has expertise in an array of real estate projects: resort/hotel, office/commercial/mixed use, residential, and government/consulting.

Those projects include The Resort at Squaw Creek, the first year-round destination resort and conference center to be developed in North America. HCV's management was responsible for identifying the mountain location and developing the Resort, including construction of the "links-styled" Robert Trent Jones golf course. This golf course was ranked as one of the "Top Five Resort Courses" in the United States by Golf Digest and has been featured in LINKS, the Best of Golf. By developing a resort which included a golf course and conference center, HCV maximized value for its investors by creating a property which has year-round appeal to its guests, even though the hotel is located in an area primarily known for winter sports.

HCV Pacific Partners was formed in 1989. The company combines the expertise and experience of a San Francisco-based real estate development company with the resources of Asian, primarily Hong Kong, investors. HCV pursues real estate acquisition and development opportunities in the western United States, concentrating on California. Since its inception, HCV has grown from US $17.5 million to US $275 million in assets under management.

HCV seeks to obtain optimal returns for its investors by identifying and acquiring undervalued assets and maximizing the value of these assets through repositioning, intensive management and development. HCV has been successful because of the extensive experience of its management, its knowledge of the marketplace and its commitment to quality

In 1996, HCV and its investors acquired the Hyatt Regency at Capitol Park in Sacramento. This premier luxury hotel is located directly across from the California State Capitol Building and adjacent to the Sacramento Convention Center. The Hyatt Regency is uniquely positioned to capitalize on the

growth of one of the most dynamic economies in California because of its superior location and amenities.

Recognizing that an investment in hotels is also an investment in the service industry, HCV provides close supervision and oversight of the hotel's management company through innovative management arrangements. HCV meets regularly with hotel management to evaluate property performance, develop strategic marketing and operating plans and participate in the employment decisions for senior hotel management personnel. By closely monitoring the performance of a hotel and its management company, HCV can provide its investors and lenders with a wealth of valuable information not otherwise available in a passively-managed property.

HCV also acquires and develops institutional-quality office properties. Some of the best opportunities involve purchasing property that needs to be renovated or repositioned in the marketplace. HCV believes that through intense management and leasing, these properties will achieve significant returns in the long-term for its investors. Following this philosophy, HCV has acquired non-institutional grade commercial buildings located in the heart of San Francisco's financial district and renovated and repositioned them into Class A buildings. In addition, HCV and its investors have capitalized on investment opportunities available resulting from lenders liquidating their properties. The company and its investors currently own 625 Market Street,

180 Sutter Street and 222 Kearny Street in the heart of San Francisco's financial district.

The development of single- and multi-family housing is a major segment of HCV's operations. Projects include luxury communities where HCV acquires and master plans the site, obtains permits, builds infrastructure improvements and sells finished homes, custom lots and home sites for builders.

HCV is currently involved in residential projects in Marin County, Contra Costa County and El Dorado County. In 1995, HCV and its investors formed a residential development company to develop, build and market high quality homes in its Madera del Presidio project in Marin County. The following year, the company achieved considerable success by becoming the fastest selling project in the county. HCV's largest residential project, consisting of 361 luxury homes located in the Contra Costa hills west of San Ramon, will commence in 1997 and be available for occupancy in 1999.

Since 1994, HCV has been providing real estate consulting services to the National Park Service in connection with the conversion of the San Francisco Presidio from a military post into a national park, by providing its expertise in leasing, historic renovation and economic feasibility analysis.

Hcv develops single and multi-family housing, such as Southpointe Homes in El Dorado County, California.

The Hyatt Regency at Capitol Park, Sacramento, California, is uniquely positioned to capitalize on the growth of one of the state's most dynamic economies. (Far left)

Metropolitan Electrical Construction, Inc.

David A. Lindt and
Nicholas J. Dutto,
Founders

Continuing to grow
in order to meet the
electrical needs
of our customers

In 1981 Nick Dutto was working for an electrical firm that performed tenant improvements, and David Lindt was working for contractors on large electrical projects, when the pair decided to strike out on their own. Borrowing $5,000 from family members, Mr. Dutto and Mr. Lindt formed Metropolitan Electrical Construction, Inc., and leased a small work space at 2400 Third Street.

Both the company's founders are native San Franciscans who identify with neighborhoods. Nick Dutto grew up in the Hunter's Point area, and joined the U.S. Navy in 1965 at age 17, following graduation from John O'Connel High School. He served two tours of duty in Vietnam for three-and-a-half years, on the U.S.S. Mark out of Saigon, and on the U.S.S. Yorktown off the coast of Vietnam and Korea. Dave Lindt, reared in the Glen Park neighborhood, was graduated from Balboa High School in 1960. He served in the 82nd Airborne Division of the U.S. Army from 1965 to 1967. Lindt and Dutto joined International Brotherhood of Electrical Workers #6 in 1967 and 1968, respectively.

Metropolitan began with two employees in the field, but has grown to be one of the largest electrical firms in Northern California with a total of 250 employees, 52 of whom are in-house estimators, project managers and administrative staff. The yearly volume has gone from $250,000 in the first year of operation to $36 million in sales in 1996.

The company's growth can be traced in its expansion from what is now only the reception area of Metropolitan's current physical plant. Gradually, the company leased additional space on the first floor, then expanded its operation to the second floor as well. Recently, Metropolitan purchased the 2400 square foot building.

From that almost inauspicious beginning Metroplitan has become a full-service electrical contractor engaged in design/build commercial construction, tenant improvement data communications projects, and cellular/PCS infrastructures. The company provides retrofitting to systems, customized lighting, and voice technologies. Metropolitan also provides infrastructures maintenance, a very structured type of preventative maintenance program.

As part of its continued effort to stay at the forefront of the industry, Metropolitan has recently expanded into wireless communications. Metropolitan has the capability to answer all wireless industry needs, from antenna system installation for cellular and personal communications services, to monopole erection, testing, and repairs.

Eight years ago Metropolitan made its entry into the data communications arena, and the company has experienced considerable growth into the Silicon Valley area. This work includes computer local area network/wide area network (LAN/WAN) systems installation, installation of new or refurbished switches and switch gear, and all data structures that require network cabling or fiber optic installation. Applications support include 16 Mbps Token Ring

and 155 Mbps Asynchronous Transfer Mode (ATM) technologies. Metropolitan partners with major telecommunications providers for much of their cable and fiber optics installations, offering a 15-year product warranty and application assurance for many of these installations.

Metropolitan's experienced in-house staff is capable of providing services ranging from design build to large bid construction. In-house computer-aided design (CAD) capabilities, along with full blue print services, are also available. The in-house CAD systems are very efficient in design consultation to help customers meet their design needs. These services include architectural layout preparation, electrical design drawing production, Title 24 compliance calculations, and documenting cable types and pathways.

Metropolitan's president, Nick Dutto, attributes the company's success to its willingness and proven ability to satisfy the most demanding project challenges — challenges that many other firms resist. By focusing on maintaining quality relationships with all members of a project team, while adjusting immediately to changes in scope and schedule, Metropolitan's clients are offered a broad range of operational and economic advantages.

Metropolitan is committed to building satisfying relationships with its customers, a commitment that begins by providing quality service. No job is considered too small, and thus far no job has been too large for Metropolitan to tackle. The company can respond to a request for a single outlet to a $3-5 million project. With 30 service vans, Metropolitan offers rapid response to customers' needs, 24 hours-a-day.

What sets Metropolitan apart from its competitors is the combination of turnkey operations. They can provide this by linking electrical, data, and design divisions so that customers are able to see the entire project laid out before them. This helps eliminate unexpected changes, which in turn saves a customers both money and time.

Today, Metropolitan does service work for a select clientele that includes not only architects and general contractors, but also management firms, financial institutions, and a number of other Fortune 500 companies. While Metropolitan has a branch office in Concord, it will open another branch in San Jose within the next year. This satellite office will be instrumental in serving the high-growth San Jose area.

One of Metropolitan's proudest achievements is the revamping of a San Francisco landmark, the "76" clock tower building. On this project Metropolitan handled a complete demolition of the shell and installed all new services, creating a state-of-the-art communications infrastructure as well as a new life safety system.

One of Metropolitan's greatest challenges was a project for a major telecommunications provider. The project entailed building the sites for the largest single launch in the world of personal communications system. The challenges included a combination of geography, weather, and access, but, as with all of Metropolitan's challenges, this, too, was handled with aplomb to meet the customer's unique needs.

Besides commitment to customers' needs, the company is committed to staying in the neighborhood where it's now located. Metropolitan recently redesigned a nearby neighborhood design center, creating a shopping center that is drawing people back into it the area again.

Just as Metropolitan's owners are committed to remaining in San Francisco, so are its employees deeply involved with community concerns. They offer support in the form of both time and talent to assist with 49ers Outreach, the AIDS Quilt (The Names Project), Habitat for Humanity, and in wiring local schools for computers so that the children of today will be better prepared to meet the technological advances of tomorrow.

full service design, installation, and repair for data/communications (Far left)

The National Group

In 1977, Daniel Y. Wong, P.E., founded the National General Contracting Company to serve the construction, design and development of northern California. Twenty years later, Wong's creation has grown to become a business that is firmly rooted in two continents.

The National Group now consists of the following: National General Contracting Company and USA National Construction & Maintenance, Inc., are two companies serving the public in project management, construction and project development tasks in the Bay Area. The National Group, as an architectural and engineering design and construction management firm that promotes many projects through a design-build approach, is the international company.

Daniel Wong, Chief Executive Officer and Director of the

National Group, was born in China in 1946. He studied at the University of London, received a B.S. degree in Mechanical Engineering (1972) and a M.S. degree in Ocean Engineering (1974) from the University of Hawaii, USA, and later undertook post-graduate study in a Ph.D. program in Engineering & Construction Management.

Prior to devoting full-time attention to the National Group, Wong worked with several companies that gave him diverse experience in design/construction planning and management. He began his professional career with Bechtel Corporation (1974-76), serving in the varied capacities as an Offshore and Marine Engineer, and Pipeline and Arctic Engineer. His work dealt primarily with offshore platforms, onshore and offshore pipelines, power plants, chemical plants, refineries and site master planning for industrial projects such as the Trans-Alaska Pipeline. At Brown & Root, Inc. (1976-1980), he was an Arctic and Offshore Supervisor for design and construction of Oil Gathering Centers 1, 2 and 3 at North Slope, Alaska. And at Standard Oil Co. (1980-1987), as a Lead Discipline Engineer in Project Management, he was heavily involved in the design/construction management of refinery, pipelines, power and oil distribution system and living/office facilities, as well as project sites master planning.

In its San Francisco office (company headquarters), the National Group has a professional staff, including architects, engineers, designers and project managers. There are about 30 professional staff members in the National Group's offices in China. The National Group is a truly international company.

With a long history of successful projects, the business has gained an excellent reputation. Wong credits this to customer relations, quality of

In China, the National Group tends to undertake much larger projects — $10 to $100 million — than in the Bay Area. The company started to serve Chinese projects in 1993 in Shanghai. In 1994, the company won a major international competition award for design and management construction of the Bank of China's headquarter complex in Beijing.

Two of the National Group's major projects underway in China are a $20 million combination four-star hotel and shopping center in Northern China, and involvement in the construction of a $100 million-to-$1 billion coal-fired electrical generating power plant. Other current commercial renovation and construction projects in China range from bank buildings to highways. Such projects as the power plant receive the willing backing by American investors as they tend to return an investment within a short time.

In the Bay Area, the company tends to undertake more construction than design projects. The company builds custom luxury homes in various cities in the Bay Area. While the company tends to build upscale homes, it will handle projects from $100,000 upwards. In the commercial side of the business, the National Group does con-

struction projects, seismic upgrades, renovations and real estate development in the Bay Area, specializing in the renovation of churches, hotels, restaurants and offices.

Altogether, the National Group is at the forefront of development in the Pacific Rim, the world's hottest current marketplace.

work. planning, and project management. The National Group excels in construction design and management, and stresses efficiency and customer's unique needs. Meticulous attention to detail, such as how to eco-nomize on space and use the latest technology to create a visually striking building, brings the firm new business.

In China, where a vast range of building is going on, from energy-related projects, to hotels and other building construction, the National Group has been successful in landing contracts for a number of major projects. Part of this success is traced to the company's understanding of both American and Asian customs, and its ability to build cultural bridges between two continents. The company has engineering and construction licenses in China that equip the professional staff to handle design, construction and project management there, in commercial, industrial and residential projects, and the company has gained a reputation for having an American style, now highly prized by the Chinese people. Also, the company's professional staff speak the language (Daniel Wong himself is fluent in both written and spoken Mandarin), a significant asset for a company desiring to do business in China.

COMPASS Management and Leasing, Inc.

In San Francisco, large office buildings and business facilities are owned by every kind of business but most are managed by firms with special expertise. Companies that want their property managed to run at maximum efficiency entrust it to COMPASS Management and Leasing, Inc.

As an international real estate services company, COMPASS offers expertise in property and facilities management, leasing and transaction management, finance and information technology integration, construction management, project development, and advisory services.

COMPASS was established in 1990 as a separate operating entity of Equitable Real Estate Investment Management, Inc. to focus on providing the highest quality management and leasing services to real estate owners and operators. COMPASS has offices in over 300 cities in the United States and throughout the United Kingdom, Europe, South America and Australia. The COMPASS national network of nine regions allows for each regional office to operate autonomously and for clients to benefit from a standardized approach to systems while enjoying customized service delivery.

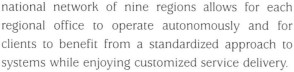

The Compass Senior Management Staff. Left to right: Jeff Reber, Gloria Carpenter, Mark Braverman, Lloyd Lechtenberg, Greg Moss, Gary Guarisco, Larry Hjulberg, Russ Morris, Paul Grafft. Seated: Mark Lucky, Patricia "Patsy" Capbarat.

The San Francisco Region, with its 180 employees, is responsible for over 30 million square feet of property located throughout the Northwest, including Northern California, Western Nevada, Oregon, Washington, Idaho, Alaska and Hawaii. Since 1990, the San Francisco Region has grown from its original 1.8 million square feet under management to over 30 million square feet. This success and growth is the result of relationships with both investment and corporate clients, including Bank of America, ORIX Real Estate Equities, KPMG Peat Marwick, ERE Yarmouth and PG&E.

Gary Guarisco, San Francisco Region Senior Vice President, believes that three factors contributed to COMPASS' success: Their culture and people, their application of technology and systems and their commitment to training.

Culture and People

The primary differentiation for COMPASS is their culture. Their mission is "...to achieve total customer satisfaction, while effectively transforming the industry...to respect their people, their opinions, and to conduct their business with the highest level of honesty, trust, and integrity."

"COMPASS owns no real estate," says Gary Guarisco. "Our employees are our greatest asset. We rely on their conduct and expertise and, as such, have instituted an exhaustive qualifying and hiring process in order to ensure that we hire the right people. We believe in employee empowerment, employee participation in the decision support process, and developing a sense of teamwork."

Application of Technology and Systems

COMPASS believes "if you can't measure it...you can't manage it". As a result, COMPASS developed and implemented technology to measure the day-to-day performance of management services. MAGNET®, the COMPASS performance measurement system, is the first and only performance measurement and analysis system in the industry. In 1995, COMPASS was awarded the Arthur Andersen Enterprise Award for Best Business Practices for "Implementing New Technology".

Commitment to Training

COMPASS believes that training is the cornerstone to developing people able to meet the demands of the real estate industry, and that the key to any successful management team begins with properly trained and challenged employees. As such, COMPASS spearheaded the formation of the National Real Estate Standards Corporation. This commitment to training, combined with their dedication to customer service, promises a consistent delivery of service to their clients.

E.G. Remodeling

In 1981, Eugene Gornitsky started a general contracting/home improvement company in Columbus, Ohio. In 1983, he moved to San Francisco. Some fifteen years later, his business, E.G. Remodeling, has developed into a full service operation which employs not only carpenters, but painters, tile installers, plumbers, finishers, electricians, and the like. Home improvement clients are able to build, remodel, or do-it-yourself, all with the security that *everything under one roof* service provides. Customers know that E.G. Remodeling will be there, "A to Z", every step of the way.

Originally from Ukraine, the Gornitsky family settled in Columbus in 1977. Here, Eugene met his wife and business partner, Ludmila. When his parents later visited San Francisco on vacation, they promptly fell in love with the city and convinced the kids that this was indeed the place to be.

Eugene worked contracting jobs with his father-in-law for several years, taking on one or two projects at a time. He worked out of his San Francisco apartment, until he decided to take a calculated risk and open not just an office, but a showroom as well. This unique neighborhood store, called Deluxe Kitchen and Bath, opened in 1987 in the Sunset District, one of San Francisco's most residential areas.

Here, people of "The Avenues" are welcome to come in and browse the full range of top-quality European and domestic fixtures, appliances, kitchen cabinets, and decorative products such as tiles, doors, countertops, and mirrors. This retail traffic is joined by wholesale suppliers who also appreciate the attention given by this independent outlet and the expert familiarity with European style combined with American know-how and craftsmanship.

Excellent design guidance, professional how-to advice, and reputable construction work is what is offered by E.G. Remodeling. But, perhaps the biggest advantage to this "one stop shopping" is that, using as few subcontractors as possible, E.G. Remodeling will coordinate the work team of contractors and suppliers so the customer doesn't ever get lost in the shuffle. "The customers deal only with our staff," explains Ludmila. "Right away that avoids a lot of headaches. We stay in touch. We really believe in communication."

Today, in addition to in-house service and follow through, E.G. Remodeling can take on four to six concurrent, new construction projects. The central location of the Sunset District headquarters provides quick, easy access to downtown San Francisco, the Peninsula and Marin County. Seventy percent of their contracted jobs are for kitchen and bathroom remodeling. The remainder is in additions, new construction, and upkeep on the classy, historic Victorian homes in Pacific Heights and Russian Hill.

Future plans include a new, expanded Deluxe Kitchen and Bath showroom to be located just down the block from the original. A second branch of E.G. Remodeling is slated for the San Francisco Peninsula, most likely in San Mateo where the Gornitsky clan currently resides.

E.G. Remodeling does it all — for any size job, any budget. Just ask their customers.

Eugene and Ludmila Gornitsky in the Sunset District showroom of Deluxe Kitchen and Bath (Upper left and bottom right)

InterOffice

Standard Office available for lease

InterOffice/San Francisco has state-of-the-art equipment and maintains the newest, most efficient advances in technology and software applications. Business services include word processing, desktop publishing, color graphics, computer services, travel services, voice mail, videoconferencing, LAN services, concierge service, and more!

InterOffice/San Francisco has a highly-skilled administrative staff dedicated to helping clients with their business support requirements. Whether it's help with business fundamentals such as setting up a personal computer, providing word processing assistance, proofreading, or urgent assistance in changing a client's travel plans at a moment's notice, there's always an InterOffice associate ready and willing to help — with a positive attitude and a personal touch.

In addition to full-time offices, InterOffice/ San Francisco has a part-time program, OfficeAccess, for individuals who need access to office space and business services on a part-time basis only. With OfficeAccess, clients benefit from professional services that are available when clients need them, but for a fraction of the cost of a full-time office.

A prestigious and convenient location, combined with advanced business support services and a first-class support team, make InterOffice/San Francisco a smart and powerful business address.

Strategically located at the corner of California and Davis streets in the heart of the central business and financial district, InterOffice/San Francisco provides furnished, staffed and equipped offices and business support services to companies nationwide. The Center enjoys one of the city's most prestigious addresses, as well as one of the most convenient.

Founded in 1985, InterOffice is one of the largest executive suite companies in the nation with 40 Centers located in every major city in the United States. Whether clients are opening a branch office, launching a new venture, or searching for a more efficient way to operate their businesses, InterOffice can help make them more productive — overnight.

Clients of InterOffice/SanFrancisco enjoy private, furnished offices (many with panoramic views of San Francisco Bay and the Bay Bridge) in a Class A building. Phones are professionally answered by dedicated telephone secretaries, and clients share tastefully appointed conference rooms and spacious reception areas with other clients.

InterOffice/ San Francisco reception area (Bottom right)

Transworld Construction, Inc.

Transworld Construction is a San Francisco corporation offering general contracting and renovation services. Specializing in carpentry and woodwork, they also provide services relative to plumbing, windows and doors. Construction projects include apartments, hotels, restaurants, schools, condominiums, hospitals and non-profit and public office space. In 1996, Transworld had revenues of $9.3 million and assets of $3.5 million.

Now celebrating its 20th anniversary, a strong family ethic informs Transworld's corporate philosophy. The company was founded in 1978 by Geomen Liu, a Taiwanese immigrant. Geomen intended Transworld to continue the legacy of his father, Han Tung Liu, owner of H.T. Engineering in San Francisco.

The family theme is apparent from their management roster. Geomen's son, Erik, who holds a JD/MBA, serves as Project Superintendent. Geomen's sister-in-law, Diane Hsia, is Project Manager and Estimator, with over 19 years experience to her credit.

Transworld extends its family philosophy to include all of San Francisco's Chinese community; their list of projects reflecting an intention to "give something back." Many of their construction projects are located in the Tenderloin district, home to many low-income citizens. Transworld creates structures that afford a quality of life to these populations, allowing them to feel good about their environment, making day-to-day living less of a burden.

Among significant new construction projects is one on Ellis Street, a low-income apartment building that features a child care center and job resource planning center. The ground floor consists of one commercial space, one laundry and 13 parking spaces, in addition to the two community rooms. In line with its community commitment, Transworld often works with non-profit funders. A prime example is the Natoma Street Apartment project, completed with the non-profit funding organization, Asian, Inc.

Renovation and seismic upgrade projects include the Lyric Hotel in San Francisco. The work entailed installation of energy saving conservation features, life safety upgrade, plumbing and electrical work. The Jones Street Apartment renovation project included reinforcement of concrete foundation walls, and installation of a new elevator and fire sprinkler system.

Seismic upgrades are ever present in earthquake-prone San Francisco, but Transworld does not limit the scope of its projects. Daly City recently retained the company to complete an aircraft noise sound-proofing project. Transworld was called upon to replace windows, doors, insulation and chimney dampers in 250 single-family houses. Speed was of the essence and Transworld completed the job in a miraculous five months' time.

The Aztec Apartments at 585-589 8th Street in Oakland. (Before and after)

In another public project, the City and County of San Francisco contracted with Transworld to perform a major demolition renovation and seismic upgrade of the Taraval Police Station, in San Francisco's Sunset district. The work included shoring of existing main building for new foundation, and addition of two three-story wings.

Another key new construction project is the Minna Street Apartments. Funded by the California Department of Housing and the San Francisco Redevelopment Agency, the project entailed construction of 24 two- and three-bedroom units.

Quality work and commitment to the community sum up the Transworld Construction, Inc. corporate identity. The Liu family looks forward to many more decades serving the San Francisco Bay Area construction community.

Sixth and Minna Street Apartments at 1518 Minna Street in San Francisco. (Bottom left)

INVESTMENT BANKING,

SECURITIES BROKERAGE,

IMPORT/EXPORT, INSUR-

ANCE, AND DIVERSIFIED

HOLDING COMPANIES

PROVIDE A STRONG

FINANCIAL FOUNDATION

FOR SAN FRANCISCO.

Business & finance

Discover Brokerage Direct

Stephen R. Miller,
Chairman and Chief
Operating Officer of
Discover Brokerage Direct

The union of two investment firms with San Francisco beginnings — one long established with roots as a family-owned business, the other young and dynamic — promises to revolutionize the way the world invests.

Dean Witter, Discover put itself at the cutting edge of online technology with the 1996 acquisition of Lombard Brokerage, one of the country's top electronic brokerage firms. Customers can take advantage of a wide range of services — they can get real-time quotes, access portfolio information, and trade stocks and options via the Internet or phone, from the comfort of their homes.

Barron's rated Lombard the top electronic brokerage firm two years in a row before Dean Witter, Discover took the bold step of adding it, making them the first large investment firm to acquire an on-line broker. The company was renamed Discover Brokerage Direct to leverage the marketing strength of 40 million Discover cardholders.

Stephen R. Miller, formerly director of Dean Witter, Discover's Pacific Region, now heads Discover Brokerage Direct as Chairman and Chief Executive Officer. A grandson of one of the company's founders, Miller has spent his entire career with Dean Witter Discover, starting as a sales trainee and moving up through the ranks over the years.

V. Eric Roach, Discover Brokerage Direct President, started Lombard in San Francisco in 1992, to offer investors superior products and services at great value.

He foresaw the merging of technology and finance and knew that a growing number of computer literate investors would flock to the most accessible technology.

Now a unit of Morgan Stanley, Dean Witter, Discover & Co., the company's goal of empowering investors by giving them the tools and information they need to make intelligent investment decisions has propelled them into a leadership position in the brokerage industry. A team of talented engineers began developing a website in 1994, and a year later it was up and running, with access to stock quotes and graphs. Growth accelerated when on-line trading began a few months later.

Customers can take advantage of a wide range of services — they can get real-time quotes, access portfolio information, and trade stocks and options via the Internet or phone, from the comfort of their homes.

It quickly became a widely popular website. The financial press took notice — the company garnered rave reviews while its website collected awards. Online trading expanded to 60 percent of the company's volume, up from 12 percent the previous year, with revenues and net income doubling in 1996.

Eric Roach noticed that customers were becoming more knowledgeable and sophisticated, and were asking for a broader range of financial products. The union with Dean Witter, Discover was a perfect match for the two companies merging Lombard's strong reputation for technology with the power of the Discover brand.

Dean Witter, Discover's 1996 acquisition of Discover Brokerage Direct follows a long line of successful mergers with firms that share goals and philosophies. The two companies combine a commitment to developing state-of-the-art technology with the ability to provide quality service to customers.

The acquisition is part of Dean Witter, Discover's overall plan to develop new businesses and expand into new market segments in both its securities and credit card services companies. Extensive research showed that do-it-yourself customers using the Internet for securities transactions made up a large, rapidly expanding market, separate from full service brokerage clients.

The development of on-line technology and the growing number of computer-savvy investors promises to bring Dean Witter, Discover and its subsidiaries together into a global, interactive marketplace. Customers could eventually view brokerage accounts from Discover sites, and vice versa.

Discover Brokerage Direct can count on the rich tradition and heritage of Morgan Stanley, Dean Witter, Discover & Co. as it eases customers into the brave new world of electronic investing. From its humble beginnings as a small, family-owned San Francisco firm, Dean Witter, Discover has held onto its long tradition of customer service while growing into a world financial leader, managing over $270 billion in assets by 1997.

Dean Witter, his brother Guy and cousin Jean opened Dean Witter & Co. from a two-room office in San Francisco's Kohl Building in March, 1924. The original partners believed in success through hard work, self-dedication and perseverance, and built a firm they could pass on to the next generation. The firm's reputation and influence grew when it landed a $1.5 million underwriting for Boeing in Seattle two years later.

The company's knack for seeing into the future and taking action began early in its history, several months before the stock market crash of 1929. Dean Witter warned customers that speculative excesses were inflating stock prices to dangerous levels. The firm sold most of its stocks, and Dean Witter & Co. even recorded a profit that year.

Dean Witter & Co. rode out the depression in good financial shape, restoring the confidence of a disenchanted public as San Francisco and the rest of the country struggled to rebuild. In 1935, it added branch offices and moved to larger quarters at 45 Montgomery Street.

"The winner and still champion this year is Discover Brokerage Direct, which garnered 22 out of 25 points and the only ☆☆☆☆ rating in the group." – *Barron's*, March 17, 1997

The firm built its reputation and laid the groundwork for future success during the 1930s, as other investment companies struggled or failed. The confidence and skill of Dean, Jean and Guy Witter and managers that joined the company made possible the remarkable growth that continues today. Even the onset of WWII didn't stop Dean Witter & Co.'s forward vision. Growth was merely put on hold as the country mobilized for war and many employees, including Dean Witter himself, joined the armed forces.

Always ahead of new developments, the company became one of the first brokerage firms to utilize systems technology when it installed an IBM computer in its New York office in 1938. Four years later, modern wire systems replaced telegraph communications, connecting San Francisco, the branch offices and the New York and American Stock exchanges. In the early 1960s, Dean Witter & Co. became the first securities firm to apply electronic data processing technology to its commodity business.

In 1945, Dean Witter & Co. laid more groundwork for future growth when it became one of the first securities firms to establish an Account Executive training program. Many of the first graduates were returning World War II veterans. Recognizing the value of attracting top employees, Dean Witter & Co. became the first major investment house to establish an employee profit-sharing plan.

> **"[Discover Brokerage] won top honors because, in our judgement, it offered the most for a client's commission dollars, with good customer service, a quietly elegant Web-site design, adequate security features and good access to research materials."**
> **– *Barron's*, May 6, 1997**

A pattern of disciplined growth and an uncanny ability for sensing opportunity created extraordinary growth. The firm spread out across the country, opening new offices in economically strategic locations and acquiring other investment houses. A history of successful mergers with companies that shared its vision enabled Dean Witter & Co. to become the international giant it is today.

The timely acquisition of W.M. Cavalier & Co., an experienced stock and bond underwriter, helped fill the personnel gap during the war and set the stage for postwar growth. In 1941, Dean Witter acquired the well-established San Francisco firm, Lieb, Keyston & Co.

A 1959 merger with Laurence M. Marks & Co. put the company in the international arena, just as international business was beginning to expand greatly. It also gave the firm a strong foothold in the institutional sales field and added the first institutional research facilities. In 1970, Dean Witter & Co. joined with J. Barth & Co., an established San Francisco firm, gaining a second research department and several branch offices.

The union of Dean Witter & Co. with Reynolds Securities, Inc. in 1978 was, at the time, the largest merger in the securities industry. The combination of Reynolds' strength in the eastern states and Dean Witter & Co.'s western presence created new opportunities for expansion. The new firm, Dean Witter Reynolds, soon became the first brokerage firm with offices in all 50 states and the District of Columbia.

Dean Witter Reynolds began a period of phenomenal growth in 1981, when it joined Sears, Roebuck and Co. as the center of its financial services network. The world's largest retailer immediately gained a huge presence in the financial services industry. The firm became the largest single bank card issuer after launching the Discover Card in 1986. Within three years, the Discover Card's record profits prompted Dean Witter Discover to make it a separate business unit.

Chart-topping growth continued in the early 1990s, when other securities firms were losing money. The company became Dean Witter, Discover when Sears made Dean Witter Financial Services an independent, publicly-owned company in 1992. It continued to reinvent the credit card industry by adding new products and services.

Expanding its influence in credit services, Dean Witter, Discover established NOVUS, a new credit card network, in 1995. NOVUS services offered a new Private Issue Card and BRAVO card as part of a strategy to reach new market segments. The next year, NOVUS Services launched an affinity card with the American Zoo and Aquarium Association, the National Alliance For Species SurvivalSM Card.

New heights were again reached in early 1997, when Dean Witter, Discover merged with Morgan Stanley, creating a global financial services powerhouse. In 1996, Morgan Stanley led the world in mergers and acquisitions, and also in underwriting initial public offerings and equity related products. The union created a firm with a market capitalization of $21 billion and leading positions in its primary business of securities, asset management and credit services.

"In the long run those firms which survive and prosper are those who maintain conservative policies and put their customers' interests first."
— Dean Witter

Opportunities for accelerated growth into the next century abound with the combination of Morgan Stanley's strengths in investment banking and institutional sales and trading and Dean Witter, Discover's in retail distribution and asset gathering. The size, strength and reputation of this new, uniquely integrated company is reflected in its 1997 theme: "winning at a new level."

The addition of Discover Brokerage Direct allows the company to market to a new kind of investor, while still focusing on clients who want to work with a broker. Its traditional full service business, built around more than 9,000 professional account executives and 3 million securities customers, will continue to be the core component of the company's securities business even as the company expands into new areas.

With the technological prowess of Discover Brokerage Direct, Morgan Stanley, Dean Witter, Discover & Co. is well on the way to achieving its ambitious plan to become the leading global securities, asset management and credit card company. The company's time-tested ability to stick to its tradition of old-fashioned customer service while forging into the future will keep Morgan Stanley, Dean Witter, Discover & Co. ahead of the competition.

As Morgan Stanley, Dean Witter, Discover's influence accelerates worldwide, it remains a powerful presence in San Francisco, with over 1,500 employees. The firm's venerable history is linked to the city's. It is the only large investment firm founded in San Francisco that still exists.

Dean Witter's last memo, written just before his death in 1967, is a legacy left in every Dean Witter, Discover office, and a testament to the principles on which the company was founded.

"The most valuable asset of an investment firm is its good name. Let us do everything we can to not allow profit to distort our judgment. We have a sacred trust to protect our customers.

"In the long run those firms which survive and prosper are those who maintain conservative policies and put their customers' interests first."

"If our survey is any indication, Dean Witter seems to have made a wise choice: [Discover Brokerage] which topped our rankings last year, remains No. 1 among the 26 firms we tested."
– *Barron's,* March 17, 1997

The folks at Morgan Stanley, Dean Witter, Discover have seen that people learn to adapt to new inventions, and that growth happens with experience. Just as the world has become accustomed to touch-tone phones, television and ATM machines, people will soon wonder what they did without the Internet. The company's foresight in bringing the advances of late twentieth century information technology to its customers promises to keep them a world leader well into the next century.

American Industrial Partners

W. Richard Bingham,
President of American
Industrial Partners

In offices overlooking San Francisco Bay from the top floor of One Maritime Plaza, American Industrial Partners is a highly prosperous investment capital firm that manages funds of $800 million. The key to their success lies in an inspired investment philosophy conceived by founding partner W. Richard Bingham.

A graduate of Stanford, with an MBA from Harvard, Bingham was an officer in the U.S. Navy before beginning his career as an investment banker on Wall Street in the 1960s. He directed investment banking operations at Kuhn Loeb & Company and went on to become a member of the Board, Head of Corporate Finance, and Head of Mergers and Acquisitions at Lehman Brothers Kuhn Loeb.

During his tenure with these large investment banks, Bingham observed that a number of their investments were not successful because they relied too heavily on financial leverage and often ignored opportunities and risks inherent in operating leverage. If they'd had investment partners who knew those industries, he reasoned, they either would not have made those investments, or would have been able to readily solve the companies' problems as they arose. It became clear to him that the most sensible way to invest in private equity transactions is to focus on operating leverage and invest alongside people who have experience with similar businesses, people who are investing their own money and are willing to become involved in overseeing acquired companies. This approach not only reduces risk, but increases opportunity, because experienced investors are in a better position to recognize opportunities as they arise.

As time went on, Bingham began to conceive of a structure to put his theories into action. After Lehman Brothers was sold to Shearson American Express in 1984, he moved to San Francisco in 1985, where he ran the company's West Coast Investment Banking division. When his contract concluded in 1988, he left to start a company of his own. He co-founded American Industrial Partners in 1989, together with Theodore C. Rogers, former CEO of NL Industries, a petroleum service and chemical company.

Rogers undertook to establish the firm's New York office and persuaded other successful industrialists to join them. The firm has six Partners, five of whom, including Rogers, are former CEOs of Fortune 200 companies. Other current and former top-level executives make up a five member Strategic Advisory Board and a ten member Executive Officer Association. Collectively, these three groups have experience running, buying, and selling companies in over sixty industries — from chemicals to electronic products to paper and food packaging. The firm's ten Principals and Associates bring additional expertise in commercial and investment banking, consulting, corporate finance, accounting, and law. Working with the Partners and others, they locate investment opportunities and perform due diligence on potential transactions.

By appealing to large institutional investors — including several of the countries largest private pension funds, insurance companies, and commercial banks — American Industrial Partners quickly raised over $217 million and bought thirteen manufacturing and processing companies, with combined sales of $1.7 billion. Demonstrating their commitment to building businesses, instead of simply selling them off, they created operating partnerships with the management at these companies, serving on their boards and contributing their knowledge and expertise. In this way they were able to improve the companies' operations and increase growth and profitability.

In keeping with this strategy, the firm also developed The Leadership Program, where they recruit recent graduates from the country's leading manufacturing and business schools to work for companies in their portfolio. Participants in the program have completed a dual masters degree in Business and Engineering from a leading educational institution, have practical business experience, and are committed to a career in business operations. They take on specific operating responsibilities at the companies, but may transfer between companies depending on need and opportunity.

Several of the companies bought by American Industrial Partners have subsequently been sold, realizing average returns on investment in the mid to high 30 percentage range. This has allowed the firm to start a second fund, in 1995, which has raised $575 million, almost three times as much as the first.

American Industrial Partners' and Richard Bingham's commitment to San Francisco encompasses the support of many of the city's cultural and educational institutions. In addition, Bingham has served on the boards of several schools and is currently Chairman of the Board of Trustees of the California Academy of Sciences.

Through its Partners group, Executive Officer Association, and Strategic Advisory Board, American Industrial Partners has experience and expertise in over sixty industries, including:

Aerospace and aircraft parts

Automotive parts

Banking

Blowers/compressors

Centrifugal pumps/ turbines

Chemicals

Construction products

Consumer products

Electrical equipment

Electronic products

Fabricated metals

Farm equipment

Fasteners

Forest products

Oil and gas

Packaging

Paper

Railroads

Rubber

Steel

Telecommunications

C. Melchers & Co. America, Inc.

Management team of Melchers America— (left to right) Erleen N. Lum, William F. O'Meara, Hellmuth O. Starnitzky (president), Chip Litten and Allan Y. Dong

Melcher's Building in Honolulu (Far right)

The 19th-century bark, *C. Melchers*

When relations between the United States and China took a friendlier turn in 1979, it was just a matter of time before the well-established international trading firm of C. Melchers & Co., whose headquarters are in the northern city of Bremen, Germany, opened its San Francisco office.

At times in the past, the trade activity of this nearly 200-year-old company touched points of North and South America, although it was only in 1981 that the USA branch, C. Melchers & Co. America, Inc., was founded in San Francisco. Of all the possible cities, San Francisco in every respect provided a true "gateway to the Pacific" through which the company has developed a dynamic operation between the United States and the Pacific Rim.

Melchers America, as the company is commonly called, engages in a broad spectrum of international trade. While China has historically been the focal point of the Melchers company as a whole, trade from the San Francisco office has expanded in recent years throughout Asia and to Europe.

The Melchers office in San Francisco continues the company's tradition of finding opportunities for foreign trade in an impressive array of industry sectors. Machinery made in America's heartland is exported to China and Vietnam. Marine hardware is imported from Asia to dealers and government agencies in the United States and South America. Almonds grown in California's Central Valley are exported to all points of the compass. Dehyd-rated vegetables are imported from Chinese pro-vinces to food producers in North

America. Building materials find their way from many states to skyscrapers in Shanghai. Furniture and other consumer items of U.S. origin are on the floors of major retail stores in many Chinese cities. Cashew nuts from Vietnam are exported to Europe. New projects surface all the time, so that Melchers America is constantly in motion, seeking and evaluating opportunities in all parts of the world. And all these transactions touch San Francisco in some way.

Anton C. Melchers started the family business in 1806. In the ensuing decades, the company operated a fleet of 32 ships, many of

which carried emigrants from Europe to America. To fill the vessels on the return trip, buying offices were established in New Orleans, Cuba and Mexico for the purchase of tobacco, rum and other products. In 1825, a whaling station was founded in Honolulu, where whales were caught, processed into oil, and the oil transported on Melchers barks and brigantines to Europe. The first stone building ever constructed in Hawaii housed the Melchers office and staff. The building still stands and is still called the Melchers Building, although nowadays it houses government agencies.

By 1864, the company divested its shipping interests and began to concentrate on the expanding trade opportunities in Asia. Two years later, Melchers Hong Kong Ltd. was established by the founder's grandson, Hermann Melchers, a man with great vision who was the driving force in the company's orientation towards Asia. The ensuing decades were periods of tremendous growth for Melchers in China. Despite interruptions brought about by war and political unrest, C. Melchers & Co. has a firmly rooted tradition of business in Asia.

There are now 17 Melchers offices around the world, with 15 of them situated west of the international dateline. No matter the site, it is

Melchers philosophy to allow each office to implement its own customized style of trading, whereby managers, on a local level, determine an individualized business plan using either country or product-oriented strategies. Each office — from Bangkok to Beijing, Shanghai to San Francisco — forms an individual profit center consisting of diverse business activities which take place simultaneously under the umbrella of the local office. The San Francisco office, for instance, is also affiliated with a manufacturing division in Ohio, Melchers Flavors of America, Inc., where food and beverage flavors are produced.

C. Melchers & Co. endorses a decentralized approach to global business. In addition, the Melchers organization likes to conduct business in a personal manner, by always making local contacts in its areas of trade and by relying on the expertise of a knowledgeable staff. For the most part, employees at Melchers speak the language and are well aware of the customs, politics and market trends of the area where they work. Approximately 1,000 employees are employed by Melchers worldwide.

Hellmuth O. Starnitzky, president and founder of the San Francisco office, has learned the protocol and intricacies of international trade starting from the time he was an apprentice in Bremen 23 years ago. He has been managing the San Francisco office for the past 16 years. During that time, he has observed the ever-changing landscape of international trade created by improved transportation and technological advances. Telecommunications alone has produced a much more competitive pace among international traders.

Yet, even in an accelerated business environment, Melchers maintains an edge because of the company's flexibility and ability to adapt rapidly to change. "Our capital resources certainly benefit both customers and suppliers alike," Starnitzky says, "however, the true longevity of the company stems from our ability to constantly seek and define our function in the arena of international trade."

There are also those intangible resources Melchers is able to utilize that make it difficult for companies with less experience and fewer contacts to compete. Melchers, over the years, has developed a worldwide network of buyers and sellers.

If it were not for the strength of its strong economic bonds, personal friendships and business integrity, Melchers would not have been able to reestablish itself in China after the disruptions experienced by all foreign companies in 1949. Before the purge, trade with China was Melchers' main business, with 12 offices and factories operating on the mainland and its headquarters, for a time, in Shanghai. The head office was eventually relocated to Bremen, even though that city and its entire commercial center had been destroyed in World War II.

In the spirit of renewal that was sweeping Europe, the Melchers organization set out to rebuild itself and its trading businesses in the Far East. During the 1950s and '60s there was an expansion and diversification, once again, into other Asian markets resulting in the opening of offices in Singapore, Malaysia and Taiwan and, later, in Thailand, the Philippines and Korea.

Melchers offices today are in Hong Kong, Singapore, Kuala Lumpur, Jakarta, Colombo, Beijing, Shanghai, Guangzhou, Seoul, Bangkok, Manila, Taipei, Saigon, Hanoi and Fairfield, Ohio, as well as in San Francisco.

Today's managing partners are Henning Melchers, family successor in the sixth generation, Matthias Claussen and Peter Kuhlmann-Lehmkuhle.

In view of the company's extensive global operations, Melchers America has established itself as an important link in the worldwide chain. And San Francisco is ideally situated between East and West.

China has a culture dating back thousands of years. One of the most lovable sides of this old culture is the Chinese habit of translating European names not only phonetically but putting a meaning into the Chinese translation, which should, ideally, say something about the person and his character. So, over 100 years ago, some unknown Chinese translator of names, foresightedly named Melchers "Mei tsui-shih," or "The eternally beautiful times."

California Federal Bank

On January 3, 1997, two established financial institutions, First Nationwide Bank and California Federal Bank, joined forces to form one of the five largest savings and loans in the country. The parent company of San Francisco's First Nationwide Bank purchased the parent company of Los Angeles-based California Federal Bank. The merged bank is head-quartered in San Francisco and although officially named California Federal Bank, A Federal Savings Bank, to locals it is simply Cal Fed.

The merger proceeded smoothly. Virtually all branch positions were maintained. Employee doubts and concerns were addressed with regular communications. Employees worked hard to provide a high level of service to customers throughout the merger process. In fact, it is this attitude towards working with customers to listen to and meet their needs that sets California Federal Bank apart from other banks.

The merger resulted in not only the typical co-mingling of employees and assets but a rich sharing of history. Mergers are nothing new to either of the two institutions (or most banks for that matter). Both have had a legacy of mergers and acquisitions.

Take First Nationwide Bank. That particular name had only been in existence for the past ten years. The bank began on the corner of Sansome and California Streets as Citizens Building and Loan. The year was 1885, the asset count at $50,000. Deposits grew to $1 million by 1925. In 1945, Citizens Federal Savings and Loan Association made the first G.I. home loan in California. The first branch office was opened at San Francisco's Stonestown Shopping Center in 1955. In 1981, Citizens (renamed First Nationwide Savings) became the first thrift to cross state lines when it purchased failed savings and loans in Florida and New York. The bank was acquired several times, including the 1985 purchase by Ford Motor Company and the 1994 purchase by First Madison Bank of Dallas, notable then as the largest acquisition in the history of the savings and loan industry. California Federal Bank's 70-year history is similar to First Nationwide's, and the banks even crossed paths over the years with the exchange of several branches. Founded in 1926 as Railway Mutual Building and Loan Association in Los Angeles, the original California Federal Bank's initial assets were $262,000. In 1937, the name California Federal Savings and Loan Association was adopted. In 1959, California Federal merged with Standard Federal Savings and Loan Association to become the largest federally chartered mutual savings and loan in the nation. With assets in the billions, the first Northern California branch opened in 1973. In 1979, the bank became the first to offer variable rate mortgages. In 1989 came the present name of California Federal Bank, and, like First Nationwide, the onset of an aggressive expansion program.

A San Francisco tradition through several name and ownership changes, California Federal Bank reflects its hometown's vibrance.
Photo by Bob Adler

The "new" California Federal Bank is the third largest thrift in the nation with approximately $30 billion in assets, 228 branches in four states — California, Nevada, Texas, Florida — and nearly 5,500 employees. The bank's wholly owned subsidiary, First Nationwide Mortgage Corporation, originates mortgage loans in 44 states and services loans for nearly a million borrowers. California Federal is privately held as an indirect subsidiary of Mac Andrews & Forbes Holdings Inc., of New York.

But statistics aren't what is important to customers — service is. It's a commodity that California Federal Bank strives to deliver. A full-service bank, Cal Fed offers the products customers want: small business banking, mortgage and consumer loans, investment and insurance products, as well as a full range of savings and checking products. Employees at Cal Fed take the time to listen to customers and find the right products and services to meet individual needs. For example, California Federal Bank has long been a leader in finding creative ways to finance home ownership and the development of rental housing for those with low to moderate income.

California Federal Bank also cares about the communities where it does business. In mid-1997, the bank was recognized in Washington D.C. as one of the most active participants nationwide in the Federal Home Loan Bank's Affordable Housing Program. The company contributes hundreds of thousands of dollars annually to support education, health care, housing, the arts, and other causes. Among the San Francisco associations the bank has supported are: Self Help for the Elderly, Meals-on-Wheels, the San Francisco Symphony, the Asian Women's Resource Center, and the San Francisco State University Foundation.

Cal Fed encourages employees to volunteer for the non-profit organizations of their choice by allocating company time of up to four hours a month per employee. Some of the major San Francisco volunteer projects the bank participates in are: Christmas in April, the annual AIDS Walk, AIDS Ride, the School Volunteer Program, and the Coastal Clean-up.

By providing services, business opportunities and support to the community, California Federal Bank is an integral part of San Francisco. President and chief operating officer, Carl Webb, summed it up: "The bank's history is woven into the city's history. The bank helped the city rebuild after both major earthquakes, has been making home ownership possible for several generations of San Franciscans, and has provided residents thousands of jobs since 1885. The bank's name and ownership have changed over the years, and we've grown into a nationwide concern. But we're still a vital part of San Francisco, and the city's vibrant culture and heritage are part of the fabric of the bank."

Through Cal Fed's award winning We Care program, bank employees volunteer their time to improve the community.
Photo by David Weintraub

Citibank California

Citibank Embarcadero Center Electronic Banking Center

Citibank is a global bank with resources worldwide to help people manage their money locally and internationally. In California, the Citicorp family of businesses includes forty different companies and over 2,000 employees serving the needs of individuals, businesses, governments and community organizations.

In San Francisco since the mid-1980s, Citibank California headquarters are in the Citicorp Center on Sansome Street. As San Francisco is the financial hub of the West and the gateway to Asia, Citibank uses its location in the heart of the City's financial district to promote business opportunities in the city and anywhere in the world.

Citibank is defining the ways people will handle their money in the 21st Century.

Global in its business reach, Citibank is also having a profoundly positive impact in San Francisco and throughout California. In 1996 the bank donated $1.5 million to various charitable causes and educational institutions, continuing its long tradition of helping Californians.

Today's Citibank offers its services in ways that reflect the tremendous diversity of its customer base. Its International Banking Center on Montgomery Street has a staff fluent in nine languages, including English, Cantonese, Mandarin, Spanish, French, German, Italian, Tagalog, and Korean. As in the bank's other branches, customers find a new type of banking when they enter: instead of being greeted by tile floors and long lines, they are greeted by a customer relations manager who answers questions and helps each customer decide if they need one of the

A winning team: the San Francisco 49ers and Citibank (Bottom right)

bank's Citicard Banking Centers (CBCs), a banking professional, or a specialized expert.

Citibank's CBC at the International Banking Center is also an improvement on the industry standard. Located in a vestibule inside the branch that can only be entered by using an ATM card as a "key," the automated teller machines offer welcome security to customers.

Citibank is the leading innovator of electronic services for consumer banking. Citibank introduced the first CBC using proprietary technology in 1977. Citibank was the first to add multiple languages to automated banking, now with a choice of 10 languages (English, Chinese, Japanese, French, German, Spanish, Italian, Dutch, Korean, and Greek). In 1992, Citibank added a special "language," which it calls VIP banking, that helps vision and learning impaired customers access the CBCs.

Mutual funds, credit card accounts and checking account records for the past 90 days can be accessed through CBCs as well. And in a move that brings customer service to new levels, Citibank has outfitted its CBCs with the means to allow its brokerage customers to check values for securities and trade stocks. CBC customers can actually buy or sell a stock — at a current price or at a limit — just as they would in a phone or in-person transaction with a broker. Providing stock trading at CBCs is a part of the bank's overall effort to give customers the power to manage

their money — 24 hours a day, whether by phone, PC, CBC, or in person, anytime, anywhere, and any way they choose.

Citibank is a subsidiary of Citicorp, a global financial services organization with over $300 billion in assets. There are more than 89,000 Citibank employees in 98 countries worldwide. While Citibank provides its millions of customers with new levels of service, the bank reaches beyond its customer base to communities where it operates with community lending and charitable contribution programs.

Low and moderate-income families realize their dreams of home ownership through the bank's Community Investment programs, which have a range of financing requirements to meet the diverse needs of people and neighborhoods.

Citibank also places emphasis on meeting the needs of community-based businesses for financing real estate, equipment, and capital improvements, in the belief that business is the lifeblood of California's neighborhoods.

One of Citibank's greatest achievements is its leadership in the area of student loans. Citibank's Student Loan Corporation is one of the largest originators of government-guaranteed student loans in the U.S., serving over 900,000 customers and representing a portfolio of over $6.8 billion in education loans outstanding in 1996.

Additionally, Citibank California makes special efforts to help minority- and women-owned companies. The bank has a program that seeks out qualified minority and woman vendors to do business with the bank and tracks results.

Just as Citibank responds to its customers' needs,

the bank responds to the needs of its communities, including San Francisco.

Typical is a $9.3 million loan to provide permanent financing to 201 Turk Street, L.P., for Tenderloin Family Housing, creating 175 units of affordable housing, with a child care center, community space, and a safe and secure courtyard, which is used by local families in San Francisco. 201 Turk Street is a microcosm of San Francisco's ethnic diversity, with more than 15 different ethnic groups living there, speaking 11 different languages among its more than 500 residents. Citibank has made 13 affordable rental housing loans over the past 11 years in some of the City's lowest-income neighborhoods — loans that have produced 635 new affordable housing units and which make the bank a significant investor in efforts to increase the San Francisco low-income housing infrastructure.

The bank has also made recent contributions to the San Francisco Renaissance Center, Jobs for Youth, the San Francisco Zoo, San Francisco School Volunteers, the new main library, and the Asian Art Museum, among others.

Citibank partnerships with the San Francisco 49ers and Pier 39 and sponsorships — such as the Black & White Ball benefiting the symphony and the San Francisco AIDS Walk —allow them to contribute to the community and provide their customers with access to key community activities and services.

A recent mission statement summed up the bank's commitment to its communities through its business and community outreach efforts: "Making our communities better. That, as much as anything, is what Citibank California is all about."

Tenderloin Family Housing provides housing for families, community facilities, a child care center and neighborhood retail space. In 1994, Citibank provided a $6.7 million permanent loan as well as a $2.6 million Federal Home Loan Bank Affordable Housing Program subsidy to this $35 million project by Chinese Community Housing Corporation.

State Compensation Insurance Fund

The California Legislature established the State Compensation Insurance Fund (State Fund) in 1914 to provide worker's compensation insurance to employers and benefits to their injured workers.

The theory behind workers' compensation dates back to the Industrial Revolution. In the English-speaking world there was simply no protection for those workers who got hurt on the job. Under the rule of "contributory negligence," an employee could not recover damages if the injury was to any degree the result of the employee's own negligence. Because of this, employees sought legal relief against their employers. Employees often lost their cases, and a "no fault" concept came into being to protect employees from having no income and to protect employers from law suits as well as loss of completed work. Germany enacted the first workers' compensation law in 1884. In 1897, Great Britain also enacted workers' compensation legislation that served as the model for most state legislation in the U.S.

Since workers' compensation is compulsory, the California Legislature created State Fund to provide an available, affordable workers' compensation insurance product. State Fund was designed to be self-supporting. (The agency receives no income from tax monies.)

California was in the forefront of states providing such coverage, and State Fund has served as a model of how private enterprise and public interest can be fused into one socially enlightened organization dedicated to the well-being of California's employers, their injured workers, and statewide economic stability. Over the years other states have looked to the successful operation of State Fund in creating their own workers' compensation programs.

Among workers' compensation providers, State Fund is unique: It is a self-supporting, non-profit based enterprise that receives no tax support. State Fund has $7 billion in assets. Since 1915, State Fund has returned all unused premiums in excess of expenses, claims costs and necessary surplus to policyholders in the form of dividends, underscoring the profitability of a safe work environment. (State Fund was attacked for "radical" and "foolish" practices when the dividend program began in 1915. Dividends would soon become a common

practice within the industry.) Total dividends declared currently exceed $4.3 billion.

Operating at cost, State Fund acts as a "yardstick" for the maintenance of fair premium rates for employers and fair treatment of injured workers. Today, State Fund is the largest workers' compensation carrier in California, insuring 240,000 policyholders. Experienced employees in 21 district offices from Eureka to San Diego provide local claims, loss control, and policy services to policyholders and injured workers.

While State Fund insures 50 percent of the marketplace, it is proud to claim 80 percent of small business employers as policyholders. In addition, State Fund works with employers other insurers often consider unacceptable, including non-profit and high risk yet essential businesses such as asbestos removal companies.

Throughout the 1980s and '90s, fraud had a devastating impact on workers' compensation providers that resulted in increased rates for employers. In 1991, the California Legislature enacted landmark legislation (the Presley Anti-Fraud Bill) that clearly defined workers' compensation fraud and imposed penalties on those involved in fraudulent activities.

Fraud legislation proved to be a turning point in a system that was rapidly spinning out of control. Well before the legislature acted, State Fund created a Special Investigation Unit and won California's first major premium fraud case. The decision in that case resulted in a $3.7 million judgment and jail for the fraud perpetrators. State Fund has referred hundreds of cases to the Department of Insurance and local district attorneys. Today, State Fund remains committed to the successful curtailment of all types of workers' compensation fraud. State Fund will continue to fight fraud and challenge suspect claims and employers.

State Fund supported the 1993 groundbreaking reform legislation that benefits employers and employees alike. This significant legislation contains many of State Fund's long-standing reform recommendations and ideas. One of the major changes of the reform legislation of 1993 was the repeal of the minimum rate law in favor of competitve rating for workers' compensation insurance. Insurance carriers may set their own rates and develop their own rating plans, but must still submit their rates and rating plans to the Insurance Commissioner. For State Fund policyholders, the 1993 legislation has resulted in a premium reduction, creating a real cost-savings for employers.

The agency's first office building at 525 Market St.

In keeping with its desire for policyholders to expect solutions to problems, not excuses, State Funded implemented a Customer Assistance Program early in 1997. This program handles any and all disputes or disagreements a policyholder may

K.C. Bollier, State Fund's present CEO

experience. While 99 percent of customer disputes are successfully resolved at the district office level, this new program assures customers that State Fund is commited to exhausting all avenues available to revolve disagreements.

As sweeping reforms have altered the entire workers' compensation system, State Fund maintained competitive rates in the new marketplace. Eighty years of specialized experience, early support of compensation reform, and a history of sound financial planning put the organization in the best position for the changing times that lie ahead.

Charles Schwab & Co. Inc.

Investing the way it should be

"In the early seventies, we started out as a discount broker — a transaction specialist. But my vision was to also provide the most ethical and useful brokerage services available," says Charles R. Schwab, Chairman and Founder.

Low-cost, people oriented services "where no one was going to sell you anything" proved to be an attractive option. Over the following quarter century, discount brokerage revolutionized the financial services industry. By 1997, Charles Schwab & Co., Inc. had become one of the nation's largest and fastest growing financial firms, serving over four million active investor accounts with $268 billion in client assets. The last ten years have seen revenues and net income growth at a compounded annual rate of 22 percent, reaching $1,851 billion and $234 million respectively.

"We have been able to enlarge our market penetration with product and service innovations and the application of leading-edge technology," states David S. Pottruck, President and Chief Operating Officer. "As other brokerage firms have faltered, we have thrived because of our unswerving dedication to high value, ethical state-of-the-art offerings. We are both pioneers and marketshare leaders in no-transaction fee mutual funds and on-line brokerage services."

Schwab opened his first office in San Francisco's Equitable Building. "It was the size of a tennis court," recalls Hugo Quackenbush, Senior Vice President. "Few thought it would grow but within five years we had occupied office space equal to five football fields."

A "fortunate" association with Bank of America made it "possible" to open more branches and to "surprise ourself with a 28 story building" at 101 Montgomery Street, now joined by the two surrounding it.

Quackenbush isn't surprised by the financial services revolution instigated by Charles R. Schwab, his childhood friend. "Chuck sets the highest standards for himself and others. Always optimistic, he had the will to make things happen and get others to buy into his vision."

The Vision and Values of Our Company, a simple guide to employee responsibility, is prominently displayed over the corporate entryway. Inside the office, Schwab takes this concept of good corporate citizenship a leap further. With the Charles Schwab Corporation Foundation double matching donations up to $5,000, employees are actively encouraged to make a difference in the community. And so they have. The Schwab team has consistently been the number one fundraiser in the San Francisco Aids Walk. Schwab is also a major benefactor of the cultural arts.

Vice Chairman, Lawrence Stupski, established a program that recruits high school and college students for Schwab internships. Now considered a leading school-to-work expert, Stupski estimates that "by the year 2000, interns will represent 5 percent of our work force."

Charles R. Schwab looks confidently ahead to the Millennium: "We are well on our way towards our goal of one trillion dollars in customer assets and serving more than ten million households by 2005."

Giving customers the very best of what will be needed tomorrow is a Schwab trademark.

Charles R. Schwab, Chairman and Chief Executive Officer of Charles Schwab & Co., Inc.
Photo by Tom Tracey

Bankers Club of San Francisco/ The Carnelian Room

The Carnelian Room, atop the Bank of America building in the heart of San Francisco, offers spectacular views and imaginative cuisine for private and business dinners that are a cut above the rest.

Named after the polished Carnelian granite that sheaths the building, the Carnelian Room's interior is reminiscent of an English manor, warm and elegant with rich walnut paneling and masterworks of 18th and 19th century art. The wine cellar features more than 40,000 bottles with a particular focus on California wineries. Since 1982, the authoritative *Wine Spectator* magazine has bestowed its "Grand Award" on the cellar.

The Carnelian Room's cuisine is exceptional. With a focus on American specialties, the menu incorporates all of California's culinary riches — fresh ingredients, imaginative preparation and fine wines. Following the season, the menu changes with the equinox, ensuring the food is the true star of the Carnelian room. Service is attentive and informed, yet never intrusive.

For business gatherings, the Carnelian Room is a welcome respite from the anonymity of the ordinary banquet hall. All eleven dining suites feature glittering views, and can be arranged to suit business needs with audio-visual and other support close at hand. For events on a grand scale, the entire room can be opened up, providing 24,000 square feet of elegant space with all of San Francisco as a back drop.

In addition to its creative cuisine and opulent views, the Carnelian Room also boasts a rich history. For decades, penthouse restaurants in San Francisco competed to claim the best panoramic view of the city and the bay. But when the Carnelian Room opened in July 1970 on the 52nd floor of the Bank of America World Headquarters Building, the competition was over. From atop the tallest building in the city, diners could relax over cocktails or dinner while savoring unforgettable views of the Golden Gate Bridge, Coit Tower, Fisherman's Wharf and other dazzling cityscapes.

Monday through Friday, the Carnelian Room is reserved at breakfast and lunch for use by the members only of Banker's Club of San Francisco, a private and exclusive business club. The Bankers Club is not only for members of the financial industry, but an elegant and exclusive place for business leaders from all different industries. Managed by ARAMARK Corporation, the club offers a very impressive surrounding for entertaining business clients in an unforgettable setting.

The 360-degree view from the Carnelian Room changes every day and from moment to moment, but in 1989, the restaurant closed for a $4 million remodeling that increased the seating capacity and enhanced the interiors.

While showcasing the best and finest San Francisco offers, the Carnelian Room attains the height in dining experiences.

The panoramic view from the windows of The Carnelian Room.

The Eye Care Network

Robert Bjorkquist, Chief Executive Officer and Aspasia Shappet, Chief Operating Officer of The Eye Care Network and Medical Eye Services
Photo by M. Christine Torrington

The executive offices of The Eye Care Network are situated on the fifth floor of a postmodern building on historic Maiden Lane. To the east is a retail store where "glasses" mean champagne flutes rather than corrective lenses. It is amid elegant boutiques and upscale shops that The Eye Care Network conducts the serious business of orchestrating vision care for more than 1 1/2 million people of California.

When a group of enlightened ophthalmologists and opticians formed The Eye Care Network in 1976, their goal was to form a panel of vision care professionals who would provide eye examinations and eyewear at reasonable cost. Robert Bjorkquist, a native of the City, whose experience had been in the field of health care insurance since his graduation from San Francisco State University, was retained to develop a business plan.

Bjorkquist knew from his many years in the health care field that vision care coverage was lagging behind other benefits being offered by employers. He had the knowledge that was needed for designing vision care plans attractive to employers, to employees and to the professionals who would agree to become participating providers. These vision care plans were made available through health maintenance organizations, insurance carriers and self-funded employer groups.

Since its inception, The Eye Care Network has grown to become the state's largest Preferred Provider Organization for vision care plans with more than 5,100 ophthalmologists, opticians and optometrists in California. The panel has expanded to include 700 participating providers in Arizona, Idaho, Nevada, New Mexico and Utah.

Medical Eye Services, a subsidiary of The Eye Care Network, is a licensed Third Party Administrator, which handles customer service and the processing of vision care claims for more than 6,000 employer groups. Aspasia Shappet, chief operating officer, is responsible for directing the activities of the claims office of Medical Eye Services in Long Beach. Additional regional offices are located in Sacramento, San Diego and Phoenix.

In 1997, more than 450,000 vision care claims were processed by Medical Eye Services. The output represented $40 million in claims payments with 98 percent of this amount distributed to The Eye Care Network's participating providers.

Medical Eye Services has developed a fast and efficient computerized system for determining eligibility and for processing claims. Over the years, technological advances have enabled Medical Eye Services to handle increased volume and to ensure a competitive edge in the vision care industry. An interactive voice response system that verifies benefits seven days a week and an imaging system that scans and processes claims information are the latest advances in administrative capability.

In 1998 Medical Eye Services became a specialized health care service plan. The product line, MES Vision, is marketed to other health care service plans and to employer groups. Bjorkquist, who serves as president and chief executive officer, says, "This new venture will provide another means that will allow both organizations to continue to play a major role in the delivery, administration and management of vision care services."

When The Eye Care Network was formed, the organization had a visionary mission — to provide quality vision care in a cost efficient manner. The plan is working... for seeing is believing.

Bank of America

At the turn of the 20th century, people from all over the world came to California — farmers, wage-earners and small merchants — people with big dreams, but little money. These newcomers were not welcome in most banks of the day which catered primarily to the wealthy, powerful and well-born. But Amadeo Peter ("A.P.") Giannini, born May 6, 1870 in San Jose, California, the son of immigrant farmers, would grow up to change the face of banking in America.

When his father died, A.P.'s mother married a produce commission merchant and the family moved to San Francisco's North Beach. Young A. P. loved working with his stepfather and got up early to sneak down to the docks before school. As he grew older, he traveled around the state buying crops, outwitting competitors and building solid customer relationships. He was so successful he became a partner at age 19. At age 30 found himself on the board of a small San Francisco bank. He suggested the bank begin making loans to workers and small businessmen and serve other immigrants besides Italians. The board refused. A. P. finally stormed out, saying, "I'll start my own bank!" On October 17, 1904, he opened the Bank of Italy in a remodeled North Beach saloon. A.P. and his employees went door-to-door explaining to people what a bank could do for them. They responded, and Bank of Italy grew.

In 1906 the great earthquake and fire devastated San Francisco. Many bankers wanted to stay closed for months, but A.P. knew people needed help immediately. He set up a desk made of two barrels and a plank and began to lend money to rebuild. Borrowers needed only character and calluses as collateral. His judgment paid off. North Beach was the first area of the city to be rebuilt. A.P. said, "We didn't lose a dollar, and we gained thousands of new friends."

A. P. created a branch system to gather resources from around the state and channel them to local communities as needed. Because of this, the bank was able to provide capital to help build whole industries such as agriculture, livestock and motion pictures. It bought bonds to fund municipal improvements for almost every community in California, including the bonds to build the Golden Gate Bridge.

A. P.'s "bank for the little fellows" had staff who spoke diverse languages — Italian, Spanish, Chinese, Russian — to better serve customers. In 1930, A.P. changed the name to Bank of America to reflect his vision of bringing helpful banking to people across the country. Later, the bank introduced Timeplan loans that made installment credit available on a wider scale than ever before.

By the time A. P. died in 1949, his mission of placing capital in the hands of working people had been an enormous success. It was copied so widely that democracy in America had been brought to a new level. A.P.'s legacy of innovation continued in the 1950s, when the bank teamed up with Stanford Research Institute to develop ERMA, the first automated check processing system. In 1959, BofA introduced BankAmericard, which became the first nationally accepted bank credit card.

Today, Bank of America serves customers in 10 Western states and 38 countries around the world. Its Community Development Bank provides special loan programs for affordable housing and small business, both essential to helping communities prosper. HomeBanking through the Internet, 24 hour customer service in six different languages and the largest proprietary ATM network in the U. S. are some of the ways Bank of America continues its rich heritage of service.

Making loans after the 1906 earthquake (Far left)

Building the Golden Gate Bridge, 1936 *Courtesy Golden Gate Bridge Archives*

PMI Mortgage Insurance Co.

Preston Martin had two goals when he founded PMI Mortgage Insurance Co. (PMI) in 1972 — to help working families buy homes and to work in San Francisco. Although Martin eventually went on to other ventures, including a term as Vice Chairman of the Federal Reserve Board of Governors, PMI has fulfilled his dreams. PMI has enabled thousands of families to become homeowners and has emerged as one of the financial district's premier companies.

Under its President and CEO, W. Roger Haughton, a Bay Area native, PMI is now the country's third largest private mortgage insurer, employing 640 people nationwide, with 19 offices in 17 states, and (in 1996) reporting more than $200 million in net income.

For its first 22 years, PMI was a subsidiary of Allstate Insurance Company. In 1995, PMI began a new era as the primary subsidiary of the PMI Group, Inc., a public company. Listed under the trading symbol PMA, The PMI Group Inc.'s combined initial public offering exceeded $1.1 billion and was the sixth largest in the history of the New York Stock Exchange.

PMI's customers are mortgage lenders, including banks, savings and loans, credit unions, mortgage bankers and brokers. By insuring a portion of the mortgages, PMI enables these lenders to offer affordable mortgages to borrowers who make down payments of less than 20 percent of the purchase price. This insurance remains in place when the insured mortgages are sold to investors, like FannieMae or FreddieMac. Consequently, PMI facilitates the sale of loans in the investor market, helping to attract billions of dollars in capital to residential mortgage lending.

PMI has also emerged as one of the leading sources of technology in the mortgage lending industry. Using sound risk management policies, PMI was the first private mortgage insurance company to create an automated system for analyzing mortgages for their relative likelihood of default. The pmiAura[sm] system is licensed to many of the nation's largest lenders and was the first to include a program for analyzing loans insured by the Federal Housing Administration and the Department of Veterans Affairs.

PMI is committed to giving anybody with the desire and the ability to own a home the opportunity. PMI works closely with lenders and community organizations, including Oakland-based Neighborhood Housing Services of America, Inc., to help borrowers in historically under-served communities. As a result, PMI can insure mortgages with down payments as low as three percent of a home's price.

As part of its commitment to home ownership, PMI enthusiastically supports Habitat for Humanity International. Annually, Roger Haughton has led volunteer teams to build houses for the Jimmy Carter Work Projects in the Watts/Willowbrook Community of Los Angeles, Pikeville Kentucky, and the Cheyenne River Sioux Indian Reservation in South Dakota, and to Habitat's 20th Anniversary "Blitz Build" in Americus, Georgia. PMI employees also volunteer with local Habitat branches throughout the U.S.

PMI is committed to helping families achieve the American Dream and proud of its heritage as part of the city where the future happens first.

PMI helps families realize the American Dream of home ownership.
Photo by Dale Higgins

BRE Properties, Inc.

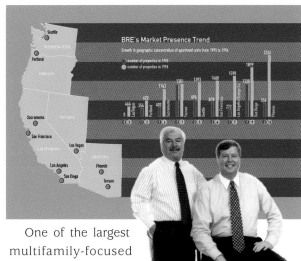

One of the largest multifamily-focused real estate investment trusts (REITs) in the country, BRE Properties is rapidly advancing its mission to become the preeminent owner and operator of apartment communities in key-growth markets of the West. The San Francisco Bay Area plays a prominent role in BRE's past, present and future business plans for building long-term shareholder value.

Founded in San Francisco, BRE began trading as a public company in 1970 as BankAmerica Realty Investors. With an initial market capitalization of $76 million, the company originally implemented a national and diversified property investment strategy.

During the last quarter of a century, BRE listed on the New York Stock Exchange, separated itself from its bank roots, redefined its core business strategies, property focus and target markets to emerge as an acknowledged model of the modern, entrepreneurial REIT.

The result? By mid-1997,

BRE's market capitalization had risen to just under $1 billion and the company's investment strategy reflected a sharpened focus on the ownership and management of quality apartment communities located in above-average growth markets of the West.

Still headquartered in San Francisco, BRE today operates seven regional property management divisions, providing services to roughly 30,000 residents in the metropolitan areas of San Francisco, Sacramento, Los Angeles, San Diego, Phoenix, Tucson, Las Vegas, Seattle and Portland.

Of all of these metros, none has more intriguing apartment demand fundamentals than the San Francisco Bay Area. The Bay Area's renowned quality of life, combined with the region's strong employment growth and constraints on new development, makes this one of the strongest apartment markets in the country.

The growth at BRE is occurring in an era of increasing public awareness of the benefits of REITs as an investment vehicle. The REIT structure has been around since the early 1960s, offering investors the type of diversification and liquidity not generally found in direct real estate ownership. It is the modern, fully-integrated REIT structure of the 1990s, however, that is attracting record levels of investment from both individuals and institutions.

What does the modern REIT look like? Successful REIT structures include all the services required to manage a company's core business "in-house". They have proven management teams with extensive public company experience. They have strong balance sheets and are prudently leveraged. Today's REITs have increasingly large market capitalization and liquidity. They have independent directors whose interests are clearly aligned with those of their fellow shareholders.

BRE has built a platform in San Francisco that includes these characteristics — a platform designed to build a solid foundation for future growth in shareholder value.

Jay W. Pauly, Chief Operating Officer and Frank C. McDowell, President and Chief Executive Officer (Upper left)

The Varandas, a 282-unit apartment community in the San Francisco Bay Area's Union City

Red Hawk Ranch, a 453-unit apartment community in the San Francisco Bay Area city of Fremont (Bottom left)

Scheidegger Trading Co., Inc.

In 1925, when Christian Scheidegger, a young Swiss entrepreneur, first opened the doors of his general store in Medan, Indonesia, he began a tradition of buying, selling, and trading that continues to this day under the Scheidegger name. Christian's store functioned like a modern department store and more — he sold bicycles, cookware, rugs, lamps, automobiles, cameras, and many other commodities that helped improve the daily lives of his fellow citizens.

Today, the company that started in his name, continues trading in much the same way but on an international scale. Scheidegger Trading Co., Inc., located in the city's financial district, exports hundreds of food items, health and beauty products, confectionery and bakery ingredients to its customers along the Pacific Rim, from Japan to Australia.

The family business, firmly anchored in Europe

since 1956 as Scheidegger B.V. in Amsterdam, the Netherlands, and in Asia since 1925, decided it was time to establish a base of operations in the U.S.A. Bjorn Scheidegger opened the San Francisco office in 1981 with the help of Mimi Murphy, now vice-president, and over the years has increased its staff to 14 highly motivated and multilingual people. Between them, they speak seven foreign languages — Mandarin, Cantonese, Japanese, Tagalog, Dutch, Indonesian, and Spanish — multinational professionals dealing with the complexities of international trade.

Scheidegger San Francisco is proud of the fact that most of its exports are sourced from American manufacturers and that it has helped promote American products in Asia. Through participation in trade fairs in Shanghai, Seoul, Tokyo, and Hong Kong, Scheidegger has brought Oregon-grown maraschino cherries to China and Korea, and California figs, raisins, and prunes to Japan and Indonesia. The search for new and exciting products to market overseas goes on!

While the success of Scheidegger's business relies heavily on hi-tech communications, it still adheres to an old principle as well: meeting the customer in person. The Scheideggers are dedicated to understanding the business of its overseas partners and learning about their country's needs. This requires investment in time and travel but is the only way of building a long-term, solid relationship. Now, more than 70 years after Christian Scheidegger extended his hand to everyone who walked into his store, his successors carry on this tradition.

Scheidegger's annual sales of $25 million attest to its extensive knowledge of the markets in which it operates, its hard work, and a philosophy of doing business on a personal yet international scale. While intent on playing a significant trading role in Asia and its emerging markets, Scheidegger, in the 21st century, is poised and ready to explore new markets in the same entrepreneurial spirit and with similar enthusiasm as its founder.

Christian Scheidegger and family, at their general store in Medan, Indonesia, circa 1925.

Sakura Bank Ltd.

In Japan, the flowering cherry blossoms — called sakura — have long been a symbol of growth, renewal, and prosperity. For this reason, Sakura Bank chose this name to represent its own commitment to the success and achievements of an ever-expanding and an ever-changing global marketplace.

Sakura Bank was formed from the merger of two large Japanese commercial banks — Mitsui Bank and Taiyo Kobe Bank — in 1990. The bank provides a full range of financial services to individuals and corporations around the world. With subsidiaries and affiliates in Asia, Oceania, America, Europe and Middle East, the company has become a major resource in the expansion of commercial enterprises and local economies. Sakura Bank offers its services to new and established businesses, and throughout its global network, helps finance a variety of industries. The company also works in tandem with other banking institutions, providing vital information and advice to prospective investors, builders, buyers and sellers.

The history of Sakura Bank can be traced back to the era of samurai warriors when Mitsui Exchange House was established in 1683, in the ancient city of Edo — now Tokyo. By the 1870s, Japan had stepped into the modern era and had opened its trading business to markets around the world. To meet the challenge, the Exchange House was transformed into the first private commercial bank in Japan — Mitsui Bank — in 1876. The bank was a pioneer in international operations. Over the years, it achieved a distinguished record as one of Japan's leading financial institutions.

Mitsui Bank and Taiyo Kobe Bank (another major corporation that had served the financial needs of Kobe, Tokyo, and cities nationwide) decided to broaden their own base of operations through merger. The new bank changed its corporate name to Sakura Bank in 1992. Sakura Bank now works as the financial core of the Mitsui Group — one of Japan's largest industrial groups, holding such prominent companies as Mitsui & Company, Toyota and Toshiba.

Sakura Bank opened its San Francisco office in 1991, and continues to provide comprehensive financial services to numerous Bay Area businesses. With its extensive knowledge and experience in the Asian-Pacific Rim, the company has gained increasing prominence among local investors and other institutions. Sakura Bank is well poised for the 21st century, showing itself as a leader in the burgeoning world of global economics.

World Headquarters Building, Sakura Bank Limited, Tokyo, Japan

Thomas F. White & Co., Inc.

A reputation for dependability and customer service, combined with the pioneering use of information technology, has enabled Thomas F. White & Company to become one of San Francisco's leading investment firms, offering full service and discount brokerage. Nestled in the city's thriving downtown, Thomas F. White & Company reaches out to institutional and individual clients through a network of brokers and its Websites. Community leaders throughout the United States have come to rely on this firm to grow their cities with municipal bonds, and people and institutions around the world are turning to them to provide financial security through a wide variety of investment vehicles.

Robert Angle, president of Thomas F. White and Co. (Top right)

The attractive business and physical climate of San Francisco lured Thomas White to the Bay Area from Cleveland, Ohio, in the 1960s. In 1978, he opened the first office of Thomas F. White & Company in San Francisco. As the city has grown in the last two decades, the company has expanded to include White Discount Securities, a discount brokerage division, and has a team of over 200 brokers working in 85 offices throughout the United States with continued growth expected. Robert Angle has been in the securities industry for more than 20 years and president of Thomas White since 1991.

Thomas F. White, the company's founder

He moved to San Francisco in the early 1970s after completing graduate school in management.

Thomas F. White and Company still caters to investors in smaller towns and cities, wherever an affluent population lives. Their typical office manager lives near a business district and has ties to the local community and leaders. These relationships have helped build Thomas F. White and Company's reputation for service and reliability, enabling them to thrive amidst inevitable economic fluctuations.

By taking advantage of technological developments, such as improvements of personal computers and the Internet, and access to a wealth of local, talented professionals, Thomas F. White & Company has been able to take their "small town approach" and expand their business throughout the United States and worldwide. Web pages are offered in a variety of languages, including Mandarin, Cantonese, Hindi and Vietnamese, and supported by native speakers of the respective languages.

A staff of dedicated Internet programmers affiliated with key technology lenders give brokers up-to-date financial information and provide Thomas F. White & Company with the capability to compete with larger investment firms. In addition to being a member of the Pacific Stock Exchange, the firm is licensed to conduct securities transactions in every state. Equity, fixed income, and option trades are placed through their trading department in San Francisco. They also offer investments in all mutual fund companies and most specialty funds.

The company's ability to take advantage of new technology makes them an incubator for new aspects of the securities business. Its forward-looking approach, combined with the more than two decades of experience of all senior managers, should keep Thomas F. White & Company in the forefront of San Francisco's securities industry for years to come.

Partners

San Francisco's

MANUFACTURING

COMPANIES ARE KNOWN

WORLDWIDE FOR

PRODUCING EXCEPTIONAL

GOODS FOR INDIVIDUALS

AND INDUSTRY.

Manufacturing

Win Fashion, Inc.

Garment manufacturing has always played, historically and culturally, a vital role in San Francisco. As a city and county industry, creating jobs and income, it is second only to tourism (a broad category which includes hotels and restaurants). Joining the ranks of such local powerhouses as Levi Strauss and The Gap, a new leader in the garment industry has emerged: Win Fashion, Inc., founded by married partners, Jimmy Quan and Anna Wong.

Choosing a name which represented a steadfast belief in the power of positive thinking, Win Fashion, Inc. was launched in 1989 in the largely industrial area South of Market, at 6th and Folsom Streets.

Win Fashion, Inc. started with 15 employees. The first local manufacturer to use automatic thread cutting machines to replace the laborious process of scissor trimming by hand, others eventually would follow their lead.

At the end of that first year, the business grew to 75 employees and generated an income in excess of $1 million.

In 1990, cutting and pressing were added. This process of building a business — buying the best machinery and adding services which in turn created jobs and increased employee productivity — became their formula for success.

By 1992, the operation had developed into a full service package which offered its customers cutting, sewing, finishing, shipping and delivery. A night shift

was added; the factory operating 24 hours a day to meet the increased demand. By the end of the year, sales were posted in excess of $5 million.

In 1993, Anna Wong started Wins of California, Inc., the focus of which would be on servicing the major fashion manufacturers. Deciding to take their business to a corporate level, local management expert, Bob Gerson, was brought on as Senior Vice President to develop global marketing. Employees now numbered 350, and earnings soared ten-fold.

In 1996, the adoption of the NAFTA agreement opened up free trade to Mexico and much controversy arose as to how American jobs would be affected. Win Fashion, Inc. opened up a processing factory in Tijuana. As a result of increased sales amounting to over $10 million, 150 additional jobs were created in San Francisco. Today,

Win Fashion, Inc. lives up to its name with 600 employees (a number that is expected to rise to 1,000 in two years) and $20 million in forecasted sales. There are now four factories (in excess of 150,000 square feet) in prime city locations, serving thousands of loyal customers worldwide.

Factory visits are encouraged. A free tour will be arranged for anyone who requests one. The factories are light, airy, and spacious. All work stations contain state-of-the art equipment, fully automated and computerized for ease of movement and operator safety resulting in a low absentee and injury rate.

At this corporation, the concept of career advancement has been introduced to the garment worker. Every employee has the potential to be trained for a higher position as a supervisor, department head, or designer.

The success of this employee incentive program, along with corporate support of the Garment 2000 recruitment and training program at City College, has extended the garment business to the next generation.

The corporate business philosophy is one of excellence in all areas, from the quality of thread on up. Cutting corners at the expense of consumer satisfaction is never tolerated. The customer deserves a well constructed garment that's long lasting.

Highly specialized computer equipment scans the design of the desired garment and creates the pattern, grading it for the various sizes. Copied for mass production, a sophisticated machine automatically cuts layers of fabric to the exact specifications.

This year their own designer label will be sold in retail locations starting locally and then expanding to fashion centers around the world. This line is to be called Wins, Made in San Francisco. The concept is that every garment sold in the Wins stores will be made entirely in San Francisco.

The corporation plans to open up the factories to the public as a bona fide tourist attraction to promote the historic local garment industry and to give workers the credit they have earned through generations of fine craftsmanship and service.

San Francisco easily lends itself to attracting customers as it represents a flawless combination of the best of both worlds — business and pleasure. The factories are 10 minutes from the airport and minutes away from the finest sights, hotels, and restaurants. Look for that Made in San Francisco label. As part of the Win Fashion, Inc. family, you may expect nothing less than quality, value, and service.

George Lithograph

W. T. George founded the George Reproduction Co., specializing in high-speed short-run reproduction.

Delivering the product — circa 1940. (Far right)

A pressman operates one of George's presses in the 1940s. (Bottom center)

Graphic arts technology has changed dramatically since 1925, the year William T. George established his printing company in downtown San Francisco. George Lithograph has continually adapted its business to this ever-changing technology — and has survived and thrived while many other veteran printing firms have faded from the San Francisco market.

George Lithograph is one of the largest commercial printers in the Bay Area and is the preeminent technical documentation printer in Northern California. Throughout its almost 75 years in business, the company has pioneered a broad range of technologies from an early photo-lithography process to current state-of-the art computerized information retrieval systems. But while its technology has changed, the company continues to print corporate brochures, manuals, newsletters and other materials in relatively small quantities and in an unusually rapid turnaround time.

George Lithograph produces essential graphics materials that its customers use to explain their products and run their organizations. These jobs are of a short-lived nature and need to be updated frequently, and the revised copies must be produced promptly and efficiently. Among its many commissions, the company produces computer hardware and software manuals, educational materials, data sheets, directories, news-letters, price lists, training manuals and brochures for large and medium-sized corporations and non-profit organizations.

Those customers include some of the best known Bay Area-based corporations, including Hewlett-Packard, Pacific Telesis, AT&T, Bank of America, Chevron, Apple, Blue Shield of California, PG&E, Cisco Systems, Computer Curriculum Corporation and Genentech. George Lithograph strives to provide the highest quality of service, ensuring that its customers receive their data in a legible and usable format that is economically produced.

W. T. George was a leader in creating technologies to produce short-run, short-term materials. George was a civil engineer in Dillon, Montana and made that state's first section map. In 1917, during World War I, he enlisted in an engineering battalion based in San Francisco.

He was eventually transferred to France, where he was placed in charge of the 42nd Division Area map reproduction unit. While there, he learned a new printing process which combined lithography and photography to produce maps. The new process enabled military mapmakers to turn out local raid maps in small quantities and in short order.

George marveled at the skill and precision of the French lithographic craftsmen. With permission from then- Colonel Douglas MacArthur, George further studied reproduction methods in French and American civil and

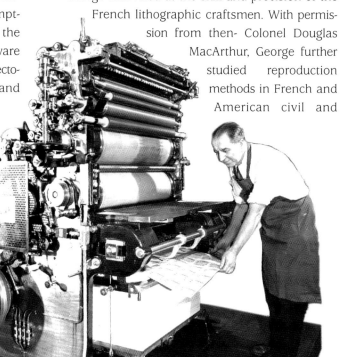

military plants. During his two months of travel and study, he found that photography and lithography were being combined in novel ways. He resolved that after the war he would go back home and apply this photo-lithography process to produce short-run low priced civilian print jobs.

George continued to experiment with the process after the war, when he worked for the Clason Map Co. and Smith-Brooks Printing Co. in Denver, and at printing companies in Los Angeles and San Francisco.

In November 1925, George founded his own firm, George Reproduction Co., which specialized in lithographing letter-size copies in runs of 50, 100 and 500 copies each, instead of the 25,000 copies which had previously been considered a minimum job order. George's pioneering efforts quickly earned his company a specialized niche in the field of high-speed short-run reproduction.

Throughout the years, George continued to test other new printing processes. In 1930, for example, his company was the first to use cold type composition to prepare railroad tariff forms.

W.T.'s son, Don George, a pilot in Italy during World War II, joined his father's company after the war. Under Don's direction, the company continued to apply the latest graphic arts technology to serve the needs of its clients.

In 1948, George Reproduction Co. entered the composition field by using IBM electric typewriters for composition. By the 1950s, the company had purchased the first prefecter press in the Western United States, and used the most up-to-date collators and other equipment to speed its work. It was also one of the first companies to use Xerography commercially for short-run printing. During the 1950s, a company brochure boasted that George Reproduction Co. had the press capacity to produce 3.5 million letter-size sheets each day, and was at its

customers' service for 14 hours a day.

The company throughout the years has devised new printing processes that are tailor-made to fit the specific needs of its clients. In the 1950s, George Reproduction Co. and the Bank of America developed a micro-encoding system to track checks.

A decade later, Don George developed a system for overnight and nightly production of the telephone intercept directories using computerized typesetting from magnetic tape and rapid production of press plates from microfilm. The company held a U.S. patent for an automated plate maker. Using this new equipment, George printed a daily phone book update for Pacific Telephone operators, for more than twenty years.

George Reproduction Co. moved to a new plant on Howard Street in 1946, staffed mainly by World War II veterans who had served in lithography units during the war. Three years later, it relocated to a larger plant on Main Street, which was later torn down when a freeway was built in the area. The company grew rapidly in the post-war years, with more than $1 million worth of sales by 1956. George Reproduction also increased its staff from 56 to 102 employees between 1946 and 1956.

The company in 1951 moved to a three-story plant at 217 Second Street. The first floor of the plant contained a bindery, press department and shipping area; the art, layout, plate making and camera departments were on the second floor. Executive offices were located on the third floor, along with a sun porch and recreation areas for employees.

In 1959, George Reproduction Co. was acquired by J. Curtiss Taylor and

The plant at 128 Main Street, where George was located from 1949 until 1951.
(Top left)

One of the presses used in the early 1950s

J. Curtiss Taylor (left), and his brothers Spaulding (second from left) and David (right) acquired George Reproduction Co. in 1959. The brothers' father, John D. Taylor (third from left), transformed The Clement Co. from a regional plant in western New York to a major national firm.

his brothers, David and Spaulding. The Taylor family owned J.W. Clement, for decades among the largest publication printers in the United States, printing *Time, Life, Sports Illustrated, Newsweek, Sunset* and *Readers Digest* and large volume commercial printing of telephone directors and Automobile Club tour books. The Taylors' grandfather and father transformed The Clement Co. from a regional plant in western New York to a major national firm with operations in Los Angeles (Pacific Press) and San Francisco (Phillips & Van Orden).

David Taylor was president of the newly acquired company from 1959 to 1966. J. Curtiss Taylor worked for Pacific Press and George Lithograph in Los Angeles in the 1960s before he moved to San Francisco to assume responsibility for the company from his brother David.

When the Taylor family purchased the printing company, George's annual sales were less than $2 million. Building on the company's reputation for rapid print production of statistical data for its clients, J. Curtiss Taylor grew annual sales to $30 million by the end of 1996.

During his 26 year tenure as president and chairman of George, J. Curtiss Taylor invested heavily in the company's technological and intellectual assets to provide his clients expertise in data management. His foresight gave the company a considerable advantage over its competitors.

In 1962, the firm's name was changed to George Lithograph. The company underwent other changes in the 1960s. It remodeled its plant at 217 Second Street in 1964, but as the company grew that plant was not large enough to accommodate its needs. George Lithograph moved to a six-story plant at 650 Second Street in September 1966. The new plant, four blocks south of its former location, contained a total of 53,400 square feet of space.

The building at 217 Second Street was

The three-story plant at 217 Second Street, George's home from 1951 until 1966.

rededicated to focus on high-volume short-run black-and-white printing and named AGS in order to give that operation its own identity. AGS was a precursor to "quick printing," which would later become an important segment of the printing industry. George Lithograph has continued to adapt new computerized technology to the needs of its customers. In the late 1970s, the company launched a sales campaign designed to increase its sales to the rapidly growing high-tech industry located south of San Francisco. The campaign emphasized George's sophisticated typesetting abilities and its investment in the latest technology.

George also created a proprietary software system which enabled it to typeset documents at low cost for its Silicon Valley high-tech customers. This software merged text and data base information directly from a client's office into George's typesetting output facility.

In the 1980s, the company worked with Apple Computer to design a new software program that transferred computer screen images to paper simply, inexpensively and with a good quality reproduction. George also developed new computerized reproduction technology for a then-relatively unknown software company called Microsoft.

George Lithograph similarly partnered with Hewlett-Packard to develop technology for printing barcodes. This process has made George a leader in barcode technology. The company can print and barcode numerous products, including individual labels, automated packing slips and pallet tags.

Once again, George outgrew its building, so it moved to a new 50,000 square-foot facility in Brisbane, 15 miles south of San Francisco. The move improved manufacturing efficiency and enabled the company to better serve its growing roster of Silicon Valley customers.

In 1984, George Lithograph printed the Democrat Convention Booklet and delivered it to convention delegates who were meeting at the George Moscone Convention Center in San Francisco. Today, George Lithograph provides total corporate document management for its clients. George offers complete project management, including warehousing and inventory maintenance, printing on-demand, binding, inventory fulfillment, shipping and distribution. It helps clients create customized electronic databases and multimedia information systems. It is a host on the Internet, providing modem access for file transmission.

George Lithograph maintains sophisticated computer systems that can immediately access memory for storage and retrieval of anything from a business card to a manual. One of its computers can store one trillion bits of information online.

George's technical specialists help clients evaluate their workflow systems and recommend hardware and software programs that can help customers archive, prepare and retrieve

data more efficiently. The company retains its long-standing commitment to inventing and applying new techniques that will help clients reduce lead times, shorten production cycles and reduce information delivery costs.

George Lithograph's Quality Assurance Program ensures that it delivers the results its clients expect and deserve. In 1996, the company received its ISO 9002 registration, attesting to its commitment to a well managed quality program. George also offers a Client Education Program, providing technical seminars to help clients maximize their productivity.

These and other programs have earned George Lithograph a coveted membership in the International Printers Network, a group of printers re-nowned for their technical sophistication and high quality. In October 1996, George was the first California company invited to join the prestigious organization.

In February 1997, a management team lead by George's current president, William P. Sloan, purchased the company from the Taylors. Sloan and his team pledged to carry on the company's long tradition of providing exemplary service and unequaled leadership in the use of advanced technologies to manage time-critical information for its clients.

George's corporate headquarters at 460 Valley Drive in Brisbane, adjacent to the company's production, warehouse, fulfillment and office facilities.
(Top left)

These state-of-the-art digital presses were installed in the Brisbane plant in 1996 and 1997. George's ability to adapt its business to ever-changing technology has enabled the company to survive while many competitors vanished long ago.

Delivering the product - 1997.

San Francisco Blues, Inc.

Both hostess and guest are attired in denim and print outfits from the 1996 *Tea for Two* collection. (Top right)

Everything this young urban cowboy is wearing from the *Sundance* collection was designed by San Francisco Blues for Fall 1997.

One of the great axioms of marketing is "Find a need and fill it." Adhering to that truism, Natalie Mallinckrodt, who saw a need for more brightly colored and sophisticated children's clothing, launched Golden Rainbow in 1982.

Now known as San Francisco Blues, Inc., the company is a leading manufacturer of children's designer coordinated sportswear. The company sells nationwide to upscale department stores including Nordstrom, Saks Fifth Avenue, Bloomingdales, Neiman-Marcus, and to boutiques and specialty stores; it also has distribution in Canada, Europe, the Middle East and Asia. In 1996, the first company-owned outlet store was opened in Gilroy, California. The company had sales of more than $7 million in 1996.

The company's original name, Golden Rainbow, identified with San Francisco by using the Golden Gate Bridge and a rainbow in its colorful trademarked label. The company changed its name in 1996 in overwhelming response to its denim label, San Francisco Blues. This label, introduced in 1987, had become the major line purchased by department stores. Although the company uses other fabrics for treatment and novelties, denim, used in fashionable ways, is the focal point of the line.

The company's launch in 1982 coincided with the growth of the two-income family of the 80s

and the willingness of parents to spend more for stylish children's clothes that reflected their own good taste. But, in the early 90s, recognizing the trend to greater value, the company cut prices by 20 percent while maintaining its high product quality and distinctive styling.

San Francisco Blues creates clothing for newborns to age 10. One chief distinction between San Francisco Blues' clothing and that of its competitors is the fact that the clothing is sized to actual age rather than to specifications set forth in the 1950s. "True to age" sizing allows clothing sized for a 12-month-old to last until the child is 18 months old.

Denim is used in many collections, and together with cotton yarn-dyed flannel plaids, knits and prints, the lines offer children a complete wardrobe. Much emphasis is placed on details such as sewn-down plackets, rolled-up cuffs, adjustable straps, and unique buttons and trims. An extra button is always attached to the cothing so that if one goes missing the garment has another button that matches. The clothing is very durable, designed to go from the dryer to a drawer or hanger — "ready to wear" and easy to maintain.

San Francisco Blues is known for its European-influenced styles and quality detailing, but the roots for such styling are not only found an ocean way, but also in San Francisco itself! San Francisco is a city that attracts artists of all types, for there is something in the environment that fosters creativity. Moreover,

San Francisco is more of a European-type city than a western U.S. city. Thus a blend of San Franciscans' creativity with a sense of European sophistication and culture is reflected in the style of San Francisco Blues' line of clothing.

"Creative environment" is a phrase visitors like to associate with San Francisco Blues' approximately 20,000 square feet office space and warehouse on Brannan Street. The light, airy atmosphere and white walls are indeed conducive to creativity. (The company moved here in 1987, after outgrowing previous office locations on Stillman and Pine Streets.)

Certainly creativity has long been the mainstay of Natalie Mallinckrodt. Mallinckrodt, the company's president and creative director, began designing clothes for Barbie dolls at age 10, and sold them to her sister's friends. She is a graduate of Mills College in Oakland, Calif.; has an M.B.A. from Simmons College in Boston; and has undertaken postgraduate study at both Parson's School of Design and F.I.T. Before starting her own company she worked six years at Levi Strauss & Co. in children's and jeans merchandising. Mallinckrodt was instrumental in developing Childrenswear SF, an association devoted to promoting the innovative childrenswear manufacturers of the Bay Area.

In 1986 the company employed 12 people with Mallinckrodt as the sole designer. In 1990 partner Jeff Zalles, a successful small business entrepreneur, joined the company as vice president and director of sales. Together, Zalles and Mallinckrodt reevaluated the business and developed the strategies that fuel the company's current success. Today, the company has a staff of 42, including two designers, a full-time merchandise manager, and 12 independent sales representatives. The company's employees represent San Francisco's ethnic and cultural diversity.

San Francisco Blues credits its success to two factors. One is its high-quality products. The collections sell well in retail trade, and buyers become repeat customers. They return to buy more clothes, saying that their children get more compliments on San Francisco Blues' clothing than that of other manufacturers. The fit is excellent, and a child's clothing often gets passed down to a brother, sister or friend. The second factor for the company's success is quality customer service. It ships on time and goes beyond customers' expectations.

In 1994 San Francisco Blues was awarded an "Earnie," the highest accolade in children's apparel, for its designs.

Education is an important ingredient of San Francisco Blues' operation. To this end, the company promotes internships. Students from area colleges such as UC-Davis, Skyline College, and West Valley College come in two or three days a week in order to earn credit for first-hand learning. Some interns have gone on to become employees. Canada College students come for tours, and due to the company's liaison with schools of international business, students in France and Belgium come to to San Francisco Blues to spend six months gaining first-hand knowledge of the industry.

Natalie Mallinckrodt is on the advisory board of Skyline College and addresses the merchandising class twice a year on the childrenswear industry.

In recognition of being based in San Francisco and of its industry, San Francisco Blues donates clothing each year to the San Francisco Clothing Bank, an agency that helps homeless children.

These boys are outfitted in San Francisco Blues' own flannel design and sherpa from the 1997 *Stadium* collection.

This colorful denim and fabric outfit represents the *California Sunflower* collection, introduced in 1994.

Schlage Lock Company

Ernest Schlage and Marron Kendrick, sons of the founders, ran Schlage Lock until 1974, when the company was purchased by Ingersoll-Rand. (Top right)

Schlage Lock produced a special handcrafted key to the city of San Francisco, which has been presented to many dignitaries, including Her Royal Majesty Queen Elizabeth II of England. (Below)

The Schlage name is known all over the world.

A coating called ULTIMA gives Schlage products the unprecedented durability. It resists corrosion and is guaranteed for 25 years not to tarnish, rust, cloud, or discolor. (Bottom left, opposite page)

Like many of America's most successful businesses, the Schlage Lock Company grew out of a dynamic partnership. Two extraordinary men — one a brilliant inventor, the other an astute businessman — joined forces in San Francisco in 1925 and found they made a solid team. Their company would one day revolutionize the door hardware industry, providing locks that secure untold millions of doors around the world, including those in the White House. The men were Walter Schlage and Charles Kendrick.

Walter Reinhold Schlage grew up in a small town in central Germany called Thuringia. His father recognized his talent for mechanical engineering early in his life and enrolled him as an apprentice in the Carl Zeiss Optical Works in Jena, one of Germany's finest technical schools at the time. He was only 14 years old.

Schlage was an exceptional student, but when he graduated four years later, he was ready for an adventure. He moved to London, where he worked for less than a year as a scientific instrument maker, then booked passage for the United States and found a job with Western Electric. Still curious about the world, he soon set sail again, as an engineer on a ship headed for Brazil, the West Indies, and Central America. He eventually worked his way to California, then to San Francisco, where he settled in 1905, once again working with Western Electric, this time at their new Oakland plant.

Schlage also rented a small shop on Bush Street in San Francisco, and for twelve years, he worked at his job during the day, then went to his shop at night and worked on his inventions — most of which involved door mechanisms. An idea occurred to him when he considered that the first thing a person does when they come home to a dark house is turn on the light. But to do that they have to find the switch on the wall. He reasoned that a better place for a push

button switch was in the door knob, already in the person's grasp. In 1909, he received his first patent for a door knob with a button in it that turned lights on and off.

From there, he saw that a door knob button could also be used to lock and unlock a door from the inside, without using a key. To create such a lock, he knew he had to find a way of fitting all the parts into two small cylinders. He also knew that this lock would require a much finer mechanism than in any existing door lock, especially if it were to be mass produced. He worked at the problem until he created what became known in the trade as the "cylindrical" or "bore-in" lock, known popularly as a "button lock." Then he improved on the concept, focusing on making the lock easy to manufacture and easy to install — two features considered vital for commercial success.

In 1920, Schlage left his job at Western Electric to design the tools to manufacture his lock and to start his own company. The company grew quickly from an initial six people to 100 employees on two shifts producing nearly 20,000 locks a month.

However, Schlage lacked the capital to market his products. In 1925, he was introduced to Charles Kendrick, who owed his fortune to a soap pad patent, and Kendrick became his primary investor. With Kendrick's capitol, the company purchased land in Visitacion Valley, a neighborhood in the southeastern corner of San Francisco, near where the Cow Palace and 3COM Park are today. On June 25, 1926, the first part of the present Schlage Lock plant on Bayshore Boulevard was formally dedicated and declared open for business.

Kendrick became President of Schlage Lock Company in 1927, and the Schlage-Kendrick alliance continued until Walter Schlage's death in 1946. "Schlage and I found ourselves an ideal working team," recalled Kendrick in his memoirs. "Walter continued to invent cylindrical locks for every purpose until the company had a full line — large and small, heavy and light; locks fitted for modest homes, fine residences, schools, hotels, office buildings, and so on."

Walter Schlage's son, Ernest, turned out to have mechanical aptitude as well. During high school, and while getting a degree in Mechanical Engineering at Stanford, he spent two months each summer working at the Schlage factory. After graduation, he worked for the company for a year, then went to graduate school at MIT. He returned to the Schlage Lock, and after his father's death became Director of Research, obtaining over one hundred patents.

Kendrick's son, Marron, joined the business in 1934. Although his formal education was in business and finance, he also had an aptitude for mechanics, and he and Ernest Schlage worked closely, like their fathers had. In 1953, when Charles Kendrick became Chairman of the Board of Schlage Lock, Marron Kendrick became President.

Schlage Lock Company began a period of expansion in the early 1950s. The goal was to offer a full line of door hardware, so that the company could bid on large construction projects. They acquired California Lock Company to add a low-cost lock to the product line; Peabody Company for custom door and luxury hardware (used mainly at the main entrance to buildings); Louis C. Norton (LCN) Closers, Inc.; and Von Duprin, a firm that had been making "panic bars," used on doors in schools and other public buildings, since 1916. By 1964, when Schlage provided the locks for the Pan American Building in New York City (the largest commercial office structure in the world at the time), the company was at the forefront of the door lock industry.

When his father died, in 1970, Marron Kendrick became Chairman of the Board of Schlage, and the family began looking for a company to acquire the business. In 1974, Schlage was bought by Ingersoll-Rand, a Fortune 150 manufacturer.

Innovations have helped Schlage Lock remain an industry leader. In 1986, they introduced two products: KeepSafer, a do-it-yourself wireless home security system, and the Intellis electronic locking system, which revolutionized security in hotels and motels by replacing the traditional room key with a programmed card. In 1994, Schlage developed a new coating for door hardware called ULTIMA, that gives its products unprecedented durability.

To better serve its customers, the Schlage Lock Company divided into two divisions in 1995: the Schlage Commercial Lock Division, which provides locks for schools, hotels, prisons, and other commercial buildings, and the Schlage Residential Lock Division, which manufacturers locks for homes. Both new companies are now headquartered in Colorado Springs, Colorado. The San Francisco location continues today primarily as a high volume metal stamping operation for component parts, that are then shipped to various plants for assembly.

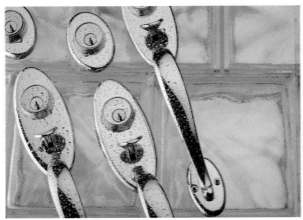

The Schlage office in San Francisco houses one of the largest historical lock collections outside of the Smithsonian.

A few of the San Francisco landmarks secured with Schlage locks:

TransAmerica Pyramid
Museum of Modern Art
Bank of America Building
University of California at
 San Francisco
California Palace of the Legion
of Honor Hills Bros. Plaza
Chevron World Headquarters
Chronicle Newspaper Building
Golden Gate Bridge
Schools in the San Francisco
 Unified School District

Color 2000

Sai Chiang, President (left) and John H. Hall, Vice President accepting an award from the city of San Francisco

Sunny Leong, Production Supervisor (right) and next to him is Sai Chiang, President, giving instructions on color correction (Far right)

Color 2000 is an innovative digital photo lab offering advanced imaging solutions. Their success story truly reflects the diversity of the San Francisco community and Color 2000's contribution to promoting commerce. The company was founded in 1975 by two immigrants, John H. Hall and Sai Chiang. When John Hall's grandfather immigrated to San Francisco in 1856 from China, he opened one of the first herb stores in the Western United States. As John was making plans for its 100th anniversary, the McCarthy era brought disaster for the family. In 1954, without warning, U.S. Treasury agents drove a truck up to his door, confiscated his entire stock, boarded up the store, and charged him with a felony — trading with the enemy! The United States Embargo Act prohibited trade with China, although John bought all his herbs from Canada. Since some of the Canadian herbs originally came from China, he was convicted and financially ruined. With little left but a camera, John took photography classes at San Francisco State University and opened his own photography studio. Dissatisfied with the quality of the color prints he was getting from local photo labs, he decided to branch out into lab work himself. This is how he met Sai Chiang in 1974.

Sai immigrated from Hong Kong when he was 14. He then served in the U.S. Marine Corps in Viet Nam, but after the war, no one would hire him. Needing to earn a living, armed only with his keen instincts about popular culture, Sai managed to obtain the exclusive rights to the images of a little-known martial artist. Coupled with his natural flair for marketing, Sai was thus instrumental in initiating the Bruce Lee poster phenomenon that later swept the country. Looking to produce the best quality posters possible, Sai was introduced to the color expert at a local lab, John Hall. The two became fast friends, and soon decided to start their own business, Color 2000.

In 1980, Color 2000 entered a rapid growth phase. Key to the success of this transition was Elnora Lee, the final partner on the management team. A native of San Francisco, formally educated at U.C. Berkeley, and a teacher at San Francisco State University, Elnora's experience in business organization and personnel development was the perfect complement to John's technical expertise and Sai's marketing skills. Sharing the same core values as John and Sai, she formalized and expanded the company philosophy that forms the basis for their principles of doing business.

Color 2000 is committed to providing job opportunities for inexperienced and hard to place job seekers such as recent immigrants, students, new college graduates, senior citizens, and the disabled. This philosophy was directly influenced by the experiences of it's founders. Their experience with unfair discrimination led to their desire to provide equal opportunity for others. Their experience with political injustice led to their committment to fairness and integrity. Over the years, the three partners, together with their team of dedicated staff, have made Color 2000 an internationally respected company. An award-winning digital photo lab, they were selected by professionals in their field as one of the top ten photo labs in the United States. Using the

latest photographic and computer imaging technologies, they produce beautiful pictures for a variety of clients; from wall-size murals and banners for major retail stores, to breathtaking reproductions for museums and visitor centers to graphic displays for trade shows and sports stadiums. With their diverse team succeeding in a highly competititve field, Color 2000 uniquely contributes to San Francisco's rich history and thriving commerce.

Partners

TRANSPORTATION, SHIPPING, ENERGY, AND TRADING COMPANIES KEEP PEOPLE, POWER, PRODUCTS, AND INFORMATION CIRCULATING THROUGHOUT THE REGION AND THE WORLD.

Networks

Aero Special Delivery

Carl Sparks served as a gunner on merchant marine ships in World War Two. One ship on which he served was sunk while making its way as part of a convoy to Murmansk, Russia. Fortunately, Sparks survived that adventure. One day in 1945 he had just been discharged from the U.S. Navy at the old Santa Rita Naval Base in Alameda County. He was hitching a ride across the San Francisco-Oakland Bay Bridge to hunt for work in San Francisco. A lady driving a Dependable Delivery truck happened to give him a lift. When he told her he'd just been discharged from the Navy and was seeking work, she hired him on the spot. The rest would become special delivery history.

Young Sparks had ambitions of his own. By the end of 1945, he and a partner embarked on a business venture and opened Sparkie's Special Delivery Service. The history of the delivery service and others like it offers a snapshot of the evolution of San Francisco and Bay Area businesses. Using couriers on foot, bicycles, and Harley Davidson motorcycles, Sparkie's picked up and delivered orders as soon as possible — the hallmark of a special delivery system. Its motorcycle fleet zipped everywhere, up and down the hills of San Francisco and across the Bay Bridge, carrying heavy wood-framed metal typeset pages to printers, metal plate engravings for advertisements, photographs, and newsruns — news services such as International News Service received news by teletype, then typed up press releases. Those press releases, which nowadays are faxed instantly from office to office, would be speeded to all the newspapers and news agencies by special delivery, to make the next edition of the newspaper. Doctors and lawyers were major clients, generating a constant stream of documents and specimens and medicines to be picked up and delivered quickly. Special delivery was part of the way newspapers, advertisers, and many other businesses functioned day-to-day — and Sparkie's and later Aero's fleet of motorcycles carried the constant flow of items on which they depended. Motorcycles were the best means of conveying special delivery goods, in the days before small pickup trucks were widely manufactured.

In late 1949 Carl Sparks sold his interest in Sparkie's. Aero Special Delivery came into being officially on tax day — April 15, 1950.

Aero opened shop on a shoestring with two motorcycles, one pickup truck, and six employees. During the first month in business the company grossed $350. But business grew briskly and by the end of 1959, Aero was earning gross revenues of $18,500 a month. Special delivery services formed an integral part of the way the city of San Francisco operated and the Bay Area is one of the most developed nationwide for the use of special delivery services.

Aero's growth paralleled San Francisco's post-War development and reflected changing technology.

To better serve clients and compete in the market, Aero adapted two-wheel motorcycles, designing and building its own sidecars with tail gates, hand trucks, and two-way radios. Using the motorcycles with specially designed sidecars, Aero could deliver anything from rolls of documents to oil drums. In the mid-60s, small trucks replaced the Harley Davidsons.

When Aero gave its delivery drivers two-way radios, The Wall Street Journal wrote up this industry first on its front page on November 12, 1956.

Another industry first, a milestone in how technology transformed and speeded up the business, was the development of special delivery computer software. In the days of keypunch systems, each

Carl and Lee Sparks, 1948

special delivery order had to be hand written and handed to the proper dispatcher. Later it was hand-priced and input by a keypunch operator. Years of work went into developing the means to enable computers to price orders, and so automate one of the most important and time-consuming aspects of the business. A major break-through came when computer memories had expanded enough and become fast enough to store all encoded addresses in the Bay Area, letting the computer instantly rate orders as they were being booked, but also consider the weight of the delivery and the type of service requested.

Comsis of Santa Clara worked with Aero for years, finally developing a viable software in the 1980s. Aero went on-line with its special delivery software in 1985 and sold Comsis the right to market it.

All rate scales were stored in the computer and with the telephone number used as the identifying key, all special instructions could be entered. Most delivery companies are now using the software first developed at Aero. The majority of special delivery services that have gone into and out of business in the Bay Area since the 1950s have had their roots in Aero, which continues to grow.

Since its inception, Aero has been the biggest special delivery company in San Francisco. Currently, the firm employs 300 and grosses over $1 million a month. The business dream of a young man just out of the Navy has come a long way.

From humble beginnings, the company has blossomed into Northern California's largest special delivery service, with branch offices in Santa Clara, Fremont, Pleasanton, Rohnert Park, and Sacramento, and delivery vehicles at every location.

Top clients remain artists, photographers, advertising agencies, printers, most city departments, and even the mayor's office, while Aero delivers vast amounts of office supplies, pallet-sized loads of printed materials, and telephone and computer parts, in addition to legal documents, medicines and specimens for attorneys and physicians. The company has also given the city of San Francisco one of its most colorful characters — the bicycle messenger.

At one point, the city fathers threatened to close the Financial District to delivery trucks after mid-afternoon because of congestion. Aero countered by developing a special bicycle and trailer for making deliveries of as much as 300 pounds. The trailer detached from the bike and doubled as a handtruck.

Serving 5,500 clients, Aero Special Delivery daily completes hundreds of miles worth of trips in San Francisco alone, making 2,500 special deliveries a day, 12,500 a week, 687,500 a year.

Aero's owners are members of San Francisco's Chamber of Commerce. Each year, the company sponsors the bicycle messengers races.

Technology is changing rapidly industry-wide and Aero remains at the forefront with a computerized dispatching system. Prospective clients can browse Aero's Internet web page. Aero constantly refines warehousing and logistics, and the use of bobtail and tractor trailer trucks to meet challenges. Meanwhile the new generation of special delivery software available to the industry can steer a delivery truck to any address by using the Global Positioning System (GPS), with electronic proof of delivery and signature facsimiles.

Bicycle and trailer
(Top left)

Aero's motorcycle delivery
fleet, 1958 - 1961.

American Airlines

American Airlines,
Something Special
in the Air.

With Charles Lindbergh as its most notable distant cousin, American Airlines can claim almost any title it wishes in the history of flying, and find it has again landed safely on the ground. Lindbergh, for instance, was an aviator for Robertson Aircraft of Missouri when that company was consolidated into the original version of American. Carrying mail was the business in those days. However, American quickly envisioned the future of aviation centering on passenger travel. Since then, it has never stopped moving forward.

San Francisco's position in American's hierarchy is not organizationally particularly high, but it serves as an excellent example of the company's commitment to serving its client base not only with air transportation, but by providing additional services to its locally-served communities. In the city by the bay, for instance, American's presence is definitely high profile. Its corporate philosophy of directing charitable aid to the arts and to health issues holds true here too.

American has been awarded the Cyril Award by the San Francisco Chamber of Commerce for its contributions to the performing arts. It directs more than a quarter of its philanthropic resources toward advancing and preserving national assets. The airline sponsors the Aids Walk and the Race for the Cure, as well as the Susan G. Komen Breast Cancer Foundation. This work, although certainly a boon to its business, exemplifies American's commitment by returning to its customers more than just safe and comfortable travel for their patronage.

Clearly one of the largest airlines in the world, American and its regional airline affiliate American Eagle fly to nearly 300 airports globally. It serves Canada, the United States, Europe, the Caribbean, Latin America, Japan and other exotic and busy destinations. Operating 642 of the youngest jets in the world, it is one of the most seriously competitive airlines, always maintaining and encouraging the newest possible flight technology available. Historically, it has always carefully defined people's flying needs and insured that it possessed the equipment to serve those needs.

It has enjoyed some of the most auspicious leadership of any company in America. Past presidents of American have included Cyrus Rowlett Smith, a former World War II major general in the Air Transport Command, Albert V. Casey, who upon retirement served as Postmaster General of the United States, and Robert L. Crandall, whose most visible claim to fame was the establishment of SABRE, the computerized information system which serves as a standard of communication excellence for the entire international travel industry. Crandall was also selected in 1991 by Financial World as a Silver Award winner in its annual CEO of the year competition recognizing superior business leadership and achievement.

Innovation is a necessity in the airline business and American has consistently lead the way with not only the newest aircraft, but with unique pricing structures and services to its passengers. The above-mentioned SABRE system originated, for instance, as an American only service, but when its potential was realized, American configured it to serve the entire travel industry and effectively marketed it to them. This information management tool secured it a pivotal position in the industry, far beyond its airline base.

Utilizing computers effectively is a hallmark of American's fame and fortune. In Tulsa, Oklahoma, it has installed underground a state-of-the-art private computer network and travel information data base second to none. Over 101,000 computer terminals today in seventy countries connect to this system.

Domestically, American has, with its American Eagle affiliate, provided the same high quality service to commuter flights as enjoyed on big airlines. Attention to such detail increased its local flights of sixty a day to nine cities from one location (Dallas/Fort Worth) to the grand sum of 1,700 flights a day to more than 170 cities in the United States, the Bahamas, and the Caribbean. With a strongly felt presence also in the Far East, American's influence is broadly based.

Its one billionth passenger flew on March 27, 1991. In 1992 it opened officially the Alliance Maintenance and Engineering Base, the first state-of-the-art airline maintenance facility to be built in the United States in over twenty years. AMR Consulting Group is a new subsidiary of American's formed to serve the growing demand for consulting services in airline-related businesses.

Commonplace items in today's travel fare which American helped foster are frequent flyer programs, private VIP lounges, and a wide variety of cargo-related products which serve commercial transport needs. These include such fascinating concepts as: garment-on-hanger shipments, which speed clothing shipments from factory to showroom floors; live animal transportation, including special handling of everything from exotic wildlife to show dogs; perishable shipments, of which the special handling of fruits, vegetables, seafood, and flowers are examples.

On an average day, American Airlines will: receive more than 343,000 reservation calls, handle more than 304,000 pieces of luggage, serve more than 196,000 meals and snacks, fly more than 2,200 flights, transport more than 270 animals and change more than 70 airline tires.

The myriad of details it handles as common place daily occurrences is staggering. But what counts is that wherever you are flying, American is likely to be there with a smiling face and a helping hand. Its

familiar blue and red colors greet you from almost every corner of the world. In the San Francisco area alone, nearly 3,000 employees busy themselves endlessly with the services necessary to please their clients in the complex business of travel.

American meets the demands of business flyers with constant attention to individual needs while always scouring the skies for distantly appearing trends in global transportation. This airline is a lot more than it seems on the surface. When American's people put someone on a plane to somewhere else they are connecting world leaders with other world leaders, doctors with patients, scientists with colleagues, entrepreneurs with allies, movers and shakers with others helping move society forward.

American's ability to have created such a fascinating company is certainly a reflection of its dedication to the needs of worldwide business travelers. Lindbergh would certainly be proud, and so may American be. It is a unique institution, and well deserves the accolades it consistently receives.

American service is tops.

Enron Corp.

As far back as its days as a republic, and ever since, California has been considered a great place for creative, innovative risk takers. This was as true of the gold-seeking '49ers who risked everything in search of fortune as it is today of companies that like to be on the cutting edge. With offices in San Francisco, South San Francisco, Long Beach, and Palm Springs, Enron Corp., one of the largest integrated natural gas and electricity companies in the world, is one such company.

From its state-of-the-art trading floor in Houston, Texas, Enron buys and sells physical and financial energy contracts. (Right)

With a net income of $584 million in 1996, Enron is the top natural gas and electricity wholesale marketer in North America, and the most successful developer of energy infrastructure in the world. It's also becoming one of the largest international suppliers of wind and solar renewable energy. Small wonder, then, that a 1996 Fortune magazine poll described Enron as America's "most innovative company" for the second year in a row.

Although the average Californian may not be aware of the company's name, Enron's involvement in California is both broad and deep. The TransWestern Pipeline Company, which delivers natural gas to California, was part of the group of companies uniting to form Enron in 1986. But even before this merger occurred, Enron had offices in San Francisco in order to deal with state regulatory issues.

Enron Wind Corp.'s innovative Z-46 variable speed wind turbine generator has a rotor with a 160-foot diameter, similar to the wing span of a Boeing 747 aircraft.

Enron has been marketing its services in California for over a decade, primarily in the wholesale business, by supplying natural gas to large utility providers — making it the unseen energy behind Californians' local utility.

Moreover, Portland General Corporation, which recently merged with Enron, was one of the original constructors of the Pacific Northwest-Pacific Southwest intertie in the 1960s, and has been doing business in California for more than thirty years.

In the developing world, new markets are emerging as governments turn toward privatization, especially in the areas of telecommuncations, transportation — and energy. In the western world, with the advent of deregulated gas and electricity, state-owned and private monopolies are giving way to competition. In North America, deregulation will open up a huge $300 billion a year market.

Enron believes that competition will reduce consumer electricity bills by 30 to 40 percent — comparable to a national tax cut of $70 to $80 billion a year. Before deregulation, utilities had no incentive to innovate because they dealt with rate payers who had no alternative choice of providers. With competition, local companies will have to be more responsive to customers' wants and needs. Competition opens the way for providers to develop new products and services. With competition, consumers benefit.

Believing that free markets work better in every case, Enron was at the table from the onset when discussion of deregulating utilities began. In the early 1990s, Enron pushed for the deregulation of the wholesale electricity market. Now, although Enron has been in the electric marketing business for only three years, it is the largest marketer of electric power coming from outside the state into California, and the largest non-regulated marketer of electricity in North America. Enron also pushed to open up the wholesale natural gas market, not only quickly but properly. It was Enron that encouraged regulators to adopt a stance that favored direct access and open markets, providing customer choice for all classes of energy users. Enron is now taking the lead in moving for deregulation of the retail electricity and natural gas markets.

Enron's success and high goals — to become the largest retailer of electricity and natural gas in the U.S., as well as the largest provider of electricity and natural gas in Europe — are guided by this philosophy: "Deregulation means greater freedom. Freedom means consumer choice. Choice means competition. Competition demands creativity — new products and solutions, new savings and services."

Enron has actively worked in 48 states and at the federal level to support deregulation, becoming a key voice in helping establish ground rules for the forthcoming competitive marketplace. In the process it has forged local business relationships that will help Enron move first and fast when full deregulation arrives. Deregulation doesn't mean the end of local distribution utilities. They continue to be of great importance in providing the benefits of competition to customers. As the market changes, Enron will be working with utilities, cooperatives, and municipal entities. Enron is committed to making tomorrow's competitive marketplace viable and strong for everyone.

Implementing this vision, Enron, through competitive processes, has already been chosen as an alliance partner by many California public utilities and municipalities — the Northern California Power Agency, representing fifteen member cities, the city of Palm Springs, and the city of South San Francisco. These choices reflect Enron's record of accomplishment as a power marketer and its leadership role in paving the way for a competitive marketplace.

With the transition to customer choice in the electric utility industry well underway in California, Enron is playing a critical role. Today, Enron continues as a major supplier of natural gas to California, but also plans to expand its marketing efforts to the retail marketplace, too. The same reliable service as a supplier of natural gas to utilities will be offered to all classes of business customers, as well as to residential customers.

With a reputation for creativity, innovation, and "breaking the mold," Enron makes a good fit with California culture. Entering the market as an independent in the electricity business, Enron has played an integral part in opening markets to competition. And, when deregulation of the electricity industry opens up retail competition in California in 1998, Enron is poised to become the market leader in new energy services. Enron recently purchased Zond Wind Energy, renamed Enron Wind Corp., the world's largest producer of wind-powered electrical generation facilities. This purchase, combined with Enron's existing 50 percent interest in the world's second largest solar energy company, Amoco/Enron Solar, makes Enron the leading renewable power company in the world.

Enron will be at the forefront of providing California customers with many choices in products and services. For example, instead of having a worker climb over a fence to read a gas meter, meter-reading may be done through an electronic system within a central office. Customers may also be able to manage their energy costs by scheduling the cost-effective use of major appliances for various times of the day. Customers may also be given "green power" options to receive solar or wind-powered energy in lieu of traditional gas or electrical energy.

Enron is the largest non-regulated marketer of power in North America.

Marine Chartering Co., Inc.

Marine Chartering Co., Inc., one of the leading international ocean transportation companies in the United States, has a significant position in the brokerage of ships and cargoes on the West Coast, in the Pacific Basin, the U.S. Gulf, and in Latin America. It is a diversified shipping company, with headquarters in San Francisco and a branch office in New Orleans. Active in the worldwide brokerage of ships and dry and refrigerated cargoes, Marine Chartering is also involved in sale and purchase brokerage, ship and projects management, and offers experienced consultancy services.

George Kiskaddon, who founded Marine Chartering, was born in Kentucky and grew to manhood in San Diego. He went to sea as soon as he finished high school. At age twenty-four, as first mate on the ammunition-laden Liberty vessel *Margaret Fuller*, Kiskaddon had to take command of the vessel when the captain had a nervous breakdown after some torpedoes broke loose from their lashings. When the command was made permanent, Kiskaddon became one of the youngest masters in the U.S. merchant marine. Later, Kiskaddon became involved with a shipping syndicate in operating a converted LST (Landing Ship Tank) that was slated to bring tomatoes from Mexico to the U.S. However, conversion work delayed the ship's departure and the spring market for tomatoes was missed. Set back but not defeated, Kiskaddon decided to move to New York to learn more about the commercial aspects of the shipping business.

Described as a man who "had an air of restless curiosity about him, supported by a gift of quick analysis," Kiskaddon sought to find a business that could sustain him while setting up an office in California. He formed his own company, Cia. Naviera Rosario S.A., registered in Panama, and with borrowed funds chartered a tanker hauling gasoline and kerosene to Mexico and molasses back to California. Kiskaddon also arranged with Johnson, Walton Steamships, Ltd. of Vancouver to start up a liner service with chartered tonnage from British Columbia to Hawaii. Kiskaddon received enough encouragement about return cargo prospects from Theo. H. Davies & Company, Ltd., of Honolulu, to set up shop on the West Coast. On May 17, 1955, Kiskaddon founded Marine Chartering Co., Inc. in San Francisco as ship-operators, agents, and brokers in a small office at 400 Montgomery Street.

In 1956, Marine Chartering promoted the formation of Pacific Reefer Service to provide transportation for frozen tuna from the West Coast of South America to Terminal Island. Two small refrigerated vessels, the Norwegian flag *Ice Bird* and *Ice Flower*, of 700 tons capacity each, were chartered, and Pacific Reefer Service's frozen tuna transportation began. At this time Dieter Tede, recently arrived in San Francisco, joined Marine Chartering and was sent to Peru to locate sources of tuna that would keep Pacific Reefer Service in business.

A series of German newbuildings replaced the Norwegian ships in 1958, and in 1962 Pacific Reefer Service became Refrigerated Express Service, Inc. As business expanded into the Atlantic, Indian Ocean and the Western Pacific in the 1960s and '70s, Refrigerated Express Service followed the fishing vessels and extended its services throughout the world's oceans.

In 1957, Jacob Nebeling, also a recent hire and appointed vice president of the company, developed a relationship with the German Oetker group on the basis of substantial shipments of sawn lumber from the Pacific Northwest to New Zealand and Australia. On the inbound leg to Los Angeles and San Francisco,

The 701 container *M.S. Polynesia* at Golden Gate Bridge. Managed by Marine Chartering, the *Polynesia* operates between Long Beach/San Francisco and Papeete/Pago Pago/Apia

these vessels brought Volkswagens. The business took on large dimensions, and Capt. A. L. Bleicher and Jorgen With-Seidelin joined Marine Chartering in 1958 to deal with the onslaught. The company also moved to the Alaska Buildng at 310 Sansome Street.

In 1962, Marine Chartering forged an important and lasting link with Interocean Shipping Corporation of Tokyo, best known in Japan as liner agents for Knutsen Lines. Interocean had already established a good reputation as brokers specializing in refrigerated transportation of fisheries products. The close business ties between Interocean and Marine Chartering have resulted in both companies providing training opportunities whereby young staff members have worked side by side in Tokyo and San Francisco. Interocean represents Marine Chartering's market interests in Japan.

Marine Chartering is active in full ship brokerage, uniting ship and cargo interests. The firm's brokerage activities include chartering bulk carriers, reefer vessels and container ships for a great variety of commodities and industrial products. Obtaining the representation of a firm, Marine Chartering sends out its business orders by electronic mail or facsimile. A number of ship owners may respond to the requirements, and Marine Chartering will then negotiate for the freight conditions, rates of loading and discharge per day, charterparty, and, with concurrence by the cargo owner, the best or most suitable ship will be selected.

Marine Chartering acts as agents and general managers for Paxicon Inc., which operates time-chartered vessels (15,000-40,000 tons) from the U.S. Gulf and East Coast to ports in Southeast Asia. Paxicon handles project cargoes such as equipment and commercial and industrial vehicles, breakbulk service (bagged, baled and unitized cargoes), and bulk shipments, such as grains, meals and fertilizers. Another related company, Marine Trading Ltd., has been active operating smaller cargo ships (3,000-20,000 tons) in the U.S. Gulf, Central and South America for more than 30 years.

Marine Chartering is also the manager of Caribbean Bulk Carriers Ltd., which owns several smaller bulk carries employed in the Caribbean and Latin American trades, and Concorde Line, a containerized line serving Central America from New Orleans and Houston.

George Kiskaddon, the company's founder, was an avid sailor and a member of the St. Francis Yacht Club, participating in both Trans-Pacific and Trans-Atlantic races. He retired in September 1973. Jacob Nebeling, who had been vice president since 1957, was named president in 1973, a position he held until his death in May 1989. Dieter Tede, born in Germany in 1933, attended the Hamburg School of Trade, and came to the U.S. via Mexico. He became vice president of Marine Chartering in 1961 and president in May 1989. Other key officers of the company are John Sylvester and Malcolm R. Cameron, as executive vice presidents, and Judith R. Smith, treasurer.

Marine Chartering moved from downtown San Francisco in 1967 to Fisherman's Wharf, and to its present Aquatic Park location in 1977.

The owners of Marine Chartering care greatly for the welfare of their staff, and early in 1961 the company launched a profit-sharing retirement plan and a health plan. Desiring to expose their employees to culture, the company sponsors tickets to the opera and symphony, a legacy that has been preserved. Today, the Marine Chartering employee family is well integrated in San Francisco's cultural life. Marine Chartering has been a closely held corporation since 1985, with all stockholders being employees of the company. There are 41 employees in Aquatic Park headquarters and 26 employees in New Orleans. Many staff members have been with the company for ten to twenty years or more. By far, they are considered the company's "greater resources."

Reception area of Marine Chartering's Aquatic Park headquarters.

The *Fortuna Reefer*, a reefer vessel of 3000 tons cargo capacity, loading frozen tuna from the fishing fleet.

TENERA Technologies

Photograph courtesy of San Francisco Municipal Railway, Cerman Magana

Public transportation is such an everyday sight in Bay Area life that it is almost taken for granted. Bright red and brown cable cars climbing city streets delight tourists and residents. BART racing through the Bay tube delivers commuters to work. Amtrak rolling down the tracks takes vacationers on summer tours. These are all familiar images.

With public transportation such an integral part of the Bay Area experience — as in many metropolitan areas — perhaps it is only fitting that TENERA Technologies, the leader in maintenance software for mass transit, is headquartered in San Francisco.

TENERA chose San Francisco as its corporate headquarters to consolidate two Bay Area offices and tap into the labor pool of the Peninsula. San Francisco, a cross-road of various mass transit systems, also enables TENERA employees to commute to work by bus, car, commuter rail, and ferry.

With its cosmopolitan, yet friendly business climate, San Francisco also provides TENERA with an internationally known corporate base. San Francisco's reputation as one of the world's most beautiful cities is a powerful magnet for attracting customers and generating business from within the global community. Both national and international customers are generally eager to visit the city. Additionally, for a high technology company such as TENERA, its San Francisco location furnishes access to the Silicon Valley, only minutes away, with a large pool of world-class programmers and a sophisticated venture capital community.

Under the guidance of Chief Executive Officer, Michael D. Thomas, TENERA is dedicated to providing solutions that will improve the safety, service, and economic performance of transit operations into the 21st century. To accomplish this goal, TENERA offers a full service program, with a team of experts to enhance the economic performance of transit providers.

TENERA takes an integrated approach to providing business solutions to the transportation industry, combining sophisticated application software products with business process and organization improvement expertise. TENERA incorporates well-proven personnel change management consulting to assist in the adaptation of the new technologies and processes by the people using them. This approach ensures the highest level of performance improvement to be realized by its customers.

TENERA software is used to maintain more bus

and rail vehicles in the US than any other software package. Some of TENERA's customers include New York Metropolitan Transit Authority, Department of Buses, Long Island Rail Road, and Subways; Dallas Area Rapid Transit; Amtrak; and internationally, world-class organizations such as British Rail Business Systems.

TENERA products address all the needs of transit asset management and operations, a fact not lost on transit organizations. British Rail Business Systems, for example, selected TENERA as its strategic partner to develop the first "Total Depot Management Solution." After conducting an extensive analysis of software capable of maintaining moving assets, BR Business Systems selected TENERA software for its power and ease of use. "We believe TENERA Technologies software is a best-of-the-class product," said Richard Bullard, Manager of Moving Assets for BR Business Systems.

Another major client is Amtrak, which chose TENERA to supply a fully integrated work management system for its "rolling stock." In addition to providing maintenance software, TENERA will provide implementation support, program management, and training services.

In addition to its San Francisco office, TENERA has an office in Hartford, Connecticut. TENERA is expanding beyond the US and Great Britain into Europe, Canada, South America, and Asia.

Like many industries, the transit industry must continually adapt and improve in order to meet the challenges of the future. Whatever the direction, transit organizations can be assured TENERA leads the way in innovative solutions.

The future outlook for the transportation industry includes a new era of global competition combined with challenges at home, such as reduced subsidies and privatization. These trends indicate that transit operations will have to learn to do more with less, and TENERA provides the solution. How efficiently transportation providers utilize their assets will separate the leaders from followers in the 21st century. TENERA can help transit operations move into the leadership position by providing appropriate tools: expertise, training, and software — for extending asset life.

With TENERA's expert services, transit operations will be able to predict and increase asset utilization, decrease unnecessary inventory, and keep assets in service. The end result: significant reduction in operating costs. TENERA Technologies does not tell a business how to run its operations. Instead, TENERA Technologies provides the power and expertise that allows a business to improve itself.

Partners

San Francisco's

booming economy

provides the ideal

setting for attracting

professionals who

provide essential

services to the

San Francisco

area and beyond.

Professions

PC World Communications

Richard J. Marino,
President & CEO, PC World
Communications, Inc.

Change is inevitable. It comes in waves, sweeping away the unprepared. But for those who can anticipate, it also brings opportunity. PC World Communications skillfully navigates changes in the publishing industry like no one else, staying on top of lightning-fast daily advancements within the high-tech industry it writes about.

Earning its reputation for staying a step ahead, PC World Communications was one of the first publishers to settle south of Market Street, in a San Francisco renaissance neighborhood known as Multimedia Gulch. With its inventive CD-ROM and computer games, The Gulch is widely recognized as the Internet capital of the world. This highly charged location, with its proximity to the Silicon Valley and key advertising agencies, attracts cutting-edge video, sound, and graphic artists hoping to make their creative mark.

San Francisco is a thriving North American publishing center. Prominent publications such as *Mother Jones*, *Bam* music magazine, *Wired* and other high-tech

publishers, and Time Warner's *Sunset* are all based here. As a result, the Bay Area has emerged as a major player in the publishing industry. The same is true for PC World Communications, now a multi-faceted media corporation. This publishing giant reaches out to service its ever-expanding audience with all forms of print and electronic media.

IDG Communications, *PC World*'s parent company, publishes over 60 foreign editions of *PC World*, the magazine of business computing. And if that's not enough, IDG also publishes 430 book titles and nearly 300 computer newspapers and magazines. Combined, these two companies qualify as the world's leading IT (information technology) media company. PC World Communications helps readers become more computer literate, from Norway to the South Pole, with a proven track record for objective reporting and service-oriented articles.

PC World has more editorial awards than any other publisher in its category. These honors include the American Society of Business Press Editors, the Jesse H. Neal Editorial Achievement Award, the Computer Press Awards and Maggie Awards. But winning accolades isn't what drives *PC World* — delivering relevant, cutting edge information about personal computers is. That's why each of its magazines is designed to be reader-friendly, in addition to providing details on the effective planning, purchase and use of PCs and computer products.

PC World Communications makes information both accessible and useful to readers, eliminating many of the frustrations associated with using a computer. This philosophy was the impetus behind its first publication, *PC World*. Premiering in early 1983, *PC World* offered an alternative to the tech journal, *PC Magazine*, at a time when IBM personal computers had just been introduced to the public. *PC World* made history as the biggest first issue ever of any computer related publication. Helpful articles such as "How the PC Thinks", and "Do It Yourself RAM" were combined with an interview of a then-young entrepreneur named Bill Gates to launch *PC World* into the limelight. This first issue proved visionary and *PC World*'s efforts were rewarded with initial circulation numbers of 135,000.

Under the guidance of President and Chief Executive Officer Richard J. Marino, *PC World* has become the world's largest monthly computer magazine. Boasting a monthly audience of nearly six million readers, its U.S. circulation base is over 1.1 million. Product ads generate almost three million inquiries a year, and the magazine's advertising sales and revenues often surpass that of the nation's top business periodicals. In 1996, *PC World* was the first computer publication to achieve status in the nation's Circulation Excellence Awards competition, a finalist to *Martha Stewart Living. PC World* outranked hundreds of others in 1997 to place in the top 30 of two leading trade magazines, *Folio* and *Advertising Age.* With such exponential growth, *PC World* has moved from being a trade magazine into the publishing mainstream, and now directly competes with the biggest of the consumer magazines.

With some of the best writers and editors in the publishing field, *PC World* works hard to keep up with its savvy readers. Its core audience consists of business managers who

Launched in 1983, *PC World* is the magazine of business computing.

have come to rely on *PC World* as not just another computer magazine, but an effective productivity tool for their business. *PC World*'s strong investigative reporting skills were validated in the "RAM Scam!" story. Reader complaints on computer memory brokers led to this news-breaking report which exposed a public rip-off in excess of one million dollars. For this investigative work, *PC World* received the prestigious 1997 Neal Award for "Best News Story".

Reader experiences are a major influence in *PC World*'s scrutiny of personal computer manufacturers. In each issue, readers are asked to complete a comprehensive survey on PC reliability and service. Based on this information, *PC World* compiles a report card on the leading manufacturers of personal computers. The data is published twice a year and incorporated into the magazine's monthly PC rankings. Each *PC World* issue ranks the Top 20 or Top 10 best PC performers, covering everything imaginable on a given product — ease of use, price, speed, etc. These information-packed charts serve to help answer the gnawing question of what to buy.

In addition to its Top 100 product reviews, every month, *PC World* includes features and special reports on topics ranging from the best places to telecommute and the top Internet Service Providers to tips for buying a new PC.
(Bottom left)

PC World Online is like having a personal library, open 24 hours a day, seven days a week. (Top right)

PC World has won more editorial awards than any other publication in its category, leading the way with seven Jesse H. Neal Awards and nine Maggie Awards.

Computer manufacturers from across the country ship truck loads of computer equipment for evaluation by *PC World*'s Test Center. Here, highly trained analysts conduct unique investigations involving hands-on or automated testing, depending on the individual criteria required. In one corner may be a test comparing online services. In another section, lab technicians and editors critically evaluate how "user-friendly" various software packages really are, carefully monitoring user reactions through a two-way mirror. The Test Center also features a modem evaluation lab which uses state-of-the-art equipment to analyze connection speed, ensuring customers can log onto the Internet easily and without long delays.

The *PC World* facility has been utilized by high-powered parties such as the National Aeronautics and Space Administration (NASA). One important NASA study used customized PC testing software, developed by the center, to study the effects of zero-gravity on PC use in space.

In an effort to reach readers outside the traditional computer universe, *PC World*

formed alliances with other major magazines, such as *Family Circle* and *Newsweek*, to produce special computer-related editions. The 84-page joint issue of *PC World*'s and *Family Circle*'s "Computers Made Easy" premiered with a distribution of 600,000. *PC World* and *Newsweek* also co-publish quarterly special reports on small office and home-office computing.

As both the hunger for more information and the PC audience grew, PC World Communications remained one large step ahead. The aggressive publisher anticipated the Internet revolution and introduced *PC World Online* in 1992. Like *PC World*, *PC World Online* was designed to reach managers who require new technology to help them at their jobs. These are the people who mostly use online media as a research and information tool. For this characteristically impatient audience, *PC World* Online provides up-to-date computer information at a glance.

PC World Online is like having a personal library, open 24 hours a day, seven days a week. Busy professionals can browse for data at their convenience, without having to leave the office. Seventy five percent of *PC World Online*'s content is created exclusively for the online user. The remaining 25 percent consists of reprinted information from PCWorld Communications' other magazines, which has been customized for the online user.

To further aid managers in making the best buying decisions, *PC World Online* offers "The Interactive Top 20 Buying Guide". This helpful service enables users to key in their personal configuration and individual specifications (i.e. budget, size requirements) to receive a customized ranking of available computer products. Innovative online information like this unique buying guide has helped win numerous editorial awards for *PC World Online*, including the 1996 "Maggie" for Best Online Publication. Continuing their pursuit of excellence, in the summer of 1997 *PC World* launched Dummies Daily, a unique series of Internet hints, tricks and user tips.

PC World Communications didn't become the publishing giant it is today by resting on its accomplishments. The same year *PC World* passed the one million mark in U.S. circulation, the visionary company launched *THE WEB Magazine*. This popular magazine was the first to recognize the cultural importance of the World Wide Web (www). Unlike the more business-oriented *PC World*, *THE WEB Magazine* was designed as an entertaining and informative guide for the millions of daily web users. Celebrity-oriented features — including interviews with Cindy Crawford, Keanu Reeves, David Bowie and Steven Spielberg — grace *THE WEB Magazine*'s covers, with pop culture ads appearing throughout this hip, irreverent publication.

In addition to editorials on everything from music and film to money and politics, *THE WEB Magazine* also reviews over 500 web sites each month.

In March of 1997, the magazine celebrated the best of these sites with the first annual Webby Awards, hosted by San Francisco Mayor Willie Brown. A stellar panel of expert writers, editors and celebrities judged web sites in fifteen categories, encompassing a broad range of interests from "Art/ Design" to "Weird".

With San Francisco at the hub of their expanding operations, PC World Communications believes in supporting their local community. The company was one of the founding corporate sponsors of Marin Day Schools' cooperative Day Care Center in the nearby Hills Brothers Plaza. PC World Communications also offers its staff the opportunity to pursue journalism classes through local University of California extension programs. In addition, employees participate in an annual Aids Walk fundraising event which generates thousands of dollars through private sponsorships and matching funds by IDG Communications.

Whatever the future holds, one thing is certain. There will be new waves of change in the computing and publishing industries. But even in rough seas, PC World Communications will rise to the top, setting the pace for years to come.

P*C World* is a corporate sponsor of Marin Day Schools, a downtown daycare center located in San Francisco's Hills Plaza.

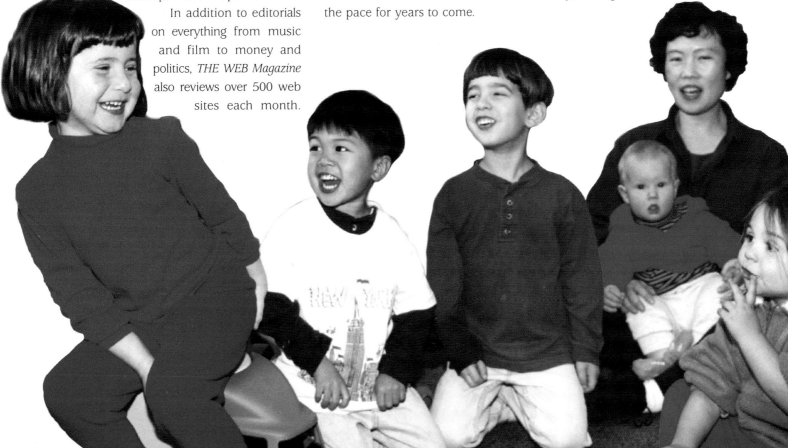

Axis Consulting International, Inc.

Graham Weston and Peter Boboff, founders of Axis

Even in today's fast-paced world of information technology, the rise of Axis Consulting International can only be described as meteoric.

In five years, Axis has grown from a small, four-man team with a tiny office in San Francisco to an international consortium with corporate headquarters at One Maritime Plaza, and branches throughout the United States, Europe and Australia.

The story of how Australians Graham Weston and Peter Boboff launched Axis onto its path to success is one of remarkable enterprise, creative thinking and gutsy maneuvering.

It began back in 1992, when Weston and Boboff, after talking with each other, agreed that business consulting was poised to enter a new age. Drawing from their combined thirty-five years of experience as computer programmers, analysts, project managers and executive management, Weston and Boboff set out to form a progressive company that would be global in scope and innovative in technique. Their company would be designed to meet the growing needs of expanding businesses by providing consulting and professional services related to advanced technology and systems integration.

Together, they envisioned Axis Consulting International, a global consultancy in which the partners would play an integral role in the day-to-day operations. In addition, partners, management and staff would form a "synergistic" working relationship, utilizing their cultural and business expertise to assess clients' needs from a global perspective. Above all, they would be highly ethical.

The big question: Could they pull off such an ambitious feat? You bet they could. And did. It was a high-stakes gamble, with both men risking everything

they had to invest in the company, that paid off. Today, Axis is a leading consulting firm in the U.S., Europe and Australia. Its client list includes prestigious multinational corporations, such as Charles Schwab & Co., Hewlett Packard Company, Intel, Bank of America, NIKE, Inc., Toshiba, Inc., Novartis, Motorola, Andersen Consulting, Mitsubishi, Microsoft, Informix and SAP America.

Axis' early days were a bit lean, however. The company's first contract was garnered through a "friend of a friend," according to Weston. It was primarily through these word-of-mouth recommendations that the Australian entrepreneurs quickly gained a reputation of being professional and highly ethical businessmen.

Another key to the company's rise through the ranks, according to Weston, was — and still is — its ability to move "resources," including high caliber consultants, around the world.

Axis takes pride in its aggressive recruiting practices. While many American consulting firms primarily hire from within the U.S., Axis draws from an "international talent pool." This recruiting policy grew out of Axis' hiring of Australians in the company's initial stages. It was a novel idea, Weston and Boboff reasoned: Bring Australians, who are highly versatile because of their smaller technical work environment and who are eager to expand their experience, to work in the U.S. The Australians were an instant success with their American counterparts, who admired the Aussies' hardworking, pioneering spirit. In return, when the Aussies were ready to return home, Axis provided them with work back in Australia or, if they preferred, in Europe.

In hindsight, this savvy recruitment plan epitomizes Weston and Boboff's "forward thinking" approach to business. Regardless of their nationality, all Axis consultants are among the most technically qualified in their field of expertise.

Today, Axis offers a wide range of services, including systems analysis, development and implementation, network design, data modeling and project management. Its consultants can supplement in-house staff or assemble complete project teams — including project managers, analysts and programmers. Whether expanding markets, streamlining operations, embarking on new ventures or renewing existing systems, Axis professionals are capable of assessing a company's needs and providing solutions for specific goals.

It's no secret that corporations that expect to thrive in the 21st century must effectively integrate technological advances into their existing framework. To address this evolution, Axis is made up of six business units, each focusing on a specific area of expertise — SAP, Database Technologies, Midrange Systems, Networking, Microsoft Solutions, and Systems Integration.

Axis employees are constantly enhancing their existing knowledge through ongoing education at Axis' development and training center, where the

Axis has branches in Australia and Europe.

focus is on the latest information about emerging technologies and product upgrades. Axis also works there with its technology partners to test applications and methodologies prior to bringing them onsite, ensuring minimal downtime for clients. By engaging Axis' services, clients can be certain their needs are met with proven technology and experienced consultants who understand the most current technological developments and business practices.

Success in today's economy lies not only in understanding technological changes, but in anticipating them. Axis takes pride in always looking ahead, anticipating demands and helping clients meet those demands. Axis' knowledgeable team prepares clients for the next generation of challenges, and provides them with the means to meet those challenges. Axis' proven ability to meet technology's rigorous demands and to swiftly and skillfully implement each client's vision has earned Axis its respected position among peers.

Time and again, Axis is chosen over competitors for the high skill level of its employees and its ability to provide resources and solutions in a timely fashion.

Whether companies plan to modify or migrate an existing application, initiate a client/server project, redesign a network or construct a World Wide Web site; whether thc needs demand the comprehensive solution provided by a complete project team or the services of a few highly skilled specialists, Axis is the solution.

Booz-Allen & Hamilton Inc.

In 1914, Edwin G. Booz contrived an idea of helping businesses by combining psychological techniques with intuitive good sense. Fresh from Northwestern University with degrees in economics and psychology, Booz started a firm in his hometown of Chicago, performing studies and statistical analyses for businesses. His emphasis was to get the right people into the right jobs

His ambition was briefly interrupted by World War I, when he was drafted into the Army. He climbed the ranks fast and was a major when he was discharged following the war's conclusion. In 1919 at age 30, he opened the *Edwin G. Booz, Business Engineering Service*, a management consulting firm conceived by a loan from an Evanston bank that thus became his first client.

In 1924, the firm's name was changed to *Edwin Booz Surveys* and a year later Booz hired his first employee, George Fry. Jim Allen came on board as a partner in 1929. Allen wanted to solve business problems, but was a bit volatile himself, having left and returned to Booz twice during the early years.

Carl Hamilton, a marketing specialist, joined the firm in 1935. A year later a new partnership was formed, *Booz, Fry, Allen & Hamilton*. During the 1930s, a client base was built, which included Container Corp. of America, US Gypsum and Johnson Wax, a continuing client well into the 1990s. The firm also worked for the American Red Cross that lead to more institutional contracts. The late-30s saw an interesting marketing campaign, with the release of brochures that had enticing titles such as "Why a consultant?" and "To the Executive Who Wants to Improve His Company's Performance." Booz was selling an idea as well as themselves, and the whole foray worked. The firm was solidifying, with a strong Midwest client base and a New York office.

When rumors of war abounded in 1940, Booz was ready, especially when Secretary of Navy Frank Knox asked them to prepare the Navy for battle. Booz and Allen sojourned to Washington DC where, once

cleared by Congress to work as civilian contractors, they organized a team for a major challenge: revamping the entire management structure of Navy department headquarters. Throughout World War II, the firm helped cut military bureaucratic red tape. When their work with the Navy proved successful, they were summoned to assist the Army as well. Their involvement with the military gave management consulting a tremendous boost, and the firm was asked to help companies prepare for a return to civilian work and the post-war "replacement boom."

By this time Fry, who balked at the Navy job and advocated civilian work, had already left the partnership over a dispute about future government contracts. Allen became Chairman of the Executive Committee and the firm's name was alas changed to *Booz•Allen & Hamilton*. Hamilton, however, died in 1946 and Booz soon retired until his death in 1951. Jim Allen remained chairman and honorary chairman until he died in 1992. By 1947, the firm had 100 employees, $2 million in billings and their first contract with the US Air Force, which plunged them into electronic intelligence and assignments with major aircraft manufacturers.

Shortly after the war, Booz•Allen secured a major consulting engagement in Hawaii's sugar cane plantations. This, the firm's first major contract outside the continental U.S., was to bring better management techniques and systems to Hawaii's Big Five companies, which included Dole, C&H and other large agricultural companies. That engagement prompted the opening of the San Francisco office in 1948, from which the firm could more closely oversee the operations. Senior partner Stuart Lowry opened the San Francisco office.

Although they had an engagement in Hawaii, the firm's first foreign contract was in the Philippines in 1953. Under Philippine President Ramon Magsaysay, the firm reorganized land ownership records. The Booz•Allen team was large, with spouses and families moving about the Philippines from project to

project. By this time, Booz•Allen planned to expand to other Far East countries, with the San Francisco office serving as a base until branch offices were opened in Asia.

The 1950s saw *Booz•Allen & Hamilton's* entry into manufacturing, electronics, chemicals and energy. The firm also alerted the communications industry to the promise of television. *Time* magazine in 1959 referred to *Booz•Allen & Hamilton* as the "company doctors" and "the world's largest, most prestigious management consulting firm." A few months later, Jim Allen appeared on the cover of Business Week.

During the 1960s, with more than 500 professionals at several offices nationwide, the consulting profession looked to Booz•Allen. Compared to other US consulting firms during that period, Booz•Allen had the largest staff, the most billings and offered the widest range of services. When the 1970s rolled in, business was booming, the market was hot and the firm went public for six years.

Warren Chinn was the San Francisco managing partner in 1972. The office employed about 25 professionals then, all men. Most of the engagements at that time involved organization, but the firm also did consulting in areas of business and marketing strategy and operations improvement, a similar mix of functional areas that occur today. Information technology was just developing and Booz•Allen was entering that field as well.

Commercial clients were mostly large corporations, such as San Francisco's Bechtel and a branch of Del Monte. The San Francisco office handled some Pacific Northwest firms, including Boeing. Booz•Allen also contracted with banks, insurance companies and energy firms. In addition, clients served by the San Francisco office during that period included state and local governments, hospitals and education systems. These institutions were growing and seeking more effective management methods.

Many of the engagements involved operations effectiveness and marketing strategy. Many clients were also making the transition from being family-owned and operated to professional management. In Bechtel's case, it was a generational shift, Steve Bechtel Jr. taking the helm from his father and planning for another era in the business.

An engagement at the Hong Kong Bank actually materialized in San Francisco because of the bank's concern with their California business. Chinn was the lead partner responsible for the assignment, which involved working with the bank locally and in Hong Kong. The engagement evolved into providing overall strategy for the bank's United States business, and culminated in the acquisition of the Marine Midland Bank in New York, which became the base of their retail banking services.

Chinn opened and led Booz•Allen's first permanent Asian office in Tokyo in 1982. The San Francisco operation was taken over by Bill Sommers, a senior partner from the Washington DC area. During Chinn's tenure at the San Francisco office, the staff grew to 60 people and became more diversified. The firm is now located on California Street.

Bruce Pasternack is the current San Francisco Managing Partner at Booz•Allen and has been for most of the past decade of rapid growth. The SF office now has more than 200 people and has expanded its portfolio of services and clients. It is working on major long-term engagements with companies in Silicon Valley, Los Angeles, Arizona and the Northwest. Services include strategy, organization, leadership models, people strategies, manufacturing operations, strategic sourcing and various services related to information technology. It has done pro bono work recently for a number of institutions, including the San Francisco Symphony, Joint Venture Silicon Valley Network, The Bay Area Bioscience Center and the World Affairs Council.

"We are committed to being a responsible corporate citizen of San Francisco," says Pasternack, and "are thrilled to live and work in this very vibrant and exciting area."

Chris Lucey and Steve Dietch training for Bay to Breakers as part of Booz•Allen's charity efforts. (Top left)

A Booz•Allen team meeting to discuss client issues. (Top right)

Bradford Staff

When Robin Bradford was 29 years old and working at a San Francisco placement firm, she considered starting her own employment firm. The thought didn't fair well with her boss, and Bradford was terminated. "It came as a big shock to me because I'd never been fired before," Bradford said. "But it turned out to be a real blessing. I think it gave me the push I needed."

No longer tethered to a full time job, the entrepreneurial Bradford, with the help of a part time receptionist, launched Bradford Personnel in 1979. Unable to procure a bank loan, Bradford invested her personal finances (all of $9,000) to start the business. From her small office on Sutter Street, she sent out 2,000 announcements to San Francisco law firms, CPA firms and major corporations to attract her first clients. Then she placed newspaper ads to acquire such personnel as secretaries and word processors. "I very slowly started getting business," she recalls,

Robin Bradford, center, and Staff

"but a number of those initial clients are still with me today." With her meager budget during the agency's developing stages, Bradford had to tediously juggle clients' income and her employees' payroll, oftentimes receiving clients' checks in the morning and paying her workers that afternoon.

Founder Robin Bradford remains President and oversees the operations from her San Francisco headquarters. Now called Bradford Staff, the highly regarded temporary employment firm has a staff of 40, an active pool of 5,000 temporary employees, a database of 20,000, four other Bay Area branches, an impressive list of clients, a specialty in providing high-end clerical personnel, an expansion into placement of temporary executives and a move to its own building in 1998.

Bradford said she discovered early on she "had a knack for picking good people," and continues in that vein today. "What we try to do," she said, "is to tap into the top ten percent of the workforce in whatever job capacity. We're very selective and that's how we sell our services to the clients."

During the firm's 18 years, two notable events changed the course of personnel placement: the recession and the computer revolution. "Before the major recession nearly all businesses suffered through, temporary agencies were thought of as a necessary evil," Bradford said. "With the massive layoffs in the early and middle 1990s, companies were short staffed but still had to get the work out. They realized what an incredible resource a great temp service could be, bringing in qualified people on an as-needed basis. It's a very efficient way of working." Bradford said her agency and its clients are "partners in hiring," which is a big benefit that utilizes resources in a more efficient manner.

The efficiency of the personal computer also had a positive impact on Bradford Staff. The agency computerized in 1982, creating a large database of personnel and client profiles, enabling quick access for a comparable match. "Before, it was how many people you could remember and how many applications fit into a file drawer," Bradford said.

Since the advent of the personal computer, workplace roles have broadened. Bradford said 15 years ago "we were losing many intelligent applicants who would have been great secretaries. They were afraid of becoming an extension of the typewriter." She said today's secretary is less of a typist and more of an administrative person, instrumental in various projects and skillful on a wide range of computer software. Bradford said the break from the traditional role of secretary makes work more interesting and increases productivity.

Bradford Staff began offering software training programs in 1992. The firm stays abreast of paramount software and can teach personnel some 32 different programs. Bradford is relieved that many word processing and spreadsheet programs have standardized, and grateful that Windows programs offer a uniform menu structure. Gone are the days when different clients used a hodgepodge of software, many obscure and difficult to learn.

When Bradford Staff relocates to its own building in 1998, the agency plans to open a formal training center. "I feel that training is the wave of the future," Bradford said, adding that the best gift Bradford Staff can give its employees is appropriate training. "That's job security, something you take with you wherever you are." Flexibility is also the key, having enough skills to be able to tackle almost any assignment. Bradford said full time jobs are "becoming modeled after the way temps have been working for years." Employers want to see their employees continue to learn and grow, picking up an array of skills. "We are here to help accomplish that, on behalf of our temps and clients," she added.

As a result of corporate downsizing a few years ago, staunch managers sought contract work on a per project basis. Many never returned to full time employment or employment in their field. Bradford Staff is accommodating this pool with their new managerial program, Bradford Executives. Instead of sending these overqualified people to clerical assignments, Bradford Executives offers them higher level positions.

How does the company get its top notch employees? "We don't have a big staff of salespeople," Bradford said. Outside of newspaper classified ads, "we grow through referral, word-of-mouth and satisfied customers. That's also my vision for our management temporary service. We're starting small, but are always growing because people are finding out about us. For me that's a very comfortable way to do it."

Bradford, now 48, said "Eighteen years ago I had no idea what I was getting into." Bradford jokes that during the start-up phase of her business she was unfamiliar with the travails of establishing and developing a new company, and she might have been more apprehensive had she known what she knows today. But in retrospect, everything turned out better than planned. "I'm a very lucky person," she said.

Burson-Marsteller

Managing Perceptions to Accomplish Business Results

Clients often turn to the Media Practice for assistance in refining their ability to talk with the media. Burson-Marsteller works with clients to develop messages that support their communications strategy and impact the perceptions of key audiences.

Legislation, regulations and other government decisions can change market conditions and make a significant difference in a company's competitiveness or an organization's objectives. Public Affairs Practice experts implement local, state and national political strategies for businesses and organizations designed to achieve clients' objectives by influencing the public policy decision-making process. (Bottom right)

At a time when most public relations firms focus only on the art of communications, Burson-Marsteller is helping its clients accomplish real business results.

Burson-Marsteller has expanded its charter — from simply leading the public relations field to becoming a perception management firm, working to positively impact its clients' futures. Where a company's stock price has languished; where a company's efforts to limit government regulation have been unsuccessful; where a brand has gone undervalued in the marketplace — Burson-Marsteller steps in with insight, innovation and creativity. Its work can support stock value, increase sales, elevate a company's point-of-view, or markedly influence audiences whose perceptions shape a company's success.

Perceptions influence how people behave. They turn political campaigns upside down, make or break product lines, create or change the tides of cultural trends. In business, perceptions are an essential operating component. It is central to the Burson-Marsteller philosophy that perceptions must be managed, just as the operational, financial and administrative aspects of a business are managed. Perceptions create or diminish value. They generate or solve problems and in so doing, drive stocks up or down, color employee reaction to company initiatives, affect consumer receptivity, even alter policy decisions. The mission at Burson-Marsteller is to use communications to manage perceptions to motivate behaviors that create positive business results.

Burson-Marsteller's work strategy begins by eliciting a vividly clear understanding of a client's desired business results. Then, a careful audit is conducted of target audiences to determine current perceptions and detail what would motivate positive changes in behavior. Finally, a forceful campaign is designed to break through communications barriers and make an audience feel the need to act.

Burson-Marsteller's clients derive competitive advantage from the firm's wealth of communications resources, state-of-the-art technologies and seasoned professionals whose experience spans a broad range of disciplines. Consider the results they've garnered in recent years:

The firm is grounded in achieving strong business results for clients like Sun Microsystems' Scott McNealy pictured at a recent B-M-managed launch.

• An integrated communications effort involving identity, advertising, publications, events and media relations changed public and client awareness of Andersen Consulting and its offerings. In the U.S. alone, awareness grew from 16 percent of the target audience to 92 percent. The result: the firm's revenues grew fourfold.

• Following a highly targeted campaign, investor perceptions of McDonnell Douglas were changed from a vision of a burdened company with a troubled future to one with critical strengths and a bright future. The result: the company's stock price more than doubled in just five quarters.

• An education campaign for Eli Lilly changed perceptions of depression among U.S. doctors and patients — altering its status from a collection of undiagnosable complaints or a personal weakness to

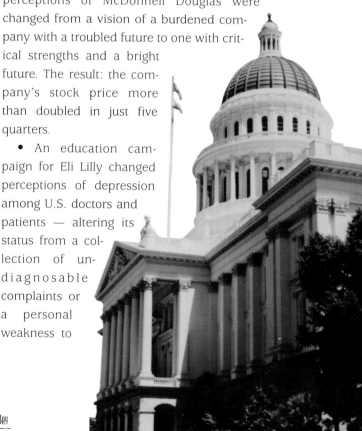

an acceptable, treatable illness. The results: awareness of depression among physicians increased by 24 percent with 35 percent expressing an increased willingness to consider a depression diagnosis. More than 266,000 patients received treatment for clinical depression as a direct result of the campaign and the U.S. anti-depressant market grew at more than twice its historic rate.

• Perceptual research revealed key strategies for shifting Hong Kong drivers to unleaded gas by linking environmental benefits with a cash payback to change driver behavior. The result: adoption of unleaded gas reached 55 percent within six months — significantly higher than the European Union adoption rate of 32 percent after a two-year campaign.

Since its founding by the legendary Harold Burson in 1953, Burson-Marsteller has set the standard by which all public relations firms are measured. Forty-four years ago, Burson set out to grow his fledgling firm. He opened his first overseas office in Geneva in 1961 and became one of just two international public relations firms in operation at that time. From then on, the firm grew at a quantum rate opening offices in Latin America, Asia and Australia.

His vision was, and still is, to maintain a "seamless company," one that operates with a uniform standard of excel-

lence, no matter how widely distributed the offices. He insists that the company's valued fingerprint of integrity be recognizable from Sydney to San Francisco.

Today, Burson-Marsteller is truly a global network. Headquartered in New York, London and Hong Kong, its staff numbers more than 2,200 with 77 offices (two in the Bay Area) in 32 countries. Linked with its New York-based parent company, Young & Rubicam Inc., more than 75 percent of its offices are outside the U.S. and the majority of its staff and clients are international.

Staff expertise is divided into "practices" — seven specialized groups working in the arenas of marketing, technology, health care, corporate affairs, public affairs, advertising and the media.

For decades, Burson-Marsteller has been the uncontested global public relations firm. Now with its focus on perception management, this is a company that measures success by the permanent bonds it forges with its clients.

Its work — and its accomplishments break all the molds.

As the world's leading crisis management consultancy, Burson-Marsteller has deployed teams around the world to help manage some of the most widely publicized crises in history.

AIDS awareness race in Bangkok. Burson-Marsteller specializes in programs that achieve greater awareness, understanding and support for government social and economic policy initiatives.
(Top left)

The Marketing Practice strives to influence buying behaviors by adding value to our clients' brands through strategic programs that reach their target audiences. It is committed to achieving measurable business results throughout the life cycle of a product — from launch to repositioning, ongoing market support, issues management, even to garnering in-depth visibility for sales promotion programs like Chevron's Toy Cars.
(Bottom center)

Career Consociates Inc.

Quality not quantity. That was Sharron Long's goal 26 years ago when she launched one of San Francisco's first "boutique" personnel agencies. Seeing the need for a service-oriented firm, the 29-year old pursued her dream of having her own business with a $2,000 loan from her family.

Long had worked for the magnate lawyer Melvin Belli for three years and, during that period, often sought employees from personnel agencies to fill available positions at the firm. At that time, it did not appear that the agencies cared about forming relationships with their clients or candidates. Their

As she continued to maintain her dedication to high standards and personalized service, referrals from these satisfied clients and candidates became the primary source of CCI's business.

philosophy seemed to be based on volume instead of service, i.e. if they sent you lots of people to interview, you would surely find one you liked. Thus Long saw the need for a highly personalized agency. In 1971 she left Belli and secured an office on San Francisco's Montgomery Street to start her own business. The young entrepreneur wasn't concerned about her shoestring budget. Like many young people of that era who were developing careers, Long said she "didn't have a high standard of living so I

The staff of Career Consociates Inc.: Shirlee Johns, Carol Foster, John Dunn, Sharron Long (center), George Matthews, Suzanne Demarais and Paula Sharpe

was able to continually put the profits back into the business."

"Consociate" means "to unite, to bring into association," a service Long has done so well. As a result of the many contacts she had developed during her years with Belli, she found she was able to rely mainly on personal referrals for both her client and candidate base instead of cold calling to obtain clients and using newspaper classified ads to locate candidates, both common practices among high-volume personnel agencies. She also chose to focus on reference checking rather than testing to qualify a candidate. This approach, Long found, was much more personal and obtained the same, if not better, information than putting someone through the traditional lengthy and impersonal testing process.

She was soon filling available positions with qualified personnel at many of San Francisco's law firms. As she continued to maintain her dedication to high standards and personalized service, referrals from these satisfied clients and candidates became the primary source of CCI's business.

During the recession of the 1990s, Long turned her focus to temporary placement. New clients, such as the Bank of America, with large temporary staffing needs helped enable CCI to prosper during this difficult time. And since their was no way to do volume temporary placements without the aid of technology, it also forced CCI to forge ahead and add an array of computers and software.

"Technology has certainly transformed the way we do business," states Long. With the advent of the computer, skill requirements began to change at such a rapid pace that it became extremely difficult to find people who had been trained on the latest software. We often purchased the equipment and/or software that our clients were using and swiftly trained personnel to meet their requirements."

The computer's impact on law firms was also substantial. Long said 26 years ago San Francisco had many small law firms. When technology first arrived, small firms "had difficulty existing because they were unable to generate paperwork as fast as the large firms could," Long said now that technology has blended in, small law firms are again able to

The company's secret to success has been their unwavering commitment to the individual needs of their clients and candidates.

compete and prosper. "Today it is significantly easier to be a small or boutique business because, thanks to the computer, you can easily generate a quality work product at the same pace as any of the large firms."

Long states that "Although the initial plunge into computers was expensive and somewhat overwhelming for a small business, it definitely forces you to pay attention. Just as you think you are catching up with technology, it takes another giant leap." CCI is currently in the process of developing their website.

Long still occupies the same space she started with 26 years ago in the penthouse of the historic Mills Building in San Francisco's Financial District and many of the law firms for whom she provided personnel in the initial start up years remain clients to this day. The company's secret to success has been their unwavering commitment to the individual needs of their clients and candidates.

What does Career Consociates plan for the future? Although the firm continues to specialize in legal placements, they have expanded their services over the years to include a balance of legal, corporate and financial staffing. Nevertheless they hope to always remain a boutique agency and to continue to offer the same level of highly personalized service that has made CCI so successful in the past.

Charles M. Salter Associates Inc.

Sound is as influential as it is invisible. Since 1975, Charles M. Salter Associates (CSA) has been making sound tangible and manageable.

Charles Salter trained in structural engineering at Tufts University, in architecture at MIT, and received an MBA from Boston College. He moved to San Francisco to lead the acoustical engineering division of a prominent engineering consultancy. In 1975, he decided to venture out on his own. In 1976, he was joined by Anthony Nash, an expert in noise and vibration measurement and analysis. David Schwind joined CSA a few years later, adding expertise in room acoustics, theaters, entertainment, and presentation facilities.

The company continued to grow and, in 1989, moved into a newly renovated floor of the Hallidie Building on Sutter Street, center of San Francisco's architectural community. At the heart of the office is a highly sophisticated acoustical simulation room, one of the first of its kind. Constructed to be thor-

oughly "soundproof," with a floating concrete slab floor and a spring-isolated ceiling, this Presentation Studio allows CSA to simulate acoustical environments using digitized sound, so that architects, developers, and other clients can experience the acoustical effect of various building materials. For example, CSA used the room to help a developer choose the most cost-effective windows for a building near the Bay Bridge. An audio-video tape of traffic on the bridge was digitized and stored it in their computer. By computing the transmitted sound spectrum, the developer heard the filtering effect of different window types while watching the video image of the traffic on a rear-projection screen built into the front wall of the room — in effect reproducing the experience of being inside the building before it was constructed.

Charles Salter has lectured on acoustics at U.C. Berkeley since 1973, and his love of teaching permeates his approach to acoustical consulting. CSA principal consultant Kenneth Graven has created two award-winning multimedia presentations — one on building acoustics and one on environmental acoustics — that are shown to clients and students from local universities in the CSA Presentation Studio.

The company is also the author of a book about acoustics published in 1997. Designed as a reference for architects, design professionals, developers — and their clients — the book uses more than 200 color illustrations and a wide variety of case studies to explain acoustical issues in an accessible way. Architects will hopefully be able to use the book as a home study course to fulfill education requirements for licensing — and take an exam supplied by CSA.

CSA professionals make numerous public presentations to describe how communities might be affected by noise generated from highways, airports, railways, and power plants. They are also called upon to present expert testimony in litigation involving acoustical issues. Voice and audio recordings are analyzed in their Audio Forensic Center, managed by Jack Freytag. For one case, they were asked to determine whether it's possible to use a recording of a gunshot from a police radio to ascertain the make of a gun. They've also helped determine the cause of a plane crash by analyzing audio information stored in the plane's flight recorder.

The CSA staff encompasses experts in engineering, architecture, design, music, and theater who apply their skills to over 400 projects a year. They design custom video-conferencing systems for corporations, sound systems to assure acoustical privacy, and complex multimedia facilities. They've consulted on the proposed Walt Disney Concert Hall in downtown Los Angeles; the screening room at Dolby Laboratories; the Rock and Roll History Museum in Cleveland; the new San Jose repertory theater; and numerous broadcasting facilities, including those for KQED TV and radio in San Francisco and Fox Broadcasting studios in six cities. They've helped create comfortable sound environments for the chambers of the California State Supreme Court in San Francisco and research complexes for IBM in San Jose, Microsoft in Redmond, and Apple Computer in Cupertino. For their work on the Lucasfilm Technical Building at Skywalker Ranch, CSA

won a 1988 Engineering Excellence Honor Award from the American Consulting Engineers Council. This has led to projects with other film studios including 20th Century Fox, Warner Bros., Disney, Paramount, Sony/Columbia, and Universal.

CSA also helps builders silence the many parts of a building that can produce noise — such as ventilation, electrical, and plumbing systems. They designed the mosque at the Riyadh Airport in Saudi Arabia so that aircraft noise does not disturb the peace inside. They helped design the Monterey Bay Aquarium to have an acceptable ambient noise environment. They've helped hospitals reduce noise-related stress. They advised the architects of San Francisco's new Museum of Modern Art on how to minimize reverberation in the atrium. They even worked with the San Francisco Zoo to design a sewage treatment plant that doesn't vibrate and upset the gorillas.

CSA is currently collaborating with architectural and engineering leaders from around the country on a new house in the Los Altos Hills to be built using state-of-the-art materials and design systems. The design of the house will address all the issues of modern living, making it a showpiece for construction in the twenty-first century.

Charles M. Salter (above), Anthony Nash, David Schwind, and Jack Freytag lead a staff of associates with the expertise to solve a wide range of acoustical problems: Robert Alvarado, Eric Broadhurst, James Chung, Thomas Corbett, Loree Curtis, Kim Emanuel, Timothy Der, Eva Duesler, Jason Duty, Harold Goldberg, Kenneth Graven, Ross Jerozal, Claudia Kraehe, Julie Malork, Marion Miles, Cristina Miyar, Marva Noordzee, Alan Rosen, Philip Sanders, Thomas Schindler, Bob Skye, Ann Suh, Michael Toy, Brenda Yee.

Deloitte & Touche LLP

A giant from every angle, Deloitte & Touche steps into the millennium a solid leader among the Big Six accounting firms.

Since opening in San Francisco in the early 1900s, there is not one industry the firm hasn't served — from shipping to banking to academia to the arts to retail and consumer products to high tech. A company ledger dated 1906 notes work for San Francisco institutions like the Belevedere Land Company, University of California, City and County of San Francisco, Pacific Union Club, Telegraph Hill Association — even San Quentin Prison. Current clients include Charles Schwab, the Gap, Pacific Stock Exchange, Kaiser Permanente, San Francisco Opera and McKesson. As the business of the city has changed from serving a frontier society to the machine age to the age of information, Deloitte & Touche has been a constant.

A company ledger dated 1906, notes work for San Francisco institutions like the Belevedere Land Company, University of California, City and County of San Francisco, Pacific Union Club, Telegraph Hill Association — even San Quentin Prison.

Deloitte & Touche clients in Northern California represent well over 20 percent of the region's 100 largest companies by revenue. Their global entity, Deloitte Touche Tohmatsu International, represents a network of over 63,000 people in 125 countries and serves more multi-nationals than any other firm. In the U.S., they do more business among Fortune 500 companies than any other firm.

But the Deloitte & Touche story is not simply one of competitive success. Their size and strength is the result of over 100 years of creative vision and quality client service.

Though the present company was formed in 1989 by the merger of two leading firms — Deloitte Haskins & Sells and Touche Ross — it represents a long succession of alliances and partnerships among industry leaders that extends back to the end of the nineteenth century, paralleling the development of the accounting profession itself.

In the 1890s, there was no income tax. Business opportunities abounded, but so did financial risk. Liquidations, bankruptcies and outright swindles made it very difficult for investors to keep track of their money. In 1893, Congress asked Deloitte & Touche forebears Charles Waldo Haskins and Elijah Watt Sells to help reform the U.S. government accounting system, which had been in place since George Washington, and was widely criticized for its inefficiency.

In the years that followed, independent accountants played a more and more prominent role in business. When their work for the government was completed, Haskins and Sells started their own accounting firm, serving clients such as Quaker Oats, the U.S. Postal Service, and several railroads. Both men were also instrumental in creating certification standards for the fledgling profession.

William Welch Deloitte made his reputation exposing frauds at railway and steamship companies in London. He opened a New York office in 1893 and began auditing Procter & Gamble — still a client today. His firm merged with Haskins & Sells in 1924. By that time, the company was headed by General Arthur Hazelton Carter, who brought in clients like General Motors and Merrill Lynch, both still clients of the firm, and also played a key role in convincing Congress to establish the Securities and Exchange Commission.

Sir George A. Touche and Philip S. Ross, both Scots, came to North America in the late 1800s with the flow of British capital. Their respective firms served clients like Pilsbury, R.H. Macy, Sun Life, and Bell Telephone. Ross was a co-founder of the first professional accounting society in North America.

But the Deloitte & Touche story is not simply one of competitive success. Their size and strength is the result of over 100 years of creative vision and quality client service.

Throughout the century, other visionary professionals have made their mark on the firm as well. One, George Bailey, is credited with expanding the company's services to include management consulting. He brought a roster of prestigious clients to the firm as well — including American Motors, Chrysler, Boeing and Sears.

More recently, the company has served as a consultant to developing countries trying to get their economics on track in an increasingly competitive global marketplace. In 1996, they were appointed project managers for Russia's massive privatization program.

The Emerson Report, an industry trade publication, has cited Deloitte & Touche as a leader in technology. The firm recently developed a windows-based software program called Visual Assurance (TM) that helps companies monitor their organization's compliance with increasingly complicated laws and regu-

lations. Other innovative software tools include "A +," the first comprehensive integrated audit support software system in the profession.

However, as a professional services firm, Deloitte & Touche recognizes that people, not technology, are its greatest asset. They tailor their services to each client by providing personnel with experience and technical skill in the client's industry and all applicable accounting functions. To do this, they go to great lengths to attract top professionals, utilizing many innovative human resources activities and standards.

The firm has won numerous awards for their pioneering work on the Women's Initiative. They launched the Initiative for the Advancement of Women in 1993, a program designed to move more women into leadership positions. The goal: to see that by the year 2000, women are represented at all levels in the firm in close proportion to their representation in the labor pool.

The firm's commitment to people extends to the community as well. Deloitte & Touche professionals are involved in a wide range of volunteer efforts in the Bay Area — from mentoring students to teaching

More recently, the company has served as a consultant to developing countries trying to get their economics on track in an increasingly competitive global marketplace.

people with disabilities, from refurbishing homes of senior citizens to reforesting national parks. In 1994, these efforts were formally recognized by the United Way, which presented the firm with the prestigious Spirit of America Award.

Executive Direction, Inc.

Executive Direction fills a special niche in today's business environment — the recruitment and consulting services of high-tech professionals in the information technology and software development fields. This need for specialized search services in building a technical work force extends not only to computer firms but virtually any business which is technology dependent.

Rick Decker and Fred Naderi founded Executive Direction in 1979. Rick Decker, a computer analyst, had moved from the East Coast in search of better career opportunities. Fred Naderi had emigrated to the United States at the age of 17 to pursue a college education. The computer revolution not yet a reality, Naderi, fascinated by its potential, obtained a Master's degree in Computer Science. Then, assisted by Rick Decker, who had moved into recruiting, immediately landed a job with a local software firm.

When Rick Decker decided to set up his own recruitment business, he offered Naderi a partnership. Decker subleased a tiny office on the corner of Sansome and Pine Streets. Naderi worked, standing up, in an adjacent kitchenette with only a wall phone and telephone directory at his disposal. With dedication, hard work and by word-of-mouth, their business grew steadily as did the size of their office. Located on the same Financial District corner for over 18 years, the firm now occupies the entire 4th floor of the prestigious Pacific Stock Exchange Building. Executive Direction prides itself on having established a trusting relationship with the best of corporate world the city has to offer, counting among their clients such established San Franciscan names as Wells Fargo Bank, McKesson Corporation, Levi Strauss, The Gap, and Pacific Bell. Neighboring Silicon Valley leaders such as Sun MicroSystems, Oracle and Yahoo have also recognized Executive Direction, as the best source for locating talented individuals. To meet the increased demand for qualified high-tech staffing, Executive Direction plans to open a second office in Silicon Valley in early 1998.

The philosophy of Executive Direction is: Don't try to be everything to everyone, the department store model, be the best at what we can offer, the boutique approach. As one of the few recruitment firms to remain independent, their emphasis has consistently been on quality work, not just big numbers. This sharp focus has led to a 90 percent referral-based business and 30 percent to 100 percent growth in the last three years alone.

Executive Direction's commitment to finding talented professionals starts with the industry expertise of their highly trained staff in all areas of technology. These employees are themselves veterans of the high-tech industry. They are intimately familiar with the type of talent sought by their clients. Striving to stay current, the staff regularly attends computer shows and studies the latest development trends in the high-tech marketplace.

Due to the influence of Silicon Valley, Bay Area companies have become highly computerized. Clients from around the globe are now looking to San Francisco and Executive Direction, having discovered that business today is increasingly

"Executive Direction Inc. has the expertise in understanding how we work and is remarkably efficient in sensing our needs. They are exceptionally adept at working, partnering, and targeting very key individuals for our specific requirements."
Michelle Rittenburg
VP Corporate IR
Sun Microsystems
(Far right)

Fred Naderi, CEO and President of Executive Direction, Inc.

dependent on technology personnel to stay competitive in a demanding marketplace.

Founder Rick Decker, now retired, is credited with the implementation of Executive Direction's database system, developing unique software to house a revolving list of over 50,000 professionals. This sophisticated system not only tracks potential employees in all ranks of technology, but the ever-changing corporate personality of the client companies as well. The database provides a complete profile of a prospective candidate, not just listed skills and employment track record, but the nontangibles in the corporate culture, such as character and personality. This emphasis on recruiting "know-how" and "fit" has become an Executive Direction trademark.

As the result of corporate restructuring and downsizing, an increasing number of companies contract with high-tech professionals on a temporary basis to augment their permanent staffing needs. Combining contract and full-time employees has helped companies to achieve higher output per worker and greatly improve their productivity and competitiveness. Highly-specialized consultants are "warehoused" by Executive Direction and delivered to clients "just-in-time" for the duration of projects necessary to complete the job. Among the advantages of contract hiring are built-in efficiency, eliminating the need for costly re-training of staff, keeping permanent staff at a manageable size, diminishing the threat of downsizing and/or wrongful termination suits and providing a smart way to excel in a technologically escalating society. This "just-in-time" temporary employment concept has become an integral component of Executive Direction services.

Fred Naderi discovered a need for career counseling after teaching computer courses through Berkeley's University of California Extension program where he found an alarming number of computer science students floundering in their careers, unsure of how to advance, or so confused they were at risk of losing their careers altogether. What Naderi calls "career architecture" is a service of Executive Direction which provides career counseling and planning for a wide range of professionals from fresh MBA graduates to seasoned executives.

Clients have found Executive Direction's use of technology combined with focused recruiting expertise exceeds expectations, and, saves crucial time and costly mistakes in staffing. The search process of Executive Direction provides clients with research, consulting, recommendations and negotiations at the final stage of selection, all with the highest standards of objectivity and confidentiality. Executive Direction's consulting service compliments full-time hiring and assists clients with the concept of "just-in-time" talent for greater productivity.

Over 500 major corporations have relied on Executive Direction to guide them to the brightest minds in the Bay Area.

"Executive Direction was a life saver for me some years ago at Pacific Telesis when I needed to put a top notch technical team together from scratch to go after an emerging market in a hurry."
Scott Teissler, Chief Technology Officer CNN
(Top left)

"Executive Direction is a customer focused organization that understands the personality of its clients and delivers qualified compatible candidates."
James A. Pappas, VP & CIO SBC Directory Operations

"Executive Direction recognizes the fine line between 'experience' and 'aptitude;' they focus on filling specific positions with the best talent in the industry."
Zod Nazem
Vice President of Engineering Yahoo, Inc.
(Bottom left)

H.J. Brunnier Associates

Henry J. Brunnier was a 26-year-old engineer when he came to San Francisco to help rebuild the devastated street railway system after the earthquake and fire of 1906. He remained in San Francisco for more than 50 years, establishing an engineering firm that has helped design many of the City's best known landmarks.

$eals Stadium (Far right)

An Iowa State University graduate, Brunnier nearly succumbed to the lure of baseball while working at his first engineering job in Pittsburgh. He spent his weekends pitching semi-pro ball, but he rejected a contract offer from the Pirates to pursue a career in engineering that eventually led him to San Francisco.

He opened his own structural engineering office in the City in 1908. Among its first commissions, the firm designed the sea wall along the Embarcadero and designed the Santa Cruz Wharf. It also provided the structural design for the nine-story Sharon Building across the street from the Palace Hotel. Brunnier's firm relocated its offices to the Sharon Building after it was completed in 1912 and has remained there ever since.

$hell Building

In his firm's early years, Brunnier entered into a long and rewarding partnership with George Kelham,

one of the City's foremost architects. In the 1910s, 1920s and 1930s, the office performed structural engineering for many of Kelham's buildings, including the San Francisco Public Library, Standard Oil Building, Federal Reserve Bank Building, Shell Building and Russ Building (which, until 1964, was San Francisco's tallest skyscraper). Kelham and Brunnier also designed the Mount Davidson Cross, built in 1912.

Brunnier, the former baseball player, also worked with Kelham to design Seals Stadium, home of the minor league San Francisco Seals (Joe DiMaggio's first team). Located at 16th and Bryant, Seals Stadium was acclaimed the finest minor league facility in the U.S. and was the first ball park to be designed for night games. The playing field was underlain with an extensive system of underground pipes to drain rain water off the field so the team could resume play when the rain subsided.

Brunnier served on the five-member board of renowned consulting engineers who supervised the design of the San Francisco-Oakland Bay Bridge, constructed between 1933 and 1936. He was selected for the board not only for his engineering expertise but also for his ability to address audiences and gain public support for the project.

In 1940, the U.S. Navy awarded Brunnier a contract to design a submarine base in Panama. Many experienced engineers were reluctant to travel to Panama, so Brunnier recruited several recent engineering graduates to work there. Four of them — Herbert Lyell, Stanley Teixeira, Charles DeMaria and Andrew Stevens — later formed the nucleus of the San Francisco firm in the postwar era, along with Melvin Klyce and longtime Chief Engineer Henry Powers, who was succeeded by Lyell.

Following World War II, the office was responsible for the structural engineering of many of the City's most prominent corporate headquarters and offices. These include the 52-story Bank of America World Headquarters, the 22-story Crown Zellerbach Building, a 22-story addition to the Standard Oil Building, the 34-story PG&E Headquarters, the 22- and 40-story Chevron office towers on Market Street, the Golden Gateway Center, the Fairmont Hotel tower and the 30-story California State Automobile Association headquarters.

The firm also designed the award winning Ice Arena for the 1960 Winter Olympics in Squaw Valley, Eastman Kodak's Pacific Northern Region distribution center in San Ramon, a major portion of the huge United Airlines Maintenance Center at the San Francisco Airport, and food processing facilities for Kraft General Foods Corp. in San Leandro.

In 1963, the office incorporated as H.J. Brunnier Associates, under the ownership of six of its engineers, four of whom began their careers working for the firm in Panama. The office continues to practice with principal Edwin Zacher, and structural engineers, David Nicholson, and Detlev Doring. In 1993, Zacher was honored by the International Conference of Building Officials, acknowledging his con-tribution to the development of building codes.

Brunnier Associates has received numerous other honors, in-cluding the American Institute of Architects' Award of Merit in 1957 and the Arch-itectural Award

United Airlines Maintenance Center at San Francisco Airport

Bank of America World Headquarters (Far left)

of Excellence from the American Institute of Steel Construction in 1970.

The late Henry Brunnier was a "landmark" citizen as well as a designer of landmark buildings. He helped establish and served on the first California State Board of Registration for Civil Engineers and was elected the first president of the Structural Engineers Association of Northern California. He was chairman of numerous committees of the San Francisco and California Chambers of Commerce.

"Bru" Brunnier also distinguished himself as president of the California State Automobile Association, president of the American Automobile Association, and worldwide president of Rotary International, a community service organization with more than three million members.

These days, the firm that bears Brunnier's name is renovating the United Airlines Maintenance Center and the Kraft General Foods' plant. The company is also involved in numerous projects for Owens-Brockway, an Ohio-based glass container manufacturer which has been a client since 1935. In recent years, Owens-Brockway has become one of the world's foremost glass container manufacturers. Brunnier Associates has been responsible for the structural design of industrial plants for Owens-Brockway throughout the United States and in Mexico, China, Australia, The Netherlands, Poland, Portugal, Hungary, Netherlands, Brazil, Chile, Peru, Ecuador and Venezuela.

Hal Riney & Partners, Inc.

Throughout dozens of commercials, Frank and Ed mixed wine coolers with social commentary.

The original Hal Riney crew, in the days when only Hal was allowed to wear a beard (Bottom right)

The history of advertising agencies in San Francisco can be divided into two distinct periods — everything before 1976; and almost everything since.

The dividing line is when Hal Riney opened the West Coast office of Ogilvy & Mather and launched a creative revolution that elevated San Francisco from its status as an advertising outpost to one of runaway national leadership.

A key move made early-on: The new agency attracted top talent across the nation by paying salaries competitive with those paid on Madison Avenue.

Some of the agency's work is part of the national culture. For example, Henry Weinhard's Private Reserve. Some of the original Henry's commercials still are seen on TV, some 15 years after they were produced — as engaging now as the day they were filmed. Students of advertising like to point out that Henry's

is, quite literally, a *product* of advertising. The agency created the name, the brand, and then the legend that surrounds it.

And then there's Bartles & Jaymes wine cooler. Most of us still can picture the earnest faces of Frank Bartles and Ed Jaymes and the quirky, down-home sincerity of their sales pitch. The ads made Bartles & Jaymes the market leader virtually overnight.

The campaign demonstrates a contrarian view that continues to this day at the agency. All research said wine cooler ads should show young people having fun, that a short product name (like "Bud") was vital, that the tone should be hip. So the agency invented a long name, added two geezers for lifestyle, and struck a tone more rustic than hip.

In 1985, ten years after opening the O&M office, Riney bought it and renamed it Hal Riney & Partners. At the time the industry was consolidating, with billion-dollar mega-agencies at one end of the spectrum; local boutiques at the other. Counter to the trend, HR&P chose its own path to become one of the largest independent agencies in America.

In later years, HR&P upped the ante for creative leadership, making Gallo, Dreyer's, John Deere,

Alamo Rent-A-Car, Serta, and Perrier unforgettable, and admired, brands.

Perhaps the most complex HR&P campaign is that for Saturn cars, recognized last year by the American Advertising Hall of Fame. When Saturn introduced "a different kind of company, a different kind of car" experts said it would fail. No new car company had succeeded in America for more than half a century; competition from imports was fierce; sales were down; consumers were turned off.

Yet HR&P created a successful brand campaign that sold cars as fast as Saturn could make them. Ads told potential buyers what to expect from Saturn and reminded Saturn people what customers expected of them. Saturn's success has changed the way cars are bought and sold in America, challenging all carmakers to put customer service first.

Today Hal Riney & Partners has a broad national base, with clients in Charlotte, N.C., Kansas City, New York, Las Vegas, Orlando, Los Angeles, Chicago, Washington DC.

On the move and growing, the $625 million agency has acquired more than $200 million in new billings in the last 18 months alone — an amount that, if it were a new agency, would be the city's sixth largest.

Which brings up another, largely unintended contribution of HR&P. *The San Francisco Chronicle* estimates 18 agencies have been started here by former HR&P staffers. That's good for the industry. More agencies means a richer infrastructure of film and print production houses, post-production editing services, media specialists and others.

To guage the overall impact on the city, compare Yellow Page listings for ad agencies and services in 1976 and 1997. Clearly *now* is the "good old days" for San Francisco's ad biz.

Though Henry Weinhard's is no longer with the agency, Riney's famous "Chuckwagon" spot still guides the current advertising.
(Top and bottom right)

After the Gallo wedding spot aired, brides-to-be flooded the winery's switchboard in search of the music.
(Top and bottom left)

IDEX Technologies

Take one part technology, one part psychology, knead in some intuition, and what do you have? A highly successful services and consulting business called IDEX. It doesn't hurt that your people are bright and from major corporations, of course, and that they are highly competent in their field. Their product: the understanding of how to use technology well to communicate and transmit information internally within companies.

How did IDEX start? In 1991, its president, tired of his previous corporate positions, decided time was ripe for a change. He broke off to provide problem-solving solutions to companies needing internal integration of their communications systems. Actually, in the case of an early client, VISA, an entire system was required, for they had as yet never thoroughly approached the problem of internal communication.

VISA had quite a staff to integrate, several thousand,

and they were constructing a new building. As they busied themselves with the over-all picture, they gave to IDEX the job of identifying the right technology for them to use. IDEX did more than this. It assessed the needs of the VISA people and constructed communications systems designed to accommodate those needs. This, IDEX acknowledged, was a question of understanding completely not only the business, but the psychological needs of employees.

IDEX's solutions were so successful that within four years they had grown from three to eighty employees. Wells Fargo hired them for a similar job. Then Mervyn's. Then Andersen Consulting. Then Nextel Communications. Then Safeway, Inc. And so on. They were on their way.

What is the business all about? According to its Sr. Vice President, Steve Collins, it's about the modern corporate downsizing trend of viewing business in an

IDEX Technology Center is located in Oakland, California.

entirely different light. Rather than viewing their function as running everything internally, most businesses these days figure their function is to generate income. Regarding management functions which incur major expenses, their job is — whenever possible — to outsource that function, to hire an expert company which is efficient in a specific discipline, and let them manage that discipline.

Valuable rewards accrue to such a conceptualization of the ancient art of business. The client company is relieved of many complex details. The service provider, such as IDEX, becomes, in essence, a partner of its client, and the two grow together. Symbiosis develops. This is apparent in IDEX. Its clients are growing; it is growing. From an original 800 feet of space, it has today 28,000 square feet in its Oakland offices. It now has 210 full-time employees servicing over 100 clients.

Although most of IDEX's clients are substantial, small clients are not discouraged. Some are as small as seven people. IDEX intuitively knows that many small clients serve large client bases of their own and that the small client functions as a reference to its larger client base. One gets to be the best in this business, it becomes rapidly apparent, when one is truly service oriented.

Referrals at IDEX have been so strong that only recently has it even created a sales team. With current revenue at $30 million annually, twelve assertive young sales people are now moving the company towards its five year sales goal of $250 million per year. The over-all culture of the firm is clearly geared for growth.

In addition to Oakland, IDEX has expanded offices now to Portland, Denver, Seattle, Houston, Dallas, and Chicago. It is aggressively heading into the

Attention to detail is always a priority at IDEX.

Eastern United States, Europe, and Latin American markets. As a full-service consulting firm, IDEX provides in-house the broadest range of technology consulting from client server to mainframe, network, voice, and voice and data cabling. Specializing in no vertical niche, the company maintains a completely horizontal approach to providing solutions to communication issues.

Its secret seems to be to keep its eye on the far horizons but to glance down frequently and make sure its feet remain firmly on the ground. Not a bad pathfinding stance for any company to take, and particularly apropos for one whose claim to fame rests on its ability to read the ever-changing book of technology and understand what it has read.

John R. McKean & Co.

Certified Public Accountants

From left to right, John R. McKean , Founding Partner: Simon S. Teng, Senior Partner- Consulting; Thomas Chu, Manager- Audit and Accounting; Terence J. Callaghan, Senior Partner- Audit and Accounting; Scott Copeland, Manager- Consulting; Richard Woodul, Manager- Tax; and Douglas G. Schultz, Partner- Tax. (Top right)

Main Conference Room

John R. McKean & Co. is a San Francisco-based firm of Certified Public Accountants serving clients in the Bay Area and throughout California, as well as other states. Now entering its fifth decade of operations, the firm is one of the largest independent CPA firms in the San Francisco Bay Area.

The firm has four partners and a significant professional and support staff that serves a growing base of clients with a broad spectrum of auditing and accounting, tax, and management consulting services, including litigation support and law firm management services. The client base includes law firms, medical services, transportation, construction, real estate, office products, financial services, wholesale distributors, retail operations and non-profit organizations.

Besides John R. McKean, the founding partner, the other partners are: Terence J. Callaghan, a senior firm partner responsible for the firm's Audit and Accounting Services Group; Simon S. Teng, senior partner responsible for Management Consulting Services to transportation and other companies; and Douglas G. Schultz, the partner who manages the firm's Tax Services Group.

John R. McKean & Co. is rated by an outside source as being among the top 25 of the 800 to 900 CPA firms in the Bay Area. It has earned such a prestigious rating primarily through its ability and willingness to take measured risks, by its depth of staff, and by the variety of services it offers. The firm's growth as a direct result of its

entrepreneurial approach to business is evidenced by its expanding clientele.

In 1992, the firm underlined its long-term commitment to the City of San Francisco and the Bay Area by purchasing and rehabilitating an office building in the historic Jackson Square area of downtown San Francisco. The extensively renovated John R. McKean & Co. building was constructed in 1907. Prior to the firm's move to this permanent location, it was located for many years at the One California Street building.

John R. McKean & Co. started business as a CPA firm of accountants and tax specialists, and it is that basis of expertise that still draws clients to it today. With today's new technologies — business problems, regulatory environments, personnel needs and demands — succeeding in business, especially for smaller companies, requires more than enthusiasm, knowledge of a market, or a good product or service. Companies need financial reports that are also useful management tools. There are problems in taxation that require not just compliance with state or federal regulations, but artful planning to maximize the client's return on investment. Problems in business systems and strategic planning require experience and analytical skills that have been hardened in a competitive crucible. It is for the above reasons that more and more clients are turning to John R. McKean & Co., for the firm's expertise allows it to contribute significantly to its clients' financial success.

For a local CPA firm, John R. McKean & Co. serves a very significant number of major law firms. Their litigation support service in evidence-gathering, fact analysis, and expert testimony is an important part of the firm's practice. Litigation came alive in the 70s, and for the twenty years since then John R. McKean & Co. has been part of a "who's who" of CPA firms that serve law firm clients in litigation support. In addition, the firm assists law firm clients in developing and using management tools for effective budgeting, cash flow projections, cost and profitability assessment, and tax planning.

Through years of hands-on experience, the firm has gained skills built upon familiarity with the practices of specific industries, so John R. McKean & Co.'s auditing and accounting services begin by assessing a client's service needs. Then, by bringing to the auditing task a team of accountants, tax specialists and business experts, the firm not only delivers a service, but becomes a useful adviser to a client's own business management team.

A team approach is also used for assisting clients' management teams in addressing the problems of financial reporting, tax planning, and managing controls and systems — all of which can affect profitability. Although well versed in such areas as production, distribution, or marketing, a business's management team may not recognize financial and management problems in their early stages. Increasingly, then, companies are turning to John R. McKean & Co. for assistance in these areas.

John R. McKean & Co. finds its tax practice functioning in several basic areas such as compliance, tax returns for corporations, partnerships, individuals, estates, and fiduciaries. By far, however, the major part of the practice revolves around tax planning and consultation for the firm's business clients. In most of John R. McKean's client engagements tax planning is integral to the services the firm provides. Tax planning — structuring a business in accordance with the tax laws to legally minimize taxes — is how John R. McKean can truly help improve the profitability of a company.

Now, as it enters its fifth decade of operations, the firm's structure is allowing the company to be slowly transitioned from John R. McKean to other partners and managers. And the high-ranked CPA firm looks forward to many years of continued success in its historic San Francisco location.

Administrative Area

Reception Area
(Bottom left)

Landor Associates

A carton of Dreyer's ice cream, the label on a Pete's Wicked Ale, the FedEx truck, the Netscape logo. These, and thousands of other corporate and brand identities, are the ingrained images of everyday life. Some a true work of modern art. All distinctly identifiable. Most designed by Landor Associates of San Francisco.

The number of Landor's local clients is astronomical — Safeway, Bank of America, Levi Strauss, to name a few. Add in the global factor — Cathay Pacific Airways, 1998 Nagano Olympic Winter Games, Union Bank of Switzerland, and the government of South Australia — for an inkling of how this major player truly covers the world.

Now the world's largest branding and design consultancy, Landor Associates was founded in 1941 by the dapper Walter Landor. One of the first to recognize the strategic business applications of effective packaging design and visual communications, Landor's insights into using design as a marketing tool proved visionary. His inspired creations moved people as never before.

In 1964, Walter Landor purchased a decommissioned ferry boat, the *Klamath*, and converted it into Landor Associates' office, where the company's headquarters remained moored at San Francisco's Pier 5 until 1987. This flagship symbol of the full-steam-ahead company endures to this day as the corporate icon. Famous for not only his business savvy but his love of entertaining and San Francisco

style, Walter Landor's death in 1995 was mourned by thousands worldwide, rating a tribute in Herb Caen's column in the *San Francisco Chronicle*.

Today, Landor Associates' international headquarters is solidly berthed in an historic, brick, waterfront building. As befitting the premier global branding and design firm, it is a modern, artistically decorated facility which was once a glass warehouse in the early 1900s. Landor's network of offices worldwide includes full-service consulting and design studios in New York, Seattle, London, Paris, Hamburg, Hong Kong, Tokyo, and Mexico City, as well as marketing and consulting offices in Chicago, Miami, Madrid, Milan, Stockholm, and Seoul. In 1989, the company was purchased by Young & Rubicam, Inc., the global advertising and communications concern.

Landor's branding consulting and design services — a multifaceted process involving research, strategic analysis, creative exploration, design and implementation — are renowned. But the firm has also established a solid reputation in product/corporate name creation. Companies looking to

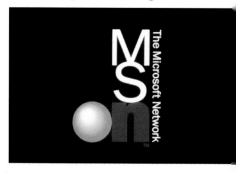

make their mark can benefit as telecommunications firm, Lucent Technologies, did when it was formed as a result of AT&T's restructuring. To distinguish itself as a separate, viable entity worldwide, this $20 billion "start up" company came to Landor to create both its name and corporate identity.

Often, the name is firmly in place, it's the image that may need revitalizing. Varig Airlines, Gerber, Frito-Lay, and Microsoft are recent examples of

major, recognizable corporations that commissioned Landor for a total redesign of their corporate identity, brand identity, or packaging.

San Francisco has contributed to Landor's own identity, one that's multicultural and cosmopolitan. In return, Landor's success has established San Francisco as an international design center. As Landor's CEO, Clay S. Timon, says: "The City has always had a unique global awareness and sensibility. This perspective certainly influenced our pioneering efforts to expand the brand consulting and design business beyond our own borders. Commitment and communication technology enables us to provide clients with a singular blend of local expertise and global resources."

Landor's philosophy is one of giving back to the community, taking on numerous pro bono works. Among the key projects are: San Francisco Zoo, Library, World Affairs Council, Art Institute, Film Festival, Sierra Club, and the Red Cross.

With a multiple award-winning talent team of approximately 200 San Francisco employees, 550 worldwide, Landor Associates' brilliant designs not only stand the test of time, they stand alone as great works of modern art.

Sandy Nash Personnel

The San Francisco financial district building where Sandy Nash Personnel is located is standard enough: the lobby of the building is tidy and business-like, and after you get off the elevator, brass, black lettered placards tell you the names of its businesses. Once inside Sandy Nash's door, however, you are hit by the difference between the book and its cover. A cozy, overstuffed sofa, coffee table with albums filled with thank-you notes, and a charming, hand-painted "welcome" sign set the tone for Sandy's unique and winning combination of warmth and astuteness, making the job seeker feel they have entered a zone of support, wisdom and skill.

With more than twenty years' experience in the personnel placement field, Sandy Nash is not just a nice woman, but a savvy consultant with a solid track record of results. As everyone knows, the personnel placement business has burgeoned incredibly over the last ten or so years, creating, especially during the recession of the early 1990s, an employers' market of unprecedented proportion. However, as these businesses were bought, sold, and merged, the "human" factor in the human relations equation was often sacrificed to a process in which any adult with a pulse would fill a job order. "We don't just throw bodies at our clients," says Sandy.

Sandy Nash, owner of Sandy Nash Personnel

Sandy started out with the modest, and at that time, easily definable ambition to be a secretary. Like many women in the 1970s, she worked in a support capacity in which a finite set of skills was required, but which offered a glimpse of the entrepreneurial possibilities increasingly open to her. Switching from a real estate to a temporary placement firm, she worked until her first child was born. In 1983, she returned to work as a placement counselor of permanent secretaries and administrative assistants.

Over the years, Sandy built up a devoted clientele, who followed close behind when she changed agencies. By 1995, buoyed by this support and encouraged by her husband, she decided to strike out on her own. Even for the respect and experience she had won through her years in the industry, the decision was a risky one, and she had to rely on credit cards and a loan with a fairly limited credit line. Cash flow was tight, and Sandy couldn't apply for an Small Business Administration loan until she had been in business for one year. She worked out of a single office for the first year.

Gradually, the orders started to pour in, and Sandy, unable to fill them all herself but wary of expanding too quickly, was faced with the crucial decision of whether to hire additional staff. A classic self-starter, this entrepreneur takes pride in being hands-on: "I am a working manager, and I wanted to stay that way." She was also determined to keep the business small, in order to maintain a manageable, high quality client base, and to avoid falling into a pattern of "throwing bodies."

Finally, she met her match for the position of Vice President of Sales and Marketing, another woman who had risen through the ranks — for IBM, no less. Originally from the East coast, Diane Berger started as a secretary for the industry giant 25 years ago, quickly ascending through the sales, finance and marketing departments. After leaving IBM, this vivacious, seasoned marketing professional found herself in the particularly vulnerable spot shared by those whose loyalty has been with one company for their adult life. That she would trust her instincts with a new, one-person office is testament to Sandy Nash's skill at locating — and landing — top-notch talent.

"We just clicked," says Diane, laughing, "and you have to remember, we're talking two women in a very small space. But we liked and respected each other, so it was perfect." In addition to marketing the

CITY BY THE BAY

312

business, she is also a recruiter. To talk to Diane is to recall something that is, sadly, rare in today's revolving-door-market: a sense of heartfelt allegiance and excitement about the company she is helping to grow. She proudly states that revenues have doubled in the last year. Much of the business comes from referrals.

Diane has set up a marketing infrastructure that matches the size, style, and goals of the business. Capitalizing on Sandy's past successes as well as her own high tech contacts, she has built a client list that is currently over 100 strong. Both women share a talent for "seeing the forest for the trees," keeping up to date with potential candidate-client matches, while looking ahead to the long-term needs of the business.

Rounding out the team are Hilary Liu, a recruiter who brings over ten years' solid administrative field experience to the Sandy Nash placement team, and accountant Jennifer Weaver, formerly an auditor for Deloitte & Touche of San Francisco. Hilary holds a BA in Sociology from UC Irvine. Having served as personal assistant to a major television star, she understands firsthand the importance of chemistry, intuition and creative problem-solving in professional matches. She worked for a personnel agency in Southern California before joining Sandy Nash as a recruiter for permanent jobs, and is noted for her proactive approach and personal attention to each candidate's needs. Jennifer's organizational and accounting skills are excellent; Sandy wonders aloud how she ever got along without her. What's more, Jennifer plays a key role with directing the behind-the-scenes, administrative details which, as Sandy Nash knows better than most, make all the difference.

Sandy's candidates know they can count on her to see past the resume and straight to the core of their skills and personality. Using a combination of skills assessment and intuition, she relies on personal, individualized interviews to gauge social skills, presentation, and a host of other nuances that testing alone would miss. In addition to keeping a database,

which can quickly become out of date, she places candidates immediately, and incredibly, she and Diane keep mental track of dozens of potential matches at any given time. Managers at companies often call back delighted about how the candidates referred meet their specific needs and desires.

The service stays open seven days a week, 24 hours a day for clients' last minute, hard-to-predict staffing needs. The results speak for themselves; Sandy estimates that during the first two and a half years in business, she successfully placed about 1,000 candidates. And the guest book attests to her accomplishments: "Thank you for your kindness and for a wonderful lunch," reads one card. "Thanks to you, I've been offered my dream job!" says another.

Healthy revenues, client satisfaction and a talented staff make Sandy Nash Personnel a success, but even these elements do not tell the whole story. Sandy makes a difference in her community. She recalls one instance when a grandmother who had been on welfare came to her for help, and she placed her in a job for a construction firm. "It's hard to come by satisfaction like that in other kinds of work," she states. Her logo depicts the pieces of a puzzle moving together, and that's how Sandy aptly sees her niche in the complex, globally competitive economy of the City by the Bay. But Sandy Nash doesn't just solve puzzles, she delivers relationships.

Sandy Nash Personnel office staff. (left to right) Hilary Liu, recruiter; Diane Berger, VP sales & marketing; Sandy Nash, owner; Jennifer Weaver, office manager

Solzer & Hail

The printing industry is an important segment of San Francisco's economy. For more than 30 years, Solzer & Hail has been providing important prepress services, such as image scanning, film separation and contract proofing to printers. Founded in May

Solzer & Hail today, where work goes on around-the-clock.

1966 by Wolfgang Solzer, in partnership with Bill Hail, Solzer & Hail is now the oldest single-owner prepress company in town.

Wolfgang Solzer grew up in Germany, graduated from the gymnasium (college), and studied economics in Hamburg. After working for a printing company he learned enough to start his own company, and being young and seeking adventure went to Australia to see the world. He worked for a printing company in Sydney, where his childhood sweetheart joined him in marriage; here their only child was born.

In 1960, the Solzers decided to visit their homeland, traveling through the United States, but when they reached San Francisco they quickly realized they wanted to spend their most productive years here. Solzer soon landed a job, and in 1964 began plans to make his dream of owning his own company come

true. He asked his friend Bill Hail to go along with the venture. Each partner put up $6,000, and in May 1966 opened business as Solzer & Hail. After only two months in business they were self-sufficient.

In its early days the business produced an annual report that was considered the best ever published in San Francisco and brought the company its sobriquet, "Best in San Francisco." The company has never lost this reputation. The business grew, and on July 1, 1975, Solzer & Hail bought the 24,000 square foot building where the company is now located, also owning an adjoining parking lot. In 1994, Solzer bought out Hail's interest.

The company has gone from manual production to a total high tech operation, resulting in many changes. Ten years ago it took five days to complete color separation; now it takes five or ten minutes! Where it once took a week to complete the color separations for a magazine cover, using a modern Linotype Hell scanner Solzer & Hail can now complete the job in minutes. A can label, which requires meticulous attention to detail in type and color, used to require two days' work; now it's a one-day job.

The Loma Prieta earthquake badly damaged the Embarcadero Freeway that ran in front of Solzer & Hail's building. Client access was limited, resulting in significant business loss for the company. The company took advantage of the freeway demolition period, however, by installing new equipment and training employees on the new technology.

When an advertising agency or design firm comes to Solzer & Hail with a job for a brochure or ad campaign poster, it comes with a completed layout, timeline, transparencies, and various files received from the client. Solzer & Hail, processing digital information, makes the color separation translations and prepares the product for printing.

Using laser optics, a Hell scanner converts transparencies into digital information for Scitex. Using a computer screen to monitor the production, workers can scan four colors at a time, adjust them as necessary, and come up with a four-color proof directly. Armed with all the information needed to create a photo, brochure or poster, a disk goes to a desktop computer or Scitex. Scitex software digitally manipulates images to alter color, positioning and content, and allows other graphic components to be added. Craftmen can convert a client's computer files from floppy disk or other digital media cartridge into a format that communicates directly from the Mac to final film output. These files can also be transferred directly to Scitex for further manipulation. Scanned images imported through Scitex and files created on a client's computer can print directly on an Iris inkjet printer, resulting in hard copy color proofs for presentation comps with quality rivaling the impact of finished pieces. Agency personnel can verify the look and feel of the finished image, allowing corrections to be made quickly and cost-effectively.

As the first West Coast operator of the Scitex image creation and processing system, Solzer & Hail helped pioneer and expand the capabilities of digital image manipulation. Solzer & Hail employees are true artists whose comprehensive understanding of lithography makes the most of the system. They can handle everything from color correction and stripping to complete page makeup. The company's Graphics Design Studio can handle special effects such as modeling 3-D shapes, stretching, bending or distoring type or images, and adding liquid, painterly blends. Experienced software personnel can provide customers with full service imaging capabilities.

Whether it's a job for advertising, packaging, sales sheets or brochures, Solzer & Hail has produced it for such notable ad agencies as Goldberg Moser O'Neil advertising, Hal Riney & Partners; Goodby, Silverstein; Saachi & Saachi; Katsin/Loeb + Partners; Pacific Group Marketing; and Foot, Cone & Belding. Other valued clients include Del Monte Foods and Electronic Arts. A company that knows Solzer & Hail's reputation for pulling off "miracles," can trust that a rush job ordered on Friday will be completed

by Monday, for the company operates around the clock with three shifts of workers, and employees will work overtime when client demand is heavy.

New technology required downsizing of the work force, requiring some hard decisions, but the company now does as much or more with 50 employees as when it had 120 eight years ago. There is little employee turnover at Solzer & Hail, partly thanks to Wolfgang Solzer's idea of profit-sharing, which he instituted in 1968 as part of his vision of a company of which the workers could be proud. The first Solzer & Hail retiree received $15,000 in profit-sharing — which took care of him during a subsequent illness. The latest retiree received $100,000 in profit-sharing.

A new integrated computer network among all departments lets employees communicate with each other without leaving their work spaces. Employees can download digital information, put it to a certain media, and ship it out. A $40,000 Canon duplicator can make full-color copies cheaper than a press operation. Internet access allows for rapid transmission of complicated film to Europe or Australia, or from those places to Solzer & Hail.

Solzer & Hail has received many awards, including the Printing Industries of America Benny Premier Print Award, Litho Club awards, Addy awards, and National Gold Ink awards. The San Francisco Green Ribbon Panel named Solzer & Hail a winner of the 1997 Environmental Achievement Award, the only graphic arts company in San Francisco so honored. Working with the Department of Health, the company has eliminated over 70 chemicals from its plant, recycles paper and fluoresecent, and has hardly any spoilage, making it truly a pleasant place to work.

The company supports numerous social, civic and academic causes, and Wolfgang Solzer is on the board of directors of Printing Industries of Northern California.

Wolfgang Solzer, whose dream of owning his own company came true in 1966

Solzer & Hail during the demolition of the Embarcadero Freeway

Watson Wyatt Worldwide

founder Birchard E. Wyatt was a passionate advocate for employee benefit plans at a time when few companies offered them.

In 1995, The Wyatt Company formed a strategic alliance with R Watson & Sons, the largest investment consulting practice in the U.K., to form Watson Wyatt Worldwide. With more than 5,000 employees, in 89 offices, in 36 countries, it is the world's third largest human resource and risk management consulting firm, advising clients in all related areas including comprehensive benefits design, retirement programs, communications and employee education, managing investments, organization effectiveness, and administrative systems. Put simply, Watson Wyatt helps companies make their business strategies work through innovative approaches to motivate, develop, and reward people.

In today's business world, an enlightened approach to human resources is essential for success. But in the early 1940s, when Birchard E. Wyatt (known as "Byrd") founded his actuarial and employee benefit consulting firm in Philadelphia, he was one of only a handful of people in the country who understood how critical benefits like retirement plans, insurance, and profit-sharing could be. He believed that providing security for employees was not only smart business, it was the key to the survival of our capitalist system. And he had the charisma and credentials — an MBA from Wharton, a Ph.D. from Columbia — to convince leading employers that he was right.

With high ideals, enthusiasm, and business savvy, Wyatt attracted other educated, driven professionals in the actuarial and insurance fields. Among them were David Luick, a successful insurance salesman, and Elmore Pollack and Dorrance Bronson, both former members of the federal Social Security Board. Within a few months, The Wyatt Company had expanded and moved from Philadelphia to Washington, D.C. New offices in Chicago, Cleveland, Detroit, and New York quickly followed. With federal income tax legislation encouraging private pension plans, it was a prosperous time for the company.

Unfortunately, it was also a tragic time. In the spring of 1946, Byrd Wyatt, then 38 years old, was diagnosed with cancer. That summer, a few days before his death, Luick, Pollack, Bronson, and four more of Wyatt's top associates, agreed to purchase his company. They knew that carrying on without him would be an enormous challenge, but in the final reckoning they believed The Wyatt Company was not only a viable business, but provided a valuable service to the public. These seven men became the Board of Directors; five would serve as company President in the years to come.

Although Byrd Wyatt led the firm for only a short time, it retained a lot more than just his name. In the early years, he developed basic principles for his company. They emphasized total client satisfaction and the importance of highly qualified personnel. The wisdom of these principles has seen the firm through more than fifty years.

Within a few years of Wyatt's death, the company

Human Resources Online

Personal Information | Health & Welfare | Pension | Savings | Life Events

Policies & Procedure | Workplace | Career | Pay | HR Q& A

had recovered enough to acquire another firm — a prominent actuarial organization dating back to 1865. It would be the first of many auspicious mergers and acquisitions. At the same time, company officers recruited a number of entrepreneurial-minded managers to open Wyatt offices near clients in other cities. Both expansion strategies have continued to serve the firm well.

But though the company has grown in every way, many elements of its corporate culture date back to the early years. One of these is a concern for public policy. David Luick, President of Wyatt from 1948 to 1961, served on the Secretary of Labors' "Committee on Pension Costs and the Older Worker" in 1952. Today, Watson Wyatt's head of Research and Information, Sylvester Schieber, is involved in Social Security reform. Continuing another long tradition, several Wyatt associates have authored books, contributing to the human resource field and to the public's understanding of workplace issues. Recent titles include *Don't Work Forever: Simple Steps Baby Boomers Must Take to Ever Retire* (John Wiley and Sons, Inc., 1995) by Steven Vernon, a senior retirement consultant, and *The Reward Plan Advantage* (Jossey-Bass, 1996) by Jerry McAdams, a senior rewards and recognition consultant.

The Wyatt Company came to the West Coast in 1962 when the firm purchased an Illinois company that had a San Francisco office. Since then, the Bay Area has been an important market for the company. With its proximity to Silicon Valley, the San Francisco office has traded on another one of Watson Wyatt's well-established strengths: the use of state-of-the-art technology. Watson Wyatt associates are experts in "Virtual HR." They help clients empower their employees by giving them easy access to information about their benefits and enrollment through the Web, multimedia kiosks, and the telephone.

Working with Bay Area companies helps keep the firm on the cutting edge in other ways as well. "San Francisco companies play a significant role in shaping corporate cultures," explains a Watson Wyatt executive. "With the Bay Area's progressive social attitudes, they often face new workplace issues before companies in other parts of the world." Watson Wyatt Worldwide helps clients handle these challenges in creative ways.

A sample online menu. Through the Web and company internets, employees can manage their own benefits, freeing human resource administrators to play a more strategic role.

Watson Wyatt helps clients transform their human resources using the latest technology. With "Virtual HR," employees can have access to information right at their desks.

Furth, Fahrner & Mason

To understand the success of Furth, Fahrner & Mason, a prestigious Bay Area law firm, one must understand Frederick P. Furth, who established the firm in 1966. A man who personifies the enterprising, pioneering spirit of the old West, where fortunes were made in another era, Furth is a self-made millionaire, who overcame obstacles to establish a renowned law firm. He is also a rugged adventurer who flies his own jet on business trips, a winery owner who produces premium wines, and an informed philanthropist who contributes to worthy causes.

Frederick P. Furth

Born and raised in modest circumstances in an Illinois steel town, Furth put himself through law school at the University of Michigan and then went on to study law at the University of Berlin and the University of Munich. After working at the Wall Street firm of Cahill, Gordon, Reindel & Ohl, Furth came to San Francisco to work as an associate in a commercial litigation firm before establishing his own law firm.

Furth's big break came in 1967 when — through his own initiative — he discovered the potential rewards of a massive class-action antitrust suit. In this case which lasted six and one-half years, Furth represented a group of building material dealers who successfully charged manufacturers of gypsum wallboard with a price-fixing conspiracy. In the final settlement of $82.9 million to the plaintiffs, Furth collected $4.2 million in legal fees.

Today, Furth, Fahrner & Mason is an internationally known law firm specializing in business litigation. Situated in the historic Royal Globe Insurance Company building — now known as the Furth Building — Furth, Fahrner & Mason works with a relatively small number of clients in order to maintain its commitment to high quality service. The firm's clientele have ranged from individual entrepreneurs and small companies to multi-national corporations such as Kellogg Company, Columbia Pictures, Chrysler Corporation, AMC and Weyerhaeuser. It has represented clients throughout the United States, Europe and China.

In addition to serving as Chairman of the law firm, Furth also serves as a director of Robert Half International, Inc., and as a director of the Center for Democracy. He is also prominent in the national Democratic Party.

Fred Furth's fierce independence, which has made him somewhat of a legend in Bay Area legal circles, extends to other areas of his professional and personal life. On business trips, for example, he pilots his own jet, a Citation X. Furth is also the founder of Chalk Hill Winery, a California ultra-premium winery in Sonoma County. Along with his wife Peggy, Furth manages the winery, which is considered one of the top 100 ultra-premium wineries in the world.

In 1969, Furth and his family established the Furth Family Foundation to assist those most in need and least able to help themselves, with particular focus on children, including those in Eastern-Bloc European countries. Since its inception, the Foundation has given grants totaling more than $5 million.

For Fred and Peggy Furth, the opportunity to help those less fortunate is one of the more rewarding aspects of success. As Furth once wrote in an article on the Furth Foundation, money provides one with the independence to "pursue matters of real interest."

Adolph Gasser, Inc.

In 1950, Adolph Gasser established a retail sales organization offering photographic equipment and supplies to individuals, companies and large organizations. Long known as Adolph Gasser, Inc., the business is considered the best source in Northern California for photographic, video, motion picture, and audio visual equipment and supplies.

After graduating from high school, Adolph Gasser, a native San Franciscan, worked for Sharman Camera Works repairing wooden view cameras and Kodak folding cameras, press cameras, and altering European cameras to use U.S. film sizes.

In 1936, Gasser decided to go into business for himself and opened General Camera Repair and developed a good reputation for quality work. He learned a lot about photographic equipment and became closely associated with Ansel Adams, Imogen Cunningham, and other noted West Coast photographers. During World War II, *Life* magazine combat photographers such as Margaret Bourke-White and Eugene Smith came through San Francisco, and Adolph Gasser repaired their equipment.

Enlisting in 1944, Gasser was assigned to the Air Corps as a camera technician, and later to the Photo Division of the 509 Composite Group at the Wendover, Utah, base that housed Silverplate, the atomic bomb unit. Gasser was on Tinian Island the night the *Enola Gay* took off to drop the atomic bomb on Hiroshima. The plane had a 9x9 K22 camera on board, but Gasser loaded a small hand-held aerial camera and showed the tail gunner how to use it. The tail gunner's pictures of the bombing were the only ones that came out.

Returning home, Gasser soon built up his business again, but didn't want to be a camera technician all his life, so in 1950 decided to risk everything and go into the camera and retail business. Mortgaging his home and borrowing money on a G.I. bill, he bought a small retail camera store on Geary Blvd. at 22nd Ave., and continued his repair work. The company was founded on the premise of understanding and satisfying customers' needs. The business grew, primarily by word of mouth, and in 1975 expanded its operation by opening a store in downtown San Francisco on 2nd Street.

On April 9, 1989, a three-alarm arson fire at the downtown store caused $750,000 damage to the building and $1.3 million in inventory loss which, fortunately, was covered by insurance. Adolph Gasser and son, John thought of their many dedicated employees and his valued customers, and decided to rebuild. Fortunately, the October 17, 1989, earthquake caused no damage, and the business fully reopened.

The 1990 recession cost the company $1 million in business, but the company is now in good shape. The 74 employees benefit from a healthy profit-sharing plan, and customers benefit from personalized service. To keep up with the digital revolution, Adolph Gasser Inc. has put in a state-of-the-art color processing lab to develop color negatives and transparencies, and color reprints and enlargements from negatives. Gasser's also house both the Kodak Create-A-Print machine and the Kodak Copy Print Station machine that allows customers self-service access to enlargements from color negatives and from original prints.

John Gasser is a full partner with his father in business, but Adolph Gasser, at age 85, still works every day. Competitors have gone by the wayside, but Adolph Gasser Inc. is still a San Francisco mainstay.

Adolph Gasser, founder of Adolph Gasser, Inc., at 85. (Top left)

Firefighters respond to a three-alarm arson fire at Gasser's downtown store in 1989. The company rebuilt immediately.

Graceful Transitions

Many people go through life as if sleepwalking — seemingly awake, but not truly conscious of their own gifts, talents and purpose. Indeed, entire industries have been built on the question: "Am I really doing what I want with my life?"

This is a familiar question for Roslyn Whitney. As a Spiritual/Business Life Coach, Roslyn helps people go inside themselves to discover their own answers — what's missing, lost or simply undeveloped. Like a metaphysical detective following clues, Roslyn passionately pursues a path to allow her clients to connect with their personal goals, ambitions, dreams and realities. In this way, she guides others towards truly serving themselves, as well as their families, friends and careers. With the approach of the millennium, more people are taking risks to feel a deeper sense of connection to themselves, their community and to the universal life chord. Through caring professionals like Roslyn, psychological and mystical tools are available to make sense out of life's often-challenging questions.

Roslyn Whitney, Spiritual/Business Life Coach

Roslyn's unique gift is the ability to literally transform people — both professionally and personally. This talent was developed out of her own path of self-discovery, shortly after she realized that her special skill was in communication. That's why she pursued a career in psychology, receiving a Master's Degree in Psycho-Social Sciences and Community Psychology from Pennsylvania State University. Called "a natural" healer by her instructor, Roslyn began to more fully realize her own role in the universe and the tremendous power of female energy. Thus began her very passionate quest to help heal the planet. By healing the person, it impacts the family, which improves the community and so on. The result is the ultimate domino effect — global transformation, one soul at a time.

From custom designing workshops to private sessions in her Bay Area office, Roslyn works with an expansive range of individuals and businesses through one-on-one and group sessions. Balancing energy in the workplace is essential for the well-being of both enterprise and employees. The setting may be a work environment, but the key is still its "spirit" — the heart of the company. So in addition to speaking to a business groups, Roslyn frequently works with top entrenpeneurs and CEOs. Graceful Transition's services are used by many savvy corporations who believe in balancing profit and work ethics. The value is full-circle and comes back through both healthier people and profits.

To dream the impossible dream? Perhaps. But even dreams can be transformed into reality with the proper tools. That's why so many different people and groups seek Rosyln's guidance. By joining hands and taking the leap of faith together, Roslyn gives others the courage to connect to their dreams and work toward making them into a living reality. Not surprisingly, many of her clients feel distinctly different afterwards. Some laugh, others cry, but each feels transformed by the experience. That's because Roslyn is a wellness professional who encourages both inward and outward growth, a synergistic approach which often results in a total life change. That's where Roslyn's practical and successful counseling tools are most effective. Graceful Transitions enables individuals to use their personal power to visualize and identify their goals in order to make positive life changes — healing the planet dream by dream.

Highway One

The dynamic nature of late twentieth century San Francisco can be illustrated by one of its leading marketing communication firms: Highway One. The history of the company's evolution parallels San Francisco's growth as an international trend-setter and world leader in many industries. The people at Highway One have had fun along their road to success, while helping a variety of clients tell the world about products and services with creative, individually tailored marketing programs.

Highway One began in 1983 with two phones, a computer and no clients. President and CEO Andrea Metzler, after heading west from North Carolina when RJR Nabisco acquired San Francisco-based Del Monte, became a "frustrated client" looking for local help to service her brands. Seeing opportunity in what she couldn't find, she decided to start her own marketing agency. She sold her house, left the corporate world and opened a small office in downtown San Francisco, over a city landmark — Tadich's Grill.

The agency's first client was Sprint, then an up and coming telecommunications company seeking a share of a newly deregulated industry. Like many of its clients, Highway One has grown over the years and is now the fifteenth largest marketing agency in San Francisco, with billings exceeding $50 million and 75 employees. Current clients include Visa, Coca-Cola, Pete's Brewing Company, Bank of America, Hewlett Packard, General Motors, Data Broadcast Corporation and The California Milk Advisory Board, to name a few.

Metzler attributes Highway One's success to her team of talented employees and their ability to create innovative solutions that help build clients' brands. The company keeps its edge by staying on top of consumer and industry trends, then designing creative campaigns using a variety of communication vehicles. Clients have come to rely on Highway One's strategic and creative use of television, radio, direct mail and the Internet to get the word out on their products and services.

The same energy that drives Highway One's marketing campaigns also goes back into several of San Francisco's non-profit organizations. The agency is actively involved in promoting the City Store, a Pier 39 memorabilia shop which funds organizations that help the homeless. By creating a direct mail campaign showing what would happen if local parks went unsupported, Highway One helped Golden Gate National Park Association raise awareness of public lands threatened by development. The agency has recently begun to work with Swords to Plowshares, an organization dedicated to helping San Francisco's homeless veterans.

In 1994 Highway One was acquired by the MacManus Group, the 10th largest global communications network, giving the agency access to international opportunities. Highway One looks forward to paving the way around the world for their clients — right into the next century.

Highway One Executive Committee: (clockwise from left) Siena Long, Vice President, Account Director; Dick Eaton, Senior Vice President, Chief Financial Officer; Phillip Feemster, Senior Vice President, Executive Creative Director; Craig Metzler, Senior Vice President, Chief Information Officer; Janna Thomas, Vice President, Director of Creative Services; Andrea Metzler, President.

Logan & Associates

Martha Logan has been a bookkeeper for so long she remembers what it was like to complete general ledgers manually, without using computers. She has been operating her business for more than a decade, and in that time her firm has become one of the largest bookkeeping services in San Francisco.

Logan & Associates caters to small and medium-size businesses. The firm performs bookkeeping services for clients in a diverse range of professions and occupations, including doctors, lawyers, restaurant owners, software developers, photographers and graphic designers. Logan & Associates also serves a number of nonprofit organizations.

Logan & Associates is a full-charge bookkeeping service, providing its clients with complete general ledgers, financial statements, billing, accounts payable and accounts receivable.

Martha Logan, owner

In many cases, Logan & Associates acts as a complete accounting department, eliminating the need for a full-time bookkeeper, and in most cases saving the client thousands of dollars each year. The firm also saves its clients money by maintaining high quality business records, often eliminating clients' needs to see an accountant more than once or twice a year.

Martha Logan began her bookkeeping service in 1983, shortly after graduating from the University of California at Berkeley with a degree in economics. From the outset, she sought to operate her business as a serious, full-time profession, not as a part-time hobby. The goal of her business has been to provide her clients with the most accurate and reliable bookkeeping service in the City.

The key to Logan & Associates' success is the hard work of the staff, who make an extra effort to keep clients satisfied with their bookkeeping systems. Logan is flexible, trying to keep what works for the clients in tune with accurate accounting records. Many clients have been using a system for years which Logan can update to integrate with high technology, without compromising the client's level of comfort.

Logan & Associates is familiar with many of the accounting systems on the market and will strive to select the appropriate package for each client. A client may see a system in operation at another company and wish to employ it at their company, but it may not be the appropriate system; Logan & Associates can help make that important decision, drawing upon the firm's knowledge of a particular industry or profession.

Martha Logan's business has grown through the years and currently employs five associates. The firm recently moved to new offices at Post Street near Van Ness Avenue in the Cathedral Hill area of San Francisco. Throughout the years, Logan and her staff have worked hard to promote and grow their business. The majority of her clients are referrals from satisfied customers.

Korn/Ferry International

In late 1969, Richard Ferry and Lester Korn started the first step on a global adventure that continues today.

So the two young entrepreneurs decided to strike out on their own in virtually uncharted territory — and became the youngest partners ever to retire from Peat Marwick, a giant accounting firm in Los Angeles. With a $10,000 investment, a secretary, and one phone, they opened the doors to Korn/Ferry International in Los Angeles.

From the very start, the two founders had a clear mission: To help companies acquire the leadership capital — the asset that sets all others in motion — needed to grow and prosper in an increasingly global environment.

In 1971, the firm has opened in New York and, on New Year's Day, 1972, established an office in San Francisco, reflecting the growth and potential Korn/Ferry saw in this market. That same year, the firm moved into Europe and then Asia and the Pacific in 1973 — the first major firm to open an office in Japan. The "international" in the Korn/Ferry name was becoming a reality.

Today, Korn/Ferry is the number one search firm in the world, with revenues of $270 million and 65 offices in 39 countries, serving about 3,000 clients a year. Since 1969, the firm has handled over 60,000 senior-level assignments for companies ranging from the major multinationals to high-growth and start-up companies.

Since its founding, Korn/Ferry has continued to reinvent the business of search, changing the ways that organizations worldwide identify the leadership

to help them stay on top. Korn/Ferry realized the potential that technology offered the business early on, starting in the mid-eighties to create a comprehensive computerized database of world-class executive talent from all around the globe. Today, consultants based in any of the offices can quickly and easily access information on over 500,000 potential candidates. Videoconferencing, too, has transformed the industry, instantly linking clients, candidates, and search professionals — and Korn/Ferry was the first to implement videoconferencing nationwide. The firm can work for its clients twenty-four hours a day across the globe.

The firm pioneered the concept of specialty practices in 1970, recognizing that clients need consultants who understand their vision, strategy, structure, and culture, and can forecast future industry developments. Korn/Ferry publishes numerous surveys and in-depth reports. A recent widely quoted study done in conjunction with the Economist intelligence unit points to the skills needed for the global executive of tomorrow.

As a corporate citizen of San Francisco, the firm is a member of the San Francisco Chamber of Commerce; is a patron of the San Francisco Symphony; and has sponsored other organizations around the San Francisco area.

The San Francisco office of Korn/Ferry continues to build on the momentum started back in 1972 — reaching over $10 million in revenues this year and executing more than 150 assignments. The growth of the office is a direct result of the confidence that Bay Area companies place in the firm — with repeat business at over 70 percent from satisfied clients that turn to Korn/Ferry again and again for its objective advice on human resource strategies.

Richard M. Ferry, founding partner of Korn/Ferry International (Top left)

David Nosal, partner and managing director of the San Francisco office of Korn/Ferry International

"Korn/Ferry has revolutionized and institutionalized the business, spawned dozens of competitors, and helped transform the way executives switch jobs." — *John A. Byrne, The Headhunters*

Romac International

Romac International is a firm that searches to find the most valuable resource for its clients — talented people.

The Bay Area's branch of Romac International, an executive search and contract placement firm, was established in 1987 by two young businessmen, John McLaughlin and Steve Reiter, who started out in a small office in San Francisco. Today, Romac International is a sprawling regional enterprise, with five offices that provide Bay Area businesses with the best and the brightest talent in the job market. Romac's clients include high-profile companies such as Hewlett Packard, Clorox, Silicon Graphics, Applied Materials, Franklin Funds, Oracle, Wells Fargo and The Gap, as well as many small and medium-sized companies.

Steve Reiter and John McLaughlin, founders of the Bay Area Romac International.

Romac's success in the Bay Area can be traced to the energy, expertise and entrepreneurial spirit of McLaughlin and Reiter, who uprooted their young families to fulfill their dream of owning their own business. After researching metropolitan areas as possible sites for their staffing company, they chose San Francisco for its "vibrant business community across multiple industries, and receptiveness to start-ups," says McLaughlin. "The Bay Area marketplace is very competitive in the search industry, but in our history here, the demand for strong technical professionals has always exceeded supply. That's a great formula for growth," add Reiter.

From the start, McLaughlin and Reiter — with backgrounds in accounting and finance — developed a simple corporate philosophy: provide highly personalized service to both clients and candidates. During the company's expansion, the two partners worked diligently to accomplish this mission, cultivating and maintaining strong business relationships with their clients while developing a reputation for highly ethical, honest interactions with their candidates. And internally, they fostered a high energy, entrepreneurial — and fun — corporate culture that gave their own employees the resources and environment in which they could find their own personal success. The individuals who joined the company in its early years are still there, and now form the core of a fine management team. As a result, Romac International is now one of the Bay Area's premier search firms, renowned for its deep understanding of the needs and goals of both the company and the candidate.

Romac focuses on two high-demand professional niches: accounting/finance, and information technology. The firm offers a wide range of placement services that include executive search, long-term contracts, short-term temporary help and career consulting. Whether a company needs a CFO or a systems analyst, Romac's extensive resources and contacts ensure prompt, successful placement. And, with offices in San Francisco, San Jose, Redwood City, Oakland, and Walnut Creek, Romac is capable of handling searches for clients throughout the entire Bay Area.

The most important key to the firm's success is the quality of Romac's internal staff. Search consultants have strong professional backgrounds, proven technical skills, and through their training and on-the-job experience at Romac grow into some of the most knowledgeable staffing consultants in their fields. After all, Romac knows that when it comes to success, a company's most valuable resource is its people.

PAGE 17
MONDAY, MARCH

THE WALL STREET

Dow Jones & Company, Inc. All Rights Reserved.

SMALL BUSINESS

More Firms Quiz Customers
For Clues About Competition

By STEVEN P. GALANTE
Staff Reporter of THE WALL STREET JOURNAL

JOHN GRUBB WANTED to distinguish his San Francisco construction company, Clearwood Building Inc., from a host of
competitors. So, in early 1983, he and his brother Robert
started talking to Clearwood's customers: the architects and
designers who hired their services.

What, the brothers asked their customers, were the worst features of Clearwood's competitors? The answer: Bad manners,
workers who tracked dirt across carpets, and
beat-up construction trucks, which high-class
clients objected to having parked in their drive-
ways.

Those seemingly small points were the
signal for a repositioning. The brothers decided
to make Clearwood the contractor of choice
among the Bay Area's upper crust. The company bought a new truck and and
its estimators donned
work crews, now

Partners

HEALTH, EDUCATIONAL,

HUMANITARIAN AND

RELIGIOUS INSTITUTIONS,

AND SERVICES, AS

WELL AS RECREATION-

ORIENTED COMPANIES

ALL CONTRIBUTE TO

THE QUALITY OF LIFE

IN SAN FRANCISCO.

Quality of Life

Getz Bros. & Co. Inc.

San Francisco Mayor Willie Brown (second from left) and some of Getz's employees celebrate the company's 125th anniversary. Brown proclaimed Sept. 11, 1996 "Getz Bros. Day" in the City to commemorate this historic event.

Getz Bros. & Co. — the nation's largest non-commodity international marketing and distribution company — traces its beginnings to 1871 and a trading post in Lower Lake, California, a small frontier town a hundred miles north of San Francisco.

Today, more than 125 years later, the little country trading post has grown to become a worldwide leader in the import-export trade, with more than 80 offices, distribution centers and production facilities in Europe, Asia, Australia and North America. In the same way that Joseph Getz's trading post bridged the 19th Century to the 20th Century, Getz Bros. & Co. is preparing to meet the challenges of the 21st Century by broadening its product base to include computer software, pharmaceuticals, medical equipment and other high-technology and biomedical products.

Getz Bros. & Co. provides global production, marketing and distributing services for consumer products, office furnishing, building products, chemicals, pharmaceuticals, biomedical and industrial equipment businesses. It has annual revenues of almost U.S. $1 billion and a staff of more than 2,200 employees throughout the world.

Getz is a member of The Marmon Group of companies, an international association of more than 60 autonomous member companies engaged in manufacturing and services worldwide. It is a Fortune 100 company with annual revenues of U.S. $6 billion.

In 1996, Getz Bros. & Co. — together with the City in which it is headquartered — celebrated the company's 125th Anniversary and the enduring growth and diversity of its operations. San Francisco Mayor Willie Brown proclaimed September 11, 1996 "Getz Bros. Day" in the City, and awarded the company a personalized plaque. Getz Bros. also received special recognition from California State Senator Milton Marks, the San Francisco Chamber of Commerce, the San Francisco Historical Society and The Honorable Pete Wilson, Governor of California.

In recent years, Getz Bros. has expanded its base of operations by purchasing Medtel, a distributor of medical devices and equipment in the Asia/ Pacific region, from St. Jude Medical Inc. Getz also acquired the Telectronics pacemaker brand name, which Getz will market throughout Asia and worldwide in the future. Also, Getz acquired Innoxa, a United Kingdom cosmetic company with plants and product distribution in South Africa and Australia, and Getz Pharma, a Pakistani-based company which develops, produces and markets ethical drugs and over-the-counter health products. With the purchase of Innoxa and Getz Pharma, Getz Bros. is now manufacturing personal care products as well as marketing and distributing them.

The company continues to broaden its businesses in new global markets and has successfully sought new business opportunities in Hungary, the Baltics, Pakistan, the People's Republic of China, Vietnam, Cambodia, Thailand, Taiwan, the Philippines, South Africa and Australia.

Every day, millions of people in more than 23 countries use one or more of the many products which Getz Bros. sells or manufactures — everything from

Some of Innoxa's anti-stress skin care products. Innoxa believes no animal should suffer for the sake of their customers' skin and has never tested its products on animals.

shampoo to pacemakers. Here are some of the many activities in which the company is engaged:

Medtel

In 1997 Getz acquired Medtel, a distributor of Medical devices and equipment. The addition of the Telectronics brand — which will be made for Getz by St. Jude under a private Supply Agreement — is significant because Getz typically acts as a marketer, taking possession of products branded by other Companies and distributing them through Industrial and Consumer channels. With Telectronics, Getz now has its own pacemaker brand to market in addition to the St. Jude pacesetter brand.

Innoxa

In 1996, Getz acquired Innoxa, a cosmetics company with facilities in Pietermaritzburg, South Africa, Sydney, Australia and New Zealand. Since 1919, Innoxa cosmetics have specialized in hypo-allergenic skin care and cosmetics suitable for even the most sensitive of skins. Innoxa's philosophy is "First Do No Harm," and the company never has and never will test its products on animals. Its choice of external suppliers reflects this philosophy — the company purchases supplies only from individuals that guarantee their products have not been animal tested. Innoxa manufactures and sells cleansing oil, lotions, moisturizers, UV protection and other skin care products.

Getz Bros. Co., Ltd.

Based in Tokyo, Japan, this division of the company develops and markets revolutionary high-technology medical equipment. These therapeutic instruments include pacemakers, artificial heart valves, catheters, centrifugal pump systems, vascular diagnostic equipment, and echo-cardiographic analyzers.

Getz Japan also produces two computer software programs. One program, GetzNet, is a software system that enables physicians and hospitals to maintain and track up-to-date medical information about their patients. The company also produces a financial information software system which is marketed to Japanese banks.

Getz Hungary

Getz has adjusted to the rapidly changing global business environment by expanding into new areas of the world, including Central and Eastern Europe. In 1989, Getz purchased Inter-cooperation Co. Ltd., a trading company based in Budapest, Hungary. One of Intercooperation's divisions markets and distributes a wide range of consumer products, including William Grant & Sons Scotch whiskey, Heineken Beer, and health and beauty care products. Another division markets flooring, tiles, insulation and other building materials.

In 1993, Getz purchased Agroker Budapesti, thus becoming the first U.S. company to purchase 100 percent of two Hungarian companies. Agroker markets and distributes products for agricultural businesses, including tractors, fertilizers, pesticides, dried fruit and frozen vegetables.

The Getz Hungarian Writer's Prize award for writing, a prestigious and sought-after symbol of literary excellence, is presented annually in Budapest by Mr. Robert Pritzker, President and CEO of The Marmon Group, Inc., and the Hungarian Prime Minister.

The Baltics

As part of its move into Eastern Europe, Getz in recent years expanded its trading operations into Latvia, Estonia and Lithuania. Getz is marketing and distributing numerous products in these countries, including automotive care supplics, health care goods and women's lingerie.

Getz Pharma

Based in Karachi, Pakistan, Getz Pharma develops, manufactures and markets pharmaceutical and biotechnology products. Three of its products are brand leaders. Others are well-positioned to capture major market share. Getz Pharma also manufactures ethical drugs and health products for major multinational pharmaceutical companies operating in Pakistan.

The company, originally called Saitex Pharmaceuticals Pvt., Ltd., was established in 1983, with technical assistance from Syntex Corporation of Palo

Getz-Japan develops and markets high-technology therapeutic instruments, including (from top) artificial heart valves, pacemakers and catheters.

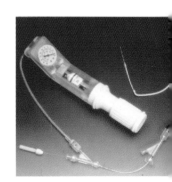

Some of the modular office furniture distributed by Getz-Singapore.

Alto, California. Getz Bros. & Co. acquired the company in 1995. Since its acquisition by Getz, the company has been provided the technological, marketing and management resources needed to meet the challenges of the 21st Century.

Getz Bros. & Co. (Singapore), Pte. Ltd: Getz has designed and constructed a state-of-the-art warehouse in Singapore. This is a "paperless" facility, with fully-computerized operations that ease storage and retrieval of a variety of products that are housed there, including building materials, pharmaceuticals, consumer goods and mattresses.

Getz Singapore also manufactures Work Place, a collection of desks, chairs, tables, shelves, storage and file cabinets, and other office furnishings. Eclipse, another modular office system, features wall panels, desks, cabinets, shelves and other items to create individual work and conference areas that allow for the optimum use of space.

Getz Philippines

This unit has two core businesses in The Philippines. One distributes health care and beauty care products, such as shampoo and hair cream. The other markets medical instruments and industrial instruments.

Intercooperation Co., Ltd., one of two Budapest-based trading companies which Getz Bros. acquired to broaden its base in the Central and Eastern European marketplace.

Milbrands, Inc.

Milbrands provides sales, marketing and distribution services for U.S. manufacturers in military commissaries, exchanges and clubs on U.S. Military bases located in this country, Europe and the Pacific. Its portfolio of products encompasses grocery products, household goods, perishable products, health and beauty aids, soft drinks, beer, wines and spirits, hardware, sporting goods, electronics and major appliances.

Getz International Travel

Getz Bros. & Co. brings the experience gained from 125 years of international trade to the management of Getz International Travel, which specializes in providing services to business travelers. Getz International Travel accesses American Airlines' SABRE system and the computerized systems of other major airlines to obtain for its clients the best schedules and fares to all international and domestic destinations for business or personal travel.

The company provides its customers with management reports to monitor their travel budget and expense levels from its main offices in San Francisco, Chicago, Indianapolis, Orlando, Phoenix, Budapest, Warsaw and London.

Getz Bros. & Co. offers unparalleled service in the area of international trade in part because the company has continually opened and maintained offices throughout the world. Getz has offices in Australia, the People's Republic of China, Hong Kong, Hungary, India, Japan, Korea, Pakistan, the Philippines, Singapore, Sri Lanka, Taiwan, Thailand, Malaysia, Cambodia, the United Kingdom, Finland, Latvia, Estonia, Lithuania, South Africa and Germany.

U.S. manufacturers benefit from Getz Bros.' expertise in a number of ways. Working with Getz enables them to move into markets they would not feel confident to enter by themselves. Getz Bros. maintains an extensive infrastructure of warehouses, trucks and equipment that enables it to effectively market and distribute products in overseas locations.

Getz's U.S. trading partners also gain from the good name that Getz has established throughout the world, particularly in Asia. Some of the brand names associated with Getz include Gallo, Heinz, Perrier, Quaker Oats, Upjohn, Massey-Ferguson, Black & Decker, Eastman Kodak, Maidenform, Helene Curtis, Eli Lilly, St. Jude Medical, Pacesetter, General Electric and Smith & Wesson.

Getz Bros. & Co. was founded by Joseph Getz and his younger brother, Max, Prussian immigrants who came to the U.S. in 1855. The brothers opened a trading business in California, and in a few years were joined by two other brothers — Solomon and Louis.

The four brothers moved their trading business to San Francisco in 1871, opening a market stall that sold meat and dairy products provided on consignment by the manufacturer to farmers in Lake County, about a hundred miles north of the City. Around the same time, Joseph Getz opened a general store in the Lake County town of Lower Lake that sold dry goods and groceries to farmers.

By the early 1880s, Getz Bros. was exporting food products to customers in Shanghai, Hong Kong, Calcutta and Madras. These shipments included canned and cured foods, some bearing the proprietary name of Getzbest.

By 1925, descendants of Joseph and Louis Getz had relinquished control of the company. The firm continued to thrive and its overseas clients remained loyal through the ensuing decades.

From left: Robert Pritzker, Agnes Gergely, the 1996 winner of the Getz Hungarian Writer's Prize, and Arpad Goncz, President of the Republic of Hungary.

The company underwent a major change in 1981, when Getz's parent company, Trans Union Corp., became a member of The Marmon Group. By re-focusing on the Getz's traditional strengths and setting new goals, The Marmon Group positioned Getz Bros. to take advantage of its incomparable knowledge of the Far East and become a leader in Pacific Rim trade.

As the new century dawns, Getz Bros. & Co. has kept pace with modern technology and business developments. It has modernized its facilities to contain the latest computerized systems and equipment. It has entered new fields of business — such as computer software, pharmaceuticals and bio-medical equipment — that reflect the changing world economy. And it continues to seek new business opportunities throughout the globe.

This ability to adapt to changing times and technologies has enabled Getz Bros. & Co. to survive and thrive for more than 125 years. This spirit of invention and innovation should enable the company to thrive into the 21st century.

Getz Pharma's manufacturing plant in Karachi, Pakistan. Acquired by Getz in 1995, Getz Pharma produces and markets pharmaceutical specialty and biotechnology products. (Far left)

Getz-Singapore's paperless warehouse is fully computerized to enable workers to easily store and retrieve a variety of products that are housed there.

San Francisco Veterans Affairs Medical Center

Impressive view of VA
Medical Center today
with the Golden Gate in
the background

Parasitic disease expert
Dr. James McKerrow
(Bottom right)

High on a bluff overlooking both the Pacific Ocean and the San Francisco Bay, encircled by dense cypress tress, is the 29-building campus of the San Francisco Veterans Affairs Medical Center. On an upper floor of one of the main buildings is the office of Dr. James McKerrow and through the window at his back is the broad expanse of the blue bay beyond.

But Dr. McKerrow's attention is on the computer screen in front of him as he studies the complex molecular pattern of a pathological organism called schistosomiasis which is responsible for a parasitic disease common in Third World countries.

Hundreds of millions of people living in the tropics and subtropics become infected with schistosomiasis each year by swimming in contaminated water. The result is a liver problem that debilitates most people and may kill children and young adults.

American men and women veterans are counted among those afflicted by schistosomiasis and other such parasitic diseases. As a result of U.S. involvement overseas, beginning with Southeast Asia, more and more veterans return home with chronic and severe physical afflictions that were seldom seen and rarely treated before World War II.

The numbers of cases of chronic fatigue, stomach and liver disorders and skin lesions have been increasing for years in VA hospitals all over the country, especially since U.S. military involvement in the Middle East and Africa.

Health officials in Washington, D.C., realizing the need for more clinical research in the treatment of parasitic diseases, four years ago allocated funds for this specialized area of medicine and enlisted the help of Dr. McKerrow and his team of experts.

The San Francisco VA Medical Center treats many cases of parasitic and other emerging infections annually. Depending on their symptoms, the patients receive monitored doses of special antimicrobial drugs. Still more effective drug treatment is being studied by VA researchers. Using computer graphics, they are able to simulate disease targets and then determine how various drugs interact. It is this kind of research that gives Dr. McKerrow a sense of accomplishment and fulfillment.

Clinical and research data are being shared with other medical facilities via the medical center's high-tech telecommunications system. The medical center has invested heavily in video conferencing equipment and now regularly conducts video conferences with other hospitals in the Bay Area. Research done by Dr. McKerrow and other specialists is also transmitted to medical and educational facilities around the world via the Internet. With technology being such a critical aspect of today's medicine, the San Francisco VA Medical Center incorporates it on a daily basis — from the operating room to library cataloging.

More than 220,00 veterans, most of them outpatients, are treated at the medical center each year.

Patients come from as far away as 400 miles for treatment — the area from which the medical center draws is from the San Francisco peninsula north to the Oregon border, encompassing the counties of San Mateo, San Francisco, Marin, Napa, Sonoma, Lake, Mendocino, Humboldt and Del Norte.

The medical center also cares for veterans where they live in communities like Santa Rosa, Ukiah and Eureka. Thousands of veterans who in the past would have had to travel to San Francisco can now receive evaluation and treatment at locations closer to home.

Two years ago, the San Francisco VA Medical

Center established a customer-friendly service called Telephone Linked Care (TLC). TLC is a call-in service that offers veterans an advice nurse, appointment scheduling, eligibility information and information on pharmaceuticals. By telephoning the medical center's TLC toll-free number, veterans can now receive assistance seven days a week, 24 hours a day right from the comfort of home. Another service making life easier for veterans is VA Autophone. Veterans can call VA Autophone's number and automatically order prescription refills.

Many VA and non-VA medical facilities throughout California, Nevada and Hawaii call upon the medical center's specialists regarding diseases and conditions that are heavily researched in San Francisco — among them — HIV/AIDS treatment.

Dr. Peter Jensen, Chief of Infectious Diseases,

treats 700 patients a year in a program that provides comprehensive health care for veterans with HIV and AIDS. He says that many of the veterans he treats are without jobs, without health insurance and without family support.

They receive the most up-to-date drug therapy available as well as counseling. The clinic has been so successful that it has increased its ability to provide care for more veterans. It now treats one-third of all the HIV/AIDS patients in San Francisco who are veterans. San Francisco has a large gay population that has been hit hard by the AIDS epidemic. Because of the depth of Dr. Jensen's program, it has become a model for VA hospitals everywhere.

When the San Francisco VA Medical Center was dedicated on Armistice Day in 1934, the medical center comprised 21 buildings and cost $1,250,000 to construct. Now, the annual research budget alone is nearly $25 million in VA and non-VA funds.

When it first opened, the medical center had only 25 doctors on staff and a total of 350 employees. Today, there are 1,700 employees working at the medical center along with 500 volunteers and 1,500 medical students. Volunteers, some even of high school age, can be seen in the corridors conducting any number of invaluable tasks. A popular location for volunteers is the medical center's modern 120-bed nursing home. The nursing home is where mostly elderly veterans who can no longer care for themselves receive long-term care. Some

Medical Center's satellite clinic in Santa Rose

Main driveway to the Department of Medical Affairs Medical Center San Francisco (Far left)

Aerial view of original veterans hospital in 1934

of the veterans, however, are not so old; instead they may be terminally ill and require quality compassionate hospice care. When the medical center opened, it had a 12-bed ward for women veterans. In recent decades, the proportion of women veterans has dramatically increased so now there is a comprehensive health center designed specifically for women veterans.

In a bright and cheerful office on the third floor of the main hospital building, nurse practitioner Rebecca Fines coordinates the care and treatment of women veterans. The atmosphere at the Women Veterans Comprehensive Health Care Center is warm and friendly, and just a little on the feminine side with pastel walls and floral wallpaper trim.

On any given day, women veterans will have the opportunity to talk frankly with their health care provider about their health concerns such as osteoporosis, breast cancer, and hypertension. They may also discuss other sensitive issues such as readjustment to civilian life and the sexual harassment that some may have experienced while on active duty.

With women veterans becoming the fastest-growing group in the whole VA system, the Women's Clinic staff is prepared to provide high-quality comprehensive health care women veterans need and deserve.

Another group that receives special attention is made up of homeless veterans, whose numbers have been growing for years; a program to address their unique needs was started in 1991.

Social Workers Julie Angeloni and Bobbie Rosenthal set up the comprehensive homeless center with the goal of linking veterans who are down and out with the appropriate treatment and referral.

Rosenthal estimates that 50 percent of the veterans who are homeless were once on the battlefields of Vietnam. They live on the streets, for the most part,

she says, because they are uneducated, lack job skills or are substance abusers. Sometimes, it is a combination of all of these factors.

Veterans who participate in the program are screened for any health problems, medical or mental, and then referred to agencies or people who can help them find jobs and get back into the mainstream.

Some homeless veterans receive a helping hand by participating in a unique VA program called Veterans Industries. This is a sophisticated program that employs homeless veterans while at the same time it provides a wide array of competitive contract services to Bay Area businesses. The homeless veterans who work for Veterans Industries are paid an

hourly wage and learn valuable skills that will help them to find employment and stay employed. The program's first business client in 1993 was a snowshoe manufacturer that Industries to pack and assemble its new line of snowshoes. In 1996, they handled a half million snowshoes making them ready for the manufacturer's retail outlets. The business has been so pleased with the quality of the work provided by Veterans Industries that it has renewed its contract for the last four years.

The medical center's Comprehensive Homeless Veterans Center helps homeless veterans in other ways, too. The homeless center manages a Compensated Work Therapy (CWT) program in which homeless veterans are employed by the medical center in any number of non-clinical jobs. At the same time, the homeless veteran is employed and gaining skills in the workforce, CWT offers him or her temporary housing if it is needed. The temporary housing program, called Transitional Residency, offers veterans a place to stay for up to one year.

The San Francisco VA Medical Center is also recognized as a leader in the adaptation of state-of-the-art technological advances such as magnetic resonance imaging (MRI) and magnetic resonance spectroscopy (MRS).

MRI and MRS permit doctors to make assessments of medical conditions previously difficult to detect. Both imaging technologies are safe and non-invasive and provide the physician and researcher with detailed medical information that a few years ago was simply not available.

In the MRS unit, situated in the basement of the hospital building, Dr. Michael Weiner and his staff use the newest in high-tech magnetic spectroscopy equipment to analyze the metabolic changes in such illnesses as epilepsy, Alzheimer's, HIV, and Lou Gehrig's disease and multiple sclerosis.

Dr. Charles Anderson, working in the MRI unit, was the first doctor on the West Coast to use magnetic resonance angiography in the study of the carotid artery. "By using this technique," says Dr. Anderson, "it is less invasive to the patient and has faster and more accurate results."

Much of the clinical research conducted at the San Francisco VA Medical Center and at other VA medical centers has not only improved the health care for veterans, but indeed, for all Americans. The Department of Veterans Affairs medical facilities have been on the cutting edge of clinical care and science for many decades and have, in fact, been leaders in some now accepted procedures such as organ transplants. Countries such as Japan and Russia have called upon the San Francisco VA Medical Center to learn new techniques for treatment of post-traumatic stress disorder (PTSD) and substance abuse. The medical center's

research program is dynamic and has been in the forefront of the treatment of sleep and neurological memory disorders, substance abuse, HIV/AIDS, PTSD, speech pathologies, cancer treatment, post-surgery care for patients at cardiac risk, and many other medical conditions.

The San Francisco VA Medical Center was one of the very first VA health care facilities to create a web site on the Internet. It was also the first to make it possible for veterans to apply for health care benefits with a click of a mouse. Now, with a personal computer, a veteran can visit the medical center's home page and easily find information about the facility, its history, and the services it offers veterans.

The San Francisco VA Medical Center has a strong and active academic affiliation with the University of California at San Francisco (UCSF). Both facilities are keenly aware of the advantages the affiliation brings to each. Approximately 1,500 medical students, interns and residents receive some of their clinical training each year at the medical center. Because the medical center is a teaching hospital, all its physicians and researchers hold academic faculty appointments at the university, thereby bringing a continuity to medical treatment, teaching and clinical research.

The San Francisco VA Medical Center offers veterans the benefits of quality comprehensive health care, advanced technologies, highly skilled physicians and nurses, and intensive and relevant clinical research. These attributes focus on the complicated health care needs of the veterans of today and prepare the medical center for the health care needs of the veterans of tomorrow.

Dr. Michael Weiner demonstrating the latest technology in magnetic resonance spectroscopy (Above)

Dr. Peter Jenson interviewing patient in the infectious disease clinic

Dr. Charles Anderson conferring with colleague in MRI unit (Far left)

Academy of Art College

Like many successful creative ventures, the Academy of Art College in San Francisco — the largest and fastest-growing private art and design college in the nation — began with a simple vision.

In 1929, a young artist named Richard S. Stephens and his wife Clara had just returned to America from Paris, where they had been living on stock dividends and the money generated from the sale of Richard's paintings. However, the stock market crash wiped out their income, forcing the young couple back to San Francisco, where they planned to start an art school that would be open to anyone with the desire to succeed as an artist.

With only $2,000 and the income Richard earned as art director for Sunset Magazine, the Stephens opened The Academy of Advertising Art in a loft on Kearny Street. It consisted of 46 students and was based on Richard's philosophy that aspiring artists and designers, with hard work, dedication, and the proper instruction, can learn the skills needed to become successful professionals.

To accomplish this goal, Stephens hired instructors who were working, professional artists, familiar with the realities and demands of the marketplace. Because Stephens believed that every successful artist must learn the fundamentals of art, the curriculum included the study of color, perspective, design, and figure drawing.

These basic principles provided the foundation of the Academy curriculum that would allow it to grow and become one of the finest private art colleges in the world.

When Richard and Clara's son, Richard A. Stephens, took over the Academy's presidency in 1951, his goal was to retain the Academy's basic tenets, but to grow and change with the times. With a master's degree in art from Stanford, he was well-qualified to guide the Academy's expansion. Over the next four decades, the Academy expanded from one to thirteen buildings, and added a wider range of courses. In 1966, the Academy officially became a college, with

Richard Stephens
and his daughter Elisa

Painting by Alumnus Veerakeat Tongpaiboon
(Top right)
Print by Alumnus Baoping Chen
(Bottom, right)

approval from the California Department of Education to grant a Bachelor of Fine Arts Degree. In another decade, the Master of Fine Arts Degree was offered.

By the mid-1980s, San Francisco residents were becoming increasingly familiar with the Academy's distinctive black-and-white signs that have since become a part of the city's downtown landscape, as familiar as the Academy's black-and-white buses used to shuttle students from classrooms, studios, galleries and dormitories.

Richard's daughter, Elisa, joined her father at the Academy in 1991 after graduating from Vassar College and earning a law degree from the Univeristy of San Francisco. She now serves as president of the Academy. Richard Stephens serves as chaiman of the board. This second- and third-generation team of Academy administration continues to carry on the family tradition of molding the college to fit today's needs. They were quick to recognize that the merging of art and technology brought by the digital revolution was creating a demand for a new breed of artist — one that can produce and thrive in a high-tech environment. To meet this demand, the Academy expanded its computer arts department and opened a new, sophisticated digital arts center south of Market Street, just blocks from the Museum of Modern Art.

This center houses state-of-the-art video and computer technology.

It virtually hums with the creative energy of students working at over 500 workstations. Due to the Academy's commitment to digital training, Silicon Graphics Inc. selected the center to be one of only eight SGI Training Studios in the nation. The Academy's job placement office works closely with these well-trained visual artists to assure that they are placed. Pixar Pictures, Adobe, Accolade, Dreamworks, Walt Disney, Hallmark and major advertising and graphic design firms all recruit graduates regularly.

More than 5,000 students, representing almost every country in the world, attend the Academy. Bachelor of Fine Arts and Master of Fine Arts Degrees are offered in thirteen majors. The Academy provides a strong "English as a Second Language" program to accommodate the large international student enrollment.

It is the Academy's ongoing mission to be a positive influence on the San Francisco community. Its local endeavors include summer youth programs, sponsorship of local and national art contests and the donation of art services to non-profit groups.

The Academy operates five non-profit galleries, featuring not only works by locally and world-renowned artists, but also the Academy's own students, faculty and alumni. This is in keeping with Richard S. Stephens' original vision — to promote and encourage the careers of visual artists.

Students studying motion picture and video production use the 20' by 30' designated blue screen room.

Sculpture by Alumnus Nils Krueger (Far left)

Digital Center

Independent Mobility Repair

Originally from Malaysia, Jeremy Chung came to the United States and San Francisco in 1985, because his wife has family here. The first of his family to come to America, he said he never dreamed of going into business. Once here, he worked repairing hospital mobility equipment. But after eight years as a repairman and a brief stint working for a wheelchair company in San Mateo County, Chung decided to leave the more corporate world. He took the plunge and went into business for himself in 1994.

The one-man shop opened on a shoestring expanded rapidly. In less than three years, the business quadrupled in size to better serve its customers, outgrowing its original location.

Jeremy Chung, owner and founder of Independent Mobility Repair Chung now owns one of the few San Francisco-based businesses that can do custom wheelchair design. Independent Mobility Repair operates from a modest Sunset district storefront, but covers the entire San Francisco Bay Area, making house calls as far north as Sacramento, as far east as Oakley and as far south as Aptos. The business is three-fold, focusing on customizing electric wheelchairs for individual clients, repairing and maintaining equipment, and installing equipment in homes and vehicles.

The shop supplies, repairs, and customizes equipment to meet the needs of children, adults, and the elderly, with staffers trained to assess each customer's special needs. Shop staffers make house calls, conduct in-house evaluations, and install equipment ranging from car and van scooter lifts and chair lifts to hospital beds and body lifts.

Independent Mobility Repair contracts to repair mobility equipment at area hospitals and to supply rental wheelchairs when available to museums and convention centers. For custom work, the shop maintains a billing consultant in Hayward.

Technology has revolutionized mobility equipment, especially chairs. Electric wheelchairs are programmed to fit a client, making them faster or slower, or more or less sensitive in response. Technological developments have given electric wheelchairs new ranges of adaptability and versatility. Infrared scanning technology used on wheelchairs for stop and go commands enables disabled children, for example, to feel more comfortable and less restricted. In fact, a man in Texas developed the infrared technology to help his disabled son. IMR has worked with the inventor from the beginning to adapt his product into wheelchairs. Pediatric electric wheelchairs, equipped with the command module or electronic brain, can also be controlled by toe commands and tongue touch commands. For those with C-2 spinal damage, in which the spine is damaged at the second vertebrae, chairs can be controlled using the chin control and bib array, while those with C-1 spinal damage, such as actor Christopher Reeve, use the sip and puff method of control. Invacare electronics products have developed to the point that control parameters can be customized and programmed to a degree of sensitivity that can match the way a client breathes. By contrast, in older electric wheelchair control systems, a chair user had to huff in a precise way at a very small, precise target to get a response from their chair. With head arrays, clients can break a fiber optic beam, which can be adjusted in widths of from 2 to 12 inches, with a nod of the head, with the chair veering according to the head movement.

Available technology serves as a sort of invisible helper for the disabled. Although IMR uses many Invacare electronic components when customizing wheelchairs, the company can adapt any manufactuer's products, mixing and matching to suit a customer's needs. Products developed by up to six different manufacturers can be combined in one custom chair. Customizing wheelchairs involves working with orthoprosthetics, the science of how seating posture affects the rest of the body, because every disability brings with it a different set of parameters for consideration.

Workers at Independent Mobility Repair see about 400 customers in a year, only 10 to 20 of whom are so severely disabled they will need the most technologically sophisticated chairs, such as that used by actor and director Christopher Reeves. The company works with paraplegics and quadriplegics, and those with multiple sclerosis, cerebral palsy and Amyotrophic Lateral Sclerosis — ALS (or Lou Gehrig's disease).

As part of a broad range of community commitments, one IMR staffer serves on the Alameda Mayor's Committee for the Disabled. In addition, IMR's occupational therapist, herself disabled, instructs San Francisco's paratransit providers in how to best serve those who require mobility equipment. Another staff member has participated in benefit fund raisers for the Recreation Center for the Handicapped in San Francisco.

IMR is a member of the Pacific Area Rehabilitation Association, a coalition of rehabilitation business owners who seek to educate the public about issues affecting the disabled, and who meet with Medicare representatives to advocate for the rights of patients and clients and allocation of adequate funding. IMR is also a member of the California Association of Medical Suppliers, a lobbying group which fights for patients and clients rights and proper funding.

In ongoing commitments to the San Francisco community, IMR has sponsored an MS walk, co-sponsored similar events with other businesses and manufacturers, and donated equipment.

IMR remains a small but vitally important company with heart and a loyal client base, part of the diverse fabric of the San Francisco business community.

Chung's philosophy at IMR has always been to do his best to help all his customers using the technology available and his own expertise. He hopes to be able to share knowledge and equipment with his Malaysian homeland — where mobility equipment is so expensive the average wage earner cannot possibly afford such products for disabled family members — either by opening another business overseas or by donating and refurbishing equipment.

San Francisco State University

Nighttime gives a different look to the Arts & Industry building.

The highlight of SFSU's 1995 commencement exercises was First Lady Hillary Rodham Clinton's address to graduates. Here Mrs. Clinton enters the university stadium with President Robert A. Corrigan.

With its long and colorful history in the City by the Bay, San Francisco State University has in a century of life gained a prominent role as a community resource and partner. The University is also known well beyond the Bay Area for the research discoveries and creative work of its faculty, its success in educating a diverse student population, and its innovative programs that link the classroom with the community.

San Francisco State has come far since its founding in 1899 as a teacher training institution whose first graduating class comprised 36 young ladies. Today, as a preeminent public, urban university preparing students to be leaders in a global and diverse society, San Francisco State offers a comprehensive academic program of 112 undergraduate and 95 graduate degrees, with fields of study that include such new areas as Jewish Studies, Vietnamese American Studies (the first such program on any major campus in the country), conservation genetics, and the nation's largest multimedia studies program. The University now graduates some 5,000 men and women each year.

With a conservation genetics laboratory equaled in the U.S. only by the Smithsonian; the nation's only College of Ethnic Studies; internationally-known programs in such wide-ranging areas as gerontology, international business, and wheelchair design; arts programs that have produced Academy Award winners, top-flight actors and best-selling writers; a computer animation program that the San Francisco Chronicle terms the "national leader," and many more areas of excellence, San Francisco State has distinguished itself as a creative, constantly-evolving institution.

The University's 96-acre main campus is located in southwest San Francisco. Through its College of Extended Learning, SFSU has a major City-center presence at its Downtown Center, which offers an extensive, credit-bearing, business curriculum; professional development classes; work-related certificate programs; custom-designed workplace education and — with "Multimedia Gulch" at the doorstep — the Multimedia Studies Program. The Romberg Tiburon Center for Environmental Studies, the only such research center located on the shores of San Francisco Bay, conducts major environmental research, with emphasis on the health of the Bay and its supporting estuary system.

An excellent faculty who combine teaching and research responsibilities have won increasing national and international recognition for SFSU. Recent instances include:

• The discovery by Prof. Geoff Marcy and SFSU alumnus Paul Butler of new planets outside our solar system capable of supporting life, "Not since Copernicus" had such a leap in our understanding of the universe occurred, wrote *Time* magazine, as the discovery resonated around the globe.

• The discovery by Prof. Tom Smith that the real key to biodiversity may be not the rain forest, but the areas surrounding it — a result which redefines our approach to conservation of species.

• The success of Prof. Frances Mayes' memoir, *Under the Tuscan Sun*, which made the best-seller lists.

• The discovery of a previously unknown creature, an "ice worm," by a team which included Prof. Alissa Arp, who also directs SFSU's Romberg Tiburon Center for Environmental Studies.

At San Francisco State, the community is also a classroom. A wide range of projects — many built into the curriculum — bring faculty and student talent to bear on the issues confronting the Bay Area. SFSU now has more than 100 centers and institutes focusing on community needs. It also has a large and expanding service learning curriculum which offers course credit for such community work. These projects demonstrate SFSU's capacity to generate new

and effective community partnerships, as they give SFSU students unparalleled opportunities to add hands-on experience to their classroom learning.

At the Mission Teen Health Center, for example, situated in Mission High School, SFSU faculty and students from counseling, nursing, and social work have joined forces with San Francisco's Department of Public Health, the School District, Department of Human Services and Kaiser Permanente Hospital to provide health care, parent education programs, internship opportunities at Kaiser, and links to City social services.

In one of many K-12 partnerships, two SFSU education faculty serve as co-principals of John Muir elementary school in San Francisco, where they have developed an innovative program that combines training for future teachers of inner-city students with an educational approach that, in two years, succeeded in lifting Muir from the School District's "troubled list."

The Mission Science Workshop, a partnership of SFSU, City College of San Francisco, the School District and MESA (Math, Engineering and Science Achievement Project) has created a hands-on, experimental lab for neighborhood youngsters. The San Francisco workshop's success prompted the National Science Foundation to award a $3 million grant to expand the program to 10 other California sites.

The newly-created Marian Wright Edelman Institute for the Study of Children, Youth and Families addresses the needs of contemporary families as it trains new generations of professionals able to develop cooperative relationships between policy makers, social service agencies and urban children and their parents.

SFSU is deeply involved in the "America Reads Challenge," President Clinton's national literacy program. Clinton named SFSU President Robert Corrigan to head the national steering committee of university presidents for "America Reads," and more than 800 campuses across the nation have so far joined the effort. In a model program, SFSU has placed 65 specially-trained student tutors in 12 City elementary schools, where they are helping very young readers acquire the skill that is the gateway to success.

Diversity — in students, faculty, curriculum and world view — is a hallmark of San Francisco State. The University is committed to educating the next generations of diverse leadership on which our state and nation will depend. Its success shows in a range of measures:

SFSU's nationally-recognized Step to College program has dramatically increased the numbers of minority students in participating Bay Area high schools who go on to college. At SFSU, "Step" students prosper, graduating at a slightly higher rate than the overall student population.

SFSU is ranked #1 in the nation among comprehensive master's degree institutions for biology undergraduates who go on to earn Ph.D. degrees, and 9th nationally in graduating students of color with bachelor's degrees. It has the highest concentration of Hispanic scientists — five, in biology — in the 23-campus California State University.

To encourage students from underrepresented groups to pursue careers in science teaching and research, SFSU has developed linked master's - Ph.D. programs with the University of California campuses at San Francisco and Davis, among others. Recently, SFSU became the only master's degree campus in the nation to receive GAANN (Graduate Assistance in Areas of National Need) federal funding for one such program.

In her 1995 commencement address, First Lady Hillary Rodham Clinton called SFSU "a great public university — a university that represents the full diversity and possibility of America — that takes the education of all people seriously. That's the kind of university I wanted to come to, to say, Thank you for doing what you do to build students and America."

As it enters its second century, San Francisco State University remains sure of its mission, confident of its worth, and ready to continue to give the best of itself to the citizens it serves.

Assistant Dean for Undergraduate Studies Mario Rivas makes a point in class. (Top right)

Students leave the Business Building after morning classes. (Top left)

California College of Podiatric Medicine

California College of Podiatric
Medicine, dedication of
Tasoine Hall in 1963.
(Top right)

CCPM early 1900s
Podiatric medical students
observe clinicians at work.

Pictured at 1975
Groundbreaking Ceremony
are: (left to right,
foreground) Leonard A. Levy,
DPM, MPH, Dean and Vice
President of Podiatric
Medical and Curricular
Affairs; Florette Pomeroy,
Member, Board of Trustees;
and the Honorable Willie
Brown. In the background
is John Howard, MHA,
Hospital Administrator.

Podiatric medicine is concerned with the prevention, diagnosis, medical and surgical care of diseases and disorders of the foot and ankle. In 1912, chiropodists founded the California College of Chiropody in San Francisco when the field required far less training and did not include surgery or drug prescription privileges.

Operating out of a Victorian in San Francisco's Western Addition, classes began in 1914, graduating five students after a year. Later, it moved in the same neighborhood to Gough Street to accommodate increasing enrollment. In 1925, the college moved to the one square block it occupies today, on Scott be-tween Ellis and Eddy Streets. By 1941, a total of 400 students were enrolled, but enrollment reduced dramatically during World War II. Today, it is back to 400.

The one-year curriculum expanded to four by 1952. Since 1978, new students have at least three years of pre-professional education and take the Medical College Admissions Test (MCAT). Virtually all hold at least a bachelor's degree, having the same preparation as students entering the United States medical school. Graduates must complete no less than one post doctoral residency year in hospitals throughout the nation and many serve two to three years.

In 1960, the college established the California Podiatry Hospital, which has since been renamed the Pacific Coast Hospital of California College of Podiatry, which was changed in 1969 to the current California College of Podiatric Medicine (CCPM). 1975 was a landmark year for the college when a U.S. Public Health Service grant permitted construction of new facilities. Then Dean Dr. Leonard A. Levy participated in groundbreaking ceremonies, attended by a local politician named Willie Brown. Interestingly, Levy left the college that year and returned in

December, 1994 as president, which he still is today.

CCPM is a private, independent, non-profit podiatric medical school, only one of seven in the country. Within the campus is the Northern California Foot and Ankle Center, with the 28-bed hospital, Primary Care Center and specialty clinics. CCPM provides outpatient and inpatient podiatric medical services to many San Francisco residents, from seniors to athletes.

Recently, a Chinese Community Podiatric Clinic was established to provide foot care to San Francisco's large Asian population. CCPM also has satellite clinics and outreach programs, where foot and ankle screenings are performed.

In 1997, CCPM developed a major alliance with the new San Francisco College of Osteopathic Medicine (SFCOM), which will enroll 60 medical students beginning in August. The presence of this new school on CCPM's campus establishes a 'virtual' university for the health sciences, with the two institutions sharing facilities, curriculum, medical library, and other operations.

Planning is underway to expand and renovate the facilities within its one block site. Surrounded by neighborhood charm and diverse cultures, CCPM plans to remain in its historic location in the heart of San Francisco.

Parent's Educational Resource Center

Financier Charles Schwab only discovered he was dyslexic when his then second grade son was diagnosed with the same problem. Suddenly, Mr. Schwab's lifelong struggle with reading made sense.

Mr. Schwab and his wife, Helen, began investigating available resources to help their son. After three years of searching, they found reliable information and coping strategies to be virtually nonexistent. Further, children with learning disabilities, of which dyslexia and ADD (Attention Deficit Disorder) are the most common, were frequently misunderstood and misdiagnosed.

To spare others the frustration they experienced, in 1989, the Charles & Helen Schwab Foundation opened the Parents' Educational Resource Center (PERC), "one stop shopping" for parents and educators working with students with learning differences. The first of its kind, this San Mateo facility directly serves 1,000 local families a month as well as tens of thousands more nationwide via a quarterly newsletter, resources such as the popular "Bridges to Reading" kit, phone consultation, web site access, and more.

PERC believes that children with learning differences can do well in school. Most are of average or above average intelligence. Many, like Mr. Schwab, are gifted. Their highly trained staff operates in a guidance, nonadversarial capacity helping parents and educators understand that learning differences impact students over a lifetime, with no quick fix.

To help children reach their full potential, a multitude of services is available for a minimal membership fee. The lending library contains recommended reading material and educational programs. In addition, an information and referral database of doctors, tutors, and educational specialists is available which connects parents with a variety of professionals.

Incoming calls, fielded by experienced educators, range from the parent just detecting their child has a problem to the parent whose undiagnosed high schooler may not graduate. Research has shown that the optimal time to begin intervention for a child with learning disabilities is before the age of seven.

Of the estimated 15 percent of Americans with learning difficulties, only 5 percent have been diagnosed. An alarming number of juvenile delinquents and substance abusers have been found to have undetected learning disabilities. Citing the critical need for early intervention, the National Ad Council has selected this issue for their 1997 campaign.

The Foundation has also initiated Teach Each, an annual Bay Area teacher's award. Nominated by the community, outstanding teachers with a proven ability to reach a wide range of learners in their classroom will be eligible for a $15,000 award, an additional $10,000 to be donated to their school.

The Schwabs continue to work towards a system which builds on a child's strengths, not weaknesses. As Charles Schwab has said: "One of the best gifts you can give your child is positive self esteem."

Mr. Schwab credits his success to his parents and the teachers who supported his interests and encouraged his dreams. Now, with organizations like PERC, every child may have the same opportunity.

Parent's Educational Resource Center: A Program of the Charles and Helen Schwab Foundation

A mother and her son visit PERC's library, the nation's largest collection on learning differences for parents and students.

Golden Gate Perfusion, Inc.

Golden Gate Perfusion's team: (left to right) Nancy Achorn, Michael Trzeciak, Avo Avadesian, Philip Crawford, Jim Aquino, and Bill Moskalik. Not pictured: Jim Sorour

Every day in the San Francisco Bay Area as many as 100 patients undergo open heart surgery. The surgical teams that assemble each morning to prepare for these procedures include perfusionists, the technologists who operate the heart-lung machine. These highly trained and specialized medical professionals assemble, operate and troubleshoot the life-support devices which take over for the heart and lungs during cardiac surgery. Similar devices are used for cardiac or pulmonary support in acute care units, cardiac catheterization laboratories, and emergency rooms. Although many perfusionists are hospital employees, the founders of Golden Gate Perfusion, Inc. became the first independent contract perfusion group in San Francisco in 1978. The three original associates of the company, which included one of today's owners, Philip Crawford, began with a case-load of just 300 patients a year at one hospital. The rapid growth of cardiac surgery programs in the early eighties presented opportunities that allowed the transformation of the company into Golden Gate Perfusion, Inc. in 1984, and the hiring of a staff of perfusionists and perfusion assistants.

One of Golden Gate Perfusion's staff members operating a heart-lung machine during an aortic valve replacement (Far right)

In a company with less than ten employees, the current owners, Philip Crawford and Nancy Achorn, naturally focus most of their attention on the delivery of service. Meeting these sometimes arduous clinical demands, while acquiring the financial principles and management skills needed to run a business, proved formidable in the early years. Today, however, GGPI is a profitable and stable business, emphasizing teamwork and patient safety. Their cardiovascular caseload, performed on a contract basis in three area hospitals, currently exceeds 1200 open-heart procedures per year, or approximately 15 percent of the open-heart surgery cases in the Bay Area. Numerous adjunctive procedures are also performed by the GGPI team, including non-surgical cardiac support and the operation of blood salvage devices, which wash and recycle a patient's shed blood, reducing the need for donor blood transfusions.

Challenges lie ahead in the guise of health care reform and hospital mergers, forcing GGPI and all health care providers to strategize ways to navigate the oncoming turbulence. Forming alliances with colleagues to share personnel, develop government-required documentation, standardize clinical protocols, and reduce costs has been an effective investment of time and energy over the past two years. In light of growing pressures on the health care system, GGPI's corporate values include a commitment to the promotion and protection of their profession, through participation in state and national perfusion organizations. They are challenged clinically, as well, by ongoing innovations in medical devices and techniques that enhance the exciting but demanding nature of the profession. By helping perfusionists provide better and safer care, these advances render cardiac surgery an increasingly viable option for a widening spectrum of patients. They also offer assurance for the cardiac patient of the twenty-first century that when he is rolled into the operating room for one of the most important events of his life, a highly trained and experienced professional will always be behind the "pump."

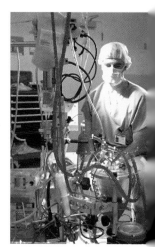

Goodwill

Goodwill Industries of San Francisco, San Mateo and Marin Counties, Inc. has helped people with disabilities or disadvantaging conditions become more employable for more than 80 years.

The Bay Area agency, the second oldest Goodwill organization in the world, was founded in 1916 by Reverend Samuel Quickmire. The agency followed the pattern set by the original Goodwill in Boston, which was organized to assist poor immigrants achieve a better life by collecting, repairing and selling clothing and household items. This process created both work and paychecks. Almost a century later, this process is still the primary means by which 186 autonomous Goodwill agencies in the United States and Canada collectively raise $1 billion annually to serve 130,000 people.

Throughout the years, Goodwill has steadfastly adhered to the philosophy that the best assistance one can give is the kind of assistance which helps people to help themselves. Goodwill does not provide charity — it provides a chance.

This simple concept of self-sufficiency guides the way Goodwill Industries of San Francisco, San Mateo, and Marin Counties, Inc. raises money to support the more than 500 people on its daily payroll and to help almost 1,000 people annually overcome barriers to employment. The agency operates 29 donation centers and 16 stores where used household items and clothing are collected and sold.

Goodwill also conducts employment, education and training programs at its main headquarters in San Francisco, at the corner of Mission and South Van Ness, and at other locations within the three-county area. A broad array of services are offered to support those who come through the doors looking for a new lease on life, including work at Goodwill facilities, skill training and job placement in the community.

Goodwill recognizes the need to look at the whole person and his or her family, surroundings and community when helping the person set forth a course of action on which to proceed. To this end, the agency provides specialized assistance to people with disabilities, homeless people, and those with limited English-speaking ability, to name a few.

Goodwill is an interdependent nonprofit agency which relies upon a broad range of Bay Area organizations, businesses and individuals to help identify, refer and support people undergoing life changes. Goodwill has solid relationships with other service providers to offer greater stability for people during this time of transition. Goodwill also partners with a comprehensive range of other services, including the San Francisco Department of Human Services, Private Industry Council, recovery programs, shelters and other agencies serving special populations.

The community can — and does — play a vital role in helping Goodwill attain its mission. This help can come through indirect means, such as contributing money or donating no-longer-needed useable household and clothing items. Help can also come through more direct means, such as offering employment for graduates of Goodwill training programs in office technology, restaurant and hospitality, and sales and service.

This profile was made possible through the Estate of Yvette G. Eastman.

From 1916, Goodwill has resold usable items to assist people with disadvantaging conditions find employment. (Top left)

Students can choose from a variety of training courses, including Office Technology.

After the earthquake in 1989, Goodwill found a new home in an old Coca-Cola facility.

The San Francisco Bay Club

The San Francisco Bay Club

Golden Gateway Tennis and Swim Club

Bay Club/ Bank of America Center

Since its opening in 1977, The San Francisco Bay Club (SFBC) has earned a reputation as a leader in the private athletic club business in the United States. When the Club opened in October 1977, the 1,500 members were delighted with the new concept: a multi-purpose, co-ed, high-quality club that catered to the emerging boomer market. The original vision for the Club was to be a community unto itself, where friends were made, professional networking and good citizenship were fostered. The San Francisco Bay Club celebrated its 20th Anniversary in 1997 and it serves 3,800 members.

Housed in what was once a cold storage warehouse, The San Francisco Bay Club is located in one of the City's first buildings in the Embarcadero/North Beach area, located on Battery Street next to Levi's Plaza. Jim Gerber and his founding partners were ahead of their time in establishing the concept of a private high quality full service athletic club catering to professional men and women. The San Francisco Bay Club was a club of many firsts. It was the first downtown co-ed multi-facilities club in the country; it was the first center for aerobics in the Bay Area; and it provided the first downtown shuttle service bringing members from the financial district to the Club.

The Bay Club/Bank of America Center (BC/BA) opened in 1991. This 20,000 square foot facility located on the concourse level of the Bank of America World Headquarters building is in the heart of the financial district. The beautiful and spacious workout environment is complete with the latest fitness equipment, free weights, group exercise classes and the option of co-ed or private men's and women's workout areas. Designed to be the financial district's premier fitness club, Bay Club/Bank of America

Center serves a limited executive membership with an emphasis on personal service.

The Golden Gateway Tennis & Swim Club (GGT&SC), on Drumm Street, opened in 1992. Situated on the waterfront in San Francisco's financial district, this unique property features an unusual urban blend of fitness facilities, nine outdoor tennis courts, an outdoor group exercise pavilion and the only two outdoor pools in the downtown area. Golden Gateway caters to the member that longs to play tennis and swim outdoors in San Francisco and has been called "the oasis in the heart of the city."

The San Francisco Bay Club, Bay Club/Bank of America Center and Golden Gateway Tennis & Swim Club are owned and operated by Western Athletic Clubs (WAC). Jim Gerber is the president of Western Athletic Clubs, a co-founder of the company and one of the top leaders in the athletic club business. Jim has accomplished a great deal in his 23-year club career; he was a founder and the fifth president of the International Health, Racquet and Sportsclub Association (IHRSA) and he was awarded the IHRSA Distinguished Service Award in 1997. Jim has built a strong value system within the WAC organization that is exemplified by its mission statement, "We enhance people's lives."

Currently, WAC owns and operates eight clubs on the West Coast and services over 20,000 memberships. Its growth in revenues has also reflected its expansion, increasing from a first year revenue level of $700,000 to over $44 million in 1997. WAC believes that each club it develops should cater to the unique tastes and characteristics of the market it serves. The clubs focus on providing their members value through exceptional member service, sparkling, state-of-the-art facilities and a variety of exciting on-site programming. Stability and the tradition of 20 years of providing exceptional facilities and member service provide the foundation for The San Francisco Bay Club, Bay Club/Bank of America Center and Golden Gateway Tennis & Swim Club.

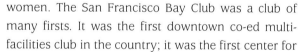

Synergy Rehabilitation Inc.

Founded by Jane Wintersteen in 1986, Synergy Rehabilitation Inc. is a collection of practitioners providing comprehensive rehabilitation services throughout California and consultant services in Wyoming and Washington state. By forming alliances, the company provides a wide range of contract rehabilitation services in acute and sub-acute care hospitals, residential care facilities, and assisted living centers, as well as outpatient care.

Synergy provides professional services in speech, occupational and physical therapy to meet facility and client needs for therapeutic intervention. Dedication to quality treatment begins with careful analysis and continues with design of individual treatments to meet patients' needs. Through a team approach, Synergy's therapeutic treatments offer patients increased mobility, functional independence, improved self-care skills after neurological injuries, reacquisition of communication skills, dysphagia management services to teach stroke patients safe swallowing skills, prosthetic training, and freedom from pain.

Wintersteen, a speech pathologist, was inspired to go into business for herself by her grandmother's example; when left a widow with a two-month-old baby, her grandmother started a business and worked until she was ninety! Wintersteen pioneered the concept of a team approach to rehabilitation (now so widely adopted by university medical schools) whereby patient, therapist, physician, nursing staff and patient's caregivers work together to meet therapeutic goals. This synergistic philosophy is behind everything the company does. Synergy is therapist owned and managed by a team of clinicians whose knowledge brings considerable expertise to the practice of therapy.

In addition to therapy services, in each contract facility a Synergy clinical consultant both supports therapists in patient care and manages on-site rehabilitation services. This expertise improves patient care and ultimately the facility's admissions and revenues. Synergy managers can handle all aspects of management, from tracking a hospital's clinical and financial outcomes and monitoring a record of patient treatment and progress, to conducting ergonomic analysis. Synergy works with hospitals to ensure financial success and efficient operation in a complex marketplace. By providing flexible staffing, Synergy helps health-care providers to be more financially cost-effective.

The focus in health care today is in prevention. In the area of ergonomic analysis (how workers cope within their marketplace), Synergy experts can make recommendations to employers on how to set up a workplace properly and also provide training and knowledge of equipment use. This examination is particularly important for individuals with repetitive stress injuries. Synergy offers regular health information clinics to the public on issues such as fall prevention, use of assistive devices for arthritic conditions, and general strengthening and balance exercises.

Synergy's convenient location at the foot of Market Street along the Embarcadero allows employees to arrive at work by ferry, BART, MUNI, or by Peninsula commuter trains. The company's 150 employees include therapists with an average of 10 years experience. Although therapists are now in great demand as the practice expands nationwide, there is very little turnover at Synergy. Synergy provides charity care for indigent persons, and its many community outreach interests include participation in a nationwide program, "Christmas in April." This year Synergy employees built a handicapped access ramp for a private home to provide access for a wheelchair-bound resident.

At Synergy, the whole is greater than the sum of its parts.

Jane Wintersteen
Photo by Russ Fischella

Toolworks

Toolworks trainee at work in lobby of historic U.S. Court of Appeals building

Dedicated to assisting people with disabilities become more independent, Toolworks is a San Francisco human service agency that has gained widespread recognition for the scope of its programs and the depth of its mission.

For more than two decades, Toolworks has been a self-supporting nonprofit corporation serving people with disabilities. Revenue for its various employment, educational and social programs comes from both public and private outside work contracts, training fees from referring agencies and occasional grants.

Bay Area businesses including the San Francisco Marriott hotel, the Bank of America, Andronico's markets and the YMCA have benefitted from hiring qualified individuals with disabilities referred by Toolworks.

Among the specialized programs that Toolworks provides are:

- Job training and placement
- On-the-job support for both the employee and employer
- Specialized services for people who are deaf or hard of hearing
- Support for independent living
- Vocational training for people with disabilities who are homeless.

Nearly 50 percent of Toolworks clients are deaf or hard of hearing. The rest are people with physical, psychiatric or cognitive disabilities.

Founder Curt Willig, a social worker with a keen business sense, was determined to find "good jobs for good pay" for people with disabilities. He began his enterprise in 1975 by negotiating a contract with Pacific Bell to repair broken tools. Hence the new agency that fixed broken tools and made them work again became known as Toolworks.

Eventually, Toolworks became a much sought after independent contractor to perform other kinds of manufacturing tasks for city businesses. Having a capable and reliable crew, Toolworks earned a reputation as a model vocational training and rehabilitation program in a sheltered environment.

However, changes were occurring in the local economy in the mid-1980s. Automation was replacing assembly-line jobs and light industry was relocating to regions beyond the city limits, thus eliminating the source of many Toolworks contracts. In response, Toolworks switched gears and focused on opportunities arising in the service industry.

Simultaneous with the economic change came a change in society's attitude about having people with disabilities integrated into the workplace. Legislation such as the Javits Wagner O'Day Act opened up job opportunities by encouraging federal agencies to set aside a segment of jobs for people with disabilities.

Toolworks received its first federal contract in 1985, providing janitorial services for the historic U.S. Court of Appeals building at Seventh and Mission streets. In the ensuing years, Toolworks continued to acquire federal, state and private janitorial and grounds maintenance contracts. These contracts have provided hundreds of good-paying jobs to people with disabilities, turning tax users into taxpayers.

Toolworks' employment programs provide evaluation, training and job placement for both individuals and groups. In each situation, a client is matched with a job according to abilities and needs, and there is always extensive follow-up by Toolworks' staff.

Toolworks is now in the process of developing new business ventures under the direction of Executive Director, Donna Feingold. An East Bay office has opened to expand Toolworks' educational and vocational programs. In addition, a new program was started to support people with disabilities who wish to live independently in the community.

Through its programs, Toolworks has made a lasting contribution to the city of San Francisco over the years, but more important, it has enhanced the lives of many of its residents with disabilities.

The Wax Museum at Fisherman's Wharf

The spirit and energy of San Francisco is manifested in the history of one of its most popular landmarks — the Wax Museum at Fisherman's Wharf. Bedecked by colorful waving flags and surrounded by a complex of gift shops and entertainment sites, the museum welcomes guests to one of the world's most visited spots. Three generations of the Fong family have kept the Wax Museum a vital and changing San Francisco attraction.

Thomas Fong opened the Wax Museum in 1963, from a renovated chicken feed warehouse which was then across the street from a handful of shops and restaurants that comprised Fisherman's Wharf. With remarkable vision, Thomas Fong saw the potential of his site to lure San Franciscans and visitors alike to the Fisherman's Wharf area and to see it as a place to spend the day, rather than just passing through for lunch. He was inspired by the wax figures at the Seattle World's Fair and decided to open a wax museum.

The museum started with 150 life-size figures in front of black curtains on the first floor and opened as the largest wax museum in North America. Now the exhibits span four floors with over 200 figures in elaborately staged scenes, carefully constructed to authenticate people at the peak of their fame with costumes, props and lighting. Many scenes were designed and sculpted by Thomas Fong's son, Ronald, who co-directed the family business in partnership with his father from its inception.

In the late 1960s, Ron and his father created a second floor for the Hall of Religions, which depicts six of the world's greatest faiths. The most popular exhibit continues to be a recreation of Leonardo de Vinci's

painting of the Last Supper. Later, the museum added a subterranean Chamber of Horrors and, in the late 70s, the Gallery of Stars. The museum debuted a replication of King Tutankamen's tomb soon after, which occupies the top floor of the museum and opened when the National Touring exhibit from Cairo arrived in San Francisco.

The Fong family has since added a collection of gift shops and attractions adjoining the museum to form the Wax Museum Entertainment Complex. The Haunted Gold Mine, a fun house, opened in 1979, and the Medieval Dungeon, a museum of ancient European history, opened in 1989.

In addition to providing entertainment for San Francisco and its visitors, the Wax Museum supports many of the city's non-profit organizations. Their belief in the importance of giving back to the community inspired the Fong family to start the Thomas and Eva Fong Foundation, which primarily supports local charities and causes that do not receive national assistance. One favorite charity is On Lok, an organization that helps Chinese American senior citizens.

Rodney Fong, representing the third generation of the Fong family, now runs most of the day to day operations of the Wax Museum. Like his father and grandfather, Rodney has the energy and vision to keep the museum a favorite of San Franciscans and visitors. Plans are underway to remodel the Wax Museum complex and expand the second floor. A growing interest in entertainment figures will bring more television and movie personalities to the museum, to join such luminaries as Bruce Lee, Mae West, Jodi Foster and all the other "stars" of the Wax Museum.

Stars of the past and present welcome visitors to the wax museum at Fisherman's Wharf

The Wax Museum entertainment complex is one of the World's most visited sites. (Bottom left)

City College of San Francisco

Serving the community as the innovative institution of learning that it has been for more than 60 years, City College of San Francisco continues to make a significant contribution to the city of San Francisco and beyond through the achievements of its students.

Among those who have attended City College since its founding in 1935 are San Francisco doctors, lawyers, even its police and fire chiefs. Other notable alumni include many civic and business leaders, television and radio personalities, government officials, renowned educators, famous chefs and acclaimed artists.

With approximately 85,000 students enrolled annually in both credit and noncredit classes, City College of San Francisco has the distinction of being one of the largest community colleges in the country, and it confers the most associate degrees in the arts and sciences in the state.

The transfer rate to a four-year college or university is 7 percent higher than other state community colleges, 8 percent higher nationally. City College transfer students typically go on to pursue professional and academic careers. Other students earn vocational certificates, giving them an edge in the Bay Area's competitive job market.

City College offers classes from accounting to zoology. There are more than 50 academic programs listed in the current school catalog and more than 150 occupational/vocational disciplines. A student can learn how to fix an automobile or an airplane, manage a restaurant, analyze computer systems or identify malignant cancer cells. The certificate programs range from horticulture to nursing, from computer programming to merchandising.

In the school's beginning, Latin was still being taught and classes were being held in borrowed space around town. Eventually, civic leaders designated a hilltop in the southcentral region of the city — where Phelan and Ocean Avenue intersect — as the school's permanent main campus. The Science Building was the first to open there in 1940, with more educational and athletic facilities added over the years. The most recent building is the Louise and Claude Rosenberg, Jr. Library and Learning Resource Center — a $22 million architectural masterpiece featuring five floors of books, journals, state-of-the-art computer equipment, learning laboratories and study areas.

In addition to the Phelan campus, there are eight other campus locations in different parts of the city. In total there are 150 neighborhood sites where classes, mainly for adults, are held primarily at nights and on weekends. Some courses are broadcast on cable television, and others are taught at the workplace. Many classes are short-term, taking only up to six weeks, instead of the traditional 16 weeks, to complete. And the best part is that the cost is only $12 per unit for credit classes, noncredit classes are free.

"Education at City College of San Francisco represents a commitment to lifelong learning," says Chancellor Del M. Anderson, who is the first woman and African American to hold that position in the history of the school.

"Our mission today," she says, "is not only to promote education but also to emphasize its value in helping people achieve better lives for themselves and for their children."

If life imitates art, then the masterly mural by world-famous artist Diego Rivera, completed in 1940 and situated in the foyer of the College Theatre, was a prediction of student life here. People of diversity, of multicultural backgrounds, and of various occupations are portrayed together, in work and at play, creating a feeling of friendship and accomplishment. That is City College of San Francisco.

Chancellor Del M. Anderson
Photo by Sharon Hall

Segment of Diego Rivera mural at City College of San Francisco
Photo by Julio Cesar Martinez

Partners

SAN FRANCISCO'S

RETAIL ESTABLISHMENTS,

SERVICE INDUSTRIES AND

LEISURE/CONVENTION

FACILITIES OFFER AN

IMPRESSIVE ARRAY OF

CHOICES FOR RESIDENTS

AND VISITORS ALIKE.

The Marketplace

Compu-Data

Computers are big business, with a large portion of the personal computing market dominated by giant chains. These huge megastores also dominate the software market aimed at small and individual home office consumers who are in the process of setting up a work area. There are few small computer stores in the Bay Area with the resources or state-of-the-art systems necessary to set up business networks.

Compu-Data's Third Street location.

One computer store that bridges the gap between offering highly personal service and robust, enterprise-wide systems is Compu-Data, a successful personal computer retailer and network service provider.

Compu-Data, a corporation with Sami Daniel as its president, is one of the premier computer dealers and system integrators in the Bay Area. Situated near the heart of San Francisco's Financial district, Compu-Data provides friendly and customized service to business and individual consumers. Although Compu-Data is relatively small, it is a big-time provider of services and products. Its store features a wide array of computer equipment, including hardware, software, accessories and peripherals. The store itself is an interactive experience. Computers on display are available for customers to try out and feel the difference between the different processors. Customers can also try out a majority of the products before buying.

In addition, Compu-Data has the resources to set up and customize a small business-oriented network that can improve a business's efficiency and productivity. It can also provide the technology and resources to build super high-performance PCs that can take their place at the top of the power charts.

Compu-Data prides itself on its excellent service. "We do not sell boxes," says Sami Daniel. "We configure a system to meet a customer's need."

Compu-Data's staff is highly informed about high technology systems, trends and issues regarding performance and cost. The sales staff also refrains from the high-pressure tactics found at large computer chains. At Compu-Data, customers can feel free to browse or chat with the staff about the advantages and disadvantages of various systems.

Compu-Data also features a top-notch "turnkey operation," where it sets up a business computing system, from start to finish. Clients range from home office users to large enterprise system administrators. Compu-Data's turnkey operation services include consultation, advice on computer systems that fit

particular needs, installation and setup and training.

Whatever the focus, Compu-Data configures the computing system to fit special business needs, such as integrating point-of-sales with accounting; or solving the problem of providing remote access to staffers such as a mobile sales force made up of sales representatives, who travel and work outside the main office.

The most challenging aspect of being a successful turnkey operation, says Daniel, is matching a customer's computing business needs while staying within the specified budget. This requires in-depth conferences with customers regarding the nature and direction of the business, taking into consideration special technological or design needs. Daniel spends considerable time education business managers about solutions that are not as well known as more expensive products, but are still efficient and affordable. "It's an are," says Daniel, "matching customers with the right systems, and bringing it all in within budget."

Compu-Data also features a division that offers a complete range of high-tech services. Its certified engineer and team of consultants can create World Wide Web pages as well as Internet and Intranet sites. Featuring top-notch service and high-quality components, they also can configure hardware, operating systems and networks such as Novell, Lotus

Notes, Unix and Windows NT. Compu-Data stands by its motto: "A Name to Trust." Therefore, it will resolve any problems. Through this division, Compu-Data extends its "turn key" operation to businesses that need a more "hand-on" approach.

Eighty percent of Compu-Data's business comes from repeat customers. "We believe in friendships, not vendor-customer relations," explains Daniel. Compu-Data's extensive support is one reason customers return for product upgrades or new purchases. To enhance its customer relations, Compu-Data provides a range of services, including providing answers to problems by phone (a boon to people in the middle of a computing crisis), supplying "loaners" while a customer's PC is being repaired and making phone calls to customers to ensure all the equipment is functioning at maximum performance.

A native of Lebanon, Daniel came to the United States in July 1986, with a bachelor of arts in business management. He enrolled in a master program at Golden Gate University. To help put himself through school, Daniel worked at a local computer store for two years, where he learned the basics of the computing retail business, including the importance of customer satisfaction. These were the early days of personal computing, when small stores were first beginning to sell PCs.

Interior of Compu-Data (Top left)

Customers feel free to browse the shelves of Compu-Data.

The Compu-Data showroom.

"At that time, PCs were sold with 256K of RAM and 20MB hard drives, which were very efficient at the time. Now, customers are asking for 256MB of RAM and 9GB of hard drive. And, they wonder if that's enough," says Daniel. "The computer industry has undergone tremendous changes in the past decade. It's fascinating to be part of such a dynamic industry."

In 1987, Daniel and a friend, Raja Srour, started a small business, using Sami's garage on Golden Gate Avenue in San Francisco to assemble computer systems. Acting as subcontractors for computer firms, they configured systems that even some store technicians were unsure how to get up and running.

In 1988, the two men opened Compu-Data on Folsom Street. In the early days, the small showroom contained the latest computer and high-tech equipment and featured extensive customer support. The two men worked long hours and performed a variety of tasks to keep the small business profitable. Both men were responsible for sales and technical equipment with Daniel also focusing on management and Srour on programming.

Together, they formed a talented partnership, developing a reputation for knowing how to set up innovative and functional office computing systems. The store began to prosper due to recommendations concerning their extensive abilities and extensive support policies. In 1992, Daniel's partner left the business to move on to new ventures. Compu-Data continued to prosper because of its strong customer base.

PSI, a systems integrator, has been a customer of Compu-Data for the past decade. Dr. Harry T. Whitehouse, president of PSI Systems, Inc., says his company has come to rely upon Compu-Data to provide the highest quality PC's, servers, components and software, all at competitive prices. Whitehouse commends Compu-Data's commitment to service. "We have positioned Compu-Data at both government and commercial client sites, and have heard nothing but praise from these client," adds Whitehouse.

In 1993, Compu-Data moved to its present location at Third Street, which is closer to the Financial district, but still part of the vibrant South of Market Area of San Francisco. SOMA, as the area is called, is home to Moscone Center, the site of numerous local, national and international computer exhibitions. Once a warehouse district, South of Market is part of the city's revitalization process. The Museum of Modern Art, once situated on Van Ness Avenue, is now part of the neighborhood, along with Yerba Buena Gardens. Both are attractions for the local community and tourists. Because of this urban renewal trend, Compu-Data now finds itself in one of the most popular, up-and-coming area in San Francisco.

South of Market is also home to many of San Francisco's software companies that are experiencing growth due to the rising popularity of the Internet and World Wide Web. In addition to breathing new life into computer technology and businesses, the Web is also changing the way America does business and, in turn, the way American businesses must set up their computing systems. In addition to a staggering new array of software products that support Web technology and corporate intranets, the Web is also creating new networking problems such as security leaks, connectivity issues and the development and maintenance of Web sites and corporate intranets.

To stay on top of this massive amount of ever-changing information, Daniel studies the market, reads computer and high-tech publications and attends seminars that offer information on advancing technology and products.

Compu-Data's highly trained staff offers business owners the freedom to do what they do best — manage their company rather than trying to absorb tech-

nology. "It's a full-time job just staying informed," says Daniel. "It would be difficult to run a company and try to stay on top of the computer industry. That's where Compu-Data comes in. We stay informed about advancing technologies so business owners can devote their time to keeping their business on track."

With all the focus on the Internet and corporate intranets, it's easy for computer retailers to place less importance on individual consumers. Yet, Compu-Data remains committed to meeting the challenges of individual computer users. "It doesn't matter it you buy one dollar of tens-of-thousands of dollars, you're treated in the same, friendly manner," explains Daniel.

Industrial Indemnity, an insurance company, is a business client that appreciates Compu-Data's commitment to service. "The 'big guys' may (sometimes) offer a slightly lower price," says J. Scott Stewart Of Industrial Indemnity. "But I've yet to find a systems vendor who has offered the kind of personal attention that Compu-Data gives."

Compu-Data's future plans include expanding into the Macintosh market, and continuing to develop services that address new technologies. Whatever its direction, Compu-Data, like the technology it works with, will remain a strong company that offers innovative and powerful solutions to computing problems.

One of Compu-Data's trained technicians at work.

Barcelino

Sharam Sharei, San Francisco's fashion Pasha, searches the world to select, design and produce the finest collection of International clothing being presented at Barcelino.

Fashion, quite often, is a mirror or reflection of the times. And no one knows this better than Sharam Sharei, the founder and president of Barcelino Continental Corp., the Bay Area's premier retailer of upscale international clothing for men and women.

Ever since he came to San Francisco in the sixties, Sharei has seen fashion trends come and go, reflecting the mood and spirit of the decade — the turbulent sixties, the jeans-crazy seventies, the upscale eighties and the "casual Friday" nineties. Despite all the fads, — from minis to midis to platform shoes to combat boots — there is one constant in fashion that never goes out of style, and that is style itself.

For many people, the idea of style is elusive. For Sharei, who has twenty-five years in the fashion business, it is easily defined. Style, he explains, is simply "good taste, which stands the test of time."

It is this concept of style — or permanent chic — that Sharei has used to create a mini fashion empire. His company, Barcelino, which started out as a single store in San Francisco's Union Square, has grown to include eight stores throughout the Bay Area. In addition, Barcelino, known as the executive menswear specialist, recently expanded to include "Per Donna," a collection exclusively for high-level career women. Besides enormous commercial success, Sharei has

also attained the well-earned reputation as an industry expert, recognized for his vast knowledge of fashion as both business and art form and for his quarter-of-a-century experience with top-quality European producers.

Sharei's Barcelino collections are renowned for being stylish, without being faddish. His men's collections are well-planned each season with clothing to take his customers from 9 to 5 to evening and also include weekend wear. To put together this sophisticated mix, Sharei focuses primarily on Italy, France and Germany as well as other European markets. Before garments are considered for the Barcelino col-

lection, however, they must meet Sharei's cardinal requirement of balance in Quality, Style and Value. These three words have become the hallmark of Barcelino — and Sharei's — corporate philosophy.

Actually, when Sharei started out in a world of giant retailers, his focus and diligent concentration paved the way for him to establish a premier small, but focused men's retail clothing business. In the early days of his retailing career — back in the seventies — when he planned on opening a men's store in San Francisco, Sharei's goal was simply to sell quality clothing at reasonable prices.

Born in Iran, Sharei

Barcelino at Stanford Shopping Center, Palo Alto
(Top)

Barcelino Per Donna, exclusively for ladies, is located in Union Square, San Francisco.
(Bottom)

came to the United State at age sixteen to attend high school and then college. After graduating from UC-Berkeley with an economics degree, Sharei went on to get an MBA from Golden Gate University. With his versatile educational background, Sharei had considerable career options, including a job offer with the foreign ministry in Iran. Instead, Sharei opted to remain in the Bay Area, where he planned to try his hand at the men's fashion business. In typical Sharei style, however, he decided first to expand his knowledge of the industry by taking fashion, marketing and design classes at New York University and England's Manchester School of Design.

In 1972, Sharei and a college friend opened a store called "Orpheus" on Union Street. This was the middle of the "hippie era," when fashion was undergoing dramatic changes, with psychedelic colors and patterns changing the way American men looked and dressed. To set Orpheus apart from the other boutiques that lined Union Street and specialized in trendy bell-bottoms, tie-dyed T-shirts and other hip clothing, Sharei imported popular European lines. This foresight established Orpheus as the first American company to represent GRUPPO G.F.T., which eventually introduced the famous Italian designer, Giorgio Armani, to the U.S. market.

After selling his half-interest in the Orpheus chain in 1983, within a week, Sharei established the first Barcelino store at Post and Mason by Union Square. His mission was to enhance the already world-famous fashionable reputation of San Francisco and the Bay Area, by presenting current collections season after season, which would exude a spirit of confidence and the feeling of sophisticated elegance, offering handsomely fresh and distinctive alternatives to an executive's wardrobe.

When it comes to fashion, Sharei's passion fills the room. "At Barcelino, we search the world to select, design, produce, and offer the finest collection of International apparel for sophisticated, fashion-conscious men who prefer natural fibers and refined, continental styling over trendy or extremely conservative looks. The styles we present are contemporary, yet classic. Our philosophy is the lasting stylish image. Our commitment is to world-class service." Because of his insight into the fashion industry, Sharei determined that designer labels did not always measure up to his standards. They generally — but not always — passed the first two tests of style and quality, but fell short on value. Designer customers, he found, had to "pay for the hidden costs of royalties, advertising and promotion." That "two-inch designer label" was an unnecessary and costly premium passed on to consumers.

Today, designer labels do not always mean exclusivity, adds Sharei. Designer lines, sold in almost all department stores, often are the same from store to store. This replication of merchandise offers customer's limited choices even among the top designers. Also, store buyers often are no longer seasoned pros schooled in "the fine art of buying," but untrained novices with little or no training in textiles and fashion design. Armed with only a "computer model," these buyers stock department stores with an array of merchandise that is the same from

Barcelino dresses the executive seven days a week. (Top left)

Season after season, Barcelino offers world-class collections with artisan workmanship and exceptional styling, providing for both comfort and a masterfully tailored look.

Sophisticated, fashion-conscious men and women who prefer natural fibers and refined, continental styling over trendy or extremely conservative looks know of the advantage projected in their lasting image while wearing Barcelino clothing.

Barcelino's collections are chosen for those who appreciate masterfully hand-tailored Italian clothing in a tapestry of richly textured world class fabrics — a unique blend that projects good taste.

store to store, or even worse, stores are filled with "merchandising gaffes" that leave customers confused at the bewildering lack of stylish clothing.

In contrast, Barcelino does not sell "silly costumes and outrageous clothes," says Sharei. "Our stores focus on stylish, well-made, comfortable clothing. Up to seventy percent of Barcelino's exclusive designs are manufactured in Europe by the same manufacturers who produce for couture designers." In addition, Barcelino offers Bay Area customers true exclusivity because it does not sell its designs to other stores in the area.

Barcelino collections are featured in seasonal fashion shows, which attract not only customers, but industry personalities interested in viewing Sharei's dazzling combination of sartorial elegance and refined style. When putting together a collection, Sharei considers design, fabric, cut and color. Fabrics, for example, must be of exceptional strength and quality. (Barcelino was the first in the Bay Area to introduce the world's finest suiting cloth known as the Super 150.) Detailing and the final touches added before a garment is finished are a Barcelino specialty. Linings must be Bamberg, and buttons natural, such as horn or pearl, rather than man-made plastics. Garments are also designed with the Bay Area lifestyle in mind, including its temperate climate. "You don't have to sacrifice style for comfort," says Sharei.

In addition, Barcelino excels at the finishing touches that make a garment look perfectly tailored. "We don't sell the right size," says Sharei, "we sell the correct fit." Barcelino staff also oversees the final custom alterations to preserve the tailored look of the garment.

The overall look — one of refined simplicity —

appeals to a high-powered mix of corporate executives, upscale professionals and international travelers. In today's ever-increasing global society, many customers find that Barcelino's clothing meets what Sharei calls the "international dress code that transcends time and borders."

The "Barcelino Image" also attracts customers who recognize the importance of personal packaging or are aware of that famous saying of Oscar Wilde's: "It is only shallow people who do not judge by appearances." Barcelino customers know the value of "being buttoned up and visually sophisticated."

Sharei contends his clothing may not be for everyone. "By no means is it inexpensive. But considering the quality and workmanship, rich fabric and exceptional styling that goes into each garment, Barcelino clothing represents a wonderful value. And there will always be a market for quality, style and value."

In today's ever-increasing global society, many customers find that Barcelino's clothing meets what Sharei calls the "international dress code that transcends time and borders."

Flax Art and Design

Phillip Flax has been in the art supply business ever since he was a mere tot sweeping the back of his Mom and Pop's Kearny Street store. A Depression spawned venture, Herman and Sylvia Flax and son, Jerome, started in 1938 with little more than $100 and hope. A general desire for creative outlets was boosted by the 1939 World's Fair, hosted by San Francisco, and a flurry of economic activity at the onset of World War II sustained the new business.

When Herman died in 1953 and Jerome left for other endeavors, Phillip took over the San Francisco store. Today, his children work alongside him and the very name, FLAX, has become synonymous with quality art supplies as other members of the family have opened stores around the country.

In the early 50s, the original store was converted into a driveway for St. Mary's Garage. Their second storefront, at Bush and Kearny, served for 15 years before a long and successful run in the historic Goldberg Bowen building on Sutter Street. In 1980, a shortage of warehouse space prompted a relocation to Market Street.

The 80s brought the computer revolution. FLAX customers had been predominately commercial clients, advertisers, draftspersons, etc. Computers changed all of that. Computer generated artwork virtually eliminated the need for basic equipment designed for handwork.

FLAX dismissed the notion of selling computers and instead compensated for the shifting business by marketing to the fine art consumer. FLAX Art & Design, then and now, prides itself on selling the finest brushes, paints and materials for the creatively inclined.

Buy why stop there? They discovered that many more Bay Area customers were particularly receptive to a well designed product. Today's FLAX Art & Design offers something for everyone: one of a kind gifts, custom framing services, presentation supplies, fine pens, journals and albums, and probably the largest paper goods selection in the world.

Flax Art & Design's eclectic store features in-store videos which offer how-to demonstrations and information on artists and museums; the retailer's collection of unusual papers include embossed, silk, stone-textured, corrugated and hand-marbled.

Many unique items are available through mail-order. The FLAX Art & Design catalog, launched in 1975, along with various offshoots such as their Collage catalog, publishes over 10 million copies.

Overseeing the warehouse operation in nearby Brisbane is son, Howard, while son, Craig, runs the Catalog Creative and Production department. Daughter, Leslie, remains at the store, preferring to work in a retail environment.

This store is a bustling attraction with ongoing arts and crafts demonstrations and seminars, complementary showings by local artists, and the annual Kid Fest Celebration where children can create and experiment to their hearts' content. Some day, one of these aspiring artists may submit the latest winning design in the annual cover contest.

In addition to renowned quality, selection, and service, this 30,000 square foot facility offers those 4 magic words for the dreamy-eyed shopper: PLENTY OF FREE PARKING! Experience spanning over a half century has made FLAX Art & Design one of the biggest art suppliers in the world. The FLAX family's vision of bringing art to the general population has been realized.

Boisset

Jean-Claude Boisset
Wine Cellar

Boisset Family
(Bottom right)

some brands, such as Christophe and Joliesse, that appeal to young, upscale consumers. In addition, Jean Charles has added a new line of craft beers aimed at grabbing a share of the booming "microbrewery" market.

Together Jean Claude and Jean Charles Boisset make up a unique father-son team that is responsible for a sprawling wine empire that reaches from France's Wine Valley to America's Sonoma and Napa valleys. And, in the classic sense of two, different personalities coming together to form the perfect working dynamics, the two men's working styles complement each other. Jean Claude, for example, avoids the limelight, preferring to maintain a low profile, while Jean Charles is one of the company's most ardent spokesmen. With their combined personalities, talents, skills and focus, they have guided Boisset enterprises to the forefront of the international wine trade.

Indeed, the Boissets' devotion to family and wine-making traditions is one of the keys to their company's

Boisset wines — like an outstanding premium vintage — is a blend of the old and the new.

The old, in this case, is France, a country steeped in wine-making traditions. It was in Burgundy, or Bourgogne as the French call it, the Jean Claude Boisset family wine story began back in the early sixties. It was in 1961, Jean Claude Boisset sold his first cask of wine and — less than forty years later — has gone on to become the chief executive officer of Boisset, one of the largest wine enterprises in France. In addition to being the top producer of Burgundy wines in the world, Boisset is now the leading exporter of French wines.

The new angle to this remarkable story is Northern California's wine country, or what the French refer to as the "new world" of wines. It is here, in Napa and Sonoma counties, that the domestic brands for the Boisset family's American division are produced. At the top of the American division, is Jean Charles Boisset, who, like his father, is determined to maintain and enhance the family's reputation for producing quality wines at reasonable prices. Since taking over Boisset's US branch at age 23 in 1993, Jean Charles has not only distinguished himself by expanding the production and marketing of the company's existing domestic brands, such as Lyeth and William Wheeler, but he has also developed

success. In the grand tradition of French vineyard owners, for example, Jean Claude Boisset maintains a family domain. Based in Premeaux Prissey, it is 120 acres of top vine-yards in the Côte de Beaune and Côte de Nuits. And, daughter Nathalie Bergès-Boisset, who has worked in the public relations and marketing division of the company, takes an active role in the Estate.

To understand the Boisset family's dedication to producing quality wines, one must perhaps travel to Brochon, a tiny village close to Gevrey-Chambertin in Burgundy, where Jean Claude grew up in a family of French educators. At age 18, Jean Claude, always an independent thinker, decided to start his business rather than pursue a higher education. His first venture was a "garage business" in the true sense of the expression. He bought a neighbor's wine and then bottled and labeled it in his father's garage.

To expand his business, Jean Claude planted his own vineyard on an upper slope, which other vineyards owners considered too steep to work. Through determination and hard work, Jean-Claude's vineyard began to pay off. Yet, the bulk of his wine business was through his role as a "négociant" or "négotiator" between wine owners and buyers. Traditionally, "négociants" have remained the "middle men" between owners and buyers, with their commissions coming from owners. Over the years, however, the role of "négociants" has evolved. Today big-time négociants, such as Jean-Claude, not only buy and sell wine, but in many cases they also buy the grapes and make the wines themselves, thus controlling the entire winemaking process.

Ever since Jean Claude set up shop in 1961, the Boisset family has maintained a controlling interest as they have built the company into a major wine-making concern active throughout Burgundy, as well as in Beaujolais, the Côtes-du-Rhône, and the Mediterranée. In the last several years, Boisset has acquired an impressive number of prestigious French houses, including Jaffelin, Bouchard Ainé, F. Chauvenet, Ropiteau, Mommessin, Thorin and L' Heritier Guyot. Today, Boisset Wine is one of France's largest wine purveyors with its wines distributed in restaurants throughout France and exported to more than 55 countries. The headquarters for the Boisset Group is at its Charles Viénot estate, a 250-year-old former convent with a stone cellar ideal for the long aging of fine vintages.

While expanding their enterprise, the Boissets have remained true to Jean Claude's original corporate philosophy of producing quality wines at affordable prices. To further this goal, the Boissets purchased their own cooperage, an important long-term investment that allows them greater control over quality and price. The Boisset winemaking facilities are a huge state-of-art winery. Situated just outside Nuits-Saint-Georges, the wine-making facility is a gleaming, auto-mated, thermo-controlled plant with stainless steel fermentation installations. But high-tech does not mean always mean high-volume. Alongside the large vats are barrels of high-quality domain wines.

Jean Claude's corporate vision extends beyond France. In 1980, he was among the first French négociant houses to venture into the Northern

Jean-Charles Boisset

Big Bang Brewery

Joliesse Vineyards

Photo by Robert M. Bruno

Wine Country Photography

Boisset Burgundy

(Bottom right)

Photo by Robert M. Bruno

Wine Country Photography

California wine coun-try, establishing a California subsidiary in 1980. In keeping with the ancestral traditions of wine-making, he appoint-ed his young son, Jean Charles, to head the American branch in late 1992.

And as the old say-ing goes, like father, like son. Since be-coming president of Boisset USA, Jean Charles has successfully introduced and expanded several domestic brands in the competitive California wine market as well as overseen the import of the popular Jean-Claude Boisset and Boisset Mediteranée Wines from France. Under his guidance, Boisset's US division has become one of the fastest-growing wine companies in the nation.

Jean Charles has also put his own personal signa-ture on his branch of the business. In just several years, for example, his Joliesse Vineyards wines have become immensely popular with young consumers. Joliesse's varietals from California include a Chardonnay, Cabernet-Sauvignon, Sauvignon Blanc, White Zinfandel, Pinot Noir and Merlot. Jean Charles also repositioned the more upscale Christophe Cellars, which feature a Sauvignon Blanc, Pinot Noir, Chardonnay and Cabernet Sauvignon.

One of Jean Charles' most challenging accom-plishments, however, was overseeing the comeback of the Lyeth Estate and William Wheeler brands, which Boisset purchased in 1993. His handling of the revival of the Lyeth wines — renowned before the death of winery founder Chip Lyeth — demonstrates his business acumen and respect for California vintages.

The first order of business in remarketing the

Lyeth wines, said Jean Charles, was to "maintain the personality and integrity of the Lyeth estate." To accomplish that goal, Jean Charles hired Bill Arbios, the former winemaker at Lyeth to retain the house style and the character of the Lyeth wines. In addi-tion, he added a popular Chardonnay and a stylish "Meritage" to the Lyeth portfolio, and marketed the wines to a broader audience. The Wheeler brands, which include the lesser-known, but highly rated Viognier, Sangiovese and Zinfandel varietals, were given new packaging that reflected their hand-crafted elegance. In return, the wines won favor with critics and consumers.

Jean Charles has also launched a more ambitious venture, the creation of a "craft brewing company," called Big Bang Brewery. Big Bang's first ale, Apollo, was released in August of 1996. Designed to compete with the popular "microbrews," Apollo, with its expensive ingredients and space-age image, has drawn praise from manufacturers and young beer drinkers. Brewed on contract, Apollo is aged on the American white oak that gives California Chardonnays their distinctive flavor and aroma. The oak, explained Jean Charles, gives the ale a "creamy and soft, yet complex flavor."

Apollo's sleek cobalt blue packaging and celestial motif, which appeal to upscale "micro-brew" enthusiasts, demonstrates Boisset's commitment to the design and marketing of Boisset products. In fact, Apollo's design has won several awards; most notably, a CLIO in 1997 as the best designed product in the beverage/alcoholic category. Other Boisset products also excel in design. The Joliesse wines, for example, employ a stylish and distinctive "sunburst" label and a clear "pop top" capsule that give the unique flange bottle and engraved cork an enticing look. The innovative package design reflects the elemental nature of the Joliesse varietals. "It's not enough to just bring a product to the market," says Jean Charles. "You have to position it correctly and then back it up with enough advertising and consumer promotion and awareness to push it along."

Boisset's commitment to its American branch includes creating more wines and partnerships. "Our goal is to secure further strong regional partnerships at the distribution level to help our products flourish in the market. We are also dedicated to importing new brands and acquiring productive wineries."

To further emphasize the company's commitment to the California wine industry, Boisset continually forms strategic alliances with large vineyard owners to ensure consistency. In addition, Boisset also has invested in its own cooperage to integrate the oak air drying process and best wood sourcing, allowing the crafting of the finest barrels available in the industry. Needless to say, aging is one of the critical parts of winemaking. "Our mission is to have a full range of French and California wines," says Jean Charles.

To accomplish this goal, Boisset depends on the expertise and skills of its wine growers, wine makers and other people that make up both the French and American divisions. Both the Boisset family and employees are committed to producing quality wines. The Boissets believe high quality depends on three important principles: control at the vineyards and rigorous selection at harvest times; respect for tradition coupled with high technology during the process of vinification; and proper storage and aging.

Jean Charles has also embarked on an industrious plan to raise money for a worthy cause. Though Boisset and his family have always contributed to worthy causes on both sides of the Atlantic, Jean Charles wanted to do something more in the United States. In 1995, he began to research possible charities. After looking at hundreds of worthy causes, he selected the "Feed the Children Campaign," an Oklahoma-based foundation that seeks to reduce hunger among American children. Founded in 1979, the group distributes food to shelters, food shelves and disaster relief efforts across the nation. Since 1994, Boisset USA has contributed a percentage of its profits on every bottle of Christophe Vineyards to the "Feed the Children" campaign. Part of the campaign's focus is to increase consumer's awareness of the child hunger problem and turn consumers into long-term donors.

It is gratifying, says Jean Charles, to be part of such an important campaign because "no child should ever feel hunger." Also gratifying is the support from back home, where his father endorses Jean Charles' commitment. "After all," explained Jean Charles, "he knows that wine can touch the heart in many ways."

Jean-Charles Boisset
Photo by Sandro Oramas

Boisset Mediterranée
(Top left)
Photo by Robert M. Bruno
Wine Country Photography

Lyeth Estate-
Meritage Wines
Photo by Robert M. Bruno
Wine Country Photography

J.J. Brookings Gallery

Bill Barrett
Eastern Memories
(Far right)

Richard McDermott
Miller
Relic II

Located next to the San Francisco Museum of Modern Art, J.J. Brookings Gallery offers visitors a varied visual art experience. Established in 1970, J.J. Brookings Gallery has consistently presented a variety of museum quality fine art that will appeal to most tastes and budgets. Visitors are impressed by the visually stimulating work that is always available — whether it is sculpture, paintings, fine photography or prints.

Tim Duran, J.J. Brookings Gallery's director, prides himself on continually having museum quality works of art available for his collectors at prices to fit the budgets of most visitors. Virtually all of the artists on view have been exhibited in museums, reviewed in critical art publications or featured in books or periodicals on fine art. Yet, Duran is the first to say, many of these works can be purchased for less than $1,000 — a substantially lower price than most people usually assume.

Duran and the staff at J.J. Brookings Gallery make a point of exploring the needs of the visitor, both visually and monetarily, and to match the art with the buyer. J.J. Brookings Gallery is one of the largest galleries on the West Coast. Thousands of individual works of art are available at any one time at the gallery. Mr. Duran is fond of saying that at any one time, maybe only 2 or 3 percent of what is actually available in the gallery is on the walls at any one time.

San Francisco residents and businesses alike have been drawn into the gallery, not only because of its location, but by referrals due to the professionalism of its staff. J.J. Brookings Gallery has a desire to go that extra step in providing art consultation, delivery and installation services, framing at the contiguous Museum West Fine Art and Framing, as well as international shipping. The gallery has worked with art consultants, architects and individuals on many wonderful projects commissioned for specific sites when existing works available at the gallery didn't meet the buyer's needs.

Beginning in fall, 1997, a new art leasing service will be available to assist those businesses who need art for the short term or who appreciate the tax advantages as well as the aesthetic and strategic importance of having fine art on their walls but whose budget constraints prevent them from an immediate acquisition.

Although new and exciting work by young artists can always be viewed at the gallery, works by internationally known or "blue chip" artists are always available, often in the "back room," where most of J.J. Brookings Gallery's art is stored when not on the walls. Photographers from Ansel Adams to Eduard Steichen to Joel-Peter Witkin, artists such Robert Motherwell, Helen Frankenthaler, Jim Dine and Andy

Warhol, and sculptors such as Bill Barrett, Bruce Beasley, George Segal and Robert Graham have been on view. Finding specific pieces of art for that certain discriminating collector from their network of art sources throughout the world has always posed a "fun" challenge to the J.J. Brookings Gallery staff.

Now open seven days a week to better serve its clients and the many visitors to San Francisco, the J.J. Brookings Gallery's staff welcome the opportunity to provide assistance, whether it is for the purchase of an individual work of art as a gift, providing an art acquisition program for a large Silicon Valley company, or leasing art to be hung throughout a 20,000 square foot financial district office. The friendly staff is helpful to anyone who visits, whether they are a casual vacationer, a member of a corporate art selection committee, or the serious collector.

Manuel Felguerez
La Pinta

Ben Schonzeit
Clear Caribe
(Bottom left)

Katherine Chang Liu
Earthly Pleasures
(Right)

Lisa Gray
Cocoon
(Bottom left)

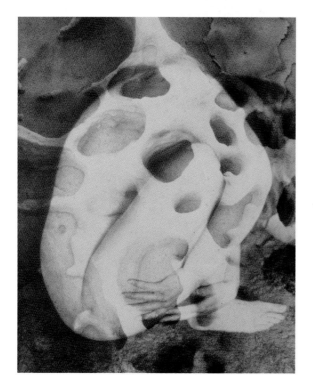

Sandy Skoglundsa
Fox Games

Trisha Orr
Still Life With Birds

Elena Borstein
Neon Courtyard

Manola Valdes
Retrato de Mujer
(Left)

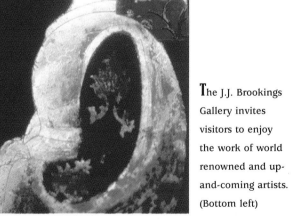

The J.J. Brookings Gallery invites visitors to enjoy the work of world renowned and up-and-coming artists. (Bottom left)

The Palace Hotel

The Palace Hotel opened its doors on October 2, 1875, debuting as the world's largest and most luxurious hotel. Occupying an entire block in downtown San Francisco, the towering seven-story structure heralded San Francisco's coming of age.

Visitors arrive through the palace's sumptuous foyer.

The Palace Hotel was the dream of William Chapman Ralston and Senator William Sharon. Ralston, founder of the Bank of California, desired to see San Francisco transformed from boomtown to booming metropolis. Envisioning his role as erecting history's most magnificent hotel in the city's center, he commissioned architect J. P. Gaynor to build a luxury hotel that would outshine Europe's finest hotels.

Alas, the $5 million price tag drained Ralston's banking empire. Just weeks before the Palace was to open, the Bank of California collapsed. The following day Ralston's body was found floating in San Francisco Bay. The Palace was opened under the guidance of William Sharon, the surviving partner.

Hailed as "The Grande Dame of the West," the Palace beckoned all to admire its majestic size and unparalleled luxury. It featured four hydraulic elevators and an electronic call button in each guest room in order for guests' every desire to be fulfilled.

Historic Palace, 1875 (Bottom right)

Only twelve days after its opening, General Philip Sheridan, fresh from his success in the Franco-Prussian War, was honored at the Palace Hotel with a three-and-one-half hour banquet and a menu that was "fit for royalty."

Almost from the day the hotel opened, a procession of presidents and potentates began streaming into the Palace's legendary carriage entrance, aptly named the Grand Court. The parade of famous guests grew to include U.S. Presidents Ulysses S. Grant, Benjamin Harrison and Rutherford B. Hayes; King David Kalakaua of Hawaii, last of the island's kings, who died at the Palace in 1891; playwright Oscar Wilde; and actress Sarah Bernhardt, who arrived at the Palace with her pet baby tiger in 1887. (President Warren Harding unexpectedly died here in 1923 after completing a cross-country good will tour.)

On the morning of April 18, 1906, a major earthquake shook all of San Francisco. Tossed out of bed by the tremors, famed tenor Enrico Caruso, clad only in a towel, fled the Palace, saying of San Francisco, "'Elluva a place, 'elluva a place, I never come back here." (And he never did.)

Even though the hotel survived the earthquake, it was soon gutted by the fire that raged through much of the city. Plans were immediately made to rebuild the landmark hotel from its ashes, retaining many architectural features of the original hotel and showcasing exciting new art. Trowbridge and Livingston of

New York were commissioned to design the new Palace Hotel; supervising architect was George Kelham.

The "new and improved" Palace Hotel opened on December 16, 1909, surpassing its predecessor in modern conveniences and glamour, but assuredly defining the standard of grand hotels for elegance, luxury and service. The cost of rebuilding the Palace was $10 million. Room rates were $2 a night.

One of the most significant changes was the transformation of the hotel's atrium carriage entrance, the Grand Court, into the Garden Court. Crowned by a $7 million stained-glass dome and shimmering chandeliers of the finest Austrian crystal, and flanked by a double row of massive Italian marble Ionic columns, the Garden Court is still recognized as one of the world's most beautiful dining rooms.

The Garden Court soon became the site for some of the nation's most prestigious events. In 1919, President Woodrow Wilson was host for two luncheons in support of the Versailles Treaty that officially ended World War I. The official banquet honoring the opening session of the United Nations was held here in 1945. The Garden Court was designated San Francisco Landmark Number 18 by the Landmarks Preservation Advisory Board in 1969. (The landmark status was later extended to include the entire hotel except for its southwest corner.)

Another addition to the 1909 hotel was the club-like Pied Piper Bar. Commissioned to paint a mural for the reopening, renowned artist Maxfield Parrish chose Robert Browning's fairy tale, "The Pied Piper of Hamlin," for his theme. *The Pied Piper* mural features the piper leading a band of 27 children. Originally installed in the Palace bar, the mural was later transferred to its namesake, the Pied Piper Bar, which was selected as "One of the World's Seven Greatest Bars" by *Esquire* magazine.

The Palace's reputation for acquiring "nothing but the best" includes its art collection. Along with *The Pied Piper* mural, The Palace owns two murals by San Francisco artist Antonio Sotomayer — the *Lotta Panel*, depicting San Francisco's favorite actress, Lotta Crabtree, and the *Emperor Norton Panel*, immortalizing the city's famous 19th-century character, Emperor Norton I, self-proclaimed Emperor of the United States and Protector of Mexico. These murals hang in Maxfield's restaurant, named in honor of Maxfield Parrish. An early 19th-century Aubusson tapestry highlights recent art additions at the Palace. Commissioned work includes portraits of the hotel's founders, William Chapman Ralston and William Sharon, a bayscape and a classical landscape by Jan Saethers, and *Palace Entry*, by Richard Chase. Other work includes *Still Life With Flowers*, by Jacquelyn McBain, and Robert Walker's *Tapestry With a Coat of Arms*.

In October 1954, Mrs. William B. Johnston, granddaughter of the hotel's co-founder William Sharon, sold the Palace to the Sheraton Corporation. In 1973, Honolulu-based Kyo-ya Co., Ltd. purchased the Palace, with the Sheraton Corporation retaining management of the hotel. The Palace is a member of The Luxury Collection of ITT Sheraton. The 48 Luxury Collection hotels and resorts, among the world's finest, are noted for personalized, individual service designed to exceed the expectations of the most discriminating traveler.

Kyo-ya's jewel-like sushi

Skylit Pool

The luxurious Palace Hotel, home away from home for a distinguished list of visitors that include presidents and potentates. High Tea (Bottom left)

On January 6, 1989, the Palace closed its doors for a $150 million renovation of all areas of historic interest and addition of modern amenities. Restored to its original splendor, the Palace reopened April 3, 1991. For 27 months, an army of specialist craftspeople from across the nation restored the hotel's stained-glass ceilings, 100 chandeliers, marble floors, antique furnishings, ornate plasterwork and gold-leaf decorations. The 550 guest rooms, including 33 one and two bedroom suites, the Bridal Suite, the Governor's Suite and the President's Suite, were refurbished with traditional mahogany furnishings and updated fixtures. The Grand Ballroom, the Ralston Room, and the Gold Ballroom, restored to their Beaux Arts splendor, lend a sense of historic importance to all functions. A new conference area and health spa were added to once again create a world-class hotel in San Francisco.

The National Trust for Historic Preservation, the American Institute of Architects, the California Preservation and the California Heritage Council all honored the Palace's restoration with a stream of design and preservation awards.

The Palace's rebirth of grandeur coincides with a revitalization of the South of Market (SOMA) area. With the building of the Museum of Modern Art, the Moscone Convention Center, and the Center for the Arts and Yerba Buena Gardens, the relocation of the California Historical Society, and the addition of many new restaurants, this area has become very respectable. Relocation of the Mexican and Jewish museums to SOMA is also in the works. Post Street, leading down from Union Square toward the Palace, has become the third most popular shopping street in the country.

The Palace's location, in the heart of the financial, shopping, convention and museum districts, draws an exclusive crowd of businesspeople for lunch. Since 1875, the hotel has played host to the nation's top business leaders from industrialists John D. Rockefeller and J. Pierpont Morgant to today's computer wizards Steve Forbes and William H. Gates.

Recognized as the West Coast's premier venue for business meetings, the Palace offers 45,000 square feet of conference and banquet facilities, including 22 separate meeting rooms that can accommodate up to 1,200 people. There are 7,000 square feet available for receptions, refreshment breaks, conference registration and related activities. The Sunset Court's expansive skylight echoes the Garden Court's legendary stained-glass dome. A full-service Business Center offers secretarial services, teleconferencing capabilities and other business amenities as well as personal computers and facsimile machines for use in guest rooms. The Palace's business comes primarily from the Bay Area, especially from the medical profession, financial institutions, and high tech companies.

The Palace's cuisine includes breakfast, lunch and dinner, as well as afteroon tea and cocktails in the world-famous Garden Court. Maxfield's features flavorful steaks, seafood and pasta for lunch and dinner daily. Acclaimed Kyo-ya serves jewel-like sushi and authentic Japanese cuisine in a stylish, elegant setting. The Palace's formal dinner service has been used at state dinners and other grand occasions, including an official dinner for Prince Philip, Duke of Edinburgh; a state dinner for President William McKinley; and a banquet for General Ulysses S. Grant.

The Palace continues to cater to an old, established crowd, and commands a good following in various social circles, including ballet and opera devotees. The debutante's Cotillion is a tradition at the Palace. The hotel's list of renowned guests includes heads of state, royalty, actors and actresses, CEOs and 10 U.S. presidents.

The Garden Court, built for the hotel's 1909 reopening, is recognized as one of the world's most beautiful dining rooms.

Yank Sing Restaurant

No ethnic group has contributed more to San Francisco's rich culture and famed cuisine than the Chinese. From the late 1800s when tiny noodle restaurants and tea houses began appearing along Grant and Stockton Streets in Chinatown, the tastes of old China took hold in San Francisco. Since then, the City has had an unrivaled love affair with Chinese cuisine.

Henry Chan's Yank Sing Restaurant is said to serve the City's finest deem sum (also spelled dim sum) — bite-sized savory and sweet dumplings wrapped in translucent rice pastry. "Even more delicate than the deem sum dishes served in China," is how Herb Caen described Yank Sing's fare. Deem sum means "to touch the heart." The phrase and extraordinary cuisine it describes are uniquely suited to San Franciscan tastes.

At Yank Sing, diners sample the tastes of ancient China in an elegant, upscale Asian atmosphere situated in the heart of San Francisco's financial district at Battery and Clay Streets just a block from the bustling Embarcadero shopping center. The generous space is divided into a warren of small dining areas and caters to a youthful business crowd of executives, stock brokers, lawyers and secretaries on weekdays and a more leisurely family crowd on weekends.

As at other deem sum restaurants, Yank Sing has no formal menu. Instead a continuous parade of carts carrying steaming food is brought to each table. On one are Mandarin dumplings; on another, minced squab, Peking duck wrapped in a thin honey-coated skin, steamed pork buns, sesame balls, succulent shrimp-filled dumplings, pungent little eggplants and grilled turnip cakes. In the end, customers experience creamy, crispy, chewy, savory and sweet tastes all in a single meal. Wise diners paces themselves, taking single portions so they can sample a wide range of flavors.

On any given day, more than 60 kinds of deem sum are served, selected from a repertoire nearly twice as large. New recipes are added monthly. Others are modified to suit changing tastes and take advantage of the freshest foods at the market.

The art of preparing deem sum reaches back more than 1,000 years to the royal court of the imperial palaces of the Sung Dynasty. When the Mongols invaded in the 13th century, the royals fled, spreading the art of deem sum as they migrated south toward Canton. By 1900, Canton had become the leader of China's deem sum tradition.

The ancient flavors of Canton are alive at Yank Sing today. Now a well established dining spot in the financial district, Yank Sing's origins were in Chinatown. In 1958, Henry Chan's parents, then new immigrants from Canton, opened a small storefront restaurant on the edge of Chinatown. Over the next 20 years, working 14-hour days, seven days a week, they built a successful business — the only restaurant in Chinatown serving exclusively deem sum. They named their businesses Yank Sing — the old name for Canton, "City of Rams."

In 1979, Henry took over the family business. And on Valentines Day 1981, he opened a much larger, more modern Yank Sing on Battery Street. The restaurant's reputation was so well established, that the grand opening boasted a list of dignitaries that included Mayor Dianne Feinstein, Herb Caen and Yul Brenner. Yank Sing was the first deem sum restaurant to open outside Chinatown and cater to a mainly Caucasian clientele. It was a bold business move that proved prophetic and extremely successful.

Dining in elegance at Yank Sing's Battery St. Restaurant (Top)

Assorted deem sum delicacies are served daily at Yank Sing. (Bottom)

The American Property Exchange

A contemporary condominium right in the heart of downtown San Francisco, a romantic cottage tucked away on Telegraph hill, a classic Victorian situated in Pacific Heights. In the not-so-distant past, business travelers and visitors to San Francisco had to settle for the standard hotel room or the generic apartment. Stylish homes and private residences could only be viewed from the outside looking in. Now, through American Property Exchange, visitors and executives can rent exclusive fully furnished dwellings, then step right in and make themselves at home for a day, week or month.

The American Property Exchange has revolutionized the concept of short-term accommodations, launching San Francisco's corporate and vacation travelers into the 21st Century. Transforming the resort town practice of renting private homes for short-term stays, American Property Exchange has taken a small-town practice and made it big business.

One of the first entrepreneurs to recognize that large American cities were ideal markets for the short-term rental business was real estate broker Zoya Smithton. Having been interested in real estate from a young age, Smithton attended college in Hawaii where she first became involved in the booming enterprise of short-term vacation rentals. Always interested in expanding ideas and never taking no for an answer, she reasoned that what worked in Honolulu would work in other markets. So, in 1984, Smithton formed American Property Exchange, a company specializing in marketing privately owned furnished apartments, homes and condominiums as hotel alternatives in metropolitan areas.

Smithton, who lives in San Francisco, focused her marketing efforts on her home city. San Francisco, she predicted, with its reputation as an international business center, thriving tourist attraction and lively entertainment area, would be the perfect market. From the start, Smithton pushed the limits of typical real estate and rental practices through her ideas and innovation. Rental properties, for example, must not only be fully furnished, they must be tastefully furnished.

Clients, both renters and owners, appreciate her dedication and determination to provide the best service and style through her unique product and real estate structure. Over the next decade, Smithton watched her one-woman operation evolve into a multi-million dollar full-service marketing and management company called American Marketing Systems, Inc. in which American Property Exchange is now just a division. Today, American Marketing Systems, Inc. is a network of companies offering clients high-quality real estate, travel, hospitality and home services on a grand scale.

The early days were far from grand, according to Smithton, who spent many long days and nights on the phone, chasing down clients and properties. If a client asked for a product or service she did not provide, this only allowed her the challenge to determine

Private inner courtyard of a condominium complex, nestled beneath Telegraph Hill and Levi Plaza

how she could make it possible. Smithton listened to the needs of her clients and never accepted defeat. Through determination and her powerful persuasive skills and personality, the company began to prosper. In typical Smithton fashion, however, she insisted her associates function as a team rather than individual, competing agents. By pooling their time and resources, they could offer clients better and expanded services. This team approach, a renegade idea in the real estate industry where companies pride themselves on the fierce competition of agents, proved to be another ingenious Smithton touch. By 1989, American Property Exchange was recognized by the *San Francisco Business Times* as one of the top 25 Women-owned businesses in the city.

From that point, business really took off. Today the company owns a four-story Victorian on the corner of Lombard and Van Ness. Furnished rental units now number more than 400. Accommodations, situated in desirable neighborhoods, offer a true slice of San Francisco life with all the amenities of home. Some dwellings feature luxuries such as spas, gourmet kitchens, panoramic views, heated pools and the most coveted of all San Francisco amenities — parking. Staying or living in neighborhoods gives long-term, and even short-term, visitors the opportunity to truly appreciate the city and its residents. Each neighborhood offers a different feeling — breezy and active in the Marina; vibrant and trendy in SoMa — its own main

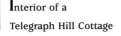
Interior of a
Telegraph Hill Cottage

street with coffee houses, restaurants, boutiques, movie theaters and public transportation that is accessible to the Financial District. So successful is American Property Exchange's short-term rental and leasing services, that the company trademark now is "We Rent San Francisco."

Smithton and company now offer a full range of real estate services under the umbrella agency, American Marketing Systems, Inc. Its companies include American Property Exchange, which has expanded to feature corporate relocation, unfurnished leasing, property management, real estate sales and vacation rental divisions; Maintain-A Property Maintenance Service, an on-call maintenance agency that also handles design planning, remodeling and renovation and licensed plumbing, electrical and general contract work; Grandma's Housecleaning Service, a residential cleaning business; The Art of Cleaning, a corporate housing and commercial service; and American Marketing and Management Systems (AMMS), a licensed travel agency. In addition, there is a Concierge Service that offers entertainment packages and an exclusive relocation book, providing information on neighborhood shops, schools, tours and services.

In the future, Smithton expects to expand beyond California and establish the company on an international level. Where ever the agency goes, you can be sure it will arrive in inimitable, Smithton style.

Noe Valley
Victorian Parlor

Interior of a
corporate rental

Ben Janken Fine Photography

Love blooms in the shadows of a flowering magnolia tree and stately columns of the Palace of Fine Arts.

From Berkeley's scenic Marina with stormy skies overhead, looking across the Bay to San Francisco. (Top right)

San Francisco has always been a city of romance, a city of love. Its rich architectural heritage, dazzling bridges, shimmering Bay and fog shrouded skyline have drawn painters and photographers for over 150 years. One of those was photographer Ben Janken, who moved to San Francisco 22 years ago.

Since 1984, Ben Janken has perfected a signature style of photography that reflects the romantic glow of lovers in the scenic grandeur of the City's land and seascapes.

A bank of fog hovers over distant San Francisco as seen from the heights of the Marin Headlands with the inimitable Golden Gate Bridge as a backdrop. (Bottom right, opposite page)

Monastic arches frame these newlyweds' romantic moment. (Top right)

The romance of old San Francisco is captured in the Garden Court Room of the Sheraton Palace Hotel. (Top left)

Stopping traffic with a kiss in romantic North Beach. (Center left)

Sunset at Seal Rock overlooking the cool, quiet Pacific Ocean. (Bottom left)

The high-tech crispness of new San Francisco as seen in the Pan Pacific Hotel. (Bottom right)

Boudin Sourdough Bakery & Cafe

The Boudin Bakery family in the 1880s, perhaps at 434 Green Street

Master Baker Steve Giraudo, credited with making the Boudin Bakery what it is today (Bottom right)

Every American city can boast of at least one thing that makes it unique. Although it might be difficult to narrow down San Francisco to one unique item, there's no mistaking that San Francisco's sourdough bread belongs in a class of its own. While several bakeries produce sourdough, the Boudin Sour-dough Bakery & Cafe product is the original sourdough bread, and it has been around the longest.

It was in 1849, when gold-seekers rushed to California, that Louis Boudin and his wife left war-torn Paris and came to San Francisco. Here Boudin created the sourdough starter by combining a wild yeast with French baking techniques. Unlike bakers whose breads were leavened from cake yeast (introduced in 1868), by using his "mother dough" Boudin allowed his bread to rise and "sour" at its own pace.

What gives Boudin sourdough bread its unique attributes? No one knows for sure. Theorists claims that it's aided by San Francisco's moderate climate, the fact that it's next to the ocean — even crediting the fog itself. Today, Boudin bakers still use the same mother dough created by Louis Boudin in 1849. Each day Boudin bakers take a portion of the mother dough and mix it with water, unbleached flour and salt to create the bread that San Francisco residents and visitors have come to love. The mother dough is refreshed on a daily basis as it has been for almost 150 years.

Louis Boudin began his bakery in the North Beach area. In 1852, his 16-year-old son, Isidore, who had remained in Paris as an apprentice baker, came to San Francisco to join his parents in the

family business. San Francisco was a good place to be for enterprising immigrants like the Boudins. The Gold Rush crowds had pushed the population from 1,000 in 1848 to approximately 25,000 by the end of 1850, and to 50,000 in 1853. In 1854 there were 11 flour mills and 63 bakeries here. Louis Boudin's sourdough bread had gained such a reputation by that time that city dwellers and gold-panners alike lined up each morning for a fresh baked loaf.

Isidore Boudin married Marie Louise Erni, a fellow French immigrant, in 1873. They ran the bakery together until Isidore's death, and then his widow, aided by her four children, Charles, Jules, Louise and Lucie, continued with the successful operation of the bakery, staying true to the original sourdough process.

After the 1906 earthquake and fire, the Boudin bakery relocated from North Beach to its present location at 10th Avenue and Geary Street, in the Richmond district. The business was then operated by Jules and Charles. Newspapers told in 1909 of the "San Francisco firm of Boudin Brothers, owners of extensive flour mills," showing that the French bakery had

developed into a substantial wholesale operation by this time. The Boudins had also begun a home delivery service, using horse-drawn wagons, which they continued until the late 1920s. The horses were trained to stroll down the center of the street as the driver ran back and forth, placing bread on nails set into door frames. In this way, San Franciscans could receive their favorite bread without leaving their homes.

Marie Louise Boudin died in 1921. Jules, who never married, died in 1925; Charles died in 1928. Charles's widow, the former Lizabelle Pomeroy, continued the operation of the business, but due to her son Paul's chronic asthma he did not join the family business, and the bakery was sold.

Steve Giraudo, Sr. arrived in San Francisco in 1935 and began work at the Boudin bakery as a union baker. In a few years he purchased the business and, with his partner, Gaspar Rivas, continued the business as it had been done since 1849, using the mother dough and the original recipe for Louis Boudin's sourdough bread.

Steve Giraudo, Sr. is credited with making the Boudin Bakery & Cafe what it is today. In 1975, Giraudo, aided by his sons, Lou and Steven, Jr., opened the first Boudin retail bakery on Fisherman's Wharf. In 1987, due to tourists' demands, Boudin began a catalog business that allows customers to have fresh-baked sourdough bread shipped to them. In the late 1980s the Boudin Bakery developed a full service cafe and began operating as Boudin Sourdough Bakery & Cafe. Menus include sandwiches on sourdough rolls, salads laced with sourdough croutons, and soups and chili served in — what else? — sourdough bread bowls. In 1996, the San Francisco Conventions and Visitors Bureau honored Steve Giraudo, Sr. with a Silver Cable Car Award for his efforts in making San Francisco internationally renowned for its sourdough bread.

Steve Giraudo's presence lives on today. Each loaf of Boudin sourdough bread is still made by bakers who hand-score each loaf, and is baked under the watchful eyes of master bakers who trained under Giraudo. Willie Jaciw, a Boudin baker for 30 years, is in charge of the Fisherman's Wharf bakery, which supplies the two retail locations there. Fernando Padilla, who has been with Boudin for 18 years, is in charge of the 10th Avenue bakery, which supplies bread to more than two dozen Bay Area locations.

Padilla's sculpted sourdough bread creations have become renowned. They include "keys to the city" for Mayor Willie Brown's inauguration; "cable car" breads for Cable Car commemorations; and saxophones for President Bill Clinton's inauguration.

In 1993 a Chicago-based specialty food company bought the increasingly successful Boudin business. Dave Barrows, president of the Boudin Bakery & Cafe since 1995, was brought in to help implement the company's plans for expansion. The company presently has over 40 locations, spread over California, Illinois, and Texas.

Boudin's roots run deep in San Francisco's history and it continues to participate in a number of San Francisco-related functions. In 1996 Boudin created a partnership with the San Francisco Giants and Project Open Hand, which feeds more than 5,000 persons living with AIDS. For every home win by the Giants, Boudin donated 300 freshly baked loaves to Open Hand — a sharing of something uniquely San Francisco. Also, Boudin regularly contributes bread and food products to San Francisco-related charities and events each month.

The original Boudin Bakery established in 1849 was located in the North Beach district of San Francisco.

Bowles/Sorokko Galleries

San Francisco, LeRoy Neiman's depiction of the Golden Gate Bridge — complete with the fog

Located near Aquatic Park on San Francisco Bay, Bowles/Sorokko Galleries is as beautiful as the art it displays. On a clear day, the gallery door offers a spectacular view of the Bay and Alcatraz Island.

Bowles/Sorokko has been in the same location for more than 25 years. Its founder, Franklin Bowles, opened his gallery in 1971, specializing in the work of Twentieth Century artists. Over the years his gallery grew into one of the finest art galleries in the world. In addition to its San Francisco location, Bowles/Sorokko owns art galleries on Rodeo Drive in Beverly Hills and in the Soho District of New York City.

LeRoy Neiman painted the Golden Gate Bridge and other San Francisco landmarks for three exhibitions which debuted at Bowles/Sorokko Galleries.

Bowles/Sorokko is the largest representative of the works of Leroy Neiman, America's most widely collected artist. Since 1964, Neiman has been the most popular painter and printmaker in America. His popularity lies not only in his bold yet harmonious colors, and the obvious passion with which he paints, but in his unrivaled ability to capture the spirit of our age.

Over the years, Neiman has painted the inductees for the Baseball Hall of Fame, the Master's golf tournament in Augusta, Georgia, and Wayne Gretsky's record-breaking 802nd ice hockey goal. He also created the magnificent portrait of Frank Sinatra that became the cover of the singer's "Duets" album.

Bowles/Sorokko has held several shows of Neiman's art devoted to San Francisco. "San Francisco by Day," "San Francisco by Night," and "City by the Bay" are the three limited edition serigraphs that represented Neiman's most successful exhibitions.

Bowles/Sorokko is also the exclusive representative of Igor Medvedev, a Russian-born artist, sculptor, writer and poet, who has lived in the Bay Area since the1960s. Medvedev has spent many months in Spain, Greece and other Mediterranean countries, seeking areas which have not yet fallen victim to cultural or architectural ruin. He has captured images of this treasured architectural and cultural legacy through his paintings, creating an awareness of the importance of the intimate and human scale of these Mediterranean villages.

Bowles/Sorokko has published a book, *A Gift Returned: The Mediterranean Light* containing reprints of some of the artist's favorite Mediterranean landscapes. The book includes an essay written by Dr. Jean Y. Audigier, one of the gallery's directors, and Edward Muenck.

Bowles/Sorokko also displays the paintings and sculptures of Mihail Chemiakin, Russia's most influential Twentieth Century artist. Chemiakin was exiled from the Soviet Union in 1971. He did not return to

his native country until 1989, when he was honored with a one-man retrospective in Moscow.

In 1995, Bowles/Sorokko co-hosted an exhibit of Chemiakin's "Carnival" series at The Hermitage Museum in St. Petersburg. The internationally long-awaited retrospective brought Chemiakin full circle. As a young man, Chemiakin had worked as a laborer at The Hermitage Museum, spending many hours studying and copying the artworks of the Western Masters, and he held his first art exhibit there in 1964.

Other artists whose work is displayed at Bowles/Sorokko include Pablo Picasso, Marc Chagall, Joan Miro, Leonard Baskin, Larry Horowitz and Pierre Marie Brisson. Over the years, the gallery has held many important shows including an installation of Chagall's Bible Suite, a stunning collection of Picasso's gravures, and an exhibit of Miro's last etchings.

The gallery's operations are supervised by three directors — Tony Pernicone, Jean Audigier, Ph.D., and Michael LaPrade.

Pernicone has long been active in the art world. A native of New York City, he worked in the theater before he moved to San Francisco and took a job at Bowles/Sorokko in 1981. A skilled art appraiser, Pernicone is a member of the American Society of Appraisers, as well as a member of the National Auctioneers Association.

Dr. Audigier for more than 30 years has been a Professor of Fine Arts at the University of San Francisco, which has one of the country's largest university collections of art.

LaPrade is in charge of marketing and promotion for the galleries.

In addition to the three directors, Bowles/Sorokko employs more than a dozen art consultants and almost as many support staff. It has its own frame shop, China Basin Design.

The galleries' directors and consultants regularly travel to France, Italy, Germany, Russia and other countries throughout the world to scout out interesting and significant art work. Bowles/Sorokko displays works by known artists who are making unique personal statements, and who demonstrate the technical expertise that will enable their work to endure. The galleries are also interested in artists whose works have a popular appeal and is proud that the public has enthusiastically responded to its exhibitions.

Bowles/Sorokko stages between six and eight installations of new work each year. It has hosted numerous art shows which have been attended by San Francisco's mayors and other prominent citizens. The gallery also holds an annual auction every February, in which a wide variety of art work is available to prospective buyers.

The galleries' proximity to Ghirardelli Square and other Fisherman Wharf landmarks makes it a convenient stop for a procession of visitors to San Francisco, who are impressed by its high-quality art work, as well as its unusually high ceilings and bright and airy atmosphere. The location also attracts artists from all over the world who want to display their work there. Two or three artists stop in each week, hoping their work can hang alongside the paintings of Picasso, Chagall, Miro, Medvedev, Chemiakin and other artists in the attractive San Francisco-based galleries with the worldwide reputation for excellence.

Block 1430, one of Pablo Picasso's Soixante gravure etchings which were exhibited at Bowles/Sorokko

Santorini Narrows, one of Igor Medvedev's Mediterranean landscapes. Bowles/Sorokko is the exclusive representative for Medvedev.

The Carnelian Room

The panoramic view from the windows of The Carnelian Room

For the ultimate dining experience 52 floors above it all, the Carnelian Room is literally the top choice for dinner. Situated atop the tallest building in San Francisco, the Carnelian Room offers glittering views of the city and bay as well as innovative and beautiful cuisine.

For decades, penthouse restaurants in San Francisco competed to claim the best and most expansive panoramic view of the city. But when the Carnelian Room opened in July 1970, on the 52nd floor of the newly completed Bank of America World Headquarters, the competition was over. Rising from the heart of the Financial district, the building's design evokes the towering rock formations found in California's High Sierra. The Building's crowning jewel is the Carnelian Room, where diners can relax with a cocktail at sunset, when the views of San Francisco and the Golden Gate Bridge provide a breathtaking backdrop. In the evening, diners can savor the excellent cuisine amidst a magical city stage of flickering lights.

Named after the polished Carnelian granite that sheaths the building, the Carnelian Room's interior walls, imported from an 18th century French chateau, are accented by antiques and paintings from the eras of Louis XV and XVI. Sprays of colorful bouquets in elegant vases grace the dining room, which features generously spaced tables, some placed right next to the floor-to-ceiling windows that showcase the

breathtaking views. Besides the main dining room, there are 11 dining suites available for as many as two diners or groups of up to 1,500 guests.

On a clear evening, diners can see the twinkling lights of the Fairmont Hotel and the hazy glow of Telegraph Hill and Coit Tower. In addition, there are sparkling views of the Transamerica Pyramid, Fisherman's Wharf, the Golden Gate Bridge and the lighted Bay Bridge. To complement this magical setting, above one of the world's most beautiful cities, is the creative cuisine of Ron Garrido, who specializes in simple, yet elegant food.

The Carnelian Room's wine cellar is one of the five best cellars in the nation, if not the best. Containing between 40,000 and 50,000 bottles, the Carnelian Room's cellar is certainly second to none in the Bay Area. It is particularly strong in first- and second-growth Bordeaux's that date back to the 1920s, California Cabernets that go back as far as 1928, and Grand Cru and Premier Grand Cru Burgundies. In addition, the cellar features a strong selection of premium vintages from California wineries. Since 1982, the *Wine Spectator* magazine has awarded the Carnelian Room's wine cellar its "Grand Award" for one of the greatest wine lists in the world.

From the day it opened, the Carnelian Room has attracted celebrities and high-profile dignitaries. Former President Jimmy Carter and Senator Dianne Feinstein entertained guests in the Carnelian Room.

Joe Montana, Don Johnson, Melanie Griffith, Leeza Gibbons, John Tesh and Rob Reiner are just a few of the many sports celebrities and entertainment stars who have dined on the 52nd floor.

The Tamalpais Room, a small suite with a table for two, offers one of the most remarkable and romantic settings in the world for dinner for two. The Tamalpais Room attracts a large following of romantics; some who proclaim their love with messages trailing from a small airplane at an appointed time. Completing the room's appeal is the sweeping view of the Golden Gate Bridge, discrete call button, fine cuisine, and attentive staff.

For large gatherings, the Carnelian Room is a welcome respite from the anonymity of the usual banquet hall. All the dining suites feature dazzling views, and can be arranged to suit business needs with audio-visual and other essential support close at hand. The private dining office is available to help plan parties. For events on a grand scale, the entire room can be opened up, providing 24,000 square feet of elegant space with all of San Francisco as a setting.

Whatever the occasion, diners will appreciate the Carnelian Room's exceptional menu and imaginative cuisine. Centering around American specialties, the menu features a selection of locally harvested fruits and vegetables, seafood, fowl and beef. Following the seasons, the restaurant changes the menu with each equinox to ensure the freshest ingredients prepared at their peak. Menu hallmarks include selections such as California Rack of Lamb, Braised Rabbit in a Phyllo Purse, live Maine Lobster and Squash Ravioli with fresh Black Truffles. The 360-degree view from the Carnelian Room changes every day and

moment to moment, but in 1989 the restaurant closed for a $4 million remodeling that increased the seating capacity and enhanced the interiors. The new decor, combined with the restaurants continuing commitment to its culinary team, has earned the Carnelian Room a prestigious DiRoNa Award since 1993. The Carnelian Room also holds a place on Epicurean Rendezvous' list of the 100 best restaurants in San Francisco/ Northern California.

In addition to dinner, the Carnelian Room offers a spectacular Sunday Champagne Brunch that includes a wide variety of fresh and tasty breakfast and lunch selections. Monday through Friday, the Carnelian Room is reserved at breakfast and lunch for use by the members only of Banker's Club of San Francisco, a private business club. Owned by ARAMARK, Corp., the Carnelian Room is managed by a top-notch professional staff.

In a city known for its cuisine, the Carnelian Room rises above the rest and offers an unparalleled dining experience.

Dinner and the twinkling lights of the City and the Bay Bridge from the main dining room of the Carnelian Room.

Cathedral Hill Hotel

Occupying a full block of Van Ness Avenue between Geary and Post Streets, the Cathedral Hill Hotel (originally the Jack Tar Hotel) serves more than 150,000 guests a year who come to San Francisco from over 20 countries around the world. It offers convenient, quality accommodations at a reasonable price — and a long colorful history as a San Francisco landmark.

When Texas financier Charles A. Sammons built the Jack Tar Hotel and office complex in the late 1950s, there hadn't been a new hotel in San Francisco in 30 years, not since the Sir Francis Drake was built in 1928. San Francisco needed a new hotel, and the Jack Tar — with its 400 beautiful guest rooms, 450-car garage, and modern convention facilities — filled that need. Nevertheless, among many San Franciscans who compared the building's boxy, functional architecture to the elegant Nob Hill hotels,

the Jack Tar was quite controversial.

Originally decorated with red, white, and blue panels and topped with a revolving sign that said "Jack Tar Hotel" in letters nearly 20 feet high, the building had a strikingly modern, even futuristic look. People who liked it thought it was "cheerful" and "colorful;" people who didn't thought it was "garish." Before long it became the building Herb Caen loved to make fun of. The year the hotel opened Caen called it "that Texas monstrosity," and wrote in his column: "I don't object to the Jack Tar Hotel as such. I can think of a dozen cities where it would look right at home. Here, well, do you carry a plastic handbag with a sable coat?" He felt much the same way about the Hilton Hotel, built four years later, which he called "The box the Jack Tar came in."

The hotel's original President, Ed Leach, was also a favorite topic in the San Francisco media. A 6 foot

When it opened in 1960, the Cathedral Hill Hotel was painted red, white, and blue — a color scheme that was quite controversial among San Franciscans. In 1979 the hotel was painted white, and the interior has since been renovated as well.

3 inch, 300-pound Texan, who never went out without his cowboy boots, Leach had worked in the hotel business since he was a teenager. His first job was to spread fertilizer on the lawn of a major Texas hotel. He went on to become a dishwasher, a short-order cook, then manager of that hotel's coffee shop, and finally Maitre d' Hotel. By time he arrived in San Francisco, he was President of the entire chain of 13 Jack Tar hotels, and his rags to riches story had won him a Horatio Alger Award.

Leach welcomed the attention the hotel was getting, believing in the adage "All publicity is good publicity," and the Jack Tar proved him right. The hotel was immediately successful. It booked millions of dollars in convention business before it even opened in 1960, and its grand ballroom soon became a popular venue for parties, fashion shows, and society luncheons.

The Jack Tar offered all the latest modern conveniences. It had free parking, two bars, two restaurants, and several attractions that were new to San Francisco. It was the first hotel in the city to have an outdoor swimming pool and ice skating rink (positioned side-by-side on a lush two-acre garden patio); it was the first hotel in San Francisco to have air-conditioning (another sign of Texas influence); and it was one of only a few hotels in the country with its own wedding chapel.

It was also the most electronically innovative hotel in the world. Long before such devices were common, the Jack Tar had remote control units for its televisions, message lights on its phones, and an electronic maid call system. A closed-circuit television network meant that guests could look in on convention meetings, without leaving their hotel room. Another invention allowed guests to register and check out without even going through the hotel lobby. All they had to do was step into a booth in the garage and converse with a hotel clerk on a closed-circuit TV monitor. Money, keys, etc., were sent back and forth via a transport tube.

Of course, the hotel has changed with the times.

The lobby and restaurants have been completely renovated. The revolving sign came down in 1978, and in 1979, the colorful panels on the outside of the building were all painted white. The name was changed from the Jack Tar to the Cathedral Hill Hotel in 1982. After a fire in 1983, the hotel closed for six months, and reopened with one of the best safety systems in the hotel business. At a cost of more than $10 million, all the rooms were outfitted with fire-retardant drapes, carpet, and furniture, as well as smoke detectors, sprinklers, and a sophisticated public address system.

The building itself is one of the most structurally sound in the city. Unlike many other hotels which have had to be retrofitted, the Cathedral Hill was originally constructed with expansion joints so that it could serve as a bomb shelter, and since it opened it has been listed on maps as one of the safest places to be in San Francisco in an earthquake.

This proved true in the Loma Prieta earthquake in 1989. Not only did the building come through unscathed, but the hotel staff had just completed an emergency preparedness training a month before. Guests were so impressed that hotel management received dozens of letters complimenting them on their staff's calm, professional manner and thanking them for the extraordinary efforts they made during the aftermath — including serving 400 people dinner and breakfast without electricity.

In 1992, a few years after the death of Charles Sammons, the hotel was sold to Cathedral Hill Associates, an independent company headed by Ki Yong Choi. Mr. Choi, a Korean born businessman, has operated the hotel since that time. In 1994 a major renovation was begun and continues into 1998. This historic and privately owned hotel has attracted a long list of celebrity guests — from Hank Aaron to Clint Eastwood to Huey Lewis — and many loyal business customers who have been holding their annual conventions there for more than 30 years.

Divisadero Touchless Car Wash

It's where you're likely to find a lot full of Rolls Royces, Lamborghinis, Ferraris and Mercedes' any day of the week. It's not a country club, nor valet parking at the Ritz. It's Divisadero Touchless Car Wash, at Divisadero and Oak in San Francisco. Founded in 1987, Divisadero Touchless is the only car wash in San Francisco, and one of only a handful in the Bay Area, utilizing the miraculous "touchless" technique. The "touchless" technique is revolutionizing the car wash industry and is considered to be the wave of the future.

The "touchless" system works entirely without brushes or spinning cloth wheels. Both these traditional automated car wash techniques imply a possibility of scratching the finish. Once a glaze is scratched, it takes a great deal of effort to restore its original splendor. Owners of luxury cars and specialty finishes have typically been limited to hand washing their vehicles, at great cost in terms of time. The "touchless" system was designed with the discriminating car owner in mind. Though Divisadero Touchless' service costs as much as 60 percent more than the traditional automated car wash, it saves car owners time, requiring only 15-20 minutes to complete. And the sophisticated technology is remarkably consistent, providing nearly flawless results every time.

The Divisadero Touchless car wash tunnel consists of a computerized system of sensors, pressurized solutions, hot water and hot air that cost $750,000 to build. Even the order-taking system is computerized. And Divisadero Touchless has scads of satisfied customers to show for it. It is featured on Best of the Bay lists year after year in San Francisco daily and weekly publications. It is fast developing an almost cult-like status among local residents.

The Divisadero Touchless treatment entails an unbelievable degree of care, including the best

An army of as many as 75 car wash attendants go about their cleaning and drying duties with great care.

efforts of as many as 75 attendants before and after the car is driven through the car wash tunnel. To start, a customer chooses from among an amazing range of services, including Rust Guard, underbody cleaning, Poly Bond, air freshener and Wheel Brite services.

Before a car even approaches the tunnel, attendants vacuum the interior and perform the optional Tire Brite service. They then remove from the exterior as much dirt as possible by hand. Inside the tunnel, the main computer relies upon a network of sensors to activate each step of the wash. First, a pressurized soap solution is applied. Then, there is a freshwater rinse. The computer then activates not one but two separate wax-applying mechanisms. Finally, a system of oscillating hot air dries the car.

Once a car reaches the end of the tunnel, the dedicated army of attendants swings back into action, drying off any remaining water from the exterior. They then dive into the car, wiping down the dashboard and door jambs. The very last step in this highly customized service is the optional tire dressing, recommended because it adds as much shine to the tires as the double-wax process has imparted to the vehicle glaze.

Divisadero Touchless realizes that for many customers, even the 15 minutes it takes to complete the service may seem a long time. They decided to create a gift shop to keep waiting clients occupied. The gift shop offers everything from T-shirts and sweatshirts to cards and sunglasses.

Divisadero Touchless also takes care to give back to the community. They regularly donate significant sums to Child Abuse Prevention Councils in the San Francisco Bay Area.

Divisadero Touchless Car Wash looks forward to many more years serving discriminating car owners in the Bay Area.

A luxury car proceeds through the Divisadero Touchless tunnel, a series of pressurized hot air, water, and cleaning and waxing solutions controlled by a sophisticated computer system.

A long-range view of the busy Divisadero Touchless lot during a typical day serving discriminating automobile owners.

Driving Obsession

What do biomechanists, orthopedic surgeons, chiropractors, physical therapists and physicists have to do with golf? These days just about everything. At least, that's the story told by David Mutton of the highly innovative golf instruction firm, Driving Obsession.

In 1993 David was teaching golf and realized there had to be a better method than traditional instruction to help golfers improve their performance. His desire turned into a search among the latest technology of the day. Developments in body motion measurement that originated in medicine would create a new way to assess and train golfers.

In 1994, he and a partner opened in San Francisco the most advanced high tech golf instruction firm in the world. Today, Driving Obsession has locations in San Francisco, Denver, Chicago, and Minneapolis. The first quarter of 1998 will see the opening of the first franchises operating under the Driving Obsession name and administered by Driving Obsession Franchising Inc., a subsidiary of Driving Obsession Inc.

What is the Driving Obsession teaching system? That requires a look at the problem it solves. Historically, golf instructors have had two obstacles to face. First, how do you accurately assess a golfer's swing? It's really impossible to see with the naked eye, or even with video. And it's harder still for the instructor to understand exactly what each golfer can do, given the wide range of individual abilities and physical constraints.

The human body makes complex motions and moves in three dimensions when swinging a golf club. Driving Obsession's system measures and records

A Driving Obsession Professional instructs a client wearing motion analysis sensors.

three-dimensional body motion through a series of sensors attached to the golfer's body. The computer records the information and then provides output to a screen, which gives the instructor the information needed to determine exactly what each client must do physically to correct her or his swing.

The golfer can step outside his or her body and see on a computer screen exactly what is happening during the golf swing. The motions of the body are seen in a skeletal model, viewed from any angle. Golfers can see the progression of the motion and view the body's range of possible motions.

Once the instructor can accurately assess the golfer's current performance and goals, a personalized training program with measurable goals is developed. Drills are designed to correct the swing and improve performance.

Mutton points out that most golfers hit the ball well occasionally, but few do it consistently. Driving Obsession provides the way for attaining that much sought after goal. It helps the golfer find the elusive "tweak" or "fix" for an imperfect golf swing. Driving Obsession clients become far better at the game, faster.

Driving Obsession's database of golf swings, measured with their 3-D swing analysis system, is the most comprehensive swing collection of its type in the world. Tour player swing data is compared to that of average golfers to determine the critical issues that differentiate the groups. By studying the physics and bio-mechanics of the golf swing, Driving Obsession's instructors can identify the exact causes of swing problems and tailor an improvement program to the individual golfer.

Many other teaching methods have tried to come up with the "Perfect Swing" but through an intensive study of the Driving Obsession database, it can be seen that one person's "Ideal Swing" is another person's "Nightmare." Unless a person's unique range of motion is determined, catch-all swing diagnosis allows too many errors to go undetected.

Most golfers look to improve their game by spending money on the latest fads in golf clubs. Even the most technically advanced clubs won't help improve your game if you still have the underlying fundamental problems. Driving Obsession's instructors will quickly diagnose your problems, identify the elements you need to work on and teach you the drills that will reshape your swing. You'll learn to practice correctly so you'll get better results from less practice time.

It's likely you've heard of the system because Driving Obsession has been featured on the Discovery Channel, CNN, major network news and in a wide range of newspapers, magazines and sports publications.

Who should look into Driving Obsession golf training? Anyone who plays ten times a year or more, says Mutton. It will help golfers lower their score, hit farther, have better form and generally look and feel better about the game. Driving Obsession's range of clients includes several PGA golf pros, top-ranked amateurs, avid weekend golfers, juniors, seniors and physically challenged people.

Each year, Driving Obsession donates over $10,000 in gift certificates to charitable organizations to be used as prizes and auction items. Driving Obsession instructors have also donated countless hours to high school golf programs. Many teenagers who take up golf in high school have benefitted from the advanced analysis and instruction methodology developed by David Mutton and taught by instructors at all Driving Obsession locations. Driving Obsession also works closely with civic organizations such as the Oakland Municipal Chamber of Commerce to organize clinics for Chamber members who do not play golf but who would like to participate in future Chamber golf tournaments.

If you have the golf bug and want to improve, the leading technology of the day is on hand from Driving Obsession.

FAO Schwarz

For children of all ages, a trip to FAO Schwarz toy store in San Francisco's Union Square is a special treat.

Both youngsters and oldsters alike are delighted when they walk into FAO Schwarz and hear the "Welcome to Our World," theme song, and see the magical "clock tower" that rises up to the second floor. With its colorful and intricate levels of fantasy worlds such as Jack and the Beanstalk and Humpty Dumpty, and the moving mechanisms such as a whistle blowing, and Dorothy's red dancing shoes, the clock tower is a rousing welcome to what is often called, "the finest toy store in the world."

For children, FAO Schwarz is virtually a wonderland of toys, including everything from basic crayons to Star Wars action figures to sophisticated computer games and electronic gadgets. For adults, a visit to the store can spark memories of special childhood events and gifts, such as a Madame Alexander doll — now a collectible toy — or a Steiff teddy bear. For generations of children, a trip to FAO Schwarz symbolizes the ultimate outing, the place to go to buy special gifts or to just browse.

Ever since Frederick August Otto Schwarz and his three brothers opened the first store in 1862, FAO Schwarz has been a company with vision and charm. Today, with 40 stores across the nation and World Wide Web sites on the Internet, FAO Schwarz stores continue to carry out Frederick August Otto Schwarz's original mission of creating toy stores that feature quality toys and stellar service.

The FAO Schwarz store in San Francisco, one of the company's five flagship stores, opened its doors in 1968 at a small store on Post Street. In 1989, the store moved a couple of blocks to its present location at the corner of O'Farrell and Stockton Streets. Situated in fashionable Union Square, the three-story store features all the FAO Schwarz hallmarks such as a full line of entertaining toys, Barbie Boutique and personal shopping service. San Francisco's version of the clock tower even includes a miniature cable car built with Lego blocks. Like all FAO Schwarz stores, the San Francisco store is a popular destination. Near special holidays, such as Christmas and Hanukkah, the store fills with shoppers, who are sure they will find one of the best collection of toys in the world all under one roof. It is the quality and quantity of toys in this collection, which sets FAO Schwarz apart from other toy stores and chains.

To amass this amazing collection, FAO Schwarz buyers travel all over the world, seeking

out unique, innovative and outstanding toys. When store buyer's don't find what they are looking for, they commission the toys to be made. In fact, more than one-third of all FAO Schwarz toys are exclusive, designed especially for the company and sold only in its stores. The remaining two-thirds of the assortment represents the best that the industry offers.

This dedication to innovation and service is a running theme throughout FAO Schwarz's history. Frederick August Otto Schwarz, for example, was one of the first toy merchandiser's to publish a catalog, mailing out his first store catalog more than 120 years ago. Today, the catalog is still a hit with customers; the classic "wish book" to look at again and again. This commitment to quality is a direct reflection upon the founding mission of Frederick August Otto Schwarz, who opened his first store in 1863, just six years after he arrived in America from Westphalia, Germany.

Schwarz operated his shop in Baltimore, Maryland, where he remained until 1870 when he moved to New York to open the Schwarz Toy Bazaar on Broadway. With the help of his three brothers, who were in constant touch with Europe's finest toy makers and sources, the FAO Schwarz store prospered. In 1880, FAO Schwarz moved to larger quarters in New York's Union Square, which was then the fashionable shopping center housing such stores as Tiffany's and other leading merchants. FAO Schwarz moved three more times until 1986, when the company established it current store headquarters at 767 Fifth Avenue. Now owned by KBB, a large Dutch retail group, FAO Schwarz currently has 12 branches across the U.S. in addition to flagship stores in Manhattan, San Francisco, Orlando, Las Vegas and Chicago, and 23 "mall flag ship" stores that represent the direction of future growth for the company.

With this continued growth, FAO Schwarz stores still provide highly personalized services, such as a personal shopping program, toy authority hotline, infant and children's gift registry, toll-free catalogue shopping, delivery anywhere in the world, corporate gift buying, in-store special events and complimentary gift wrapping.

The stores also remain focused on FAO Schwarz's original mission of providing toys of quality workmanship and whimsical attraction. San Francisco's FAO Schwarz, like all the stores, features a dazzling array of toys and several special department such as the Barbie Boutique, where shoppers will find "everything Barbie," including dolls, apparel, fashion accessories, home furnishings, videos and more. One of the best-selling toys since her debut in 1962, Barbie comes in many guises, from doctor to lawyer to President.

In addition to the Barbie Boutique, there is also a large "hands-on" Lego display, where children constantly rearrange the Lego blocks into an ever-changing monument to creativity. Star Wars fans will find a huge assortment of action figures and memorabilia items, some from the original movie sets. Small children and toddlers will delight in the interactive toys and stuffed animals that make up a colorful, huggable displays of furry creatures. Collectors even have their own special department, which features classics such as Gumby and GI Joe.

And for customers longing for simpler times, or a chance to finally own Park Place, there's always Monopoly, just one of the many board games in FAO Schwarz's collection of timeless toys.

FAO Schwarz: Serious about play

All photos by S. Rose

House of Prime Rib

Robert Louis Stevenson's genius once immortalized a cow in a poem. Joe Betz, founder of one of America's most unique restaurants, has done Mr. Stevenson one better, because he has immortalized a portion of the animal: the ribs. Comparing his accomplishment with Mr. Stevenson's might be pushing creative license too far, but not much, for Joe Betz is — in his own right — a poet of food. And as excellent poets select a few choice words to convey their meanings in a sonnet, Joe selects a few choice ingredients to produce culinary haiku.

His philosophy, he says, is "to do ordinary things extraordinarily well." He certainly succeeds. The uniqueness of Joe's "House" is not that he produces incredibly complex dishes, like the French, but that he has invented a uniquely attractive genre of dining: the prime rib dinner. Its trademark is essentially to serve prime ribs in an elusively contagious and simple style.

What are the ingredients of a prime rib dinner? The finest corn-fed prime ribs, sparsely marbled with delicate veins of fat which enhance the flavor and quality of the lean, savory meat, potatoes, spinach, Yorkshire pudding and mixed green salad. From these, something just short of a miracle occurs.

Take the prime ribs, which are completely coated in rock salt before being baked to perfection. The purpose of the salt is not to introduce its saltiness into the meat, but rather to lock in all the inherent flavor and juices of the beef ribs themselves. As with all of the restaurant's dishes, optimum cooking time of the ribs is a matter of precision, measured down to the minute.

A variety of lettuces, watercress, chopped eggs, pimento and other ingredients make up the salad. Its cream dressing requires two weeks to complete and the ingredients remain a closely guarded secret. Spinach and potatoes are carefully selected and closely monitored to ensure only the freshest reach the dining tables. Both the chef and the manager personally taste test all batches of creamed spinach, mashed potatoes and Yorkshire pudding.

The House recognizes that a fine restaurant also requires an equal serving of show business. Carvers, sporting voluminous white Chef's caps and white aprons, uniforms of their skillful trade, maneuver glistening aluminum-covered serving tables throughout several dining rooms. Guests select from these heated tables the precise cuts of meat they wish.

§erving Cart and Carver

A waiter tosses and dresses the salad at the table, verifying its freshness. The potatoes, spinach and Yorkshire pudding too are served at the table, piping hot and delicious almost to the point of ecstasy.

Pretension, however, is not served at the House of Prime Rib. Although suits, dresses, even tuxedos and gowns may occasionally be present, equally at home and welcome are blue jeans and sweat suits. Next to a teenage football player may sit a local politician. A Chinese family may celebrate the birthday of a young daughter in her colorful Asian silk finery while casually clad locals lounge at the bar in khakis and tennis shoes.

Quality, diversity and informality are simply Joe Betz's style. After all, he has run restaurants in San Francisco for 35 years. He is a local celebrity in his own right, and seems to feel no need to put on any airs. He just wants you to enjoy your dinner and feel at home. This, one senses, rewards him as much as the financially good trade the restaurant enjoys.

Joe formally studied the restaurant business at school in his native Munich and worked in others' restaurants in Holland and Switzerland, and on the Holland American line, before shipping to the United States. In 1968 he bought the Hoffman Grill, then Heide's Bank Exchange, Park Exchange (a disco) and eventually ran all food service in San Francisco's Transamerica building. He opened the House of Prime Rib in 1986. Selling all other interests in 1990, he has since concentrated his energy on the House.

Joe has resisted expanding the highly successful restaurant, choosing rather to hone its single location to perfection. It has clearly been a winning formula; annually the restaurant serves over 210,000 pounds of Prime Rib.

His 21-year-old son, Steven, works in the restaurant, presently sharing various tasks with the 50- person staff which operates the business. Co-managers Mr. Cohen and Gus have worked, respectively 20 and 45 years, Gina, the bookkeeper, over 20 years and the various kitchen people, waiters, hosts, and hostesses, also are longstanding members of the Prime Rib team. People like to work at the House as avidly as people like to eat there.

Joe also has been a Director of the California Restaurant Association since 1989. Wherever and however his original concept arose, he certainly seems to be running a food conspiracy designed to kidnap you and fill you with his wares. Beware, if you enter his place, for his trap is well laid. And bring a hearty appetite, for, although served with Asian haiku simplicity, the food poem Mr. Betz produces is truly more akin to a Beethoven symphony.

Main Dining Room
(Bottom left)
All photos, by
Andrew McKinney

Just Desserts

In 1974, the husband/wife team of Elliot Hoffman and Gail Horvath started their gourmet bakery with just one dessert, Grandma's irresistible cheesecake. As it turned out, this lone cake launched not only 12 Just Desserts stores, but a San Francisco institution.

Today, this multi-award winning, retail/wholesale operation of Just Desserts is a household name in the Bay Area. The place to go for Cake Extraordinaire. Just Desserts' quality products offer something for everyone. From that little bit of sweet with your coffee to Mayor Willie Brown's one-of-a-kind birthday cake. From an elegant wedding cake to the spectacular Embarcadero waterfront replica (roughly the size of a hotel room) commissioned by the Hyatt Regency to celebrate their grand remodeling.

In the 70s, Elliot and Gail spent months literally peddling their mouthwatering cheesecake door-to-door. Upon building a loyal

Poppyseed Cake
(Top right)

Gift Box Cake
(Bottom left)

clientele of restaurants, they expanded their list of wares to include chocolate fudge cake and carrot cake, and opened their first store on Church Street. This Castro District cafe with the North Beach "feel" soon became quite the hang-out counting among its regulars, rock stars' Crosby, Stills, Nash, and Young. Actors John Travolta, Danny Glover, and musicians Boz Scaggs, Grace Slick, and Paul Kantner were among the number of celebrities who frequented Just Desserts original stores.

The Church Street bakery was the pioneer of the "coffee cafes," so prevalent today. Customers would crowd the shop in the morning, read the newspaper, and relax with a delectable pastry over coffee. Then, return in the evening in droves for some after dinner respite. They're still swarming to Just Desserts, their cakes as popular as ever with the discerning San Francisco public. The nostalgic carrot cake is still going strong, ranked the #2 favorite choice overall. But the current winner, perhaps a reflection of 90s decadence, is the chocolate fudge.

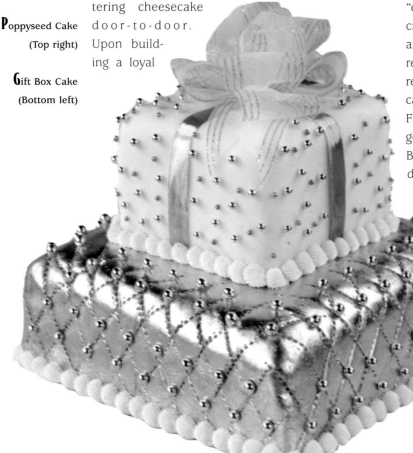

Not satisfied to rest on their laurels, the management team of Just Desserts is in constant touch with their customers via taste tests of new products and consumer satisfaction updates. When the emphasis on low fat/no fat first came into vogue, the Just Delites line was introduced. But feedback on these products supported the theory that it's human nature to splurge on occasion, calories or not.

In desserts, people want the real thing. That's exactly what you get at Just Desserts. A whopping

50,000 pounds a month of pure butter (they're the biggest San Francisco user) goes into their classic, non-refrigerated cakes, refrigerated sophisticakes, and custom decorated wedding/special occasion cakes.

Just Desserts' business philosophy is simple: Never cut corners. Same day shipments serve the entire Bay Area as well as the outlying regions of Sacramento, Santa Cruz, and Napa. Only the freshest, most natural, finest ingredients are used in Just Desserts products. And, as one of the remaining stalwarts that bakes the old fashioned way, totally from scratch, "the difference is delicious."

The San Francisco-based bakery headquarters is a 24 hour operation. Many employees are long-timers; some having been with the company since Church Street. The Just Desserts fleet of trucks is a welcome sight on Bay Area streets and highways. Drivers are greeted with a smile and often a request for a free sample.

Just Desserts is nationally known as "a company that cares." Daily donations of surplus baked goods are distributed to nearby churches and homeless shelters. Elliot is a highly visible figure at City Hall, making an impact as a small business advocate and encouraging others towards the use of business to promote social concerns.

One of the company's most rewarding involvements has been with the Garden Project. This training and counseling program for ex-offenders from the San Bruno County jail was started in 1990 by Director, Catherine Sneed, and Elliot Hoffman with the support of Sheriff Michael Hennessey. Elliot Hoffman helped the group convert an abandoned, garbage-filled lot behind the Just Desserts bakery to a half acre, working organic garden. Local companies purchase produce cultivated here by Garden Project students. Students also work on urban renewal, planting trees and doing charity work. Many Garden Project graduates have secured permanent employment with Just Desserts.

Just Desserts' dedicated team of 325 employees is proud of its San Francisco heritage and the cultural diversity of its workforce. Stubbornly resistant of lucrative franchise offers, the very name, Just Desserts, has earned recognition as a distinguished brand equity.

For nearly 25 years, Just Desserts has shared with Bay Area residents in the celebrations of their lives. It's all been a joyful process for the Hoffman/Horvath partnership. Some might even say, a piece of cake!

Chocolate Cloud Chiffon
(Top right)

Strawberry Cloud Chiffon Cake
(Far left)

Carrot Cake
(Bottom right)
Photos by Lats Lavis

LesConcierges

When a well known investment banker needs conference planning assistance in the Napa Valley, 45 yard line tickets in Dallas, a travel itinerary to the U.K., one-of-a-kind corporate gifts, or an out-of-print jazz recording, he makes just one telephone call.

LesConcierges, the world's leading corporate concierge organization, delivers extraordinary results in such wide-ranging service areas as travel and destination management, conference planning, gifts and incentive programs, tickets and entertainment planning, client visit coordination, esoteric research and personal needs — all with the ease of a single telephone call.

Originally conceived as a luxury private membership service for pampered Bay Area executives, LesConcierges now accommodates over 600,000 customers across the nation. LesConcierges delivers on site corporate concierge programs to such innovative leaders as Sun Microsystems, Microsoft, Netscape, and Texas Instruments. Concierge teams at Sun, for example, handle everything from company picnics for 2,000 employees to weekend getaway planning; from wedding ceremonies to tracking down a toddler's lost toy; and from short notice birthday parties to finding rare trading cards. Employees quickly become addicted to this key workplace amenity, and hot recruits find it a compelling reason to join a successful, forward-thinking company!

Concierge assistance is also provided via telephone to American Express Platinum Card members, Diners Club, General Motors OnStar, 25 U.S. airlines, and VISA U.S.A. Comprehensive services and gifted LesConcierges teams add demonstrable value to the products and services offered by these leading U.S. companies. When a customer calls en route to the Caribbean, panicked that a passport has been left at home, LesConcierges uses its skill and vast network to retrieve the item from the caller's home and immediately courier the article to the customer's last American stopover city before departing the U.S.

American Express Platinum Card members can place a call from anywhere in the United States, and receive immediate concierge assistance with dining, entertainment, gift, and travel arrangements — while at their home or office, or while in a car or airplane seat! Passengers on most major U.S. airlines can call upon LesConcierges while airborne at 30,000 feet, and request that two bottles of their favorite champagne be gift-wrapped and delivered to their connecting gate at Kennedy Airport, within an hour!

Concierge assistance is also offered on-site at luxury office buildings from Honolulu to Boston. LesConcierges works with property and asset management firms to create programs that will both attract and retain tenants. Concierges organize lavish-looking tenant appreciation parties on tight budgets, arrange brilliantly themed broker outings to help sell vacant office space, secure great accommodations at sold out hotels for key tenants, and become a travel/conference/meeting/event/gift planning expert for thousands of appreciative customers in each building.

Founded in 1987 by Bay Area entrepreneur Jane Winter, this premier San Francisco-based company now employs over 110 concierges throughout the United States, and provides global assistance to a diverse client group that includes Fortune 500 organizations, cutting edge technology companies, small organizations, and private individuals. Whether a

Jane Winter, Founder and CEO of LesConcierges, the nation's leading corporate concierge organization.

client needs a three day conference planned in Munich for several hundred European participants or just a bouquet of roses delivered during a blizzard, LesConcierges relies upon its expertise, contacts, and a certain "magic" to exceed even the most demanding expectations.

Premised on the idea that time is precious and that smart assistance is invaluable, LesConcierges picks up where sophisticated personal assistants of another era left off. They build detailed profiles on their customers; anticipate needs rather than simply react to them; produce complex events and manage minute details. LesConcierges has built an extraordinary network of contacts and clout to secure coveted reservations at top restaurants, hotels, and at major performing arts and sports venues around the world.

Are key customers arriving unexpectedly? No problem. LesConcierges will create a savvy itinerary that includes perfect accommodations, special amenities and lodging services, door-to-door transportation, preferred seating at top restaurants, spousal arrangements, customized tours and entertainment, gifts, language services, and personal assistance — seamlessly managed to let LesConcierges' clients focus on their customers, and to enhance business success.

In an era of streamlined staffs and intense global competition, LesConcierges also functions as a key workplace amenity. Charged with planning employee appreciation parties, incentive programs and personal gifts, client and family visits, personal services, and leisure travel, LesConcierges' experts understand both the immediate need and the larger goal. Dedicated concierge teams build great morale, save time and energy, and help make the workplace rewarding and more productive. Whether the client's industry is financial services or software development, LesConcierges understands why a key executive needs tee times at a prestigious club or why a new recruit needs help finding an apartment fast.

How does LesConcierges accomplish these service feats? Jane Winter credits her company's success to a passion for service excellence, an investment in terrific talent, and a commitment to provide the training and technological resources necessary to develop her team and to best anticipate the complex needs of a global client base. Then she adds more training!

"It's a way of life for most of our concierges — they have an uncanny ability to listen well, to think quickly and creatively, and to want to do an outstanding job. We try to provide as many tools as possible — from training seminars on planning complex events to motivational seminars led by world renowned customer service experts. As a service industry leader, you simply cannot commit enough resources to good recruitment, training, and staff development. The greatest compliment we receive is when our customers simply expect extraordinary and sophisticated service, anywhere in the world. It means that we are living up to our credo and making a difference."

This young, entrepreneurial company boasts a set of superlative statistics. In addition to 50 percent annual growth, LesConcierges is the largest retail flower buyer in the country; the third largest sports, theater and event ticket buyer; and the largest coordinator of restaurant reservations in the world. The team offers fluency in over a dozen languages, 24 hour a day service capability, and fully customized programs to meet the unique needs of each customer. "Service beyond expectations" is not only LesConcierges' credo, it is the reason why this San Francisco company enjoys cutting edge success.

"Wherever in the world life takes you"... LesConcierges delivers perfect results and service beyond expectations™.

MacKenzie Automotive Parts Warehouse

Gordon MacKenzie, Sr. began the Battery Distributing Co. in the 1930s, operating the business from his home at 41st and Quintara. The business originally sold batteries and battery accessories. Anna MacKenzie handled the bookkeeping, while Gordon traveled around the Bay Area selling and delivering products. In the 1950s, MacKenzie secured a contract with Union Oil to be a distributor of their branded products to their Union Oil gas stations. Products sold were batteries, chemicals, accessories and basic tune-up/oil change auto parts.

Gordon MacKenzie, Jr. began working with his father in the Battery Distributing Co. in the 1950s, but in 1960, after Union Oil decided not to renew independent distributors contracts, Gordon, Jr. established the Gordon MacKenzie Warehouse at 34 Page Street. The company sold Accurate Tools and EIS brake parts, and the business operated on the three-step distribution system: Manufacturers sold to a warehouse; the warehouse sold to an auto parts store (jobber); and the auto parts store sold to both the public and the automotive repair facility. Gordon MacKenzie Warehouse did wholesale business only with auto parts stores in the Bay Area. Gordon, Jr. serviced customers and delivered merchandise; his wife, Anna-Maria, and mother (Anna) handled the bookkeeping; and his father (Gordon, Sr.) helped with daily warehouse activities and deliveries.

As the business grew the family added employees to help with warehousing, customer service and deliveries. In the late 1960s, the older generation moved into semi-retirement. (Gordon MacKenzie, Sr. died in 1976; Anna MacKenzie in 1986.)

MacKenzie Warehouse purchased its first computer in the late 70s. That was not only the significant change to the business, however, for in 1970 MacKenzie Warehouse was one of the first auto parts warehouses to purchase a line of replacement parts for Japanese cars known as SBH (Lazorlite). Japanese cars were then considered to be a fad that would eventually disappear.

In the 1970s and 80s Gordon and Anna-Maria MacKenzie reinvested company profits into the business and increased the availability of products for the growing business, which was relocated to a 15,000 square foot building on 17th St. Colin MacKenzie, son of Gordon and Anna-Maria, began working full-time in the warehouse following high school graduation in 1981, and then took a position as a salesman. Colin's sister, Michelle, also began working full-time for the business after high school graduation in 1985, first as a driver, then in other positions until her switch to a management/ administration position in 1987.

In the mid-1980s, Gordon MacKenzie believed he would be able to better control the flow of distribution if he owned his own auto parts stores. He saw this as a more reliable, guaranteed way to assure the flow of volume needed to maintain a warehouse inventory. Accordingly, he first purchased McCulloch Auto Supply, which Colin MacKenzie managed until its closing in 1992. In 1986, Gordon went into a partnership and purchased Pacifica Machine & Parts. In 1987, Gordon took over Menary Auto Supply, and went into a partnership in the Auto Plus Stores in Oakland and San Pablo. In 1989, he purchased the inventory and machine shop of Whitie's Auto Parts in San Bruno and began McCulloch #2. McCulloch #1 on Valencia St. was moved into the 17th Street warehouse.

Anna and Gordon MacKenzie, Sr., who began Battery Distributing Co.

At that time the distribution chain began to condense. Larger auto parts stores began to buy directly from the manufacturer, and warehouses began to sell directly to the automotive repair facility. Shrinking profits from the three-step distribution system caused MacKenzie Warehouse to change its business philosophy in 1988. Gordon and Michelle MacKenzie began closing the company's auto parts store locations; this was completed in 1993. In 1989, Gordon began handing over the management of the business to Michelle.

Gordon and Michelle consolidated the inventory and personnel at MacKenzie Warehouse on 17th Street and began selling directly to auto repair facilities. In essence, the business was starting over again as it had to establish an entirely new customer base. Changes in business were painful, but positive results began to show by 1990. Gordon wanted a less active role, and when Eduardo Menendez joined MacKenzie Warehouse in 1990, the present-day management team was started.

"Customer service" became the business' primary concern, and new systems and services were introduced to help attain that goal. The company redefined its marketing area to the San Francisco Peninsula through San Mateo. An "on demand" delivery system put parts in customers' hands within an hour after they called in an order. In 1993, MacKenzie Warehouse joined a buying group that allowed it to be more competitive by lowering its acquisition costs.

In March 1996, a new computer system allowed for "electronic cataloging" of all inventory, as well as "electronic ordering" for customers to transmit their orders directly from their computers to MacKenzie's.

In 1992, Colin MacKenzie decided to pursue other interests and became a San Francisco firefighter, and in April 1995, Gordon MacKenzie Jr. died, but MacKenzie Warehouse still remains a family business. Anna-Maria MacKenzie has daily responsibilities in the return department; Michelle MacKenzie is president of the corporation, and her husband, Eduardo Menendez, is vice-president and Operations Manager. Brothers-in-law Raul and Gustavo Menendez serve as Customer Service Manager and Delivery System Manager, respectively.

Since 1990, the business has quadrupled. In 1990, there were two delivery vehicles; in 1997, there are 30 drivers to ensure rapid delivery six days a week. In 1990, the company employed 25 employees; there are now 95, and the company has annual sales of more than $12 million. MacKenzie Warehouse carries 50 different parts brands and 12 chemical brands. Its large inventory of quality products is being updated constantly. The company also makes available a library of technical and informational videos at no charge.

The company's continued growth and success is due to the hard work and participation of the management team and all employees of MacKenzie Warehouse. Michelle comments, "It all comes down to the fact that we enjoy doing what we do and we feel proud to be working with each other and our customers. We genuinely want to help our customers prosper."

MacKenzie Warehouse moved to its present location on Mariposa Street in May 1997. The 52,000 square foot facility, with its ample warehouse space and parking, allows the business to operate more efficiently, with greater time management, than before. This move has allowed the company to gear up for the deployment of new marketing strategies and expansion into different marketing areas — steps that will help shape the direction of MacKenzie Warehouse for the next generation.

Pacific Marine Yachts

Marti McMahon turned her love of entertaining, gourmet cooking and yachting into the Bay Area's premier luxury yacht charter company. All four of Pacific Marine's yachts bear her personal touch, and Marti is frequently on board to welcome her guests.
Photo by Michael Mustacchi

The fleet of Pacific Marine Yachts is the most elegant on SF Bay and can serve up to 1,000 people a day. The staff custom designs charters for weddings, product launches, regattas, holiday parties, or whatever it takes to make the client's dreams come true. All four yachts sail from Pier 39.
Photo by James D. Northey (Bottom right)

Hard work, an eye for beauty, a love of entertaining, and pleasure in yachting. These qualities have enabled Marti McMahon to become the owner of San Francisco's most elegant yacht charter company and hostess to multinational companies, blushing brides, and numerous heads-of-state.

What began as entertaining family and friends has grown into a $5 million business with a fleet of four yachts, a staff of up to 100 and the capacity to feed 1,000 people a day. All four of Pacific Marine's yachts are U.S. Coast Guard-certified and licensed, and staffed by uniformed crews. The yachts are decorated with luxurious appointments selected by Ms. McMahon, and equipped with customized galleys so the Cordon Bleu-trained chef can prepare fresh gourmet food.

It's all a far cry from the early days when Marti cooked the food, did her own flowers, made her own tablecloths and put her neighbors to work as hostesses. She first found her sea legs when she and her former husband bought a derelict yacht, fixed it up and sold it at a profit. Marti then continued refurbishing larger and larger boats.

When Marti was a child, her mother taught her how to turn something inexpensive into something beautiful. After her family moved from El Salvador to Chicago, her mother taught her how to make tissue paper flowers. When she was seven, Marti started her first business selling the flowers door-to-door. Her love of color and design and her flair for salesmanship won her friends and supporters. Even then, McMahon knew she would make a difference, although she didn't know what the future would hold.

Ms. McMahon started Pacific Marine Yachts in 1979 with a 49-passenger yacht. In 1980 Pacific Marine became a fleet when McMahon acquired the 83 foot, 97-passenger *Pacific Spirit*. Marti designed her two newest boats herself, and built a handsome boat dock at Pier 39 where the fleet is berthed. Her company is now one of the Bay Area's 100 largest women-owned businesses and one of the country's 500 largest Hispanic-owned businesses.

Like all entrepreneurs, McMahon loves what she does. And it shows. Each boat is elegantly inviting, combining the warmth of a private yacht and the luxury of a first-class hotel. Each meal is delicious and impressive. Marti and her staff at Pacific Marine have customized cruises to host executive meetings and receptions, fashion shows, VIP events, high-tech seminars and bridal fairs. Depending on the client's needs, these perfectionists can provide a midnight salsa party or a five-course formal French dinner. Movie and TV location scouts often call Marti for the ideal yachting shot. Don Johnson and his crew recently filmed a Nash Bridges episode on the *California Spirit*.

Pacific Marine Yachts' planning expertise, impeccable service, award-winning cuisine and stunning views of San Francisco have been enjoyed by dignitaries, celebrities and sports stars. From Joe Montana to the Prime Minister of Russia, from Mick Jagger to Kristi Yamaguchi, a growing list of stars have cruised San Francisco Bay aboard one of Marti's yachts. Even Mayor Willie Brown has taken the helm of the *San Francisco Spirit*.

McMahon spends her days making sure all four boats are looking their best. She's on hand to welcome such diverse clients as the CEO of Seagrams, William R. Hearst, III, the Prime Minister of Hungary, or you and me.

The first yacht McMahon designed was the *California Spirit*, which accommodates 149 passengers. During the planning stages, thirteen banks turned McMahon down for financing. Even after she secured a loan she still had to put a second mortgage on her home, borrow money from her dad, max out her credit cards and sell her 49-passenger boat to make her dream boat a reality. Nonetheless, thanks to her indomitable spirit, the *California Spirit* sailed under the Golden Gate Bridge in 1988. Business boomed. And when she set out to build her showpiece, the five million dollar *San Francisco Spirit*, financing was not a problem.

The 150-foot flagship *San Francisco Spirit* was christened in 1991 by San Francisco Chief of Protocol Charlotte Maillard Swig. It features three decks, marble dance floors, a grand staircase, three gorgeous bars, and the capacity to serve 550 guests a formal dinner. Or 700 guests can enjoy cocktails and hors d'ouevres. Clients can charter one deck or the entire yacht.

Marti has risen to the many challenges of being successful in a male-dominated industry, and has the distinction of being the only female who is the sole owner of her fleet in the Passenger Vessel Association. She believes being different is an asset, and she's living proof that a woman does not have to give up her femininity to be successful in business.

Through necessity and desire, McMahon has included her family in the business. Her children sailed with her through the Panama Canal when they were 8, 10 and 12, and grew up eating gourmet leftovers. Currently her daughter Danielle is on Pacific

Marine's Board of Directors, her son Derek is Assistant Food and Beverage Manager, and her son Darren works there part-time.

After 12 years of working out of her home, Marti now has bright and cheery offices across from Pier 39. She prides herself on the diversity of her employees, believing a good mixture provides balance. Her president and comptroller both happen to be women, although that was not a requirement. These days McMahon enjoys being able to concentrate on sales and community involvement, and her gift for networking and promotion make her Pacific Marine Yachts' biggest booster. She also devotes her time to ensuring the yachts' decor is freshly up-dated and bears her personal touch.

Ms. McMahon currently serves on the board of the S. F. Convention and Visitors Bureau and on the Hospitality Board of the University of San Francisco. She is a member of the National Association of Women Business Owners and was named the Woman Entrepreneur of 1989. And because she believes women should be encouraged to start their own businesses while young, she also supports "An Income of Her Own," a mentoring program for girls 14 to 18 years old.

Marti McMahon dreams of building even more vessels, and eventually expanding to other ports. But for now she's content with creating memorable events for parties of 2 to 700. And it shows right down to the last orchid-topped napkin.

San Francisco Marriott

The hotel that is a work of art in itself

In 1976, Mayor George Moscone had a dream for San Francisco, a dream many dismissed as impossible. His plan called for a major development between 3rd and 4th Streets, South of the Slot as it was called. The Slot being Market Street, the central divider between the "good" part of town to the north (i.e. Financial District, Union Square) and the "bad" part to the south.

This project for a mixed use center to draw the business the city desperately needed was first broached in 1967 but it was Moscone who took action. Phase I, the construction of the Moscone Convention Center, was completed in 1981, in memorial to the mayor who was assassinated three years earlier.

Phase II called for a grand hotel. Mr. Marriott had a vision of his own and the San Francisco Marriott, the first new building in the Yerba Buena Redevelopment Project, was conceived. Marriott saw the potential for turnaround South of the Slot. Dan Kelleher, Director of Marketing for the San Francisco Marriott, attributes his boss' success to instinct: "It's a knack he has. He can look at an area and get an incredible feeling for it."

The San Franciscan architectural firm of DMJM put pencil to paper and after years of bureaucratic finagling, a team of local engineers and construction firms finally broke ground in 1986. 60,000 yards of concrete, 20,000 tons of steel, and 39 months later the San Francisco Marriott arose to the sky like a magnificent spotlight. An entire city took notice.

Controversy erupted immediately. Like the Eiffel Tower, or closer to home, the Transamerica Pyramid, now city landmarks, approval came slowly. Defenders of the new structure raved of its modern design, how its fan-shaped mirrored windows beautifully reflected life around it, and how its fluent, tiered levels so smoothly diminished the vastness of its 1.5 million square foot size. Nonadmirers were not so eloquent.

When San Francisco Chronicle columnist, Herb Caen, coined it "the jukebox," he actually did the hotel a tremendous favor. Abiding by the old adage that "any press is good press," the Marriott's marketing staff used the term to promote the hotel. The campaign took off, especially with the international set. Suddenly, everyone wanted to come see "the jukebox."

The Marriott was forced to prove itself again on its opening day of October 17, 1989, a day familiar to all San Franciscans as the date of the massive Loma Prieta Earthquake. Distinguished as "the shortest hotel opening in history," the Marriott,

built "earthquake proof" on rollers, sustained zero structural damage. No one was hurt. A senior group partying on the top floor did get their spirits literally dampened when the sprinklers went on and the liquor bottles crashed to the floor.

Two hundred registered guests spent two nights on cots in the underground Golden Gate Room. "A little panic," Kelleher says. "But people were comforted because it was the newest building in the City and pleased with the way we handled the safety system."

The hotel re-opened in record time, less than a week later. Today's San Francisco Marriott is considered, not only one of the safest, but, the finest in a city *Conde Nast Traveler Magazine* ranked in 1996 as the #1 travel destination in the country, #3 in the world.

The reasons a reservation at the Marriott is sought after are as varied as the features of the hotel itself. Its proximity to the Moscone Convention Center — it is the closest hotel — naturally lends itself to conventioneers. Kelleher cites the statistics: "Any convention that comes here meets or exceeds their attendance by 5 to 20 percent."

The Marriott is a huge hit with business travelers having won the coveted "10 Best Corporate Hotels in the World" by *Business Travel Magazine*, among other awards. Understandable with over 100,000 square feet of meeting facilities and the largest number of suites in town, Kelleher credits "the staff and the level of service they provide."

Standing in the immense lobby, thoughtfully interspersed with cozy spots for private reflection, you are acutely aware of the large number of foreign visitors. Rivaling New York City as a global magnet, The Marriott, with its multilingual staff and translation services, accommodates everyone with the same ease and respect, from the sightseer to Mikhail Gorbachev.

The panoramic skyline views, the restaurants offering some thing for everyone, and the generous ballrooms are just a few other factors in its success. Fund raisers, such as for the American Cancer Society, do immensely well at the Marriott. The hotel prides itself on its community involvement with such organizations as the Aids Emergency Fund, forming focus groups to support local charities in what Kelleher refers to as "a good mix."

The surrounding neighborhood, now called SOMA (South of Market) has undergone an incredible urban renewal likened only to New York City's Lincoln Center Project in 1970. Rapidly emerging as the official Arts District of San Francisco, only befitting a city known for its creativity and free expression, SOMA is thriving with new businesses and people flocking to the now fashionable side of Market Street.

The Marriott is no longer the only rose among the thorns. "Every year it just gets better and better," agrees Kelleher. The stunning Yerba Buena Gardens, Center for the Performing Arts, and world-class Museum of Modern Art have been added to rave reviews. The near future holds plans for a monument to Dr. Martin Luther King, Jewish and Mexican museums, and a 350,000 square foot Sony Entertainment Complex complete with interactive center and movie theaters. One sector of society traditionally neglected in city planning hasn't been forgotten this time — the children. With plans for a Children's Center with a museum, ice skating rink, play centers, and child care, SOMA has evolved into a cultural playground the whole family can enjoy.

The San Francisco Marriott is the crown jewel in this new Arts District. Not only is there 1.5 million dollars worth of original art in the building, the hotel has gained widespread acceptance as "a work of art in itself." Mayor Moscone's dream of a San Francisco renaissance has come to life.

Shapur
Mozaffarian

Fine Jewelry Since 1883

𝑆hapur's location on Post Street

Shapur Mozaffarian's world renowned jewelry store, on Post Street right off Union Square, houses a fortune of traditionally unique artistry. Each of Shapur's awe inspiring and one-of-a-kind pieces carries with it the imprint of generations worth of expertise and superior craftsmanship.

Shapur travels the globe in search of the most spectacular stones to adorn the jewelry which he, himself, designs. His original pieces are coveted worldwide, as evidenced by the celebrity testimonials discreetly tucked among the objets d'art throughout the Post Street shop.

San Francisco happily celebrates Shapur's renowned establishment, one which can be traced back to 1883, which marks the date when the first records were kept by the family business in Persia. Family legend, however, dictates an even longer history, originating sometime before the 1800's. This rich history is also reflected in the fact that Shapur's long-run family business was one of the very first to

Visitors to the City can find original jeweled artistry at Shapur's location in the lobby of The St. Francis Hotel.

manufacture enamel objets d'art. Continuing to uphold this tradition, Shapur's manufacturing of enamel jewelry has earned nothing but enduring popularity and irresistible appeal.

In 1970, Shapur brought this legendary history to the charming city of San Francisco, the city he fell in love with. As the proprietor of this family business, Shapur set up a permanent shop in the classy section of Post Street, an area now regarded worldwide as the core of San Francisco's jewelry district. He soon established a reputation for custom-made pieces and for offering the best selections of the finest Swiss timepieces in the world.

In addition to his Post Street jewelry store, Shapur has opened two relatively new boutiques in the elegant lobby of the St. Francis Hotel, in order to accommodate his many loyal customers. The city of San Francisco has been gifted with the superior craftsmanship and honorable historicity of this age-old family business.

The Rafael's

Is Fashion Art?

Carmel and Mona Rafael, owners of the The Rafael's Fashion

Owner David Rafael

Mona Rafael looks up from behind her desk at The Rafael's boutique. With a knowing smile, she answers in quick affirmation, "Art is not always painting."

How could Mona have known when she studied art in Europe how much the great masters of painting and sculpture would influence her future career in the fashion business? Or even that she would have a career in fashion?

A walk through The Rafael's is a veritable walk through a gallery. There is color and line, texture and style. The clothes and accessories for women are exquisite and many times original.

Opening night at the opera, dinner at a downtown restaurant, a meeting of the board of directors at the Embarcadero or a walk at Ocean Beach, a lady would be able to find just the right thing for any occasion at The Rafael's. The garments displayed are classics with a stroke of elegance and a dollop of panache.

The Rafael's opened its doors in 1978 on Post Street. Mona and her husband, Carmel, and Carmel's brother, David Rafael, started the business with the intention of featuring custom designers and manufacturers from Europe and America who were creative in their approach to ladies fashion, but not well-known.

Thus began The Rafael's concept in retailing that has continued through the years and has developed the family's thriving and successful business.

The Rafael's mission is: to offer to the public high-quality fashion and excellent personal service.

Merchandising of fine clothes and accessories is a skill born of experience and a certain intuition. Carmel began his retailing career in the garment district of New York, where he worked while attending school at New York University to prepare himself for a career in civil engineering. David also had planned to work as an engineer, only an industrial one. But as chance would have it, Carmel and David took the opportunity to go into the fashion business in California. The Rafael brothers are natives of Iran.

Mona was born in Ukraine of Hungarian descent. She grew up speaking Hungarian, Russian and Hebrew and later learned German and Persian. She met Carmel in the late 1960s, when they had both lived in Israel as students.

Mona traveled to Cologne, Germany, to continue her art studies. Carmel encouraged her to abandon a European bohemian life for the beauty of San Francisco. After marrying, they decided to set up shop together, with Mona taking care of clients and Carmel doing the bulk of the administrative work.

David is the master of the art of easy conversation. He always enjoys a convivial chat with his customers while guiding them in the selection of styles that are both fashionable and flattering.

Selecting the designers and manufacturers to be represented in the boutique, it is a trilateral agreement always, for all three partners to keep informed of the latest trends.

The Rafael's on Market Street in the Sheraton Palace Hotel is close to the Marriott and ANA hotels. This downtown location is convenient for business travelers, tourists and local residents.

A large segment of the clientele is career-oriented, and Mona is sensitive to the needs of women who might require a tailored business suit for an important meeting as well as a sharp-looking outfit for a weekend in the wine country.

As for style — that's where Mona's artistic flair shows itself best. She can evolve "the classic look" into a definite fashion statement by coordinating accessories and accents to add the finishing touches whenever needed. Belts, jewelry, handbags and scarves are available at both The Rafael's. Experience and knowledge are critical. Each staff member of The Rafael's at either boutique is prepared to work personally with clients, providing each and every one of them fashion advice and counsel.

David Rafael, for instance, over the years has been fashion mentor to many movie stars and celebrities. Both he and Mona maintain files for regular customers — recording sizes, taste, color preferences and the like. Because many of their clients are sophisticated shoppers, having addresses in St. Moritz, Hong Kong, La Jolla or San Francisco, the Rafaels feel that it is important to be there whenever a client needs them. At times, it is even necessary to send something afar — either in person or by express delivery service.

Exterior of The Rafael's shop located on Market Street within the Grand Sheraton Palace Hotel

It's not a place, though, but really a state of mind that determines the true customer of The Rafael's.

Clothes here range in price from moderately high to very expensive, therefore the typical Rafael's client is a person who understands the meaning of quality and service. The cost of some garments may be in the thousands.

Yet, if a designer has searched the flea markets of Japan to locate a particular grade of silk for the bodice of a dress or if another designer has hand-dyed fabric the exact shade of an antique Kilim rug to trim an evening gown, the end result is not just an outfit. It is art.

Such pieces are included in The Rafael's collection.

The Rafael's is a marketplace of silk and cashmere, velvet and chiffon. The boutique is a palette of colors and fabrics having labels from noted clothiers of Paris, London, Milan, Bologna and New York. These designers and manufacturers are not the corporate giants whose emblems are instantly recognized all over the world. Instead, they are among those who belong to a more intimate club of people who work in the fashion-clothing business.

The Rafaels make it their business to seek out designers and artisans who bring originality and fine craftsmanship to their designs. They are always searching for people in the fashion world who complement their sense of style and reflect the truly cosmopolitan nature of the city.

A glittering chandelier highlights The Rafael's on Market Street at the Sheraton Palace Hotel. (Far left)

Britex Fabrics

Photos by Mark Stephenson

San Francisco, a city of landmarks, has one unique landmark that houses a dazzling array of incredible fabrics and accessories. People from all over the world visit Britex Fabrics, legendary for having the widest selection of quality fabrics for fashion and the home found anywhere, all under one roof!

Located on Geary Street, just a half-block from Union Square, Britex Fabrics attracts show business personalities, motion picture costumers and theater groups always in search of unique fabrics. An endless variety of quality fabrics and accessories draws shoppers on all kinds of quests — from matching a silk blouse or wool skirt, selecting fabrics for a prom or bridal gown, customizing a garment by adding the right trim and buttons to redoing an entire room.

With four floors of woolens, silks, linens and cottons, Britex is a mecca for those who value high quality and unusual colors and textures. The latest styles in fabrics can be found here, yet the atmosphere of this family-run business is a throwback to an era when service was as important as value. It combines the friendliness of a neighborhood fabric store with the excitement of a Paris fashion show.

Britex was born in San Francisco in 1952 when Martin and Lucy Spector, who owned a fabric business previously in New York City, discovered an ideal location for a fabric store in the heart of San Francisco. After Martin passed away in 1966, Lucy developed the store into the Britex we know today. She continues as chief "curator" in what many consider to be a museum of fine fabrics!

The vast and inviting inventory of Britex reflects the discerning tastes of Lucy Spector, who travels to mills in Italy, France, England and Switzerland to hand-select fabrics. Trips to Seventh Avenue in New York to buy fabrics from top designer houses offer the customer selections in top quality and couture design.

A high level of customer service also sets Britex apart from others. A knowledgeable sales staff of over 50 people — who together speak 18 languages — is always available to assist customers with their fabric needs.

Each of the four floors of Britex has its own flavor:

The first floor has over 5,000 bolts of luxurious woolens, plus thousands of elegant silks. English men's suitings, Italian brocades, French laces and countless couture fabrics excite the senses.

On the second floor, Britex dazzles the eye with over 1,000 sumptuous home decorating prints and tapestries. Interior decorators in search of hard-to-find upholstery fabric or those just wanting to change the look of accent pillows will find what they need at Britex. The second floor also houses a huge bridal section, cottons, linens, and easy-care fabrics for creating the latest clothing styles.

Bargain hunters head to the third floor, where remnants are cut or left over from the store's stock of regular merchandise and found at greatly reduced prices. Fabulous fake furs, vinyls, sequins and imported designer knits also line the walls of the third floor.

Those in need of that perfect button or accessory will find it on the fourth floor. A fantastic collection of over 30,000 buttons, plus trims, ribbons, braids, flowers, tassels and accessories crowns this one-of-a-kind fabric store.

In an era when franchises and computerized inventories are the norm, Britex Fabrics retains an Old World commitment to running a business "by hand." The result is a store — a San Francisco landmark — that reflects the style, beauty and friendliness for which the City is renowned.

Barbary Coast Pedicab

What has three wheels, speaks more than one language, and hauls human cargo between the Northern Waterfront area to Chinatown and North Beach? Barbary Coast's pedicabs and their drivers, that's who! Founded in 1981 by Jeff and Helena Sears, Barbary Coast does more than just cater to the transportation needs of tourists; it has enlivened San Francisco's Wharf area, while offering a fun, environmentally sound, elderly- and disabled-friendly alternative to bus, boat, and other diesel-fueled tours. With its main staging area located at the foot of Powell Street in front of Pier 41, the company offers tours and shuttle services that start with a breathtaking view of the Golden Gate and encompass the entire northern waterfront area.

The business was a response to the new feasibility of transportation systems following the Wharf's expansion to Pier 39, which was completed in the late 1970s. The Sears began with four pedicabs; they currently operate about forty along the waterfront. Not to be deterred by the decreased tourism that followed the Loma Prieta Earthquake in 1989, the company expanded, and is now enjoying the renaissance of the embarcadero waterfront area, which is more pedicab-friendly than before. Barbary Coast also manufactures pedicabs for domestic and international sales, and has seen demand grow, especially in urban areas, as other areas begin to create pedestrian zones that restrict vehicles and promote non-motorized vehicle transportation.

Most pedicab drivers are college students, including several foreign exchange students during the summer months. These savvy guides can offer translations of "Irish coffee," "sourdough" and "steamed crab" in their native Russian, Italian, German, French or Spanish, while helping to finance their education abroad. The Sears takes enormous pride in the companys' contribution to these students' welfare. Keenly interested in how the business fits in with the past and present needs of the Wharf area, the Sears see the pedicabs as reinforcing San Francisco's

quirky, rugged image with tourists. "The pedicabs take us back to those wild, Barbary Coast days," Jeff Sears says.

It was exactly that "wildness" which initially worried other Wharf merchants, who were a hard sell when it came to convincing them of the benefits of pedicabs in their midst. The Sears were twenty-one when they started the business, and point to style differences with these older, more traditional merchants, who at first resisted the added pedestrian flurry of the pedicabs and bikes, for safety, traffic and aesthetic reasons. Eventually the pedicabs' charm and convenience won over their detractors, however, in the city which celebrates the marriage of tradition and individualism.

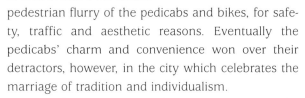

A Barbary Coast pedicab tour takes in some of the scenery along the waterfront.

Young businesses struggle to carve out a niche without stampeding a neighborhood's historical flavor, and that struggle is a quintessentially San Francisco one. Jeff and Helena thank both City Supervisor Wendy Nelder for pushing through legislation that legitimized the pedicab industry, and Angela Alioto, who was particularly effective in lobbying for the 1992 legislation that placed the authority in the hands of the Port to regulate the pedicabs' staging areas. The Sears happily report that they are now a member of the Wharf Merchants Association.

Few other cities in the country can boast companies that offer tourists such an entertaining, smog-free means of getting around — but then, few cities are like San Francisco, with its Old World, edge-of-the-frontier ambiance. Weary travelers can take a load off by hopping into one of Barbary Coasts' vehicles, and the entire wharf area has lightened up, thanks to the buoyant charm of the pedicab.

The Sir Francis Drake Hotel

"Beautifully positioned," says Marketing Director Tom Pucci, of the historic Sir Francis Drake, "where the energy level is in The City." Nestled atop trendy Union Square — Chinatown, the Theatres, Financial District, and Fisherman's Wharf are a stroll or a cable car jaunt away. This sparkling location may draw the business and leisure traveler alike, but it is the timeless beauty of the hotel itself that compels its guests to return.

The Drake was originally designed as "a working man's Mark Hopkins," complete with panoramic room on top, viewing the Bay its namesake narrowly missed discovering in the 1500s. Opening in 1928, the Drake attracted a glittery clientele of movie stars and local luminaries. Wry observer, columnist Herb Caen, aptly christened one particularly boisterous lounge, "The Snakepit."

The atmosphere turned somber with World War II. The mezzanine was converted to soldier quarters and renamed the Truman Lobby, in honor of one well known guest.

The most photographed man in San Francisco
Photo by Kimpton Group

Hardships followed, culminating in a Bank of America foreclosure in the 80s. In 1993, San Francisco's Kimpton Group assumed control and the Drake was revived. Local designer, Michael Moore, blended the dignity of the old with new conveniences, creating an inviting look of gracious comfort.

One element of the Drake's classy image that no one would dare tinker with is that of, 20 year veteran doorman, Tom Sweeney.

Tom, as he is known to all, has become a beloved symbol of San Francisco, parlaying an entry level position into a phenomenon. "It's his charm," says Pucci. "Tom never forgets a name. He's always up. He's created that job."

Dressed in full Beefeater regalia, Tom's ever smiling image adorns T-shirts, posters, even the hotel key cards. "You can't get into your room without me."

When he says, "this job has opened up a lot of doors for me," he's not kidding. Tom's appeared on talk shows, a soap (The Young & the Restless), even movies. Cheerfully submitting to the demands of an admiring public, Tom poses for up to 300 pictures a day. Always "on stage," he has run the Bay to Breakers in uniform. "Got a lot of miles out of this uniform."

Tom has as many stories as he does one-liners. Once a socialite asked him to fetch her dog out of her car. Tom's typical positive spin on discovering that Fifi was freeze dried: "At least I didn't have to worry about getting bit."

In 1982 Tom singlehandedly captured two robbers. He was awarded the Key to the City for "Best Tackle" by Mayor Dianne Feinstein. 49ers Joe Montana and Dwight Clark were honored too — something about "The Catch" and their first Super Bowl.

Tom is just the beginning of the "small hotel experience" the Drake prides itself on providing all its guests, from the conventioneers mingling in the 20,000 square feet of meeting space to the wedding parties in, what many claim as, the most romantic ballroom in the Bay Area. At the Sir Francis Drake,

The Futon Shop

The futon is a soft cotton pad originally designed in ancient Japan for sleeping on the floor. In the mid-60s, American architect, William Brower, took this concept a step further and created fine wood frames. Viewed as modern art, these beautiful futon sets were subsequently displayed in New York City's Craft Museum.

During this period, there was a growing interest in the Japanese-influenced macrobiotic lifestyle. Two such proponents were Suzanne and Arthur Diamond. As young parents living in Los Angeles, they sewed futons for their family and friends. In 1976, they moved to the Bay Area. Recognizing the opportunity to mass market Brower replicas, they opened their first tiny store in Marin, to become pioneers of the retail futon business.

Soon outgrowing their original warehouse in San Francisco's Mission District, The Futon Shop eventually settled in the Potrero Hill area. Here, all futons, covers, pillows, are manufactured in house and sold factory-direct to customers worldwide. There are now 19 stores throughout California, three in San Francisco alone. A family atmosphere prevails as employees are valued not only for their contributions to this team effort enterprise but the greater community as well.

In the 70s, futons became synonymous with the college "Crash Pad" scene. But today's futons are for everyone, from children to retirees. Designed to fit every lifestyle and budget, there are chairs, bunkbeds, flat beds, and, their specialty — the convertible sofa bed; all available in a variety of wood selections, futon styles, and hundreds of designer fabrics.

The Futon Shop family

The advantages to a futon are many. The convertible models offer an ideal solution for tight spaces. Futons are easier to transport, maintain, often less expensive, and with interchangeable covers, decidedly more versatile, than a traditional sofa or bed.

The Futon Shop's mattresses are made from the highest quality California staple cotton and virgin wool. As the Diamonds strongly believe that "it's what's inside that counts", visual displays are located in each store so customers can examine the grades of cotton and choose accordingly. Due to a regenerative surface which contours to body shape, futons are being increasingly sought out as a health aid.

Ironically, The Futon Shop's biggest customers outside of California, are the Japanese. Accustomed to a traditional bed of a scant 1.5 inches, the luxuriously thick, Futon Shop imports provide unparalleled warmth and comfort.

Anticipating customer needs and pride in commitment to quality is what has made this trend-setting San Francisco company the largest futon retailer in America.

100% Staple Cotton. Its what's inside that counts... The Futon Shop's futon mattresses are made from the highest quality California staple cotton and virgin wool. (Far left)

The Futon Shop has nineteen stores throughout California; three in San Francisco alone

Hard Rock Cafe

The 225-seat restaurant displays an extensive collection of rock and roll memorabilia. (Far right)

The entrance with the distinctive Hard Rock Cafe logo

Down home American cooking, seasoned with a healthy dose of rock and roll.

That's the recipe for one of San Francisco's most popular restaurants — the Hard Rock Cafe.

The San Francisco eatery has been serving hearty food at reasonable prices in a rocking and rolling atmosphere since September 1984. Located on the corner of Van Ness Avenue and Sacramento Street, the cafe is easily recognizable from the street by its distinctive Hard Rock logo.

Inside, the 225-seat restaurant is undergoing its most extensive renovation since it opened for business. Guitars, gold records, clothing and other artifacts belonging to just about every rock musician from Elvis Presley to Alanis Morissette are displayed on the walls.

The restaurant's San Francisco Wall contains memorabilia hailing from the psychedelic 1960s, when the City's Haight Ashbury district was home to hundreds of hippies and many of the era's best known rockers. Photographs of Janis Joplin, a guitar signed by members of the Grateful Dead, and posters advertising rock shows at the Fillmore West, Winterland and other San Francisco venues are included in the collection. One of Jimi Hendrix's guitars and one of his tambourines is also displayed, as are guitars belonging to Frank Zappa and Bo Diddley.

Another wall features Beatles memorabilia, including a photo of John Lennon

and Yoko Ono from the couple's personal collection. There are also four Bobbin' Head Beatle dolls, circa 1964, as well as a Beatles' lunch box and wig from the same period.

Other items of note include Elvis Presley's walking cane, Elton John's pink panama hat adorned with a pink plastic Eiffel Tower, and Madonna's black sequined bustier and hot pants.

Along with the rock and roll decor, and the rock music playing in the background, the Hard Rock Cafe offers a wide variety of dishes, served in large portions and at reasonable prices. Some of the more popular items listed on the guitar-shaped menu include chicken, steak, fish, fajitas and cheeseburgers.

The San Francisco restaurant is part of a worldwide network of 76 restaurants. The first Hard Rock Cafe opened its doors in London on June 14, 1971, ushering in a new era of culinary entertainment.

Along with treasuring rock and roll's past, the Hard Rock works hard to remain true to its mottos: "Love All — Serve All," "Take Time To Be Kind," "All Is One," and "Save the Planet."

The San Francisco restaurant has been recycling its cardboard, bottles, cans and other refuse ever since it has been in business. Twice a week, the restaurant donates leftovers to Food Runners, a San Francisco organization that donates food to needy people. And each year, the cafe serves a free Thanksgiving dinner to more than 500 people.

Hard Rock Cafe is available for private functions and has hosted some of the music and film industries' top events.

These activities, combined with the food and unique decor, have made the Hard Rock Cafe a Number One Hit with San Francisco diners.

Golden Years Medical

Not far from the ocean in San Francisco's outer Sunset District, one of the City's most well established residential neighborhoods, is Golden Years Medical, a company that provides a full spectrum of high quality home care products and respiratory services to elderly residents living around the corner or as far away as Miami.

A start-up company with nothing but an empty warehouse and an ambitious dream 10 years ago, founder and CEO Ronnie Naiker, then a new immigrant to this country, carved out a crucial niche in the home health care business. Today, Golden Years Medical is by far the largest supplier of disposable products for the elderly in San Francisco and one of the top three suppliers in California.

Golden Years serves Bay Area hospitals and nursing homes as well as private patients who are temporarily or permanently incapacitated at home or in board and care homes. The company sells an extensive line of disposable products for incontinence — diapers, underpads, bed protectors and skin care products such as creams and washes. The largest segment of their business, Golden Years moves more than 2,000 cases of disposables each month to a client base of more than 3,000. Their five-truck fleet makes more than 100 deliveries each working day.

Even after 10 years, Ronnie Naiker still micromanages the $2.5 million business he built from scratch. But he never loses sight of the big picture. Born and raised in South Africa at a time when apartheid made life for people of color quite difficult, Ronnie is a man much more interested in setting an example with his own life than accumulating wealth and awards.

Golden Years is a family and neighborhood business in the deepest sense. Both Ronnie's children work closely with him, and the neighborhood is his lifeblood and network. A well known figure in the community — past president of the Neighborhood Merchant's Association and an active board member on the Stonestown YMCA — Ronnie makes a point of getting to know his local clients. This is where he finds fulfillment. Although there are many others who would do it, he's usually the one who answers the phone at 2 a.m. when a patient's oxygen regulator is giving her trouble. He makes the trip to comfort the patient and adjust the equipment.

In many ways, it is the personal service Golden Years Medical provides that sets them apart from other home health care providers. Trained staff provide in-home evaluations at no cost to the patient. The company's most important goal is to educate their clients to help them decide what equipment works best for them in their daily lives. This could mean fitting them for undergarments and diapers, evaluating whether they need an adjustable guard rail for their toilet, grab bars or a shower chair in their bathtub.

Golden Years also sells and rents durable medical equipment — hospital beds, wheelchairs, canes, crutches, lift chairs, commodes, scooters, walkers and a wide range of the most up-to-date home health car products on the market.

founder and CEO Ronnie Naiker (Far left)

Golden Years Medical is the largest supplier of disposable products for the elderly in San Francisco.

Ideas Unlimited / Unlimited Ideas

The classic European concierge was always on call to serve clients' needs, no matter how unusual or urgent their demands. Superimpose this service concept upon today's diverse business needs worldwide, and you begin to describe Ideas Unlimited/Unlimited Ideas, which bills itself as "Concierge-at-Large."

IU/UI is the unique brainchild of Philip F. Schneider, who is the original, key concierge of his San Francisco-based business. His singular ability to

Concierge at work

be a master of many diverse occupations is the firm's proprietary market niche. This came about, curiously enough, not by chance, as one might suppose, but by design. Using the skills learned in his two previous lives — elementary teacher, television instructor, curriculum supervisor, principal, college instructor (in the public sector) and consultant, sales manager, and manager of marketing services (in the corporate world) — he created his new service business.

While at Houghton Mifflin for twenty years, his natural flair for solving multi-faceted problems was depended upon by his co-workers, supervisors, and other managers in many areas — meeting planning, trade booth design, travel arrangements, advertising, marketing, computer systems, phone systems, etc. Long intending to turn this talent for diversity into a business, Schneider got his chance when Houghton Mifflin eliminated his job category.

Exactly what does IU/UI do? What doesn't it do? It solves almost any outstanding problem that plagues you. It is your travel agent, event planner, trade show booth designer, advertising specialties distributor, personal shopper, research assistant, tutor. You have a need, IU/UI fulfills it.

Unusual requests? One of Schneider's first was to find a missing person. A friend asked him to locate a neighbor who had moved. Phil leapt at the challenge, and within two days the friend was found. Once a business associate asked him to find an authentic Bocce Ball set, used in the popular Italian pastime. Within hours, the set was at his side. He has even designed a haunted house room for a trade show booth — complete with special effects, props, actors, and staging.

IU/UI thrives on diversity and deadlines. In this world of specialists, IU/UI seems to be exactly what busy people need: an infinite source of expertise managed by a man with an infinite capacity for resourcefulness and creativity. Ideas Unlimited/ Unlimited Ideas hopes your obscure problem becomes their next exciting challenge.

Hotel Triton

The nation's historic love affair with San Francisco has none of the tarnish of old love. It has the constancy and vibrancy of invigorated love as the City's tourist industry continues to grow. Last year, an estimated 3.5 million tourists and conventioneers stayed in San Francisco's hotels, a seven percent gain over the previous year.

One of the City's most popular hotels is the Hotel Triton, a small, upper-end, three-star full service design hotel. Conveniently situated in the City's French Quarter just two blocks from Union Square and the financial district, across the street from Chinatown's dragon gate entrance, Hotel Triton is surrounded by some of the City's finest galleries, sidewalk cafes, theaters, shops and restaurants.

Called the place where Greek mythology meets Alice in Wonderland, Hotel Triton blends the warmth and intimacy of a European hotel with the stunning design and gracious ambiance unique to San Francisco. Its chic decor is the collaborative work of a team of local artists, guided by the creative force of Michael Moore, an icon of San Franciscan interior design.

The recently renovated building dates back to the turn of the century. Its earlier heyday as a hotel was in the 1950s and 60s. Since its purchase by the prestigious Kimpton Hotel Group and subsequent renovation in 1991, the Hotel has experienced a renaissance. Last year, they had the highest occupancy rate per room of any hotel in the City.

Its success is due to its professional staff of 40, inviting decor, and playful spirit. Every guest is treated as a celebrity. "We're no longer in the business of selling sleep, we're selling fun," is part of the hotel credo. Always blending innovation with inspiration, guest rooms are adorned with hand-painted faux finish walls and custom-crafted furniture. The hotel's top floor is specially outfitted as an EcoFloor™, an ecologically purified environment for those who wish it — 24 rooms with purified air, natural cotton bed and bath linens, energy-saving light fixtures,

hypoallergenic amenities and biodegradable soaps. The hotel has a spacious conference room opening onto an outdoor patio, perfect for an outdoor buffet, San Francisco weather permitting. Each of the hotel's 140 guest rooms has a fax, a fully stocked honor bar, luxury amenities and, in the spirit of European luxury and San Francisco's foggy mornings and evenings, an over-stuffed comforter on every bed. Complimentary morning coffee and evening wine service take place daily in front of the main lobby's fireplace.

In keeping with its exotic splendor, the Hotel has five designer suites, each created by a celebrity guest at the Triton. Each suite is outfitted with limited edition artwork and customized textiles that reflect the tastes and atmosphere of its namesake. The Carlos Santana Suite, for example, is designed with a palette of serene and subtle colors and features a meditation corner, capturing the vitality and warmth of this legendary guitarist. The Wyland Suite, named for the famous marine muralist, boasts a 100-gallon saltwater aquarium and fabrics adorned with images of dolphins and whales.

Named for Triton, son of the mythical Poseidon, Greek god of the sea, this Atlantean "EcoChic" hotel has forged a reputation for its witty irreverence and incomparable charm — a place where the service cannot be surpassed and the surprises never stop.

Designed to mimic the ornate beauty of a jewel box, Hotel Triton's richly appointed main lobby features handcrafted lamps, tables, and the hotel's signature "Dervish" chair, here framed between undulating gold-leafed pillars.

Jeffrey's Toys

Owning a toy shop is not just a business for Mark Luhn. It's a destiny. He has spent 44 of his 50 years working in family-owned toy shops. With his ability to find unusual toys and gizmos he has created a store that is a haven for children and adults alike.

As the owner of an unconventional toy shop located in the historic Hearst Building in downtown San Francisco, Mr. Luhn couldn't be happier. Jeffrey's, which he describes as a "museum of toys," is stacked with items from its floor to its unusually high ceiling.

One of the walls contains children's activity books, coloring books, paper dolls, educational skill books and similar materials. Another wall features an extensive collection of stuffed animals and hand puppets.

Mark Luhn (right) and his father, Mannie and the family business— toys for children of all ages.

Jeffrey's sells dolls — not the usual Barbie dolls, but a selection of dolls from around the globe representing a range of nationalities and ethnic groups. There are puzzles, boardgames, Star Wars collectibles, science kits, dinosaurs, farm animals and comic books — just about every item you'd expect to find in a toy store, and then some.

The toy business has always been and always will be — in Mr. Luhn's blood. His family has been selling toys for five generations. His grandfather, Morton Luhn, opened the first store, Birdie's in San Leandro, with his sons, Mannie and Joel, when Mark was just a toddler. Mark began learning the toy store business from his father, Mannie, when he was five years old; by the time he was six, he needed a Social Security card.

Years (and many stores) later, when Mark was serving in the U.S. Army in Vietnam, his father opened the first Jeffrey's Toys at Serramonte Center. When Mark left the military in 1968 he immediately returned to his first love. He worked in his father's store and, in time, Mark and Mannie opened three other stores in San Francisco at Union Square, Ghirardelli Square and the Embarcadero Center.

Business was good and the toys on the shelves set the image for Jeffrey's Toys in the 1970s and 1980s. Mark traveled to Europe and Japan frequently to acquire toys that were years ahead of the competition. Smurfs, Japanese space toys, electronic games, transformers, paper models and die-cast planes from West Germany's Schabak Co., were just a few of the stores' popular toys.

Then on October 17, 1989, everything changed. After the Loma Prieta Earthquake, tourists stopped coming to San Francisco, and, to the Luhns' toy stores. Mannie retired in 1990, letting Mark continue the business. But without tourists, the business began to crumble. The Union Square and Ghirardelli Square stores closed, and Mark lost the lease to the Embarcadero Center shop.

Mark relocated his business to the Hearst Building at 3rd and Market Streets on May 1, 1994. Since then, Jeffrey's Toys has once again become the place for residents and tourists to shop for yoyos, slinkys and hundreds of unusual gifts.

Jeffrey's Toys means a lot to San Francisco, but it has always meant much more to Mr. Luhn and his staff. Or, as Mark Luhn likes to say, "If you took an X-ray of my insides, you would see little trucks and trains running through my blood."

M.G. West

A stable, family-run firm with a knack for meeting the changing needs of customers over time, M.G. West has provided fine office and institutional furnishings, office design and full facility management services to prominent Bay Area business and institutions for nearly a century.

Monroe George West founded the company in San Francisco in 1905 and became a distributor for custom-made heavy equipment (safes and vault doors). After the 1906 earthquake, many government offices were gutted, and West established a thriving business by designing and installing large metal "roller shelf" cases for storing maps, ledgers and property register books. Under the leadership of Ross West, Monroe's older son, the firm continued to grow during WWI, and supplied document storage cases and furniture to government offices throughout Northern California and to all the Federal Reserve banks in the West.

As office furniture manufacturers began making more standardized desks, chairs and file cabinets, M.G. West expanded into the general office furniture business — in time to supply the building boom in San Francisco in the 1920s. Interior designers joined the staff in that period, and by the time Ross West's younger brother, Kirby, took the reins in 1940, M.G. West was doing full-service space planning and office design for most of its clients.

The M.G. West company remained in the West family for three generations. Kirby Jr., grandson of the founder, took over as General Manager in 1951 and moved the company in 1967 into a renovated landmark building on Second Street where 32,000 square feet of office and warehouse space allowed them to keep a large inventory of fine office furnishings and fill orders immediately. The firm moved again in 1982 to their present location — an even

larger space consisting of 55,000 square feet of office, showroom and warehouse — on Hubbell Street.

In early 1985, the firm was purchased by Don Sullivan, the current Chairman of the Board and CEO. Carrying on the legacy of excellence and family tradition, his son, Andrew Sullivan, joined the firm in 1987 as head of a newly established company, MGW Asia, Ltd., with headquarters in Hong Kong and offices in Jakarta. In 1995, Andrew also became President of M.G. West.

Productivity, ergonomics and the integration of lighting, electronics and acoustics into office furnishings dictated a move to technology in the 1980s and 1990s. As more businesses have chosen to outsource their move planning and facility management functions, M.G. West has changed from a product- to a service-oriented business.

Technology has kept M.G. West at the cutting-edge of the industry. Their space planning and designs are all computer-generated (CAD) to the customer's specifications, saving clients time and money. A specially designed computer program creates a custom flow-chart for each client to track all aspects of their work.

M.G. West's client list is a testament to their diversity, with such prestigious names as Aetna Health Care; Bechtel; Chevron; Contra Costa County; Hewlett Packard; Wilson, Sonsini, Goodrich & Rosati; and hundreds of others — local, national and international.

They offer a complete range of facility services — from space planning, project management, move/relocation management, warehousing and inventory/asset management to the fine art of furniture refinishing and maintenance. They proudly represent over 300 high-quality furniture manufactures headed by the Knoll, Kimball and HON Companies. All are elegantly displayed in their offices and showroom on Hubbell Street.

As they move into the next century, M.G. West will continue to focus on quality products and customer services.

MG West Showroom — 1916

San Francisco store — 1929 (Top left)

Current MG West Headquarters

Wine Impression

in learning the wine business, from operating a chain store's wine bar program to becoming department manager for the major West Coast grocery chain.

Rusty Albert, an eighth generation English German descendant, became a Wine Impression partner in 1997. He became involved in wine while working on a doctorate in plant taxonomy at the University of Nebraska. After managing fine wine shops in Nebraska, he moved to San Francisco and became a buyer-salesman at a famous neighborhood wine and grocery store before joining the Wine Impression team.

A love of wine brought the partners together. They renovated an old, run-down liquor store and turned it into a light and airy shop that handsomely showcases a wide variety of wines, spirits and cigars. Keeping only the 1940s flamingo mural, they added a wine bar, attesting to their commitment to fun, education and service.

Part of Wine Impression's success is due to location: a prominent neighborhood shopping center whose demanding clients are well-traveled, have sophisticated tastes and expect quality products, value and service. Customers follow-up their purchases in the center with a stop at Wine Impression, and usually ask for recommendations.

In a 1994 nationwide survey conducted by Wine & Spirits magazine, Wine Impression received the top rating of three stars along with only seventeen others. Importantly, the partners are committed to the notion of "selling satisfaction," which includes the service, selection, value and meeting the customer's needs — not just the products.

The store's inventory includes a wide range of hand-selected, hard-to-get and rare wines; nonetheless, one can choose from among a hundred wines under $10.00 for everyday and large or casual gatherings. To the community, Wine Impression is not just a one-stop shopping place. It is a focal point, a resource place where the "oil of civilization" can be found in an enthusiastic, neighborly store committed to customers' expectation for quality and value.

Wine Impression- A place to meet friends, taste and share.

Wine Impression, a Laurel Heights full-service wine, spirits and cigar shop, is as culturally and ethnically as varied as any in America, since the three owner-partners represent first, second and eighth generation Americans. Collectively, they have over sixty years of retail beverage experience and participation as wine judges, consultants and lecturers. All arrived at their interest in wine by circuitous routes.

Adel Shalabi studied accounting at Egypt's University of Alexandria while spending his summers traveling in Europe and working in French and Italian vineyards. After graduation, he spent two years in New York City, working in restaurants and learning about wine. He arrived in San Francisco in 1980 with $520 in his pocket. Within three years he had opened a grocery store and wine shop.

Raymond Fong, a second generation American-Chinese, was completing his master's degree in political science when he took a week-long trip through Burgundy in 1976. He thereafter immersed himself

Washington Square Bar & Grill

The Washington Square Bar & Grill celebrates its 25 year anniversary in 1998. Somehow, a mere quarter of a century doesn't seem long enough for this popular fixture to San Francisco's historic North Beach district. Forever seems more likely.

This timeless appeal of the Washington Square Bar & Grill attracts hundreds of thousands of customers each year making it as much of a destination as the nearby tourist attractions of Chinatown and Fisherman's Wharf.

Along with the terrific food and drink the Washington Square Bar & Grill offers, is the exciting prospect of spotting a celebrated local. Beloved man-about-town, Herb Caen, was one whose presence is greatly missed. Caen endorsed the restaurant so routinely in his daily column at the San Francisco Chronicle, that he had the name officially shortened to The Washbag. It is now known worldwide as such.

The Washbag was one of the first bar and grills in San Francisco. Its walls, highlighted with sports and musical memorabilia, attests to a long history of community involvement. But new owner Peter W. Osborne, an enterprising man in his late thirties, feels his customers are entitled to "receive more than laurels can provide."

Keeping all the things that made the Washbag great, Mr. Osborne increased the focus on contemporary food and wine, taking advantage of the abundance of local produce and seafood readily available. The updated menu proved both successful and crucial. As San Francisco has gained a worldwide reputation for fine food, the atmosphere among its establishments, no matter how heralded, has become increasingly competitive.

This fresh approach combined with a respect and preservation of the past is what San Francisco is all about. As a result, the Washington Square Bar & Grill has evolved into a gathering spot for city dwellers and locals, older generations and their families, movie stars, journalists, sports figures, government and city officials.

Peter Osborne has discovered that his loyal clientele, while enjoying some new changes, yearns for the traditional. One of the Washbag's more enduring traditions is its softball team, Les Lapins Sauvages (The Wild Hares). These urban warriors travel the world spreading goodwill as well as playing locally with other restaurants and organizations for charitable events.

Pitchers of another type participate in the annual St. Anthony's Penny Pitch. In this event, promoted by Mayor Willie Brown and held at the Washbag for the past 21 years, 100 volunteers relive the bygone days of city sidewalk games to raise money to benefit St. Anthony's Dining Room.

Today's Washington Square Bar & Grill is a combination of Cheers, private club, and tourist attraction. Live jazz is performed seven nights a week with such acts as Norma's Boys, a trio of devoted sidemen who enjoyed a 20-year association at the Washbag with the late, great Norma Teagarden. Equally entertaining is the colorful staff. Where else but at the Washbag would you find a hostess named Boom Boom or a tuba-playing bartender?

The Washington Square Bar & Grill *is* San Francisco. Just sit back, relax, and enjoy the show.

A Select Bibliography

THE SUBSTANTIVE RESEARCH FOR *CITY BY THE BAY* WAS ACCOMPLISHED THROUGH THE EXTENSIVE historical files of the San Francisco Public Library's San Francisco History Room in the Main Library, the files of the San Francisco *Chronicle* and San Francisco *Examiner*, the files of documents of various public agencies of the City and County of San Francisco, city businesses and organizations, and in interviews with innumerable San Franciscans who have been involved in events and processes during the more than half century of San Francisco history which I have attempted to describe in this book.

The following is a selection of books that deal with some specialized areas of San Francisco's history, mostly its political history, during the last half century.

Bloomfield, Arthur. *Fifty Years of the San Francisco Opera*. San Francisco: San Francisco Book Co., 1972.

Cavan, Sherri. *Hippies of the Haight*. St. Louis: New Critics Press, 1972.

Chatfield-Taylor, Joan. *San Francisco Opera: The First Seventy-Five Years*. San Francisco: Chronicle Books, 1997.

Daniels, Douglas Henry. *Pioneer Urbanites: A Social and Cultural History of Black San Francisco*. Berkeley, CA: University of California Press, 1990.

Davidson, Michael. *The San Francisco Renaissance: Poetics and Community at Mid-century*. Cambridge [England]: Cambridge University Press, 1979.

Davis, R.G. *The San Francisco Mime Troupe: The First Ten Years*. Palo Alto, CA: Ramparts Press, 1975.

DeLeon, Richard. *Left Coast City: Progressive Politics in San Francisco, 1975-1991.* Lawrence, Kansas: University Press of Kansas, c. 1992.

Dorsey, George. *Christopher of San Francisco.* New York: Maxmillan, 1962.

Finch, Phillip. *The 49ers, Champions of the West.* Englewood Cliffs, N.J.: Prentice-Hall, n.d. [1973].

Fracchia, Charles A. *Fire and Gold: The San Francisco Story.*

French, Warren G. *The San Francisco Poetry Renaissance, 1955-1959.* Boston: Twayne, 1991.

Gaskin, Stephen. *Haight Ashbury Flashbacks.* Berkeley, CA: Ronin Publishing, Inc., c. 1990.

Hartman, Chester W. *The Transformation of San Francisco.* Totowa, N.J.: Rowman & Allanheld, 1984.

Hartman, Chester W. *Yerba Buena: Landgrab and Community Resistance in San Francisco.* San Francisco: Glide Publications, 1974.

Karagueuzian, Dikran. *Blow It Up! The Black Student Revolt at San Francisco State College and the Emergence of Dr. Hayakawa.* Boston: Gambit, 1971.

Lapham, Helen Abbot. *Roving with Roger.* [San Francisco: Cameron, 1971].

Lewis, Alison, Carolyn McGovern, and Beverly Sykes. *The Lamplighters: 25 Years of Gilbert and Sullivan in San Francisco.* San Francisco: Opera West Foundation, 1977.

McGloin, John Bernard. *San Francisco: The Story of a City.* San Rafael, CA: Presidio Press, 1978.

Perry, Charles. *The Haight-Ashbury: A History.* New York: Random House, c. 1984.

Pottenger, Dennis. *Great Expectations: The San Francisco 49ers and the Quest for the "Three-Peat."* Rocklin, CA: Prima Pub., 1991.

The Quake of 89': As Seen by the News Staff of the San Francisco Chronicle. Introduction by Herb Caen and an epilogue by Randy Shilts. San Francisco: Chronicle Books, 1989.

Richardson, James. *Willie Brown: A Bibliography.* Berkeley, CA: University of California Press, 1996.

Schneider, David. *The San Francisco Symphony: Music, Maestros, and Musicians.* Novato, CA: Presidio Press, 1983.

Scott, Mel. *The San Francisco Bay Area: A Metropolis in Prospective.* Rev. Ed. Berkeley: University of California Press, 1985.

Selvin, Joel. *Summer of Love: The Inside Story of LSD, Rock & Roll, Free Love, and High Times in the Wild West.* New York: Dutton, 1994.

Shepard, Susan. *In the Neighborhoods: A guide to the Joys and Discoveries of San Francisco's Neighborhoods.* San Francisco: Chronicle Books, 1981.

Shilts, Randy. *The Mayor of Castor Street: The Life and Times of Harvey Milk.* New York: St. Martin's Press, n.d. [1982].

Steinberg, Cobbett. *San Francisco Ballet: The First Fifty Years.* [San Francisco]: San Francisco Ballet Association: Chronicle Books, [c. 1983].

Stryker, Susan and James Van Buskirk. *Gay by the Bay: A History of Queer Culture in the San Francisco Bay Area.* San Francisco: Chronicle Books, 1996.

Sykes, Beverly and Alison Lewis. *The Lamplighters' Story: 1977-1987.* San Francisco: Opera West Foundation, 1989.

Watson, Steven. *The Birth of the Beat Generation: Visionaries, Rebels, and Hipsters, 1944-1960.* New York: Pantheon Books, c. 1995.

Weiss, Mike. *Double Play: The San Francisco City Hall Killings.* Reading, Mass.: Addison-Wesley Pub. Co., 1984.

Wiley, Peter Booth. *A Free Library in This City: The Illustrated History of the San Francisco Public Library.* San Francisco: Weldon Owen, 1996.

Wirt, Frederick M. *Power in the City: Decision Making in San Francisco.* Berkeley: University of California Press, 1974.

Index

McLaughlin, Ken, 102
McMahon, Clarissa, 78
Meltzer, David, 39
Memorial Gym, 162
Mendocino County, 83
Mercer, Mabel, 40
Merola, Gaetano, 188
Merry Pranksters, 55-57
Meschery, Tom, 162
Metropolitan Opera, 188
Meyer, Linda, 183
Micheline, Jack, 39
Mieuli, Franklin, 162-163
Milhaud, Darius, 41
Milk, Harvey, 85-86, 88, 90, 129-130
Miller, Henry, 35
Mills College, 41
Mingus, Charlie, 41
Miracle Mile, 20-21
Mission San Juan, 134
Mission Bay, 119, 139
Mission District, 17-18, 52, 109, 129,
    149, 156, 172
Mission Dolores, 146, 184
Mitchell, Jim, 102-103
Mitchell, Artie, 102
Modern Jazz Quartet, 41
Molinari, John, 111, 116
Molotov, V. M., 26
Montana, Joe, 161
Monterey Pop Festival, 61
Monteux, Pierre, 192
Moore, Brew, 41
Morabito, Tony, 160
Morris, James, 188
Morris, Mark, 183
Morrison, Jack, 78
Moscone Convention Center, 75
Moscone, Mayor George, 83, 85-86,
    110-111, 115, 129, 157
Mount Zion Hospital, 68
Mural Room, 23-24
Murphy, Turk, 41
Museum of Modern Art, 167, 198
Muzio, Claudia, 188
Naked Lunch, 39
National League Championship, 157
National Historic Landmark, 29-30
NBA, 163
NBC, 62
New Age, 54, 59-60, 101, 104
New York Giants, 156

New Yorker Magazine, 33
Newhall, Scott, 195
Newhart, Bob, 40
NFC, 161
NFL, 161
Ng, Peter, 169, 173
Nichols, Mike, 40
Nob Hill, 19, 23
Noe Valley, 108
Nolan, Milton Van, 21
Norman, Thomas, 90
Normandy Lane, 19
Norris, Frank, 32
North Beach, 18, 33-36, 39-40, 100-
    102, 106-109, 139
Oakes, Richard, 83
Oakland Athletics, 134
Oakland Coliseum, 163
Opera House, 26, 32, 70, 100, 182-
    183, 188-189, 192-193
Operation Abolition, 49
Orey, Kit, 41
Orinda Station, 77
Orlovsky, Peter, 33, 39
Owens, R. C., 160
Ozawa, Seiji, 192
Pacific Coast Stock Exchange, 141
Pacific Islanders, 108
Pacific Heights, 17, 19, 28, 30, 65,
    104, 108, 196
Padilla, Darcy, 116
Palace Hotel, 41
Palooka, Joe, 19
Panama Pacific International
    Exposition, 45
Paramount Theater, 22
Parent Teachers Association, 95
Parker, Harry, 166
Parkmerced Towers, 46
Pavarotti, Luciano, 189
Pavloff, Nicholas, 198
PBS, 183
PCL, 153, 156
Pei, I. M., 96
Peoples Temple, 85
Perls, Fritz, 104
Perry, Charles, 62
Perry, Joe, 160
Persian Room, 23
Peterson, Betty, 68
Philadelphia Warriors, 162
Planning Commission, 65, 114

Playland-at-the-Beach, 23-24, 64-65
Police Officers Association, 89
Polk, Willis, 21
Pool, Fleishhaker, 64
Pope John Paul II, 95, 97
Port of San Francisco, 81
Portsmouth Plaza, 45, 69
Potrero Hill, 17
Presentation High School, 186
Price, Leontyne, 189
Produce District, 72
Prokofiev, Sergei, 183
Proposition E, 30
Proposition F, 114
Proposition H, 120
Proposition I, 119
Proposition K, 114
Proposition M, 100, 113-116, 119-120
Proposition O, 113
Proposition P, 117, 119
Proposition V, 119
Proposition W, 117
Pryor, Richard, 40
Psychedelic Shop, 62
Purple Onion, 40
Queer Nation, 131
Quinn, Archbishop, 97
Quintet, John Handy, 57
Recreation Park, 153
Red Dog Saloon, 56
Redevelopment Agency, 65, 70-72, 75
Reich, Wilhelm, 104
Rexroth, Kenneth, 35-36, 38
Ricciarelli, Katia, 189
Richardson, Bobby, 157
Richmond District, 107-108
Richmond-San Rafael Bridge, 141
Rincon Point, 72
Ringman, Steve, 173
Riordan High School, 188
Robinson, Mayor Elmer, 31, 76, 109
Rogers, Carl, 104
Roos Brothers, 19
Rosen, Al, 157
Rosenberg, Jack, 105
ROTC, 81
Rubin, Jerry, 59
Runnicles, Donald, 189
Russian Hill, 64
Russian River, 23
Ryan, Leo, 85
Sacred Heart High School, 147

Partners in San Francisco Index

LeRoy Neiman